ARISTOCRATS

Also by Lawrence James

Raj: The Making of British India
Imperial Warrior: The Life and Times of
Field-Marshal Viscount Allenby
The Iron Duke: A Military Biography of Wellington
Warrior Race: A History of the British at War
The Rise and Fall of the British Empire
The Golden Warrior: The Life and Legend of Lawrence of Arabia
The Middle Class: A History

Aristocrats
Power, Grace, and Decadence: Britain's Great Ruling Classes from 1066 to the Present

Lawrence James

St. Martin's Griffin

New York

To the memory of Wellesley
a Newfoundland dog

www.stmartins.com

The Library of Congress has cataloged the hardcover edition as follows:

James, Lawrence, 1943–
    Aristocrats : power, grace, and decadence : Britain's great ruling
classes from 1066 to the present / Lawrence James.—1st U.S. ed.
        p. cm.
    First published in Great Britain by Little, Brown, 2009.
    Includes bibliographical references and index.
    ISBN 978-0-312-61545-1
    1. Aristocracy (Social class)—Great Britain—History. I. Title.
HT653.G7J36 2010
305.5'220941—dc22

                                                        2010013041

            ISBN 978-0-312-58379-8 (trade paperbacks)

        First published in Great Britain by Little, Brown

        First St. Martin's Griffin Edition: May 2011

P1

Contents

· Contents ·

Acknowledgements

First I would like to thank my wife Mary for her encouragement, patience and helpful suggestions. My gratitude also extends to Dr Ian Bradley, Geordie Burnett Stuart, Richard Demarco, the Earl and Countess of Dundee, the Earl of Glasgow, Professor John Haldane, Michael and Veronica Hodges, Edward James, Henry and Ruth James, Viscount Kelburn, Yvonne Mallett, Dr Roy Oliver, Professor and Dr Anna Patterson, Professor Nick Roe, Dr Jane Stabler, Andrew and Sarah Williams, and Percy and Isabel Wood. All have offered suggestions and enlightenment.

I would also like to thank John Forster the archivist at Blenheim Palace and Greg Colley of the Bodleian Library for their assistance, as well as the staff of the British Library, the National Archives, the National Archives of Scotland, the National Library of Scotland and St Andrews University Library. Guidance and support have come from my agent Andrew Lownie, and Steve Guise, Iain Hunt, Tim Whiting and Richard Beswick of Little, Brown for which I am grateful.

Material from the Blenheim Palace archives appears by kind permission of His Grace the Duke of Marlborough.

Introduction

This is a history of the British aristocracy and their now almost vanished supremacy. It explains how and why a tiny elite exercised such a vast and pervasive influence over the course of our history. Aristocrats created the constitution, made laws and commanded armies and navies. They rearranged the landscape to accord with their notions of beauty and to satisfy their passion for hunting. Their patronage dictated patterns of taste until recent times and aristocratic manners established codes of conduct for the rest of society which remained in place until recently.

The word aristocracy appeared late in our language, arriving via France in the mid-sixteenth century. It was a compound of the Greek 'aristo' (the best) and 'kratos' (government) and defined an Aristotelian notion of the distribution of political power in an ideal state. Aristotle's aristocrats were men of learning and wisdom whose wealth gave them the leisure to devote their lives to government and the general welfare of the rest of society. This concept of aristocracy was highly flattering to an already dominant elite, which, since the eleventh century, had been called the 'baronage', 'nobility' and latterly 'the peerage'.

The Aristotelian notion of aristocracy reinforced an already deeply rooted sense of superiority and public responsibility which justified power and privilege.

This new word assisted the long process of collective self hypnosis by which aristocrats convinced themselves that their distinctive qualities made them indispensable to the nation. In 1484 John Russell, Bishop of Lincoln, told Parliament that the nobility represented 'virtue and ancient riches' and was the sheet anchor of the country. The Whig political theorist Edmund Burke said much the same in the 1770s when he praised the 'upright constitutional conduct' and 'public virtues' of the aristocracy. Virtue was genetically transmitted as the Marquess of Curzon assured the House of Lords in 1910. The 'hereditary principle' he insisted had given Britain 'an upper class which, on the whole, had honourably trained itself in the responsibilities of government'. In 1999, when the hereditary peers were about to be expelled from the House of Lords, Lord Hardy, a former trade union leader and Labour life peer, recalled the long history of dedication to the public good of one noble dynasty in his native Yorkshire.

The Aristotelian concept of aristocracy has had a long life and, on the whole, aristocrats have been highly successful in convincing the world that they were qualified to undertake the affairs of state, were supremely useful and that things would somehow fall apart without their guidance. Their conviction and its manifestations comprise the central theme of this book. Aristocrats did not, however, always have everything their own way: from time to time the aristocratic principle has been challenged, sometimes violently. I have, therefore, paused to examine the opinions and actions of those men and women who rejected aristocratic authority as irrational and unjust.

Antipathy to the theory of aristocracy raises the question as to why it was tolerated for so long by so many. One explanation offered in this book is that there were always enough aristocrats who understood that consent to their power ultimately depended on its being used for the public benefit. From the Middle Ages onwards, aristocrats had encouraged the perception of themselves as robust, independent-minded fellows who would take up cudgels to protect the people from overbearing monarchs and elected governments with authoritarian instincts. The House of Lords was 'like the Home Guard, ready in case of danger', observed Winston Churchill, the grandson of a Duke. Within the last decade, the Lords have opposed legislation designed to overturn ancient legal freedoms in the name of the so-called 'war' against terrorism.

I have argued that the consent of the masses underpinned the ascendancy of the aristocracy and its survival. This consent was almost withdrawn during the Reform Act crisis of 1830–2 and the row over the reduction of the powers of the House of Lords during 1910 and 1911. Yet there were aristocrats, most notably the first Duke of Wellington, who recognised that compromise was infinitely preferable to extinction. In the final sections of this book, I have tried to show that submission to public opinion and flexibility paid dividends. By shedding some of its powers, the aristocracy discovered that it could thrive and still exert some influence within a democratic and egalitarian society.

I have interwoven the political history of the aristocracy with an exploration of the ways in which its members used their prestige to dictate aesthetics, literature and music. Aristocrats also dominated the world of sport. A thread of hearty muscularity runs through the history of the nobility: aristocrats hunted, bred horses and raced them, and patronised boxers and cricket teams. Sporting mania was surpassed by an urge to gamble, often recklessly.

The sporting aristocrat with his devil-may-care panache fascinated the rest of society. Since the eighteenth century, middle- and working-class newspaper readers were fascinated by his antics as relayed by the press. This audience was also enthralled by the dazzling rituals of the London season and shocked by the frivolities and vices of wayward noblemen and their wives, sons and daughters.

Thanks to the newspapers, their lives and indeed those of the rest of the aristocracy became a form of public entertainment. This engagement with the world, I have argued, may help explain why the nobility was accepted as part of the fabric of society. In her *Lark Rise to Candleford*, Flora Thompson likened the aristocracy to kingfishers, brilliant colourful creatures briefly glimpsed but remembered with wonderment.

Eccentricity was central to the aristocracy's mystique. It was inventive, often disconcerting and entirely natural to a self-confident caste which knew that it was different. Aristocrats were free to indulge their whims. Once at a supper party a ferret emerged from the cleavage of the late Lady Strange, approached her plate, gnawed at a lamb chop and then returned to its refuge. The other guests continued to eat without remark. Aristocratic quirkiness was not always so charming: the second Lord Redesdale flirted with Nazism and his daughter Unity fawned over Hitler. Her father was a visceral anti-Catholic and once interrupted a performance of *Romeo and Juliet* with a loud warning to 'beware of the priest'. At various stages of this book I have found room for aristocratic eccentricity and perversity.

On the other hand, Redesdale was a contemporary of aristocrats who used their leisure and wealth to advance scholarship and the arts. Lord Bertrand Russell studied and wrote about mathematics and philosophy, Lord Berners composed music and Lord Carnarvon sponsored the excavation of Tutankhamun's tomb. All represented a long aristocratic tradition of patronage which stretched back to the Middle Ages and was extended to playwrights, poets, philosophers, artists, architects, composers, musicians, actors and scholars. Aristocratic patrons cherished the arts and dictated their development. I have argued that the British aristocrats were always cosmopolitan and their extended love affair with the Continent was the means by which the great European aesthetic movements took root and made headway in this country.

Finally and to make sense of what follows, I must say a few words about now unfamiliar and often bewildering subjects: the nature of former social structures, status and titles. The best starting place is perhaps Chipping Campden church in Gloucestershire. On the chancel floor is the ambitious brass to William Grevel, a rich wool exporter, who died in 1401. He invested in land and his descendants were knights with estates in nearby Warwickshire. They called themselves 'Greville', which suggested Norman blood, and, by the end of the sixteenth century, the family had been ennobled by the crown with the title Lord Brooke.

The upwardly mobile Grevilles had flourished in a fluid society. Its profile was conical with a broad base and a narrow apex. At the top were men and women who were 'gentle' and they included the aristocracy. Within this elite there were gradations which, in ascending order, were gentlemen, esquires and knights and then the hereditary peerage. This group too had its own hierarchy which had evolved by about 1400. At the top were dukes and then marquesses, earls, viscounts and lords. Titles could be accumulated through marriages to heiresses and were shared among eldest sons and even grandsons if there were enough to go round: the eldest son of John de la Pole the second Duke of Suffolk (d. 1491) was Earl of Lincoln. Much later the daughters of dukes and marquesses were allowed the honorary title of 'Lady'.

A porous frontier divided the gentle from those beneath them. Although a wool merchant, William Grevel had a coat of arms on his brass to announce that he was a gentleman. Another local boy who made good, William Shakespeare, a glover's son, also ended his life as a 'gentleman' with the right to be addressed as 'esquire'. Proof of his rank was a coat of arms he had purchased from a herald. Cynical contemporaries of Shakespeare remarked that anyone who lived by his wits could call himself a gentleman and have their presumption endorsed by a herald.

All aristocrats were by definition gentlemen, even if they neglected the moral codes by which gentlemen were expected to live. Charles II joked that a king could make a lord, but not a gentleman, an aphorism that was repeated by the Duke of Wellington who took a lofty view of the public duties of the aristocracy. However they chose to behave, peers were unlike other gentlemen. They enjoyed a superior public status and expected deference from all inferiors, gentle or not.

The aristocracy have always been an open elite. New blood was welcomed and assimilated. Yet aristocrats emphasised their superiority by never letting slip the chance to announce that their virtue and superiority was genetic. Like the finest bloodstock, they were all thoroughbreds. Close to William Grevel's brass in Chipping Campden is the flamboyant marble monument to Charles Noel, second Lord Campden, who died in 1642 fighting for Charles I. According to his epitaph, Campden was 'a lord of heroic parts and presence', while his wife was 'a lady of extraordinary adornments both of virtue and fortune', qualities that were passed to her 'numerous and gallant issue'. Yet Campden sat in the House of Lords alongside the sons and grandsons of lawyers, civil servants, judges and merchants like William Grevel. These noblemen too would commission monuments which proclaimed an illustrious ancestry and its concomitant, accumulated honour.

PART ONE

ASCENDANCY
1066–1603

1

———◆———

A Game of Dice:
The Growth of
Aristocratic Power

The history of medieval England, Scotland, Wales and Ireland is of four embryonic polities engaged in a prolonged struggle to achieve order, stability and prosperity. It was a difficult, slow and frustrating task because political power was inseparable from military, and those who possessed it used it promiscuously. A king was the first warrior in the realm: he defended it from its external and internal enemies and was ready to uphold the laws he made by force. Immediately below him were a body of men who enjoyed his favour and owed their elevation to their skill in war. Before the Norman Conquest of 1066 they were called 'thegns' and afterwards, 'knights', but their function and status were the same. The Crown granted them land that was cultivated by a peasantry which was largely unfree. Their labour supported the knight; it gave him the leisure to train for battle and it paid for his warhorse, armour, sword and lance.

From childhood, the knight mastered their use, inured himself to the weight and discomfort of armour, and learned how to control an often temperamental charger which had been bred for weight, strength and ferocity. Stamina and training made knights the masters of the battlefield; one can see them in their element on the Bayeaux Tapestry. They also appear mounted alongside a nobleman on an eleventh-century stone cross now in Meigle Museum in Angus.

The Norman, Breton and Flemish knights who won at Hastings were more than fighting machines. They upheld the authority of the Crown and defended the kingdom they had helped to conquer. Kings were always paramount, but they were bound by obligations imposed by God. In one thirteenth-century romance an archbishop tells the newly crowned King Arthur that 'Our Lord has shown your are His elect' and, to confirm this, the King had to swear 'to protect the rights of the Church, keep order and peace, assist the defenceless and uphold all rights, obligations and lawful rule'. William the Conqueror (1066–87) would have understood this and so would his knights. They too were the servants of God. Speaking for them in 1100, Robert de Beaumont, Earl of Leicester and Count (Earl) of Meulan in Normandy, reminded Henry I (1100–35) that 'we . . . have been entrusted by God to provide for the common good and the safety of the realm'.

De Meulan was a distinctive kind of knight, he had the title 'Earl'. It was a gift of the Crown, and at that time was not necessarily hereditary, but it marked him out as an owner of larger than average estates. He was, therefore, richer than a knight and could devote some of his wealth to the creation of a following of knights. They were given land and, in return, pledged loyalty to their overlord and promised to serve him in war or in his household for the customary forty days. An earl's retinue of knights was vital if he were to perform his function as a servant of the Crown. He was a local strongman whose military resources enforced the king's authority, particularly in lawless or frontier areas. Earls and their castles guarded the southern coastline of England and its borders with Scotland and Wales until the fourteenth century.

However powerful they were in their locations, earls were subjects of the King. Allegiance to the Crown overrode all private obligations. In 1124 Henry I ordered the blinding and castration of two knights who had joined their immediate overlord in a rebellion. The king was both the ruler of his kingdom and its landlord. His legal powers were extensive: an earl or a knight needed royal permission to inherit their lands and the king charged a fee for granting it. On taking possession of his estate, the heir paid public homage to the king. If a knight died leaving an underage heir, the boy was made a royal ward. Orphaned heiresses likewise were placed under royal protection and the king had the right to select their husbands. The power of the king as a landlord and a ruler often overlapped; if an earl or a knight wished to build a castle, he needed a royal licence.

Tension was inevitable whenever kings strapped for cash pressed their legal rights to the limit, and, if they were desperate, beyond. Early-medieval domestic politics revolved around the creation of a balance between the legal prerogative of the Crown and the rights of all landowners. This was vital since the Crown needed their cooperation in government: they enforced his laws and collected his taxes. Those whom the Crown had honoured as 'earls' or 'barons' were royal advisers. It was axiomatic that good government was the result of reasoned debate among wise men. They included bishops, who were often civil servants, and the greater landowners, who were experienced in war and, in many cases, administration.

Kings chose their councillors, but custom and common sense dictated the selection of men whose goodwill was vital for government. Many were called 'Earl' or 'Baron' in the writs which commanded them to attend the royal council, but these titles were not yet all automatically hereditary. In 1295 Edward I (1272–1307) ordered eleven earls and fifty-three barons to attend his Parliament, and in 1307 writs were delivered to seven earls and seventy-one barons.

These magnates were a fledgling aristocracy. All had substantial estates, many held offices under the Crown and some were the king's councillors, intimate companions who ate, diced, jousted and hunted with him. They were also gradually coming to think of themselves as representatives of all the landowners within the kingdom with a responsibility not just to counsel the king, but to remind him of where his duty lay and, if necessary, compel him to undertake it properly.

Hereditary monarchy has always been hostage to genetic accidents which produced kings who were temperamentally unfit or intellectually deficient and, therefore, a danger to their high office and welfare of their subjects. The character of a king mattered, for the warrior class admired kings who were made in their image and showed leadership, courage and open-handedness. Richard I (1189–99) had all these qualities, which excused but did not alter the fact of his neglect of his domestic duties. The Lionheart spent a greater part of his reign as a Crusader fighting to recapture Jerusalem, which immeasurably enhanced his reputation as a knight.

Richard's younger brother John (1199–1216) had no martial charisma and was a spasmodically idle and supremely unlucky monarch. His endeavours to stay solvent and twist feudal law to fill his coffers, and the favours he showered on mercenaries and adventurers of low birth, alienated his barons. A substantial number of them formed a coalition (backed at various times by the papacy and Philip II of France) to save John from himself. In

1215 they forced him to concede Magna Carta, a lengthy document contrived to rectify the pent-up grievances of the preceding fifty years. The charter drew the boundaries between royal power and established the inalienable legal rights of all freemen – everyone, that is, who was not a serf. Excessive feudal fines, burdensome tax demands and unlawful imprisonment were outlawed. Magna Carta was a landmark: it clarified relations between Crown and subjects and gave an additional legal weight to the concept that kings ruled by consent and were bound to pursue what was to the common good of their subjects.

Another principle was implicit in Magna Carta. The great men of the realm had a duty to represent the nation as a whole and call fickle or overbearing kings to account. There was a contract between the Crown and the kingdom, and the magnates had the power and the men to enforce it. They did so again in 1264 after Henry III (1216–72) extended lavish favours to imported French favourites, cold-shouldered English barons and misspent his revenues. Simon de Montfort, Earl of Leicester, led an armed protest and looked beyond the usual allies of the magnates to enlist support from the commercial community of London.

After defeating a royal army at Lewes, de Montfort summoned a parliament in which the barons and earls were joined by representatives of the counties, cities and boroughs. The voice of the kingdom thus extended beyond the barons to knights and merchants. This experiment provided the model for all future bicameral Parliaments in which earls, barons, bishops and the richer abbots sat in what became the House of Lords and elected Members of Parliament sat in the Commons. The theoretic consent by which kings ruled now became actual; although elected by men of property (a tiny proportion of the population), parliament could claim to be the authentic voice of the kingdom. Its powers soon ceased to be advisory and by 1340 it had secured control over direct taxation.

The House of Lords was now a permanent feature of the legislature. Past custom was regularised so that territorial magnates who had hitherto been summoned as 'barons' and 'earls' were now, if the king wished, allowed to pass on their titles to their eldest sons, who were henceforward guaranteed seats in the House of Lords. Land was the principal quali-fication for this honour, coupled with proven loyalty to the Crown. This could be expected from members of the royal family: King John's younger son Richard became Earl of Cornwall and was succeeded by his son, Edmund Crouchback. Yet the policy did not always work as intended, for kinship was never a guarantee of allegiance. Thomas, Earl of Lancaster, a grandson of Henry III, was the mainstay of baronial opposition to his cousin Edward II (1307–27). Undeterred by this example, Edward III (1327–77) substantially reinforced the royal power base in the Lords by giving dukedoms to four of his sons and arranging their marriages to the richest heiresses on the market. Edward's fourth son, Thomas of Woodstock, Duke of Gloucester, was Richard II's (1377–99) most intransi-gent and vindictive adversary. Kinship was never a guarantee of loyalty.

The fourteenth century saw the emergence of an aristocracy in an Aristotelian sense. The House of Lords contained bishops, respected for their learning, and noblemen whose virtue lay in their distinguished ancestry, courage and wisdom. 'The more we bestow honours on wise and honourable men, the more our crown is advanced with gems and precious stones,' declared Richard II in 1397 after he had ennobled his Beaufort cousins. This fitted the ideal of rule by the best, although cynics won-dered whether handing out titles to the King's more distant and, in some cases, poorer kinsfolk was a device to create a more tractable House of Lords. Well-established peers felt that their status had been devalued and dismissed the new creations as 'duketti', petty and inferior dukes.

By the close of the fourteenth century a hierarchy had emerged within the peerage. At the top were dukes, then followed marquesses, earls, viscounts and barons. It became common for the eldest sons of peers to have 'courtesy' titles, a notch or two lower in the scale than their fathers. Status was indicated by the fur trimmings of a peer's robes and the design of coronets. There was a correlation between rank and wealth. A rough guide compiled early in the next century indicated that a duke should have annual revenues of at least £5000, an earl £2000, a viscount £1000 and a lord £500. There were exceptions: Thomas, Earl of Lancaster, had an income of over £10,000 a year, as did Edward III's fourth son, John of Gaunt, Duke of Lancaster.

At the bottom of the scale, Lord Ogle got by on £200 a year and often less, for his estates lay in the war zone between England and Scotland. If a nobleman's revenues were insufficient to maintain his status, his title could be forfeit. In 1484 Parliament stripped the impoverished George Neville of the dukedom of Bedford on the intriguing assumption that 'a lord of high estate' without the wherewithal to maintain his dignity would resort to crime to raise money. Maybe this judgement said something about Neville's character.

The aristocracy of the fourteenth century upheld the political traditions of their predecessors. They were vigilant and obstreperous whenever the Crown attempted to impinge on the legal rights of property. Whenever a king showed undue partiality towards one or more individuals, aristocratic hackles were raised. Favourites were an anathema simply because they soaked up the royal patronage which kings were expected to spread evenly. Edward II and Richard II did not and each faced coalitions of disgruntled peers.

Edward II's infatuation with his favourites Piers Gaveston (his homosexual lover) and the rapacious Hugh, Lord Despenser provoked three baronial rebellions, all designed to bring the King to heel and restore good and disinterested government. The lords complained that Gaveston's promotion to the earldom of Cornwall was inappropriate for so 'slight' a man. This insult was compounded by Gaveston's rudeness: he called Thomas, Earl of Lancaster, 'an old Jew' and Guy de Beauchamp, Earl of Warwick, 'the black dog of Arden'. Worse still for peers proud of their blood, Gaveston was a good jouster. They and their allies were revenged in 1312 when Gaveston was kidnapped and murdered. Edward II found other favourites, the Despensers, and in 1327 he was deposed by a cabal of lords led by his wife Isabella of France and her lover, Roger Mortimer, Earl of March. Both houses of Parliament endorsed the coup and the succession of Edward's son, Edward III. His father was imprisoned in Berkeley Castle in Gloucestershire, where he was murdered. Living kings, even if under lock and key, were always a focus for a counter coup.

Resisting royal tyranny was an aristocratic duty and, some believed, a hallowed one. This made Thomas, Earl of Lancaster, the implacable leader of opposition to Edward II into a martyr in the eyes of his adherents. He had been beheaded in 1322 and five years later they had begun a campaign for his canonisation on the grounds that he served God by resisting tyranny. Miracles were claimed at his tomb in Pontefract and Lancaster's 'martyrdom' was painted on the south wall of South Stoke church in Oxfordshire.[1] Rome, however, withheld the Earl's sainthood.

Ultra-royalists, including Richard II, responded many years later by seeking the canonisation of Edward II as a martyr slain for his defence of the God-given authority of kings. It was a cause close to Richard's heart and his interpretation of his divine powers provoked a series of clashes with the nobility which ended in 1399 when he was deposed. Charges against Richard included deviation from the laws and customs of the kingdom, intimidating those councillors who 'dared to speak the truth', and announcing that the laws 'were in his mouth'. In short, Richard wanted his own way, just as John and Edward II had done.

Richard's abdication was confirmed by Parliament, which then approved the claim to the throne of his cousin, Henry Bolingbroke, Duke of Lancaster, the leader of the coalition which had unseated Richard. Propaganda issued by the new king, Henry IV (1399–1413), represented himself and his allies as the genuine voice of a country exasperated by Richard's caprice and misrule. This was partially true. Bolingbroke had been guided more by ambition and opportunism than patriotism. The wealthiest landowner in England, Bolingbroke's first intention had been to recover his property, which had been illegally confiscated by Richard, an act that had frightened the nobility. The King's temporary absence in Ireland, the disintegration of an army raised from the royal estates in Cheshire and Richard's surrender convinced Bolingbroke that a coup was both possible and likely to succeed. He had the King imprisoned and his and his allies' retainers were sufficient to scare off any resistance by Richard's former followers.

Twice within a century a coalition of noblemen had assumed the collective right to correct and then dethrone a king whom its members considered headstrong and incorrigible. It was a power which proved mischievous, intoxicating and addictive. Between 1400 and 1408 there was a sequence of aristocratic rebellions against Henry IV. In 1415 a handful of peers plotted to assassinate Henry V (1413–22) on the eve of his departure for France and replace him with his cousin, Edmund Mortimer, Earl of March.

The deposing of Edward II and Richard II had been blows to the power of the Crown and an advancement of that of the aristocracy. Both kings were largely responsible for their misfortunes, not least in their inability to reach any understanding with their nobles and their extreme sensitivity to any form of criticism. For their part, the aristocrats had radically departed from their role as a force for stability within the kingdom and become instead a disruptive element. Yet it was only the peerage who possessed the capability to restore just government and equilibrium to England. This was the chief thrust of their propaganda, which, in the crucial years 1327 and 1399, had presented them as selfless figures reluctantly driven to arms to save the country from the consequences of wayward and inadequate monarchs.

There was some truth in this, but the lords who posed as tribunes for a misgoverned nation were also driven by private jealousies and dreams of future advancement. The most trenchant and persistent critics of Edward II, Richard II and Henry IV were peers who considered themselves undervalued or displaced in the pecking order of royal patronage by upstarts like Gaveston. Their private grievances mutated into public causes, but coalitions of the envious and discontented were always fragile. 'The love of magnates is as a game of dice, and the desires of the rich like a feather blown upon the wind,' observed the unknown author of the *Vita Edwardi Secundi*.

Whether exercised for the public benefit or private gain, the power of the aristocracy was in the ascendant at the beginning of the fifteenth century. Two factors determined its nature and application. There was individual temperament, which made some peers prone to resort to violence or the threat of it whenever a political crisis seemed imminent. This, in turn, was influenced by the assurance of military support in the form of readily available soldiers, arms and armour. Both were in evidence in January 1400 when Richard II's half-brother John Holland, Earl of Huntingdon (a former 'duketti' with the title Duke of Exeter), joined a conspiracy to overthrow and murder Henry IV. A rash and impetuous nobleman, Huntingdon had little to lose, for he was tainted by his former attachment to Richard II and could expect no favours from the new regime.

Huntingdon had extensive lands in the South-West and he instructed his estate officials and servants to mobilise his tenants. Affection and fear were appealed to in equal parts. One volunteer declared that he would stand by his landlord with 'all my body' and in Saltash the Earl's bailiff threatened the hesitant with immediate beheading. In Exeter a canon of the cathedral who was one of Huntingdon's close advisers raised forty archers.[2] Armour and weapons were freely available from the Earl's arsenal. They were never used, for he and several other plotters were seized and lynched by the townsfolk of Cirencester before the uprising had gathered any momentum.

Territorial, political and military power were inextricably linked. A lord's network of estate officials could be transformed into recruiting sergeants who could bully tenants with threats of future victimisation or cajole them with promises of future favour. These methods yielded the largely untrained and ill-equipped rank and files of the baronial retinues, but what counted in terms of political leverage was the number of knights a lord could rely on in a crisis. Their numbers and their loyalty depended on the depth of the lord's purse, for they were either his salaried household servants, or men under contract to him and paid annual fees.

From the eleventh to the thirteenth centuries the feudal overlords of the aristocracy had used legal power to summon their knights, but the compulsion of custom proved a less efficient way of raising men than signed and sealed indentures. By 1300, these documents had spelt out the reciprocal duties of the lord and his retainer. The gist was always the same: the lord promised an annuity and, in return, the retainer pledged his service and that of his servants in war and peace. A caveat was always added which excused the knight from taking up arms against the Crown.

Indentured retainers were the sinews of aristocratic power. In 1312 the outstandingly rich Thomas, Earl of Lancaster, had ridden to Parliament at the head of two-and-a-half thousand men, including fifty knights. He was a maestro of political stagecraft who used the spectacle of an armoured cavalcade to impress the world at large, hearten his allies and browbeat Edward II. Thomas's private army was an expensive luxury which cost him between £1500 and £2000 a year, just under a fifth of his yearly revenues. His bluff was finally called in 1322, when thanks to slipshod generalship he was defeated at Boroughbridge by a royal army. Only two of his knights had refused to serve against the King.[3]

Paradoxically, the system of retaining gave aristocrats the means both to overawe the Crown and uphold royal authority in the countryside. Retainers were part of a nationwide latticework of personal alliances whose struts were compacts between the nobility and lesser landowners. It also offered the Crown a means to raise armies for foreign wars: when Edward III invaded France in the 1340s, he invited his nobles to mobilise their retainers into contingents whose wages and transport costs were paid by the royal exchequer.

At home, retainers were vital for the maintenance of a decentralised regional administration and the enforcement of legal disciplines. Every magnate had a semi-viceregal role in the area where his lands were concentrated and was expected to serve as a conduit for the authority of the Crown. His prestige, his estates and the knowledge that he was the king's man-on-the-spot commanded obedience and deference. This dispensation of power in the provinces was bluntly explained in 1452 by John Mowbray, third Duke of Norfolk, in an open letter to the inhabitants of that county. 'We let you know that next [to] the King our sovereign lord, by his good grace and licence, we will have the principal rule and governance throughout the shire, of which we bear our name.' He named local lawbreakers and warned them that 'though our person be not here daily, they shall find our power at all time'. The Duke's retainers and servants were his visible and vigilant presence.

Such men exercised power as sheriffs, under-sheriffs, justices of the peace and assessors and collectors of taxes. The names of local aristocrats headed the lists of knights and squires commissioned by the Crown to investigate matters such as flood defences and the state of the roads. A lord might not be present during the proceedings, but what mattered was the prestige of his name. Serious problems required direct intervention by noblemen; in 1414 Henry V ordered his cousin Edward, Duke of York, to preside in person over an enquiry into chronic lawlessness in Shropshire.[4] As a general rule, areas furthest away from London were the most prone to disorder.

The devolution of royal power reinforced that of the nobility by giving its members virtual control over local government. The system worked so long as royal supervision was thorough and peers respected (and feared) the king. Absolute honesty and impartiality were unattainable because an aristocrat's status and personal honour compelled him to defend his own and his dependants' interests with vigour. A willingness to concede or compromise were signs of irresolution which harmed a peer's local standing. Compliant sheriffs packed juries and rigged parliamentary elections. The system encouraged corruption, but it worked after a fashion and was better than none at all.

Local ascendancy strengthened a peer's national political power. Between 1386 and 1401, seven out of the eleven MPs for Warwickshire had close links with the Beauchamp Earls of Warwick who dominated the West Midlands. One of these Members was Thomas de Crewe, a country squire and retainer of the Beauchamps since 1387, when he appeared under their banner in an army raised by Thomas de Beauchamp to resist forces raised by Richard II's favourite, Robert de Vere. Crewe was a bureaucrat with some legal training rather than a warrior, and so he served the Beauchamps as an adviser and estate manager. Efficient and trustworthy, he served many times as a justice and under-sheriff. De Crewe was so proud of his service to the Beauchamps that he had their arms set on his magnificent brass in Wixford church, which, ironically, equalled in scale that of his former employer Thomas Beauchamp in nearby Warwick.

De Crewe had been one link in a chain of authority which stretched upwards through the earls of Warwick to the Crown. Just as kings needed the assistance of the nobility, they, in their turn relied upon professionals like de Crewe to manage their business affairs and fulfil their public responsibilities. Yet, it is worth remembering that de Crewe was willing to risk his life for his master when he challenged Richard II.

The number, physique and dress of a lord's retainers and servants were public advertisements of his status. In 1471 John de la Pole, second Duke of Suffolk, declared that it was beneath his dignity to ride from his seat at Ewelme in Oxfordshire with just twelve servants, all that were then available.[5] The frame and stature of these outriders were also important. One servant was recommended to a peer's household because he was 'a very tall gentleman and has good conditions [i.e. features]'.[6]

Sturdy, well clad and sometimes armed and armoured, servants riding in cavalcades behind their lords were the visible expression of the political and social dispensation of medieval England. In a country where the bulk of the population lived in small towns of fewer than five hundred inhabitants or villages, the local nobleman or his agents were the representatives of the state and most people's only contact with it. In a fourteenth-century version of the romance of the legendary Guy of Warwick, the hero meets an earl on a pilgrimage, who announces:

> I was a knight of rich lands
> And castles and towers in my hands.
> Of goods, I have great plenty
> All that land had dread of me.

Kings, too, had to cosset such creatures or else risk their thrones. A contented aristocracy was a biddable and cooperative partner in government. Its happiness depended on royal patronage in the forms of gifts of land, offices and favours not only for individual peers, but their strings of kinsmen and women and retainers. Vanity as well as greed had to be satisfied and peers had to be entertained in the grand style. A magnificent court with lavish feasts, tournaments and hunting in well-stocked royal parks won hearts.

Charismatic warrior kings Edward I and Edward III knew exactly how to satisfy their noblemen through patronage and entertainment, although it helped that the former was a frightening man with a ferocious temper. Both monarchs appealed to the aristocratic imagination by deliberately projecting themselves as second Arthurs who would restore the chivalric dreamworld of Camelot. The message was clear: there was peace and harmony in Camelot only so long as the King and his lords kept faith with each other and gladly performed their reciprocal obligations for the benefit of all.

———•———

Manners with Virtue:
The Cult of Chivalry
and the Culture of
the Aristocracy

Chivalry explains the mind of the medieval aristocrat. It was a blend of moral truths, theology and romantic, chiefly Arthurian, legends. Together they constituted an ideal to which all knights aspired, and chivalric precepts governed their relations with each other and the rest of the world. Above all, chivalry was the touchstone of honour, that abstraction which both guided the knight and set him apart from lesser beings.

All the ideological strands of chivalry are drawn together in the spectacular chapel built to contain the tomb and effigy of Richard Beauchamp, Earl of Warwick (see plate XX). Secular and religious imagery combine to reveal the nature of the universe Warwick inhabited and justify his exalted place within it. The onlooker is confronted with a visual celebration of the power and self-confidence not just of one nobleman, but of the aristocracy as a whole at a moment in its history when its influence had reached an unprecedented peak.

Richard died aged fifty-seven in 1439 after a career of service to the Crown as general, diplomat and administrator. Chivalry had been the driving force of his life, as it had been that of Chaucer's knight. According to his epitaph, Warwick was 'one of the most worshipful knights of his days' and a model of 'manhood and cunning [i.e. intelligence]'. His devotion to the ideals of knighthood share equal prominence with the list of high offices he had held, including the lieutenant governorship of Normandy, where he had overseen the trial and execution of Joan of Arc.

The essence of knightly perfection is conveyed by Warwick's copper-gilt effigy. He wears a suit of armour in the latest Milanese fashion, which combined function with elegance. His features are handsome and may possibly be a portrait since a surgeon and a painter were consulted when the tomb was being designed. Whether or not a likeness, the Earl's figure indicates an athletic, well-proportioned man with long, delicate fingers.

In death the medieval aristocracy were always depicted as a physical elite and many were in life. A modern autopsy on the skeleton of Sir Bartholomew de Burghersh, who died in 1369 in his sixties after a lifetime of campaigning, revealed a sturdy man of nearly six foot with strong, muscular limbs. His physique was the result of regular exercise and a diet rich in protein, although his teeth were eroded by the grainy bread he had eaten. By contrast, analyses of the bones of the mass of the population reflect stunted growth and infirmities caused by inadequate diet and back-breaking labour.

Knights were not just taller and stronger than their inferiors. Popular chivalric romances constantly drew attention to the fine features and fair complexions of noble heroes and heroines. Fiction often reflected reality. Sir Thomas More described Arthur Plantagenet, Viscount Lisle (an illegitimate son of

Edward IV), as 'princely to behold, of visage lovely, of body mighty and strong; and clean made'. His contemporary Edward Stafford, third Duke of Buckingham, was likened to 'a Paris and Hector of Troy' as he performed in the tiltyard. Aristocratic manners would have been impeccable, their movements graceful and their speech fluent. In 1483, when Buckingham's father tried to persuade Londoners to accept Richard III as king, his unconvinced audience noted that his words were 'well and eloquently uttered with so angelic a countenance'.[1]

War was integral to Warwick's life. As a young man he fought for Henry IV at the Battle of Shrewsbury in 1403 against Harry Hotspur and against Owain Glyndŵr's Welsh rebels. In middle age the Earl had commanded armies and fleets during Henry V's conquest of Normandy and, in the final years of his life, he helped resist the French counter-offensives. Warwick's courage, fighting skills and horsemanship were assayed many times in tournaments in England and on the Continent. He jousted with French, Italian and German knights and gained many victories which enhanced his prestige and honour. Chivalry was an international brotherhood bonded by common values and such shared pastimes as jousting and hunting.

Prowess on the battlefield or tiltyard were the traditional accomplishments of the knightly order, one of the three so-called 'estates' of the feudal society which had emerged in Europe in the tenth and eleventh centuries. The terrestrial social dispensation was a mirror of the Heavenly, and Paradise was an absolute monarchy with God ruling over a layered hierarchy of angels whose rank and function were denoted by their apparel and crowns. This was a paradigm for human society, where princes ruled by God's grace and power flowed downwards through a stratified society. It had three inter-dependent orders or estates: the knights who defended society and the Church, whose clergy provided salvation through prayers and ministering the sacraments, and the peasantry who laboured to sustain warriors and priests.

Theologians and secular writers on chivalry agreed that the knights were the earthly equivalent of angels. It was a highly flattering conceit which appears on the sides of the Warwick monument, where angels alternate with figures of the Earl's noble kinsfolk.[2] One, his son-in-law Richard Neville, Earl of Warwick ('the Kingmaker'), became a byword for grasping ambition and perfidy.

Above Warwick's tomb the divine and earthly paradigms are represented in stained glass by angels playing musical instruments and creating harmony. This orchestra is a reminder that by discharging their worldly and largely political responsibilities men of Warwick's rank were fulfilling God's purpose. It was a point repeatedly made by preachers and theologians, many of whom used chivalry to reinforce their arguments. Indeed, the cult of chivalry had its roots in the eleventh-century Church's attempts to persuade knights to undertake their sacred duties.

It had been a difficult task, for it had first required knights to suppress their predatory instincts which had so often led to outbreaks of anarchy in which peasants, their homes, crops and livestock were killed and destroyed. Chivalry taught knights to abhor wanton violence and fulfil their hallowed obligation to protect the poor and weak. It was the catalyst which gradually transformed muscular raptorial knighthood into muscular Christian knighthood. In 1096 the Church had produced its masterstroke: the crusading movement. The crusader was Christ's own knight, fighting to recapture the saviour's land from Muslim infidels, and so qualifying himself for Paradise. The idea captured the imagination of knights and enhanced the spiritual status of knighthood.

Christianity and chivalry were welded together to raise the self-esteem of the knightly estate and convince them that they were truly an elect chosen by God. Knights of the Order of the Bath were reminded of their sacred vocation by a vigil of prayer and symbolic cleansing before they were knights. Theologians contrived a version of history which stressed the importance of knights in the unravelling of God's purpose: the establishment of Christian Europe, and at every stage in its development, knights or their counterparts had been unconscious agents of divine Providence. Christianity had spread through the Roman Empire thanks to the order imposed by Roman 'knights'. Commanded by the Emperor Vespasian, pagan Roman knights were the unwitting instruments of God's will when they avenged Christ's crucifixion by the destruction of Jerusalem in AD 70.[3]

God always needed his knights. Outstanding faith and devotion to the ideals of chivalry combined in the legend of St George. According to an early sixteenth-century life of this martyr, he was an exemplary knight who:

> . . . had manners with virtue,
> Noblesse, courage, wisdom and policy.

The same qualities were accredited to Warwick in his epitaph.

The Earl's moral forebears included classical heroes such as Hector and Alexander, reinvented by the authors of popular romantic fiction as proto-knights who had lived by the codes of chivalry. Classical antiquity validated knighthood in an age when Greece and Rome were revered as unrivalled sources of knowledge, wisdom and examples of correctness in every area of human affairs. An heir in spirit to the heroes of the ancient world, Warwick could also claim a direct and illustrious pedigree which linked him with the paladins of chivalric legend.

Warwick's feet rest on a muzzled bear, the badge of the Beauchamps, which, according to legend, had been worn by one of Arthur's knights. On the Earl's helmet is his crest of a white swan, a device which shows his descent from the Knight of the Swan. His legend was first related in tenth-century Germany and underwent many variations, all of which were immensely popular. In essence it was the story of an enchanted knight who appears from nowhere in a boat towed by swans. He rescues a widowed duchess and her daughter from an over-bearing lord and marries the girl, by whom he has a child, Ida. He vanishes and his daughter marries Eustace, Count of Boulogne.

Fairy story and fact became entwined. Every variant of the legend of the Knight of the Swan provides him with historical descendants, most famously Godfrey de Bouillon, one of the commanders of the crusading army which captured Jerusalem in 1099. The blood of the Knight of the Swan, and with it an atavistic propensity for honour, flowed through the veins of a select body of European knights. In England, the Beauchamps shared this distant ancestor with the de Bohuns and the Staffords, and each family boasted the connection by displaying swans on their tombs, heraldry, seals and the badges worn by their servants.

The supposed blood of the Knight of the Swan had made Richard Beauchamp genetically predisposed to virtue and courage. Honour was transmitted across generations: a poet reciting the deeds of Sir Ralph de Tony (an ancestor of Warwick's) during the siege of Caerlaverock in 1300 insisted that he fought with astonishing valour *because* he was descended from the Knight of the Swan.[4] Warwick would have under-stood this and all that it implied for his own conduct. He was also acutely aware of another legendary ancestor of outstanding bravery, Guy of Warwick. His father had added a tower to Warwick Castle in Guy's honour and hung his great chamber with tapestries depicting his ancestor's exploits. Amazingly, while on a pilgrimage to Jerusalem in 1408, Richard Beauchamp encountered 'Sir Baltirdam, a noble lord' in the service of the

Egyptian Sultan who was acquainted with the legends of Guy of Warwick and anxious to meet his descendant. He entertained Richard, who repaid his hospitality – chivalry could cross even the boundaries of faith.[5]

Richard Beauchamp's ancestors and living family are represented on his tomb by their coats of arms. Ferocious beasts like the de Bohun and Plantagenet lions, the Monthermer eagle and, of course, the Beauchamp bear reveal how heavily the heraldic imagination relied on images of feral strength and savagery. All are appropriate to a caste whose origins were warlike and whose members were expected to display fearlessness and ferocity in battle.

Heraldry was the cipher of ancestry. It said who you were, where you came from and with whom you were connected by blood and marriage. The coat of arms was the insignia of gentle birth and it could be assumed by anyone who considered themselves qualified and felt confident that their pretensions would be accepted by the world at large. Faked pedigrees were sometimes produced as evidence of gentleness, and so at the close of the fifteenth century the whole business was placed in the hands of a semi-official body, the College of Arms, whose heralds decided who was or was not a gentleman and issued coats of arms accordingly. Their principal criterion was an applicant's ability to pay their fees. The colours and images of the coat of arms were described in an archaic Anglo-Norman vocabulary (gules [red], sable [black], vair [a stylised representation of fur]) which implied antiquity and ancient blood.

A family's coat of arms also charted that family's economic fortunes. Nearly all the shields on the Warwick tomb are quartered, evidence of marriages to heiresses and the acquisition of their lands. Between 1300 and 1500 one in four aristocratic families failed in the male line, their estates passing either to daughters or collateral heirs [nephews, nieces and cousins], a process which meant that many accumulations of land were broken up.[6] Infertility and infant deaths thus acted as a natural brake on any one dynasty's engrossment of land, and with it, political muscle. Warwick's only male heir died in 1446, some seven years after his father's death, leaving a daughter who died three years later. The Beauchamp inheritance was split between Richard's four daughters and their respective husbands.

On Warwick's calf is the Order of the Garter, a token that he was one of an exclusive knot of peers and knights who enjoyed special royal favour. It had been founded in 1348 by Edward III as part of his self-conscious promotion of the Arthurian cult, contrived to raise the prestige of the monarchy and signal to the world that Camelot had been restored. The order was dedicated to St George and confined to twenty-six distinguished lords and knights each of whom was '*un gentil homme de sang et chevalier sans reproche*' ('a gentleman of lineage and a knight beyond reproach'). All were bound by the Order's motto *Honi soyt qui mal y pense* ('Shame to him who thinks ill of it'), which was a coded warning against perfidy and faction. The Earls of Arundel and Huntingdon, who had objected to royal policies some years before, were not invited to join. Knights of the Garter were to keep faith with each other and their King. Not that Edward III was likely to provoke unrest among the nobility; his French wars were enriching them and his tournaments gave them the chance to add lustre to honour won on the battlefield.

Jousts were the theatre of chivalry and propaganda for the social and political order. One fifteenth-century tournament opened with the declaration that it was a celebration of 'Chevellerie . . . by which our mother Holy Church is defended, kings and princes served and countries kept and maintained in justice and peace'.[7] This assertion justified the ascendancy of the entire knightly order and the aristocracy which stood at its pinnacle. Its wealth and mystique are conveyed by the spectacle of knights in burnished armour with jewelled accoutrements riding massive caparisoned and armoured warhorses and attended by squires and pages. Such wonderful sights and the thrilling mock combats supplemented the iconography of the Warwick chapel.

Popular, secular romances taught knights and noblemen how to behave. This literature proliferated after 1300 and was widely read for diversion and instruction. Scenarios encompassed fantasy with fairy tales and magic (like those of the Knight of the Swan) and familiar reality with temperamental clashes within families, sibling jealousies, forced marriages, kidnapped wards, sexual desire and profitable marriages. As in Chaucer's *Knight's Tale,* there were battles, and prolix descriptions of armour, clothing, jewellery and the menus of feasts.

Readers were constantly reminded of chivalric propriety and custom: in Sir Thomas Malory's *Le Morte Darthur*, which was first published in 1485, when Gawain first meets Arthur, the King promises to 'do unto you all the worship that I may, for I must by reason you are my nephew, my sister's son'. Family obligations mattered and without doubt Warwick would have behaved in a similar fashion to any of his kinsmen and women. He would also have appreciated how fictional knights accumulated honour through valour, uprightness and the daily exercise of such knightly virtues as 'mesure' (inward restraint and moderation), generosity and courtesy.

The perfect knight was also a creature of aesthetic sensibility. According to the literary chivalric ideal, he was a fearless warrior distinguished by his taste and creative accomplishments. He lived surrounded by objects of beauty: tapestries, intricate gold and silverware, jewellery and illuminated books filled his home. He commissioned the building of castles and churches and the objects which adorned them.

Noblemen practised as well as patronised the arts. Chaucer's squire 'could make songs and poems and recite' as well as dance, draw and write. This virtuoso would have been welcomed in any noble household. Open-handed hospitality was a chivalric virtue and it was incumbent upon a host to offer sophisticated entertainment to his guests. 'A dalliance of damsels' who read from chivalric romances diverted the guests of Sir John Berkeley, a Leicestershire knight who died in 1398.[8] Visitors to Wressle Castle in Yorkshire in the early sixteenth century were treated to 'interludes', religious and secular plays and concerts performed by the Earl of Northumberland's musicians and choristers.[9]

Providing such entertainment was a sign that a host possessed that equipoise between refinement and bravado which was so prized. Berkeley had acquired it: he had won honour on the battlefields of France, was a celebrated huntsman and maintained a cultured household. For the aristocracy, there was never any incompatibility between cultivation of the body and the mind and senses. Moreover, and this is too often forgotten, noblemen had to be literate in order to read the accounts and legal documents involved in the running of their estates.

Berkeley's distant cousin Thomas ('the Magnificent'), fifth Lord Berkeley, simultaneously raised pheasants, hunted, commissioned illuminated books, founded a grammar school and was the patron of the Cornish scholar, John Trevisa. He lived with his patron in Berkeley Castle in the Vale of Gloucester, where he translated theological texts into English and, at Lord Berkeley's insistence, injected them with anti-clerical opinions.[10]

After his wife's death in 1392, Berkeley ordered a finely executed brass from a London tombmaker. It remains in Wotton-under-Edge church and its now lost inscription contained the touching lines:

In youth our parents joined our hands, our selves, our hearts,

This tomb our bodies have, the heavens our better parts.[11]

This monument must have deeply impressed Berkeley's neighbours, for two (a knight and a wool exporter) chose the same workshop for their brasses which equalled his in scale and quality.[12] A cultural trend was already underway: the aristocracy dictated patterns of taste which those below were eager to imitate, particularly if they were on the way up in society. What pleased the eye of Lord Berkeley was, for that reason alone, an object of desire.

Berkeley was one of a growing number of peers with literary and intellectual interests. Although historically remembered as a political bruiser, William de la Pole, first Duke of Suffolk, wrote love poetry in French and English and his library contained French romantic fiction, a Latin treatise on statecrafts and English religious handbooks.[13] Anthony Woodville, Lord Rivers, translated various French works into English, some of which were printed by his protégé, William Caxton. Printing first came into England by way of aristocratic patronage.

Architecture has always been about power. Medieval cathedrals and castles were blatant statements of the spiritual supremacy of the Church and the temporal supremacy of the Crown and the aristocracy. The sheer size and the richness of the ornamentation of these buildings demanded awe and supplication from all who approached them. All required onlookers to look upwards.

Castles were first built in the decades after the Norman Conquest, and were like nails driven into the countryside: they were where knights and barons lived and they were also places of refuge and defence. The magnate could defy the world from his castle and to prise him out of it required a time-consuming and expensive siege. By the late fourteenth century, the growing efficiency of artillery had made the castle militarily redundant. But it kept its grip on the imagination of the aristocracy. Massive gateways, high towers and battlements were the prime ingredients of the aesthetics of power, and so peers continued to build castles until the early sixteenth century.

New styles and new materials were applied to an old concept by Ralph, Lord Cromwell, who demolished his ancestors' defensive castle at Tattershall in Lincolnshire and began building a new and very different one in 1434. The second Tattershall castle was a four-storey tower block built in brick with airy rooms lit by broad windows and heated by massive fireplaces with painted heraldic stonework. Cromwell's badge of a tasselled purse was prominent and reminded visitors that he was Treasurer of England, one of the highest offices in the state. Valence tapestries hung on the walls, adding to the impression of colour and sumptuousness. A fastidious peer who enjoyed comfort, Cromwell had a fireplace in his bedroom and a private lavatory, and he and his wife slept in a four-poster bed hung with cloth of gold and blue damask.[14]

When completed and furnished, Tattershall was one of the first examples of the architecture of pure prestige. Its turrets and crenellations were misleading: this was not a stronghold, but an edifice that puffed Cromwell as a rich aristocrat with local and national power. Similar declarations of social and political eminence would be made on an even grander scale by aristocratic houses over the next four hundred years.

Cromwell's pride and egotism were tempered by that chilling sense of sinfulness which the Church insisted haunted everyone, whatever their rank. Without direct heirs to inherit his fortune, he diverted large swathes of his estates for the construction of a collegiate church in which priests and choristers would sing masses for his soul in perpetuity. Charity accelerated the soul's ascent heavenwards and so Cromwell endowed almshouses for the infirm poor. A free grammar school was attached to the college and Cromwell funded scholarships to Cambridge for its brightest pupils. Ignorance was evil: it hindered Christians from understanding the scriptures and reduced the flow of clever young clerks into the Church and those professions and trades for which literacy was essential. The advancement of learning was a social and religious duty for all noblemen.

What does the still impressive ensemble of castle and church say about the nature of aristocratic taste and culture? Cromwell was certainly vain, anxious about his salvation, aware of his obligations to society and driven by a strong sense of dynastic pride. He was the last and most illustrious member of a line which deserved a permanent memorial to command the respect and wonderment of posterity. Memory mattered to all noblemen, which was why Richard Beauchamp allocated several thousand pounds to his tomb and chapel at Warwick.

Cromwell got at Tattershall what he and other aristocrats wanted: an imposing church in which the arrangement of space, light and colour conveyed a sense of holiness, and prompted admiration for the piety of the man who had footed the bill. As for the overall design, this was dictated by the prevailing Perpendicular style, which lent itself to spectacular displays of stained glass. Large windows were filled with images of Bible stories, legends of the saints and representations of the sacraments and the creed. Heraldry told the onlooker who had paid for this religious instruction. Tattershall's now sadly depleted glass was purchased by the foot: images of the Seven Sacraments cost eighteen pence, the Magnificat fourteen pence.[15] Individual designs were left to the glaziers, who relied on stereotypes from pattern books. Here, as in the overall design of a church, the aristocratic patron was happy with conservative convention.

Meticulous care was taken for the preservation of memory. Its constituents were honour, ancestry and devotion to chivalry. All were rendered on tombs with effigies of the deceased in stone, brass and the less durable wood, which fell out of fashion in the early fourteenth century. These tombs were striking objects in churches and cathedrals: effigies were gilded and painted and brasses burnished and inlaid with enamels. Funeral iconography proclaimed the chivalric virtues. Knights appeared as young, strong men wearing the most up-to-date armour with swords hung at their hips and spurs on their heels. At their feet were lions, symbolising courage, or hounds, symbolising loyalty. Their wives too were young, elegantly dressed in the most fashionable gowns and with elaborate and often jewelled headdresses.

Patrons wanted images which proclaimed status, and artists responded. James Reames, a London marbler with a string of aristocratic and noble patrons, knew exactly what they desired and provided it. In 1466 he agreed to make a brass for Richard Willoughby from Wollaton near Nottingham. He had asked for 'the image of a man whole armed except the head in the best harness [i.e. armour]' with his head on helm with the Willoughby crest of an owl and standing on the Willoughby badge of a whelk. His wife was to be portrayed 'attired in the best with a little dog with bells about its neck at her feet'. A design had already been prepared and there were detailed instructions as to the shields of arms on the tomb.[16] This rare contract confirms all the iconographic evidence as to the conventional features of honourable memory. Physical verisimilitude was ignored: the armoured figure of Willoughby was a standard pattern which Reames used for other clients. What mattered was the inference of earthly perfection, the inscription and, of course, the heraldry.

An idiosyncrasy appears on the effigy of an unknown, early fourteenth-century knight at Pershore in Worcestershire: he holds a hunting horn in his hand. It was a symbol which had a triple significance. Hunting was the exclusive pleasure of knights and lords, who had legal rights of ownership over the beasts, birds and fish which inhabited their parks, woodlands and ponds.

This allowed them to eat venison, hares, rabbits and wildfowl, delicacies forbidden to lesser men and women. The right to kill and consume game set knights and lords apart from other men, a distinction they were determined to uphold.

Wild animals, birds and fish were a very vulnerable form of property which was protected by a sheaf of Game Laws passed by Parliament from the mid-fourteenth century onwards. This legislation was a blatant case of the nobility's selfishness and was deeply resented by peasant farmers and labourers, who were banned from snaring rabbits and hares. Poachers were criminals and were punished for a form of theft that challenged the social dispensation and sometimes was a satisfying revenge of 'us' against 'them'. Revealingly, in 1451 a large gang of yeoman farmers and labourers calling themselves 'servants of the queen of the fairies' and disguised by false beards and blackened faces broke into the first Duke of Buckingham's deer park at Penshurst in Kent. They were good archers and they shot and carried off eighty-two deer. This was profitable vengeance on a peer who had been prominent in the judicial retribution after Jack Cade's rebellion and had had a part in hanging many Kentishmen.[17]

Hunting was a pastime which filled the abundant spare time of the nobility and enhanced individual status. The accomplished huntsman basked in the admiration of his peers, and in the private satisfaction of knowing that he had acquired in the chase that nerve, hardiness and coordination of mind, eye and muscle that were invaluable on the battlefield. Hunting prepared a martial elite for the rigours of war, and for this reason alone the right to pursue game had to be the monopoly of knights and noblemen.

The chase also stimulated all the senses. A fourteenth-century narrative of a young knight setting out one May morning in search of deer conveys the exhilaration and thrills of hunting. He watches the sun rising over the mist, there is dew on the daisies and primroses. Cuckoos, thrushes and wood pigeons are singing, 'each fowl in that woodland more joyous than the other'. The huntsman sees a high-antlered deer in a glade and 'stalked [it] full stilly no sticks to break'. At last he is within range and a single arrow slays the beast, which the hunter then cuts up in the correct manner.[18] Art mirrored reality; this huntsman's historic contemporary, the second Lord Berkeley, would spend nights in the open with his brother, waiting for daybreak and the chance to take deer, hares and foxes.[19]

Hunting acquired its own arcane rituals and mystique. The knowledge and practice of these were as important in distinguishing men and women of noble blood as their coats of arms. Towards the end of the fourteenth century, an encyclopedic account of the lore of hunting and fishing was compiled by Dame Juliana de Berners, a knight's daughter. It was printed in 1496 with the title *The Boke of St Albans* and proved immensely popular. Like so many textbooks it froze contemporary practice and made it permanent.

Dame Juliana has not received the attention she deserves. Her veterinary advice to the huntsman, the falconer and the angler gives an insight into contemporary aristocratic attitudes, not least because the hierarchies of the human and animal world run parallel. The hunter's quarry possessed admirable human qualities: the salmon was a 'gentle' fish and the bream was 'noble'. Like their owners, dogs who scented and chased game were part of a stratified hierarchy. There were aristocratic, thoroughbred alants (forerunners of the modern mastiffs) and far, far below them were mongrels, who were tainted by their 'churlish nature and ugly shape'. The rules of precedent dictated the ownership of falcons and hawks. As sovereign of all raptors, the gyr falcon could be flown only by a king, the peregrine was reserved for earls, merlins were for ladies and at the base of the avine ladder there was 'a kestrel for a knave [i.e. servant]'.

Dame Juliana laid down the correct terminology to be used in hunting. References to a 'bevy of quails' or a 'deceit of lapwings' (these and other of her collective nouns have passed into the language) identified the speaker as a true cognoscente and, therefore, of gentle blood. The dexterity with which a nobleman butchered the carcass of a deer revealed additional proof of rank and ancestry. He took the best meat for his own table, the liver and kidneys went to his huntsman and his dogs consumed the entrails.

Legend posing as history, Christian doctrine and artistic conventions had been enlisted to underpin and perpetuate the ascendancy of aristocrats. All contributed to the cult of chivalry, which had transformed a purely martial elite into one which convinced itself and the rest of the world that it had hereditary virtue. This was innate and required careful cultivation, usually within the household of a knight and nobleman; the attainments of Chaucer's squire had been acquired in his father's household, where, among other things he had learned to be 'lowly and serviceable'. Aristocratic superiority, like that of Dame Juliana's thoroughbred hounds, was ultimately natural and, since the universe operated on principles laid down by God, legitimate.

3

---•---

Their Plenty was Our
Scarcity: Resistance

Aristocratic power was always conditional. It rested ultimately
on the consent of the vast mass of the population which worked
for a living and in various ways paid to support lords and knights.
For all their skill at fighting, building castles and amassing servants, the nobles were always massively outnumbered: in the
early fourteenth century, when the population was about 4.5
million, there were roughly forty hereditary peers and two thousand knights and squires. Submission to superiors was the will of
God and the Church preached quietism to the masses, reminding them that riches and power were no passport to Paradise and
that Christ cherished the poor.

In June 1381 the masses suddenly and violently withdrew
their consent to the social order. For four days the nobility

trembled as they never had before. Upwards of ten thousand peasants had occupied London, seized the Tower and murdered royal ministers and officials. Individual noblemen were insulted. Suddenly, the world seemed to have been turned upside down and for a few moments it seemed as if this arrangement might become permanent. At Smithfield, then just beyond London's Walls, Wat Tyler, the leader of the insurgents, confronted the fourteen-year-old Richard II and demanded a social revolution. The rebel's mood was nervous and menacing. He demanded the extinction of the nobility: 'No lord shall have lordship in the future, but it should be divided among all men, except the King's own lordship'. Churchmen would be stripped of their estates and, to complete the new order, all men would be free to fish and hunt game. A few minutes later, Tyler became involved in a scuffle with one of Richard's attendants and was mortally wounded. The King rode forward instantly and calmed the rebels, convincing them that he would now be their leader.[1]

Ironically, given his future fate, Richard II had saved the social order and with it the nobility. It was already preparing a counter-attack, for, while he was winning the hearts of the insurgents, a detachment of armoured knights and squires appeared. Two days of humiliation and impotence rankled and some asked the King permission to behead 'at least two hundred of the criminals as a warning to posterity that the knightly order was of some worth against the rustics'. Richard forbade a massacre because he thought that many of the victims may have been present under duress. Judicial and extra-judicial chastisement followed, with noblemen and knights to the forefront. A poet later wrote:

> Man beware and be no fool:
> Think on the axe and the stool!
> The stool was hard, the axe was sharp,
> The iiii [fourth] year of King Richard.[2]

Had the social system been in jeopardy at Smithfield? Or were already dramatic events embellished by clerical chroniclers determined to reveal the sheer evil of an uprising directed against God and the Crown. After all, a royal herald was reported to have seen two devils among the insurgents. Fearing for his soul, Jack Straw, who was Tyler's lieutenant, confessed on the scaffold that the rebels had planned to kill all the King's escort and any lords who opposed them. Straw's admission confirmed Tyler's ultimatum: the rebels wanted an egalitarian society, proof that they were the enemies of God.

Straw's revelations confirmed the worst fears of the nobility and clergy. As with terrorism today, the Peasants' Revolt spawned paranoia and alarmism. There were suspicions of a secret, diabolic conspiracy. Its guiding spirit was John Ball, a vagrant priest who had served as the rebels' prophet and chaplain. Since the 1360s he had been preaching seditious sermons on the couplet:

> *When Adam delved and Eve span,*
> *Who was then a gentleman?*

This challenge to the scriptural sanction for human inequality was indirectly complemented by the contemporary academic theologian, John Wycliffe. He argued that God could not give 'civil dominion' to a man and his heirs, which threw into question the validity of a hereditary aristocracy. Yet he urged submission on the poor: 'if you be a labourer, live in meekness and truly and willingly do thy labour'. Nonetheless, it suited the Church to connect Wycliffe's heretical doctrines with sedition and depict his followers, the Lollards, as enemies of both itself and the state. Heresy and sedition went hand in hand and by suppressing it the nobility served its own interests.

Some clergymen blamed the 1381 uprising on a collective moral lapse by an aristocracy which had neglected the moral obligations of chivalry and succumbed to the sin of the rich and self-indulgent Dives. The point was eloquently made by the Dominican Nicholas Bromyard, who imagined the poor appealing for justice at the gates to Paradise:

> Oh just God, mighty judge, the game was not fairly divided between them and us. Their satiety was our famine, their merriment was our wretchedness, their jousts and tournaments were our torments, because with our oats and at our expense they did these things. Their plenty was our scarcity. [3]

God had punished an aristocracy which had forfeited its authority through overindulgence and callousness towards the poor.

Historians have disagreed on precisely what the peasants wanted in 1381, and, more importantly, on whether they were all of the same mind. One cannot be certain that the chroniclers faithfully reported the exchanges at Smithfield or whether Straw spoke the truth on the scaffold. What matters is that contemporaries were so scared by the events of 1381 that they were willing to believe both. A surprisingly level-headed analysis was offered by Sir Richard de Waldegrave, the Speaker of the House of Commons, which assembled in the autumn. Addressing both houses, he conceded that the 'poor commons' had endured 'great outrages' at the hands of 'various servants of our lord the king and other lords of the realm'. This stifling oppression had goaded 'the mean commons to rise and commit the mischief they did'.

There had certainly been provocation. Moreover, and this is astonishing in the light of what had occurred in 1381, landowners had believed that the docility and forbearance of the peasantry were limitless. The poet John Gower summed up this attitude when he likened the placidity of the peasants to that of the oxen and pigs they tended. When the lords and knights reasserted their military power at Smithfield, observers revealingly noted that they herded the cowed peasants like sheep. Yet for a few days the peasants had been like wolves, a metamorphosis which gave the knightly order a brief but profound psychological shock.

Nonetheless, anyone who owned land would have been all too well aware of the changing temper of the peasantry during the massive economic disruption of the previous thirty years. Rent rolls and the records of manorial courts presented a stark picture of dwindling revenues and bloody-minded peasants. 'Sheep died of murrain, husbandry at great loss and tenements ruinous' was the surveyor's report on the condition of John of Gaunt's once flourishing fenland manor of Methwold in the 1380s.[4] Like the rest of the country, Methwold was slowly and painfully convalescing from an unprecedented sequence of natural calamities. There had been intermittent harvest failures and famines between 1315 and 1322, the Black Death pandemic of 1348–49 and subsequent, lesser outbreaks over the next thirty years. In 1300 the population had been between 4.5 million and 5 million, and by 1400 it had fallen to 2.25 million. It did not begin to rise until the end of the fifteenth century.

Demographic disasters played havoc with land, labour and food markets. As a result the economic balance of power shifted away from landowners to tenants and labourers. Most important of all, chronic depopulation knocked away the main prop of economic feudalism, hereditary serfdom. Serfs had never been efficient labour units, for they required close supervision and undertook obligatory duties to their overlords resentfully. From 1350 onwards, masses of serfs liberated themselves; they fled from manors to compete in an open labour market in which wages were soaring. The most ambitious hoped to acquire capital and tenancies.

Landowners reacted with legislation to outlaw the free market in labour. Using their dominance in Parliament, they passed successive Statutes of Labourers which froze wages at pre-1349 levels. The criminal and seignorial courts enforced serfdom, and captured serfs were dragged back to their manors where they had been born and where the law demanded that they stayed. Lawyers sifted manorial records to uncover evidence of the ancestry of serfs who alleged that they were freemen. All these efforts to put back the clock failed. The machinery of coercion could not cope with the problem and the routines of agriculture compelled landlords to make the best bargains they could with employees. The alternative was unploughed fields and unharvested crops.

Attempts by landowners to deploy legal sanctions to reverse economic trends created a steady accumulation of frustration and anger among the peasantry. These were exacerbated by the poll taxes of 1377, 1379 and 1380 which placed intolerable burdens on the poorest. The cash was needed to fund the war against France, which had entered a disastrous phase. French and Castilian warships cruised unopposed in the Channel and launched amphibious attacks on south coast ports. Noblemen and knights were blamed for having neglected their duty to protect the kingdom and the lives and homes of its weakest subjects. Economic and military feudalism were failing.

Minatory tax officials collecting the poll tax in Kent and Essex triggered the insurrection in May 1381. As it spread, peasants directed their animus towards overbearing landlords (in particular the abbeys of St Albans and Bury St Edmunds), middle and lower-ranking royal and manorial officials, and judges and magistrates who had enforced the Statutes of Labourers. Wherever possible, insurgents burned manorial documents and with them evidence of serfdom. A day before he made his radical demands at Smithfield, Wat Tyler had asked Richard II for the abolition of serfdom and a uniform rent of four pence per acre for arable land. He also demanded a repeal of the detested Game Laws. The King agreed.

A very strong case can be made for saying that what most peasants wanted was the removal of legal barriers to their future prosperity. Some eyewitnesses to the events in London claimed afterwards that many rebels began to go home once the King had made these concessions. At the same time, the insurgents were eager to pay off old scores against their immediate persecutors. They singled out one aristocrat: John of Gaunt, Duke of Lancaster, who was the richest peer in the country and uncle to the King, whom he allegedly plied with bad advice. The insurgents looted and burned down his London house, the Savoy palace, but could not get their hands on its owner, for Gaunt was in Scotland.

Charters extracted from Richard under duress were rescinded once the rebellion had been broken. Nevertheless, the uprising had taught the landowners that it was dangerous folly to use political and legal powers to preserve their economic ascendancy. A mood of resignation to economic reality replaced intransigence and intimidation. Reviewing estate policy in 1401, the Countess of Warwick's officials concluded that 'until the world recovers better' they would have to lease lands on the best terms they could get. In the same year, the steward of Archbishop Arundel's manor at Wrotham raised labourers' wages 'so that they should conduct themselves better in their lord's service'.[5] The Statute of Labourers was a dead letter, so too was serfdom, although a handful of landowners occasionally tried to enforce it in the fifteenth and sixteenth centuries.

The withering of serfdom ended economic feudalism. Henceforward, all landlords relied on cash rents and entry fines (paid in instalments) due from tenants after they had agreed new leases. For most of the fifteenth century, when holdings exceeded potential lessees, agreements tended to favour tenants rather than landlords.

In the meantime, sheep kept the nobility solvent. Aristocrats responded to the extended agrarian crisis by resorting to what we now call diversity. Thomas the fifth Lord Berkeley abandoned direct farming and rented out his rich grasslands in the Vale of Gloucester to cattle graziers.[6] His neighbours the Beauchamp earls of Warwick adopted the conventional policy of turning arable land into pasture and investing in sheep. Their fleeces were sold to a Cotswold dealer William Grevel, an agent for Florentine importers. (Grevel's descendants became landowners and, in the sixteenth century, earls of Warwick.) Sheep saved the aristocracy as they did the rest of the landowning class. Foreign and domestic markets for wool expanded during the fifteenth and early sixteenth centuries and canny landlords responded by turning more and more arable land to pasture.

'Beware for vengeance of trespass' one poet warned the nobility after the 1381 rising. In common with the rest of the landowning class, the aristocracy had gone too far and used its power selfishly and, as events turned out, recklessly. It tried and failed to isolate itself from the economic upheavals and it nearly came unstuck. The aristocracy's position had briefly been exposed as precarious and it had survived thanks to the presence of mind of the young Richard II and a later willingness to compromise.

This being said, it is extraordinary that the 1381 rebellion remained a one-off phenomenon which never really became implanted in the historical consciousness of either the nobility or the masses. It was a revolution which never happened, because ultimately the insurgents were satisfied by an adjustment to economic relations with their rulers rather than a root-and-branch change to the social order. As the events of the fifteenth century proved, aristocrats' greatest enemies were themselves and not the peasantry.

4

Weeds Which Must Be Mown Down: The Wars of the Roses 1450–87

The Wars of the Roses were an aberration. The Crown and aristocracy lost sight of their primal duties: the preservation of just government and the maintenance of stability. Both were damaged by thirty-seven years of intermittent civil wars in which there were no ultimate winners. The Crown emerged in 1487 with its prestige and authority intact and enhanced, while a traumatised aristocracy had undergone a salutary lesson about the risks of going too far in the pursuit of power for its own sake. Thirty-five died in battle or on the scaffold and the victors confiscated the estates of the losers. The phrase 'never again' summed up the mindset of the survivors.

In an attempt to make sense of the conflict I have dealt with the wars in two parts. This chapter attempts to unravel the events and the next dissects the motives of the principal peers involved and the sources of their power. It is mostly about human vanity and selfishness; chivalry was seldom in evidence during the wars.

Shakespeare was right about the Wars of the Roses. The dramatic hurly-burly of the second and third parts of *Henry VI* and *Richard III* may distort the chronology, but they tell us what happened and, more importantly, offer insights into the minds of the protagonists. Temperamentally, fifteenth-century aristocrats differed little from their Elizabethan successors with whom Shakespeare was familiar. Both were proud, quarrelsome, ambitious, jealous of their honour, inclined towards intrigue and prone to exaggerated gestures. At a tense moment during the Battle of Towton in 1461 the bombastic Richard Neville, Earl of Warwick (the Kingmaker), declared with a flourish that he would kill his horse to prove his willingness to stand and fight. On hearing of the death of the Earl of Huntingdon in 1595, the Earl of Essex 'tore his hair and all his buttons broke with the swelling of his stomach'.[1]

As for individual characters, the sheer nastiness of Shakespeare's Richard, Duke of Gloucester, fits the historical nature of the man. Just before Christmas 1472, when he was twenty, Richard set about extorting property from the aged dowager Countess of Oxford. He bullied her in person and, unmoved by her 'great lamentation' and weeping, ordered her abduction from a nunnery to his London lodgings. There he and his henchmen broke her will by threats to kidnap and imprison her in Middleham Castle in Yorkshire, knowing that the 'great journey and the great cold' would kill the frail old lady.[2] A creature of this stamp would have no qualms about murdering anyone who got in his way, and, of course, he did.

Shakespeare also understood that aristocratic haughtiness was an expression of lineage and honour. Listen to the Duke of

Suffolk's refusal to ask for mercy after he has been captured by pirates:

> Suffolk's imperial tongue is stern and rough,
> Us'd to command, untaught to plead for favour.
> Far be it we should honour such as these
> With humble suit: no, rather let my head
> Stoop to the block than these knees bow to any,
> Save to the God of heaven, and to my king:
> And sooner dance upon a bloody pole,
> Than stand uncover'd to the vulgar groom.
> True nobility is exempt from fear: . . .[3]

William de la Pole did not speak these words, but he would have applauded the sentiments.

The historical Suffolk was beheaded with six strokes of a rusty sword on the gunwale of a boat in May 1450 after he had been captured on his way to exile in France. He was the first aristocratic casualty of the Wars of the Roses. A considerable proportion of his countrymen, including the House of Commons, had made Suffolk the scapegoat for all that had gone wrong in the country since Henry VI had come of age in 1436. This was an exaggeration; what was not was Suffolk's ambition, ruthlessness and ability to prevail upon a naive and tractable King. Henry stood by his favourite, halted the Parliamentary bill for his impeachment and banished the Duke for five years.

Henry's intervention incensed his subjects across southeastern England, who briefly usurped the role of Parliament by rebelling and demanding a thorough purge of Suffolk's cronies from the government. When the king prevaricated, Jack Cade's insurgents killed those they could get their hands on. Later, when the shipmen who had murdered Suffolk were charged, they defiantly claimed that they had acted for 'the community of the realm'.[4]

Shakespeare presents the rebel leader Cade as a cats paw of Richard Plantagenet, Duke of York, who in a surreptitious and crablike way is aiming to overturn Henry VI and make himself king. The friends of Cade's victims suspected something of the sort. They subsequently procured the indictment of York's steward Sir William Oldhall for overseeing the writing and distribution of seditious literature during the spring and summer of 1450. This propaganda was produced to convince the public that York alone could save Henry VI from Suffolk and a pack of rapacious courtiers who plied him with bad advice and plundered his revenues.

The squibs and doggerel verses are instructive. They indicate the existence of public opinion among the literate (who encompassed most clerics, landowners and men and women engaged in commerce) and a willingness of an aristocratic faction to enlist it. Cade's followers mouthed York's propaganda; an early example of the aristocratic political movement seeking allies wherever it could find them. The stratagem worked, for, from 1450 onwards, the Yorkists convinced a large number of people that they alone could and would save the kingdom.

It was not too difficult a task, for the House of Lancaster had never been wholly secure. The legitimacy of Henry IV's title had been challenged by aristocratic factions during his reign. Reopening the Hundred Years War offered a lifeline to the Lancastrian dynasty because it would simultaneously raise the prestige of the dynasty and concentrate the minds and energies of the nobility on a quest for glory and riches. As Shakespeare's Henry IV advised his son:

> Be it thy course to busy giddy minds
> With foreign quarrels; . . .

Giddy minds sobered at the prospect of fortunes. In 1412 an army commanded by Henry IV's second son, Thomas, Duke of Clarence, returned from France with £35,000 which was shared among the thirteen noblemen who had accompanied the expedition. Revealingly, several had left home heavily in debt.[5] The Agincourt campaign showered honour on Henry V and his lords, but they had to wait until the start of the piecemeal conquest of Normandy in 1417 to acquire the dividends they expected. These soon flowed freely as the Crown parcelled out French lands and titles. The Earl of Warwick became the count of Aumâle, the Earl of Stafford became Count of Perche, the Earl of Dorset became Count of Mortain and the Earl of Shrewsbury became Count of Clermont. French baronies and manors were scattered among lesser captains.

The new Anglo-French aristocracy quickly dissolved after 1440 as the Lancastrian empire in France disintegrated. It had always been underfunded, since English taxpayers were averse to underwriting enormous bills for wages, equipment and shipping, and so the Crown had borrowed heavily, creating a spiral of debt. Overstretched English forces were pushed back towards the Channel, and, with Henry VI negotiating from a position of strategic weakness, peace talks came to nothing.

War had failed to strengthen the Lancastrian monarchy by uniting and enriching the nobility; rather, it left them disgruntled, shamed and, in the case of the Duke of York, out of pocket. Recriminations were inevitable and varying degrees of blame were attached to the Dukes of Suffolk, Somerset and York. None was an outstanding commander or diplomat, but even if they had been, they had to contend with a King without political acumen or charisma.

Henry VI's father, Henry V, had epitomised that heroic, Arthurian brand of kingship which seduced the hearts of noblemen. Warrior kingship was not for Henry VI; he was withdrawn, torpid and preferred pious meditation to the tiltyard or hunting field. He had been born in December 1421 and astrologers blamed his dull humours on the baleful influence of the moon.[6] The moon king stood five feet and nine inches tall and was utterly without presence, so much so that some of his humbler subjects likened him to a child or a simpleton, for which impertinence they were hanged. Their diagnosis had not been too far off the mark, since between August 1453 and August 1454 Henry suffered a physical and mental breakdown which deprived him of his senses. When he recovered, he discovered (allegedly to his amazement) that he had fulfilled that most basic of royal duties, fathering a son and heir.

Clysters, enemas and bloodletting may somehow have cured the royal distemper, but the nobility failed to contrive a remedy for a lethargic and fallible king. The upheavals that followed the downfall of Suffolk were a prelude to a decade of increasingly bad-tempered bickering between aristocratic factions. All agreed that Henry VI could rule only under tutelage, but who could be trusted as his mentors? On one side stood his wife, Margaret of Anjou, the high-spirited and wilful daughter of a French princeling who was rich in titles (he was titular King of Naples) and poor in revenues. A few months after their marriage in 1445 Margaret had persuaded Henry to surrender the French provinces of Maine and Anjou. The King was under her thumb, an arrangement which suited those nobles who believed her preferable to York, whose integrity and disinterest were questionable.

York saw himself as an ideal protector by right of blood (he was descended from Edward III through both his parents) and he was the richest peer in the country. He was allied to two other super-rich lords, his kinsmen, Richard Neville, Earl of Salisbury, and his son Richard, Earl of Warwick (Warwick the Kingmaker). All three possessed extensive estates in Wales and the Scottish marches which provided reservoirs of soldiers. But while York could threaten his fellow peers, he could not unite them.

Whatever faction they followed, or even if they took refuge in neutrality, individual noblemen became increasingly anxious about their security. The attempted murder of Ralph, Lord Cromwell, in Westminster Palace at the end of 1449, the killing of Suffolk and three other ministers during the next year, and York's claims that a knot of courtiers had planned to assassinate him as he travelled back from Ireland generated a sense of paranoia. Violence became part of public life and its presence justified aristocrats of all affinities summoning their dependants whenever a political crisis seemed imminent. Fearful lords backed by armies were disinclined to compromise.

Humphrey Stafford, Duke of Buckingham, sensed the new mood. In 1450 he was prudently purchasing gunpowder and during the next ten years repeatedly summoned his retainers, who, in turn, called up their servants and tenants. The Duke could muster two thousand fighting men, all distinguished by the Stafford livery of scarlet and black jackets and the badge of the Stafford knot. They did not save him or his eldest son from being injured in 1455 when York, Salisbury and Warwick confronted Henry VI at St Albans. Exasperated by royal temporising, Warwick stormed the town and captured the King, who had been wounded in the neck by an arrow. The dead included York's enemy Edmund Beaufort, Duke of Somerset, and the Nevilles' northern rivals, Henry Percy, second Earl of Northumberland, and Thomas, Lord Clifford. These killings were calculated. They added the element of vendetta to political life.

Long before St Albans Henry had become a monarch to whom things happened rather than a ruler who made them happen. After St Albans he was under the thumb of the Yorkist peers, but by 1458 the Queen had reasserted her authority. Queen Margaret's aims were to preserve the dynasty and sustain an aristocratic party strong enough to withstand the Yorkists. Their elimination offered the best hope of security and it was temporarily achieved in 1459 after York's defeat at Ludford in Shropshire. Immediately after the battle, the Coventry Parliament passed acts of attainder stripping all prominent Yorkists of their titles and estates. Henceforward, they were fighting to recover their livelihoods and, in the following year, they won the Battle of Northampton and once again captured the King.

Shakespeare's insight into York's character suggested that he had long coveted the crown, which is probably correct, although he proceeded with circumspection, setting an example which would be followed by his fourth son, Richard, Duke of Gloucester. With Henry his prisoner, York claimed the throne in October 1460 and triggered several months of intermittent fighting in which he and Salisbury were killed and Margaret regained control of her husband. They lost the final assay at the Battle of Towton in 1461, which confirmed York's nineteen-year-old eldest son Edward, Earl of March, as King. Margaret hustled Henry towards Scotland and exile. In 1464 he was persuaded by former Lancastrian partisans to return, was taken and imprisoned in the Tower.

Edward IV's propaganda exploited the commonplace notion of England as a garden (it was used by Shakespeare in *Richard II*) that had been untended and become overgrown with 'weeds which must be mown down'.[7] Edward carried a scythe and, at the same time, was bent on reviving heroic kingship. One of his scribblers declared:

> *Of a more famous knight I never read*
> *Since the time of Arthur's days.*[8]

The rhetoric had some substance. A tall, courageous and likeable prince, Edward did all in his power to govern wisely, promote the welfare of his subjects and achieve solvency. Yet the cold reality was that he owed his throne to a coalition of noblemen who all wanted to be rewarded, none more than Warwick the Kingmaker. The conflict had also created a body of alienated lords who had lost kinsmen and forfeited titles and lands by attainder. Over a hundred landowners were deprived in this way, though they could regain their assets through conspicuous loyalty and good behaviour.

Just over half the aristocracy (thirty or so peers) had taken an active part in the fighting between 1459 and 1461 and, of these, Yorkist partisans were a minority. Edward had, therefore, to reunite the peerage, secure its cooperation and create a knot of lords dependent on his favour as a counterbalance to Warwick. He more or less succeeded, but seriously underestimated Warwick's rapacity, egotism and intoxication with power.

The Earl parted company with Edward IV and common sense in 1469. He stage-managed three small-scale uprisings against the King in which the insurgents claimed that Edward had fallen under the spell of an upstart nobility, most notably the relations of his queen, Elizabeth Woodville. She was the daughter of a minor Lancastrian peer and the widow of a Lancastrian knight who had been killed at the second Battle of St Albans in 1460. It was not her connections which angered Warwick, but the fact that her family were elbowing the Nevilles aside in the queue for royal patronage.

Indirect pressure having failed, Warwick cobbled together an alliance with Edward's capricious younger brother George, Duke of Clarence ('false, fleeting perjur'd Clarence'), Margaret of Anjou and various Lancastrians peers who had joined her in exile. This consortium of old antagonists briefly restored Henry VI to the throne in 1470 and compelled Edward to flee to Flanders. He returned in 1471, quickly rallied his supporters and defeated the Lancastrians at Barnet and Tewkesbury. Their leaders, including Warwick, who was cut down 'somewhat fleeing' from Barnet, were killed or executed after the battles. Henry VI was murdered in the Tower, and his son, Edward, Prince of Wales, had died in the fighting at Tewkesbury. An unprecedented blood-letting was a warning to the nobility.

Unlike the earlier phase of the Wars of the Roses, which had been fought over the issue of how best to rescue the country from Henry VI and install honest and efficient government, the contest between 1469 and 1471 was no more than selfish aristocratic power-broking. Before and after the tumults, Edward had an excellent record of kingship.

Edward's death at the age of forty-one in 1483 opened the final stage of the wars. Again, the conflict revolved around a blatant struggle for power; no issues were at stake. Within a week of the King's death, his brother Richard, Duke of Gloucester, and Henry Stafford, second Duke of Buckingham, agreed to try their hand at kingmaking. Each was rich, amoral and ruthless. Richard had long cultivated a sense of his own destiny. 'What am I Lord and what is my family that thou has brought me this far – then has raised me to this,' he declared in the preamble to the charter for his college at Middleham in 1478.[9] He had much to thank God for: he was a royal Duke, the richest and most powerful man in the kingdom and could rely on the retinues of his northern clients.

Alleging that Edward IV's marriage to Elizabeth Woodville had infringed canon law (but not laying the claim before the Church courts), Gloucester and Buckingham deposed the thirteen-year-old Edward V and imprisoned him and his younger brother Richard, Duke of York, in the Tower of London. Both Dukes overawed London with troops summoned from the North and the Welsh Marches and intimidated the nobility by the summary executions of Lords Grey and Rivers (kinsmen of Elizabeth Woodville) and William, Lord Hastings.

After a rushed coronation, Richard III (1483–5) doled out rewards to his accomplices: the dukedom of Norfolk and the

Mowbray estates were given to Lord John Howard. The title and lands had belonged by marriage to the Duke of York, who had been betrothed to marry Lady Anne Mowbray when they had been six and eight, and the Prince's rights to the dukedom had been confirmed by statute. Howard's promotion and enrichment at the young Duke's expense confirmed what was widely rumoured: that he and his elder brother had been murdered in the Tower on Richard III's orders.

Richard's cynical and brutal manipulation of power shocked the country, divided Yorkist supporters and, since he had overridden the laws of property and inheritance, alienated landowners of all ranks. Richard's moral claim to the throne was as flimsy as his legal; there was no reason whatsoever to imagine that Edward V would have proved an incompetent king when he came of age. Fear and anger led to a number of localised uprisings in the autumn of 1483 in favour of Henry Tudor, Earl of Richmond, a Lancastrian exile with a tenuous but valid title to the throne. Buckingham defected to the king-in-waiting, but was caught and executed. He had been deserted by his Welsh tenants, who refused to risk their lives in the madcap adventure of a notoriously tight-fisted landlord who needed an armed escort whenever he visited his lands in the Marches.

Richard III's authority remained precarious and fell apart quickly in 1485. Richmond landed on the western coast of Wales, marched unopposed to Market Bosworth in Leicestershire and defeated Richard in a short battle on 22 August. The King's supporters fought with little or no enthusiasm and two commanders of large contingents, the Earls of Derby and Northumberland, showed a benevolent neutrality towards Richmond. The pitch of hatred towards Richard was so intense that the victors broke with hallowed tradition and abused his corpse.

Legend has it that Derby found Richard III's crown in a thorn bush and handed it to Henry VII (1485–1509), a symbolic reminder that, like his Yorkist and Lancastrian predecessors, he owed his throne to an aristocratic faction. He kept it, although a tiny rump of diehard Yorkists with nothing to lose attempted a comeback with a bogus Richard, Duke of York (in fact one Lambert Simnel, a craftsman's son), and were beaten at the Battle of Stoke-by-Newark in 1487. Henry VII followed the policies of Edward IV and national recovery was swift. Stability was restored and the nobility was grateful.

5

As a True Knight: Honour and Violence and the Wars of the Roses

Stable government equalled security for all forms of property. For this reason alone, the aristocracy had most to lose from civil wars. Why, then, did the English nobility jeopardise its lands and its lives by resorting to the politics of the sword? Shakespeare blamed a collective insanity. 'England hath long been mad,' declares Henry VII at the end of *Richard III*. It was a simple diagnosis that accorded with the commonplace metaphor which likened a nation to the human body. Its organs, limbs and brain worked in unison and its internal humours, which governed the emotions and its overall health, were balanced. In late medieval England the body politic seemed infected with recurrent spasms of lunacy. Its symptoms were most virulent among the aristocracy, who functioned as the country's brain. They were accomplices in the inflation of violence and the proliferation of disorder and rejected the notion that the nobility had a duty to protect the kingdom from anarchy.

Unravel the motives of those noblemen who began and prolonged the Wars of the Roses and two questions emerge. Did the men produce the times, or did the times the men? Some modern parallels offer clues. The characters and careers of the big players – Suffolk, York, his sons Clarence and Gloucester, and Warwick the Kingmaker – suggest that they would have flourished in Chicago during the prohibition era, or as entrepreneurs in post-Communist Russia. They were ambitious, tough, ruthless opportunists, and, in the cases of Gloucester and Warwick, probably psychopathic.

A pack of blackguards perhaps, but they persuaded other aristocrats to join them in hazarding lives, titles and lands in what were always potentially fatal enterprises. The odds of survival were discouraging. Between 1455 and 1485 seven dukes, nine earls and nineteen lords were killed in action or beheaded after battles. Losers suffered Parliamentary attainder, which deprived them of titles and lands. Nearly four hundred landowners were penalised, although about two-thirds of the attainders were eventually rescinded. In the meantime, their estates were distributed among the winners. When the losers recovered their property, they often discovered that it had been exploited or neglected. Thomas, Lord Roos, whose Midland manors were returned after twenty-four years in 1485 found that they had been mismanaged by their interim owner William, Lord Hastings, who had even stolen the lead from the roof of Belvoir Castle in Leicestershire.[1]

While Roos was contemplating his dilapidated home, James Blount, Lord Mountjoy, was compiling a balance sheet of the gains and losses of the aristocracy during the wars. He concluded that it had fared badly, but the experience had been instructive. Blount warned his two sons against taking the 'state of baron' and urged them to suppress any 'desire to be great around princes, for it is dangerous'.[2] High politics were nasty, dangerous and best shunned. The Blount boys were infinitely better off away from court and looking after their own affairs.

Those noblemen who had ignored the perils of political engagement in an age of faction, or tried to sidestep it, believed that they were in the hands of God. He was omniscient, opaque and perverse, insofar as his dispensations did not always conform to what humans considered best for themselves. What outwardly appeared as caprice was in reality the unfolding of a divine providence whose ultimate purpose was hidden. This consoled Sir John Paston after he had backed the defeated Lancastrians at Barnet in 1471:

> God has shown himself marvellously like Him that made all, and can undo again when Him list [wishes]; and I can think that by all likelihood shall show Himself as marvellous again and that in short time . . .[3]

He did, but not as Paston had hoped. The Yorkist victory at Tewkesbury less than a month later turned out to be another Yorkist miracle. As one court rhymester wrote afterwards, the battle proved that God had intended Edward IV to be 'the true inheritor of the crown'. Sir John survived his error of judgement, but the family did not tempt fate again: in 1485 his son ignored a call to arms to fight for Richard III.

Supernatural forces could penetrate the future. Necromancy and astrology had a considerable hold on the aristocratic imagination, understandably in precarious times. In 1441 Eleanor, the wife of Henry VI's last surviving uncle, Humphrey, Duke of Gloucester, consulted a witch to discover whether he would succeed the still childless King. Regal ambitions may have prompted George, Duke of Clarence, to dabble in witchcraft in 1477. At various times he, his brother Gloucester and Warwick accused Elizabeth Woodville of using sorcery to seduce Edward IV. As Richard III, Gloucester went a step further and had the Queen formally denounced as an enchantress during the 1484 Parliament.[4] He did so on the twin assumptions that the charges were credible and that witchcraft could be efficacious.

Those who pored over prophetic literature for an insight into the future accepted that history was preordained, although its precise direction was not easy to trace, given that many ancient prophecies were couched in obscure language. Those attributed to Merlin were lucid enough when they predicted the distant triumph of an unknown Welsh prince. This was perfect propaganda for Henry, Earl of Richmond, the grandson of a squire, Owain Tudor, who was imagined to be descended from the legendary Welsh prince Cadwalader. Before and after the decisive Lancastrian victory at Bosworth in 1485, Henry VII's apotheosis was depicted as the fulfilment of a predestined history whose culmination would be the onset of a golden age. Its arrival was confirmed in 1486 when he named his first son Arthur.

All who probed the after times were ultimately concerned with self-preservation and material advantage. These decided whether men fought and which side they joined. Sir Paston's faith in a benevolent Providence may have reassured him when he threw in his lot with the Lancastrians, but what pushed him into the war was the fact that his family's enemies were Edward IV's friends. In 1470 a prominent Yorkist, John Mowbray, Duke of Norfolk, sent his retainers, equipped with artillery, to besiege

Caister Castle in Norfolk. Its bombardment and capture was the climax of an extended legal dispute between the Pastons and Norfolk. Justice was beyond the Pastons' reach: Edward IV's throne was still insecure and he needed Norfolk's goodwill. The Pastons had therefore to choose between enduring their losses stoically, or hitching their fortunes to those of another local lord, John de Vere, Earl of Oxford, a diehard Lancastrian.

The Pastons' dilemma was repeated many times. Since 1440 the legal system had been paralysed by Henry VI's lassitude and lack of judgement. The nobility lost faith in the Crown's impartiality. They ignored traditional legal arbitration and litigants increasingly resorted to force to get satisfaction. This resulted in sporadic outbreaks of anarchy in the provinces which increased in number and scale during the 1450s. Small private wars between landowners eventually merged with the wider national conflict. A new moral climate was being created: lords who routinely used violence to settle their personal differences had no inhibitions about applying it in public affairs.

Many were genuinely appalled by encroaching anarchy, but detachment was impossible. Consider Ralph, Lord Cromwell, the rebuilder of Tattershall Castle, an Agincourt veteran, sometime Treasurer and long-serving royal councillor who was proud of his own and his ancestors' honourable service to the Crown. A grateful Henry VI publicly acknowledged his integrity in 1453, but the King could no longer protect Cromwell from his local enemy, Sir William Tailboys.[5] He was Cromwell's neighbour and could gaze from the parapet of his tower house at South Kyme and see Cromwell's recently completed castle. It overlooked the surrounding fenland and was a solid reminder that Cromwell was the dominant figure in Lincolnshire. It was a sight which aroused Tailboys's envy and rage.

He was a devious psychopath determined to topple Cromwell and make himself supreme in a county where his ancestors had lived for centuries. Tailboys had prepared the ground by gaining the favour of Viscount Beaumont and, through him, the Duke of Suffolk and Queen Margaret. Their friendship was tantamount to immunity from prosecution. By 1449 he was confident enough for a trial of strength. It was provoked when one of his servants was arrested, imprisoned in Tattershall and threatened with hanging by Cromwell. Tailboys appealed to Beaumont for help. If the man was executed it would be the 'greatest shame that might befall' since his own and the Viscount's standing would be diminished. If Tailboys had permission to mobilise Beaumont's followers and rescue the prisoner, their honour would be upheld and everyone in Lincolnshire would see where power lay in the county.[6]

The operation to save the captive probably miscarried, which may explain why Tailboys attempted to murder Cromwell while he was attending the House of Lords at the end of 1449. He failed, but escaped arrest after Suffolk's intervention. A brief spell in gaol followed after Suffolk's downfall, but Tailboys was soon free and determined to pursue his feud with fresh vigour and ingenuity. He conspired to blow up Cromwell's London lodgings with gunpowder (a novel form of murder) and circulated rumours that his enemy was a covert traitor, in the knowledge that similar libels had helped destroy Tailboys's former patron Suffolk the year before.

Cromwell was terrified. Even at Tattershall he dared not walk or ride abroad without an escort of at least thirty armed servants.[7] He could expect no help from the law, for Tailboys had secured two formidable new patrons: Queen Margaret and Henry Holland, Duke of Exeter. He was an unstable, hot-blooded young man, short of money and bent on securing Cromwell's castle and a manor at Ampthill in Bedfordshire. Exeter's servants beat, bribed and bullied local juries to procure verdicts favourable for their master and his allies. As Cromwell lamented, Exeter was a 'prepotent' lord in the county who could do what he liked. [8]

Beset by powerful and vicious enemies, Cromwell desperately needed security. He was in his fifties, had an annual income of over two thousand pounds and was childless. Apparent deliverance came through an alliance with York and the Nevilles, sealed by marriages between his two nieces and co-heiresses and a younger brother of Warwick and the son of a Yorkist peer, Lord Bourchier, though both bridegrooms were later killed in battle. Cromwell also loaned money to his new friends.

More was demanded of him in 1455 when York and the Nevilles confronted the King at St Albans. Cromwell hesitated; rebellion was a step too far for a lord who had devoted his life to the service of Henry V and his son. Cromwell's misgivings may have been the reason why his contingent arrived too late for the battle. Afterwards, a furious Warwick accused him of backsliding. Early in 1456, Cromwell died from a stroke in his newly fortified mansion at South Wingfield in Derbyshire. Those present at his deathbed said mass and then made a frantic search for the key to the strongbox where his will was kept. Among those expecting a bequest was his new friend John Talbot, Earl of Shrewsbury, a prominent courtier, and he was well satisfied.[9] Cromwell's adversary Tailboys remained a tenacious partisan of the House of Lancaster and was executed and attainted in 1464. Within ten years his family reclaimed his estate.

Cromwell's misfortunes coincided with a period when violent aristocratic feuds were increasing. Most were rooted in disputes over land ownership and impatience with the serpentine, expensive and lengthy processes of litigation. Why wait years for judgement when it was possible to seize a disputed property and collect its rents? This was what the Duke of Norfolk did when he besieged Caister in 1470.

Norfolk's honour was also at stake. No one could defy the Duke with impunity, certainly not arriviste gentry like the Pastons. Honour required a lord to protect his dependents. The news of Suffolk's arrest in 1450 had been a signal for a gang of

Norfolk's followers to break into his deer park at Eye and kill a dozen bucks and three does.[10] This was more symbolic poaching, for it proclaimed the end of the de la Pole ascendancy in East Anglia. The once feared Duke could no longer even protect the beasts he had preserved for his pleasure, let alone his allies and servants.

Honour was precious and to preserve it a noble was always willing to risk his life. In 1455, exasperated by years of rancorous and sometimes bloody bickering between them, Lord Bonville challenged the Earl of Devon to a duel. 'I shall in myself in proper person upon my body in that quarrel fight and make it good,' he told the Earl, adding that the latter did not merit this trial of honour, for he was a coward and traitor. Devon replied 'as true knight' and accepted the challenge of his 'false and untrue' enemy.[11] The language of violated honour was always hectoring and overblown. At the head of their retinues, the two peers fought as arranged at Clyst St Mary, a few miles south-east of Exeter, and Bonville was routed. Eight men died and afterwards the victors entered the city and looted the cathedral.

Honour was at the heart of the Berkeley–Talbot dispute over the ownership of several manors in Gloucestershire. It had spluttered on since the early 1450s and, at various stages, involved kidnapping, intimidation and forcible entry. In March 1470, with Edward IV fighting to regain his crown and effective royal authority suspended, William, Lord Berkeley, challenged Thomas Talbot, Lord Lisle, to settle their differences once and for all in a battle. 'I will appoint a short day to ease thy malicious heart and thy false counsel: fail not to be at Nibley Green at eight or nine of the clock.' Lisle agreed in a letter scornfully addressed to 'William called Lord Berkeley'.

Watched by a crowd of rustics, including children who had climbed trees to get a good view, Berkeley appeared with about a thousand men, some hurriedly recruited in Bristol and the Forest of Dean. The two sides exchanged volleys of arrows and one fired by 'Long Will' struck Lisle in the cheek, for his visor was raised. Berkeley and his men then dirked the wounded Lord between the ribs. His men scattered and Berkeley's forces sacked his house at Wotton-under-Edge and stole vital legal documents.[12]

'Lamenting like a virgin and girded in sackcloth,' Lisle's widow protested to Edward IV. But what could the King legitimately do? Berkeley and Lisle were peers of ancient blood and Lisle had agreed as a man of honour to put his claims to the assay of arms and, implicit in this, the judgement of God. The King had recently submitted to the same jurisdiction at Barnet and Tewkesbury. Convention demanded that Lisle accept the challenge; to have done otherwise was an admission that he was a poltroon and his cause mendacious.

The skirmishes at Clyst St Mary and Nibley Green were about honour as expressed through aristocratic spheres of influence; today we might call them incidents in the 'turf wars' between criminal monopolies. So too were the other minor engagements between aristocratic retinues in East Anglia and Northern England during the 1450s and between 1469 and 1470. They dramatically illustrated the political fact that when royal authority was in eclipse, that of the nobility was omnipotent. Under-mighty kings had over-mighty subjects.

There was something distinctly theatrical about the events at Clyst St Mary and Nibley Green. The appeals to honour, the challenges, the mustering of retainers and their convergence at the pre-arranged battlefield resembled the stage-managed, ritualistic tournaments held to celebrate coronations and royal weddings. These were part of that theatre of power in which the nobility played the lead parts, performing before an audience both dazzled and overawed by the trappings of wealth and authority.

Manpower and political power were synonymous. This was exemplified when the Yorkist lords staged a minatory demonstration of their military muscle early in 1454. They converged on London at the head of impressive cavalcades preceded by carts crammed with armour as an earnest of their readiness to fight if they were checked. York was accompanied by his household, who were reported to be handsome and 'likely' men, and his son Edward, Earl of March, rode at the head of 'a fellowship of good men'. One hundred and forty knights and squires attended the Earl of Salisbury and it was rumoured that his son Warwick was bringing at least a thousand men. The Duke of Norfolk assembled a retinue 'according to his estate'.[13]

Where did these men come from and what did they hope to gain from what for many was a long, uncomfortable winter journey? An informed spectator would have identified two species of retainer from their appearance and bearing. There were knights and squires, either attached to a lord's household or bound to him by contract. If fighting had broken out, they would have worn armour, either suits of full plate or, for comfort, velvet-faced brigandines, which were flexible coats of steel plates, and carried swords and poleaxes. Padded jackets (jacks), sallets (helmets), bows, bills and lead-tipped clubs (mauls) were the equipment of the second type of retainer. They were tenants and domestic servants and, like their betters, were distinguished by their master's colours or badge.

While the Yorkists were on the march, the Lancastrians James Butler, Earl of Wiltshire, and Lord Bonville were inviting the men of Taunton 'to go with them and serve them' for sixpence a day, over twice a labourer's wage. Aristocrats were never fastidious when it came to raising armies and were happy to trawl the margins of society to fill out their forces with jobless labourers and artisans, petty criminals and ruffians, who, in the vivid phrase of one contemporary indictment, had 'no other occupation but riots'.

Like everyone else involved, the criminal underclass offset the fear of battle with hopes of profit. After the second Battle of St Albans in February 1461, three soldiers from the Duke of Exeter's contingent carried their spoils (including a horse and armour taken from Warwick's men) to a house in Totteridge and left it there. This trio survived the Lancastrian defeat at Towton a month later and had the chutzpah to return south and reclaim their loot. Lancastrian troops plundered civilians in Hackney and in Bedfordshire and Lord Roos's servants robbed a York parson, alleging he was a traitor. These bandits took their cue from their betters. Sir Robert Clifford and Sir William Lancaster stole goods worth three hundred pounds from the house of Lord Vescy at Wymington near Bedford and deposited their pillage 'trussed in a fardel' with the Abbot of St Mary's, York.[14] In these cases, the victims took the trouble to seek legal restitution, but there must have been others for whom it was not worth the expense and bother.

Common bonds of obligation and expectation linked everyone who fought in the Wars of the Roses. The Taunton weaver lured by Wiltshire and Bonville looked for pay, food and drink and hoped his commanders would turn a blind eye to larceny. Knights, squires, gentlemen, yeoman farmers and household servants were likewise paid and victualled. If their lord was fighting for the Crown, it would pay the reckoning for his retainers' wages and rations. The exchequer might also clothe and arm them: during the 1470 campaign Edward IV provided a thousand jackets of blue and murray embroidered with his badge of the white rose, as well as armour and weaponry.[15]

Knights and squires expected specific favours, either from the Crown, or the lord to whose service they had pledged themselves by written contracts or verbal promises. In 1478 Gervase Clifton agreed to be 'faithful and true' to William, Lord Hastings, and render him 'true and faithful service' in peace. In war Clifton was to provide him with as many men as he could raise, all 'defensively arrayed' and prepared to fight any man save the King. Hastings would pay their expenses and promised to be 'a good lord' to Clifton and show him 'special favour'.[16] Two peers and sixty knights and esquires made similar agreements with Hastings between 1461 and 1483; some appeared in arms when he joined Edward IV at Barnet and Tewkesbury.

Good lordship was all that Hastings promised Gervase Clifton, but it was a valuable commodity since Hastings was the coming man, cherished by Edward IV as a friend and, so gossip ran, fellow philanderer. Hastings was one of a new Yorkist aristocracy created by the King to both buttress and cement support for the dynasty in areas formerly under the sway of Lancastrian lords. His power base was in the East Midlands. Edward IV showered his favourite with grants of local estates and offices (many once held by attainted Lancastrians) and Hastings asserted his new eminence by starting to build an imposing castle at Kirby Muxloe in Leicestershire. Its scale, ornament and gunports proclaimed his pretensions. His political influence was gauged by the numbers of his retainers who were returned to Parliament, served as sheriffs and sat on the bench as justices. Hastings could direct royal patronage towards men like Clifton. As Justice Shallow observed in Shakespeare's *Henry IV, Part II*, 'a friend at court' was an asset for a provincial squire.

There were limits to aristocrats' string-pulling. In 1481 Clifton was considering litigation to recover a manor recently seized by servants of Francis, Lord Lovell, a courtier. He soon dropped his plan, informing the property's owner, the Bishop of Winchester, that he dared not meddle with Lovell, 'considering he is a lord, I may not so deal'.[17] Shifting balances of power at court had a direct influence on what a lord's retainers might expect in the way of favour, or how far he might go to assist them. This was why so many of the Pastons' London correspondents sent reports home of the latest political alignments at court. Such knowledge was crucial for the ambitious: a servant of John de la Pole, second Duke of Suffolk, once told John Paston that he 'would forsake his master and get him a new, if he thought he should rule'.

'Beware of lord's promises,' cautioned another Paston correspondent. Lords too had to be watchful and circumspect. Hastings's political antennae failed him in June 1483 when he was betrayed by his steward William Catesby, who had secretly switched his allegiance to the Dukes of Gloucester and Buckingham. Hastings was executed, the first victim of Gloucester's coup. His retinue dissolved instantly; as one eyewitness drily noted: 'all my lord chamberlain's [i.e. Hastings's] men became my lord Buckingham's'. No one worships the setting sun nor expects warmth from it.

By making a compact with a lord a retainer did not sign away his independence of mind or freedom of action. In 1455 Sir William Skipwith, a retainer of York, 'refused to assist the Duke's rebellion in that journey to St Albans', for which he forfeited his twenty-pound annuity and stewardship of York's estates at Conisburgh and Hatfield.[18] In what was a final appeal of despair, Warwick pleaded with his retainer Henry Vernon in 1471: 'Henry, I pray you fail not now as ever I may do for you.'[19] Vernon knew political folly when he saw it and stayed put in Haddon Hall. Both he and Skipwith died in their beds.

The bad nerves or common sense of retainers were constraints on aristocratic power. Nonetheless, the ranks of armoured men wearing their lords' liveries must have seemed awesome, even terrifying on the battlefield or parading through towns under enormous war banners with such intimidating devices as the black bull of Clarence, the white boar of Gloucester and the yale (a tusked antelope) of Beaufort. Onlookers could have been excused for imagining that they were witnessing the zenith of aristocratic political power.

But was it? Events strongly suggest so. Between 1399 and 1487 aristocratic coalitions deposed Richard II, Henry VI (twice), Edward IV, Edward V and Richard III. Noblemen had also conspired to unseat Henry IV, murder Henry V and replace Henry VII with a pseudo-prince. Aristocratic propaganda had endeavoured to justify these actions as undertaken in the best interest of the country. There was a degree of truth in this in the case of Richard II, although his high-handedness hurt the nobility more than his humbler subjects. Henry VI's utter incompetence was a far greater threat to the stability of his realm and the safety of his subjects, but in the other instances the self rather than the public interest of the aristocracy was uppermost. Warwick, Richard, Duke of Gloucester, and Henry Stafford, Duke of Buckingham, attempted coups because they knew they could get away with them. They did in the short term, but the regimes they created were shallow rooted, lacked legitimacy and were short-lived.

The fate of would-be kingmakers did not wholly chasten the aristocracy, and old habits died hard. In 1503 news that Henry VII was suffering from a severe illness prompted a group of officials to speculate on the succession. They wondered whether either the exiled Edmund de la Pole, Earl of Suffolk, or Edward Stafford, Duke of Buckingham, might succeed and bypass the King's only surviving son, Henry, Prince of Wales.[20] Intelligent and well-informed men still believed that an aristocratic *coup de main* of the kind that had occurred in 1483 was a possibility, even after two decades of efficient government and domestic stability. As it was, Henry VII died in 1509 and Henry VIII succeeded unchallenged. Athlete, huntsman, jouster and warmonger, he was soon the darling of the nobility.

The violent changes of dynasty during the previous century had left the balance of power between Crown and aristocracy unchanged. The royal prerogative remained, as did the structures of conciliar and Parliamentary consultation. Edward IV and

Henry VII repaired and adjusted the machinery of the law and achieved solvency. Statutes passed in 1468 and 1504 outlawed the giving of liveries to yeomen, artisans and labourers (the cannon fodder of armies during the Wars of the Roses), and made the retaining of men above the rank of gentlemen subject to royal licence. Many were granted by the Tudors, who, like their predecessors, needed the nobility and their retainers for military service and, in an emergency, public order.

Most important of all, the Wars of the Roses had not shaken the philosophy which underpinned the political order. Chancellor John Russell, Bishop of Lincoln, reiterated it in 1484 when he addressed the Lords and Commons. 'Noblesse', he argued, was 'virtue and ancient riches' and its possessors were like firm rocks in a turbulent sea. 'The politic rule of every region well ordained stands in the nobles,' the Bishop concluded. His reassurances were welcome after thirty years of aristocratic violence and listeners who recalled Gloucester's bloody seizure of power a year before may have been sceptical.

6

In Foolish Submission: Irish and Scottish Aristocracies

Medieval England was an expansionist state which preyed on its neighbours. Territory equalled power and profit for kings and their noblemen. There were four areas open to conquest: France, Wales, Ireland and Scotland. France with its greater wealth and population was the most attractive objective, but in the end its superior resources always told, and occasional dazzling English victories like Crecy (1346) and Agincourt (1415) were followed by long and unwinnable wars of attrition. Normandy, Aquitaine and Anjou, all acquired by the Norman and Angevin kings, had been lost in 1214 when King John's army was defeated at Bouvines. Only Gascony was retained and its defence was a headache for Edward I and Edward II. Edward III launched a concentrated counter-offensive, but this had petered out by the 1370s. Henry V tried again in 1415, but within forty years England was left with just a toehold, Calais.

When the going was good, the aristocracy were enthusiastic partners in enterprises which yielded honour and profit. Richard, Earl of Arundel, made over £72,000 from plunder and ransoms during Edward III's French campaigns.[1] This was exceptional, but it explains why the nobility so strongly supported the Crown's efforts to establish a Continental empire. Hope triumphed over experience and in 1513 and 1542 Henry VIII invaded France. Again, funds ran out and in 1558 Calais finally was recovered by the French.

The subjugation and absorption of the polities on the fringes of the British archipelago was equally hard and success was limited. The piecemeal conquest of Wales was complete by 1282, but progress in Ireland was slow and by 1500 large tracts of the island still remained under its independent Gaelic rulers, whose allegiance to the English Crown was brittle. Scotland proved an even harder nut to crack. Edward I's attempt to annex the kingdom ended with his son's defeat at Bannockburn in 1314 and a sequence of destructive incursions into England by Robert the Bruce, whose brother Edward opened a new front against the English in Ulster.

Henry VIII fared no better when he attempted to unite the two kingdoms in 1542 through an offer of the marriage of his son Edward to Princess Mary (Mary Queen of Scots) backed by a large-scale invasion of the Lowlands. English prestige soared after victories at Solway Moss and Pinkie, but so did the bills, and by 1550 the treasury had run out of the means to pay them. Costs included the wages of noble commanders in search of esteem. 'I hear you are come to the Borders to win honour,' a friend told Henry Manners, first Earl of Rutland, in 1549.[2]

Manners was fighting against men like himself who believed themselves born warriors and rulers. The principles of aristocracy were deeply rooted in the hierarchical Celtic culture. Welsh

bards constantly associated rank and political authority with illustrious ancestry, qualities which interestingly distinguished both
the ancient rulers of Wales and their Anglo-Norman successors.
The latter brought to Wales alien legal notions of feudalism, but
the indigenous culture warmed to the incoming lords because
they were men of honour and ancestry who lived according to
ancient traditions of fairness and generosity. William Herbert,
first Earl of Pembroke, was praised by a bard as a 'chieftain in
rank'. He was also a patron of Welsh poets.[3]

Aristocratic assimilation in Ireland was more complex and
fraught. When Henry I had first invaded the country in 1170
armed with a papal bull which granted him overlordship, his
propagandists announced that his purpose was 'correcting evil
customs and planting virtue'. Imagined Irish barbarism seduced
some of the conquerors, and in 1297 the Dublin Parliament
introduced the first of many laws designed to discourage the
Hiberno-Norman nobility from speaking Irish, wearing Irish
dress, marrying Irish women and employing harpists and story-
tellers. Isolated from their original homeland, outnumbered and
confined within what came to be known as the English Pale, the
imported aristocracy was going native.

Survival required a degree of assimilation that raised questions
of identity and loyalty which continued to perturb the Anglo-
Irish nobility for the rest of its history. Were they English, forever
clinging to their Englishness in an alien and potentially hostile
country, or were they the hybrid offspring of two cultures? Seen
from London, any sign of ethnic eccentricity among Anglo-
Irish landowners was interpreted as evidence of a political
independence that had to be suppressed. An insurrection by
Gerald FitzGerald, the ninth Earl of Kildare, in 1534 was one of
the reasons why Henry VIII formally declared himself King of
Ireland seven years later, the first step in the introduction of the
machinery of centralised government. Thereafter, and whether
they liked it or not (and most did not), the Anglo-Irish and

Gaelic aristocracies were to be corralled into the English polity and subordinated to English laws. In 1542 one bard lamented:

> O'Neill of Oileach and Earhain [Macha]
> the King of Tara and Tailté
> In foolish submission has exchanged his kingship
> for the Earldom of Ulster.[4]

This demoted descendant of kings was a Gaelic patriarch who owed his status to his lineage. He was the head of a clan whose members were connected with him through blood and were obliged to serve him in war. Clansmen and -women worked the clan's lands, shared its collective honour and, when it was slighted, were always ready to take revenge with fire and sword. Blood feuds were endemic in Gaelic Ireland and Scotland, often enduring for generations. Status and honour rested on a capacity for immediate and bloody revenge. In Scotland in 1570 a band of MacGregors plotted to ambush the laird of Glen Urquhart, a relation of Archibald Campbell, fifth Earl of Argyle. It was as if the Earl himself had been the target, for, as a friend reminded him, a conspiracy against one of his kin was 'an offence against your Lordship's self'. Swift and 'grievous punishment' was imperative to teach the 'world' the perils of meddling with the Campbells.[5]

Archibald Campbell needed no prompting in such matters. He could muster at least three thousand Highland fighting men and owned a string of castles, an artillery train and a flotilla of galleys. Campbell influence on the west coast and among the isles was growing (Argyle fancied himself 'King of the Gaels') and he was once likened to the wild ash of the glen which 'grows fast and fair, but kills all living things in its shadows'.[6] Seen from the outside and through an official lens, clan chiefs like Argyle and their counterparts in Ireland were rulers of states within a state with a vast capacity for mischief. This increased during the second half of the sixteenth century when Protestantism became the state religion of England and Scotland. On the whole, Gaelic Ireland and Scotland remained Catholic. Argyle was an exception, which was one reason why his ascendancy was tolerated.

Religion was one of the reasons why the governments in London and Dublin convinced themselves that collaboration with the old Anglo-Irish and Gaelic aristocracies was neither possible nor advantageous. Uprooting or emasculating these elites became a matter of urgency as England drifted into a war with Spain in the 1580s and the presence of thousands of armed Catholic clansmen became a threat to national security. Moreover, permanent stability required a docile aristocracy; a modern, centralised state could not tolerate the existence of semi-independent lords, their private armies and incessant tribal warfare on its peripheries.

The Elizabethan re-ordering of Ireland required the introduction of a stratum of imported English landlords, the richest of whom would provide the seedbed for a new, utterly reliable nobility whose sympathies and outlook were English. A glimpse of the future was provided by Walter Devereux, first Earl of Essex, who, in 1573, led an enterprise for the colonisation of Antrim, which was subscribed to by several other English noblemen. Their aims and methods were close to those of the Spanish conquistadores in the New World. Essex's venture miscarried (there was fierce local resistance from the Gaels), but others followed in Ireland and Virginia. As in the earlier wars against France, aristocrats were active partners in what turned out to be a new wave of English expansionism.

Soldiers benefited, as they had done after the Norman conquest of England. Many who served in Elizabeth I's wars of pacification were rewarded with lands. According to a champion of the new Irish order, the poet Edmund Spenser, the colonists were physicians who would cure the moral depravity of the native Irish and their 'Popish trumpery' with 'strong purgations'.[7]

The patient rejected this therapy and the outcome was a sequence of wars. The longest, against a confederacy of the O'Neills, O'Donnells and Maguires, lasted from 1594 to 1603, involved forty-three thousand soldiers levied in England and cost two million pounds. The Irish pinned their hopes on help from Spain, but when it arrived in 1598, it failed to tip the balance. In 1607 the battered remnants of the old clan elites went into exile. It was a signal for a flood of immigrants from England and Scotland, including fifty men of the Graham clan from Eskdale whom James VI (1566–1625 in Scotland, 1603–1625 in England) deported from the Borders. They were settled on the Roscommon estates of one of Ireland's new aristocracy, Sir Ralph Sidney. This precedent was followed later in the century when criminals from both England and Scotland were shipped to the New World plantations as labourers.

Evicting troublemakers from a region long convulsed by feuding and cross-border raids was part of James VI's efforts to impose 'perfect civility and obedience' throughout his kingdom. Politically, Scotland had long resembled a sandwich, with the comparatively peaceful Lowlands squeezed between the two areas of chronic disorder: the Highlands and the Borders. Both were largely infertile upland regions where agricultural productivity was low and whose inhabitants traditionally turned on their neighbours to supplement their livelihoods. From the top downwards the economic necessity of predation was glorified by the rodomontade of the honour of clan and the septs into which the clans were divided. Raids and massacres became the stuff of heroic minstrelsy, which, like chivalric romances, set examples of courage for warriors.

Like the rest of the Scottish nobility, the clan chieftain belonged to a divinely ordained social order. When worshippers in St Machar's Cathedral in Aberdeen looked heavenwards, they saw not angels but a ceiling painted with the shields of their earthly equivalents: the Pope, the Holy Roman Emperor, the monarchs of Europe and Scotland, and the bishops and noblemen of Scotland. The honour of the King and that of his knights was indivisible claimed Sir Gilbert de la Hay, a Scottish knight who believed that only men like himself should occupy the high offices of state. James IV (1488–1513) projected himself as a king in the Arthurian mould by holding tournaments with fashionable themes drawn from Arthurian romance. Mock Highlanders playing bagpipes appeared at one tournament in 1507 to remind onlookers of the King's recent punitive expedition against the MacDonalds of the Isles.[8]

These theatrical flourishes projected the Scottish Crown as the permanent guardian of the nation's independence which had been won by Robert the Bruce. The Scottish aristocracy also saw themselves as defenders of their country's freedom. Poets celebrated the exploits of the Douglases, Border magnates who were Scotland's first line of defence against England. James, second Earl of Douglas, who was killed in the Scottish victory over Harry Hotspur at Otterburn in 1388, was praised as 'a most ferocious knight and a permanent danger to the English', while Archibald Douglas, the bastard son of the third Earl, was remembered in one ballad as a knight of 'gigantic physique' who could slay an adversary with one blow of his sword. The English dreaded him.[9]

National security compelled successive Scottish kings to accept the regional ascendancy of the Douglases and families like them. For the Scots, particularly those who lived in remote and inaccessible regions, the local nobleman was the only agent of the state's authority they knew. By the close of the fifteenth century, there were about thirty Scottish peers with a hereditary right to sit in the single-chamber Scottish parliament and their numbers rose steadily during the next hundred years through royal creations. Infertility and infant mortality led to extinctions, particularly among earls. Lords were more fecund, producing sons who founded cadet dynasties of lairds, which led to a proliferation of Gordons in Aberdeenshire and Campbells in the western Highlands.[10]

Noblemen sat with the clergy and commoners in the Scottish Parliament, which censured as well as counselled kings. The point was forthrightly made by Sir James Graham during a session in 1436 when he accosted James I (1403–37).

> I arrest you, sir, in the name of the three estates . . . for right as your liege people be bound and sworn to obey your majesty royal, in the same wise be you sworn and ensured to your people to keep and govern your law, so that you can do them no wrong, but in right maintain and defend them.[11]

As in England, a theoretic contract existed between Crown and subject and the nobles believed that in extreme circumstances they could enforce it. At the same time, they looked to the Crown for patronage that would fill their pockets and raise their prestige.

The outspoken Graham assassinated James I at Perth in 1437 at the instigation of his kinsman Walter Stewart, Earl of Atholl, a magnate with extensive local power and regal ambitions. At the very least, Atholl had hoped for control over the person of the infant James II, but the rest of the nobility spurned him and he was seized, tried and executed, a paper crown set on his head in mock of his pretensions. Graham and his fellow assassins were tortured to death.

This dramatic incident exposed a dilemma which intermittently agitated the medieval Scottish aristocracy: how did a nobleman balance public duty with private selfishness? It was an unwelcome choice that had to be made repeatedly during the fifteenth and sixteenth centuries as a result of a series of accidents which left Scotland temporarily kingless and in the hands of minority or regency governments. The English captured James I in 1406 and he was imprisoned for nineteen years, and between his murder in 1437 and James VI's coming of age in 1587 Scotland had a hundred years of rule by various councils made up of noblemen and bishops.

Their endeavours to discipline themselves and their countrymen were an object lesson in how vital personal monarchy was for national stability. The mystique of the Crown commanded reverence and obedience, sentiments which could never be aroused by a committee of lords and clerics, however well intentioned. Moreover, minorities made it harder for kings to restore their authority and practise active kingship, that is the assertion and extension of their power. James I's attempts to do this through patronage persuaded Atholl to have him assassinated.

The mid-sixteenth-century Scottish reformation made the achievement of national harmony even more elusive because it opened new fault lines among the nobility. On her return from France in 1560, the Catholic Mary Queen of Scots was confronted by an aristocracy that in large part detested her religion and had become accustomed to doing as it pleased. Aristocrats were also getting richer, for the extensive lands of the Scottish Church were gradually being annexed by the nobility and gentry. Irrespective of the depth of their theological convictions, a substantial body of landowners now had a vested interest in upholding Presbyterianism. Some were happy to make common cause with Elizabeth I, whose ministers were nervous about the presence of a French-sponsored Catholic monarch on England's northern frontier.

Mary Queen of Scots marital miscalculations added immeasurably to her problems, and she was finally forced by an aristocratic coalition to escape to England in 1568. For the next nineteen years there was another regency, during which a section of the nobility followed their instincts. An English intelligence analysis of 1577 revealed a selfish and fractious peerage. The Earl of Caithness 'follows his own profit, making always fair weather with those in authority', whom he bribed. Despite being a peer of 'no substance', Lord Forbes was pursuing a 'deadly feud' with the Gordons. The MacDonald Lord of the Isles was fickle, disobedient and often ordered raids on the mainland, which was to be expected from a man whose ancestors had made private alliances with the English Crown whenever it suited them. It was noted that quarrelsome lords were backed by gentlemen of 'their surname', that is networks of kinsmen. In 1583 another intelligence assessment concluded that the nobility and knights were the 'greatest force now in [the] Kingdom' and marvelled at the 'insolence' of the Borderers and Highlanders.[12] James Melville, a Presbyterian divine, despaired of the Scottish nobility, castigating them for their indifference to the nation's welfare.

Between 1573 and 1625 there were 365 recorded feuds between landowning families in Scotland.[13] They involved assassinations, the vengeful mutilation of corpses, sieges, skirmishes and, in the case of the feud between the Earls of Moray and the Earls (later Marquesses) of Huntly, pitched battles between armies of hundreds. The participants were not disloyal, rather they passionately believed that their ancestral code of honour was superior to the laws made by Parliament. Legislation framed to extend the civic peace and encourage commerce was utterly alien to the spirit of the tribal, Gaelic world of the Highlands with its culture of feasting, cattle rustling and clan feuds.

James VI was determined to erode and finally destroy a culture which he believed was a brake on his kingdom's progress. To transform it into a prosperous and peaceful state he needed a passive and cooperative nobility that had relinquished its old habits and the codes which gave legitimacy to violence. Tamed in spirit, the Scottish aristocracy would use its traditional authority to impose civility on its kinsmen, servants and clansmen. The royal project was endorsed by the Kirk, which needed the nobility and gentry to enforce religious and social discipline, and lawyers. There was support too from a section of aristocracy that shared James's vision and recognised the damage inflicted on the nation by its headstrong colleagues.

The royal civilising mission was a slow, uphill task. There was the carrot of royal patronage for lords who cooperated and the stick of armed coercion for those who did not. It fell heavily on the Earls of Huntly and Erroll in a string of campaigns waged between 1589 and 1595, and on the intransigent MacGregors, MacLeods, MacIains and MacDonalds in the western Highlands, whose lands were harried by royal forces. An iron fist remorselessly applied would teach the clansmen to fear the King more than the chiefs who had failed to protect them from his displeasure.

The bruised clans submitted to new laws contrived to crush their culture. The 1609 Statutes of Iona enlisted chieftains as the gendarmes of civilisation by compelling them to enforce laws made by Parliament where Lowland influence predominated. The statutes were intended to defuse the clans by banning those features of their culture which fostered violence. Chieftains had to ration the amount of whisky drunk at their feastings, prune their personal retinues and punish clansmen who wandered the countryside extorting food and drink from anyone they encountered. A prohibition was placed on giving hospitality to performers whose ballads and verses glorified and perpetuated the bloodthirsty culture of clan feuds. James also put pressure on the chieftains to send their sons to Lowland academies, where they would acquire the polish and learning which distinguished the Renaissance gentleman.

Better still, young bloods could be encouraged to undertake the Grand Tour and absorb at first-hand the manners, tastes and sophistication of the Continental nobility. Fencing classes, dancing lessons, visiting foreign courts and inspecting Roman ruins did not quite do the trick. Gaelic machismo was not easily neutered, and in 1633, when Charles I contemplated legislation to restore some of the purloined Church lands, the Scottish aristocracy was outraged. To protect their purses (and their honour) one group of peers considered dirking the royal representative 'in the old Scottish manner', a blind nobleman asking his colleagues to help guide his dagger to its target.[14] The taming of the Scottish nobility had been partial, but the process was accelerated after 1603 when England and Scotland became a dual monarchy. A steady stream of Scottish peers followed James VI southwards to London where they soon became addicted to the indulgences of competitive consumption.

Obeyed and Looked Up To: The Tudors and Their Lords

When James VI and his peers rode to London in 1603 they were astonished by the scale and ostentation of the houses of the English nobility. In Scotland the endemic political turbulence of the past fifty years had compelled magnates to live in castles for their own safety, but in England these had either fallen into disuse, or had been adapted to satisfy the prevailing fashion for light-filled rooms and galleries. Owners of new houses regarded them as jewels whose settings were knot gardens, mazes, topiary and landscaped grounds. These artificial Arcadias were 'fair and good to the eye', and proof that the lords of the soil were also masters of nature.[1] The Elizabethan grand houses with their furniture and ornaments were expressions of the visual culture of 'magnificence' which had entranced the aristocratic imagination for the past hundred years. Cultivating and paying for magnificence required a flourishing agriculture and domestic peace.

The sixteenth century had been a period of comparative stability. There were some unnerving wobbles between 1547 and 1558 when the minority of Edward VI and the reign of a woman, Mary I, were treated as a power vacuum by a handful of ambitious and reckless peers. The politics of the sword reappeared. In 1549 Edward Seymour, Duke of Somerset, Protector of the twelve-year-old King was overthrown by John Dudley, Earl of Warwick, at the head of thousands of his retainers and allies. Revealingly, Somerset feared a repeat of the 1483 coup and predicted the King's deposition.[2] Nothing was further from Warwick's mind: he planned to make the King his creature, propel the Dudleys to the forefront of the aristocracy (he made himself Duke of Northumberland) and direct England towards a Calvinist brand of Protestantism. Success depended on Edward's eventual succession, but at the close of 1552 the hitherto robust prince contracted tuberculosis. A frantic Northumberland induced the dying king to make a will by which he bequeathed his crown to Lady Jane Grey, the Duke's daughter-in-law and a pliant young gentlewoman.

This was illegal and, as in 1483, the nobility was shocked by one of its kind tampering with the laws of succession and inheritance. Mary Tudor was Edward's lawful heir, of this there was no doubt beyond Northumberland's greedy circle. She was then living in Norfolk, where she had been given the forfeited Howard estates (seized in 1546 by Henry VIII) and with them, the family's network of dependents. They formed the core of her forces which converged on London, where Northumberland's fellow councillors were preparing to welcome them. Paralysed by the scale of the opposition, the Duke dithered and then capitulated.

Within a year, the politics of violence were revived again, this time to force Queen Mary to forgo her proposed marriage to Philip I of Spain, which, it was feared, would reduce England to the status of an outlying province of the Habsburg empire.

Rebel forces under Sir Thomas Wyatt entered London and were repulsed only after heavy fighting in which the retinues of loyal peers tipped the balance. The Queen had survived, but not long after a Spanish observer remarked that her nobles were more 'obeyed and looked up to' than her.

Actual aristocratic military power was less formidable than recent events had suggested, largely because many of their followers were lukewarm or wanted no part in highly risky power games. This nervousness was sensed by Lord Thomas Seymour, the Protector's headstrong and swaggering younger brother who in 1547 advised Henry Grey, the Marquess of Dorset (the father of Lady Jane), to enlarge his retinue. The gentry, Seymour thought, would prove irresolute and so Dorset's best bet lay with tempting 'superior yeomen' who were easily flattered by gifts of wine, venison pasties and the attentions of a marquess.[3] Seymour was proved correct when Northumberland's followers refused to hazard their lives for 'Queen' Jane.[4] In 1554 when Dorset, now Duke of Suffolk, joined Wyatt's rebels, his frightened servants deserted him. Afterwards, one explained that although the Duke had been 'a good lord to them', they refused to become accomplices to treason.[5] On the other side, Lord Cobham complained that his servants and the 'commons' he had enlisted to resist Wyatt mutinied when the rebel artillery bombarded his castle at Cobham in Kent.[6]

Prevarication and backsliding were understandable, as they had been during the Wars of the Roses. Allegiance to a lord did not strip a man of his common sense, or make him careless of his life. Rebels lost their lands and lives; titled traitors were beheaded; commoners were hung, castrated, drawn and quartered. Moreover, in the mid-sixteenth century fears of civil war were more intense than ever, for there were excellent reasons to believe that it would resolve into a contest between Catholics and Protestants. Worse still, Continental experience indicated that religious wars stimulated social conflict. During the summer of 1549 it seemed briefly possible that the destructive German peasant uprisings of the 1520s might be repeated in England. The popular insurrections in East Anglia and the western counties in 1549 were a powerful inducement for all landowners to show unity. One of the charges against Protector Somerset had been his open sympathy with the rebels' economic grievances which had made him shrink from swift and condign measures against them.

A religious war of the kind then being waged in France between the Catholic and Protestant nobility seemed imminent in 1569. A cabal of Catholic peers hoped that a marriage between Mary Queen of Scots, then a fugitive in England, and Thomas Howard, fourth Duke of Norfolk, would simultaneously settle the succession (assuming the pair had a child) and reverse Elizabeth I's Protestant settlement. Two of those peers, Thomas Percy, seventh Earl of Northumberland, and Charles Neville, sixth Earl of Westmorland, reached for their swords and mobilised their kinsmen, tenants and retainers in the hope that the royal council would cave in. However, it was unshaken by what turned out to be a shambling protest that collapsed with hardly a blow struck. Protestant clergymen harangued the royal levies on the sacred duty of obedience to a sovereign and loyal peers (including crypto-Catholics) raised thirty thousand men, an impressive show of solidarity with the Crown.[7] Westmorland fled to Rome and exile, Northumberland was captured, tried and beheaded. Twenty years after, London theatregoers saw what the country had been spared when they watched Marlowe's *Massacre at Paris* and Shakespeare's *Henry VI* trilogy.

The pantomime of the Rising of the Northern Earls was the last serious attempt by the nobility to employ force to impose their political will on the Crown. The swansong of this tradition came in 1601 when Robert Devereux, second Earl of Essex, led a small band of impoverished peers on to the streets of London to bully Elizabeth I into giving them the favours they believed they deserved. It was more a riot of swaggerers led by a discarded favourite than a rebellion, and found few sympathisers. Essex was subsequently executed.

The Tudors could not govern without the goodwill and cooperation of the aristocracy, a political fact of life which they freely acknowledged and sometimes cursed. On the eve of his departure for the chivalric carnival of the Field of the Cloth of Gold in 1520, Henry VIII ordered Henry, Lord Clifford, 'to do us service in keeping the peace and good rule' of northern England and spy on local sheriffs and justices.[8] Clifford knew his duty: soon after he commanded a detachment against the Scots and held Skipton Castle against the insurgents during the 1536 Pilgrimage of Grace. The King was thankful and made this model peer Earl of Cumberland. Henry also elevated those roaring boys with whom he drank, feasted and hunted and who embodied the spirit of muscular knighthood which animated him in his youth. Yet, on the whole, the Tudors were sparing in the creation and promotion of peers, Elizabeth I strikingly so. Royal restraint and natural wastage led to their numbers falling from fifty in 1500 to forty-four in 1603. Many of the new creations and promotions were of members of the royal secretariat like the Wriothesleys and Cecils, the men who painstakingly attended to the detail of everyday government.

Peers and everyone else now addressed the sovereign as 'Your Majesty', rather than 'Your Grace', which had been sufficient for Plantagenet vanity. The inflation of language reflected an inflation of status: 'Majesty' invested the Crown with a new aura and awesomeness and extended the distance between it and its most elevated subjects. Just before Henry VIII's accession in 1509, huge statues of the kings of England from William I to Edward IV were set on the screen which separated the nave from the chancel in York Minster. Their size and prominence gave these princes parity with prophets and saints and pointed towards theories which stressed the sanctified nature of kingship. At the same time, the English monarchy assumed new political pretensions: Henry V was portrayed on his tomb in Westminster Abbey wearing an imperial crown, which was adopted by Henry VII on his coinage. The inference was clear: the English king had no earthly superior and, as Henry VIII declared when he took control of the Church in 1534, England was an 'Empire'. The eventual outcome of this apotheosis of monarchy was the notion of the Divine Right of Kings, which insisted that the authority given by God to kings and queens exempted them from their subjects' restraint or censure.

There was a political dimension to this nascent cult of sacred kingship. Between 1529 and 1536 Henry VIII constructed his own national Church with himself at its head and repudiated the spiritual authority of the Pope. Henceforward, the Crown through Parliament decided the faith of the nation and religious dissent became disloyalty. It was a revolution from above and, publicly at least, the aristocracy was content to comply with the King's wishes, although in private many peers remained attached to old doctrines. Allegiance triumphed over private conscience; but protest was treason and so fear buttoned many lips. In 1536 a jittery Viscount Lisle implored Thomas Cranmer, the Archbishop of Canterbury, to scotch rumours that he was a covert papist.[9] In the same year, the nobility of the Midlands and North obeyed royal orders to mobilise its retinues and suppress the Pilgrimage of Grace, a mass popular protest against Henry's religious policies. The fifth Earl of Shrewsbury raised nearly four thousand men.[10] One peer, Thomas, Lord Darcy, joined the rebels and was the only aristocratic martyr. There were, however, plenty of humbler people glad to die for dogma, Catholic and Protestant.

Nobles of both faiths flocked to stake claims on the confiscated Church estates, which Henry first put on the market in

1540 to fund his French and Scottish wars. Within fourteen years the Crown had raised over a million pounds in what was the largest transfer of land since the Norman Conquest. Investors were able to secure a good return and closed ranks in Parliament in 1554 to block Mary I's attempts to recover some of the former Church lands. Self-interest overrode devotional preferences, and at least one of the landowners who had helped the Queen to her throne accepted Church estates as his reward.

Between 1559 and 1560 Parliament established Protestantism as the national religion and Elizabeth I as 'supreme governor' of the Church of England. Her pretensions and the doctrines of her Church were vindicated in 1588 with the defeat of the Spanish Armada, which patriots interpreted as a victory over the Pope. Elizabeth was acclaimed as the embodiment of the spirit of a godly, united nation and courtier poets flattered her as the moon goddess Cynthia, or Diana the virgin huntress.

The ground had been well prepared for the cult of the Goddess Queen. Sir Thomas Elyot's *The Book Named the Governor*, which appeared in 1531 dedicated to Henry VIII, a popular guide to politics and morals written for the nobility and gentry, described the monarch as a sun, a source of life and illumination for all his subjects. The luminary prince gave lustre to his nobles and his 'countenance, language and gesture' conveyed a truly godlike dignity. To these qualities Elizabeth I added a feminine mystique. For the lords who attended on her, she was the aloof and unattainable lady of courtly love romances who was adored from afar. One of those under the royal spell, Sir Philip Sidney, gave her a present of a jewelled whip as a token of his submission to her will.

The Crown occupied the summit of the social hierarchy and was also its principal mainstay, as Elizabeth I had explained to the young Sir Philip. The youth had responded brusquely to an insult delivered by Edward de Vere, seventeenth Earl of Oxford, during a tennis match. The Queen was appalled and lectured

Sidney on 'the respect inferiors owed to their superiors and the necessity in Princes to maintain their creations [i.e. the peerage], as degrees descending between the people's licentiousness and the anointed sovereignty of Crowns. A gentleman's neglect on the Nobility taught the peasant to insult them both.'[11] Minus the contentious reference to the divine source of royal power, the Queen's words echoed the sentiments later expressed by Ulysses in his famous justification of degree in Shakespeare's *Troilus and Cressida*.

> *Take but degree away, untune that string,*
> *And hark! What discord follows;*

The medieval social dispensation remained intact as Catholic social doctrines were preserved by the Anglican Church. Its ordering was a replica of that of civil society with the Queen at its head and, below, bishops and clergymen whose authority derived from the Crown. Subsequent theological criticism of this arrangement was treated as a challenge to the social hierarchy and the reasoning which underpinned it. 'No Bishops, No King!' barked James I when Puritans questioned the theological justification for the first. 'Obey them that have rule over you' (Hebrews 13: 17) announced an inscription on the wall of Burton church in Sussex, placed there by a local squire. Quietism was a Christian duty and parsons regularly read homilies which warned congregations that a blow against the social fabric was a self-inflicted wound on the nation and a defiance of God.

Submission to the Crown meant submission to the nobility. Funeral processions reinforced the eminence of the nobles and the nature of the society they overlooked. Under the Church of England these were secular ceremonies which focused on the deceased's earthly status. Choreographed by heralds, the funerals of noblemen were stunning pageants in which the sombre black gowns, hoods and horse furniture of the hundreds of mourners contrasted with the dazzling gold, silver, red, blue and ermine of banners and shields.

The funeral of Edward Stanley, the third Earl of Derby, who died in 1593, was typical. First in the procession came two of his yeomen carrying black staves, followed by black-gowned paupers and choristers. Derby was a Christian peer who had fulfilled the duties of charity which the Church insisted were incumbent on all men and women of wealth. He was a figure of authority in the North-West and so next came his huge heraldic banner, a cavalcade of eighty of his household squires, fifty knights and gentlemen and the officers of his household. Behind them were mounted heralds bearing Derby's sword, shield, spurs and crested helm. Then came the Earl's coffin conveyed on a chariot and attended by his son and heir, kinsmen and noble mourners. Trumpets (symbolising the Resurrection) blared out and, if Derby had been a noted soldier, there would have been fifes and drums.[12]

In his lifetime, Derby had been an agent of Henry VIII, Edward VI, Mary and Elizabeth I, enforcing their will and their laws in a remote part of the kingdom. The knights and squires who rode in his cortege had looked for him for favours and danced to his tune, although not always with a good grace. In 1598 some Welsh landowners protested to Elizabeth I that they had no need of 'a great lord to terrify them', meaning Henry Herbert, second Earl of Pembroke.[13] The Queen was unmoved; the huntress Diana needed her pack of well-bred, energetic and loyal hounds. She had handled them firmly, but generously and they responded well. Harmony between the Crown and nobility and their sense of national destiny was a significant feature of the legend of Elizabeth's reign as golden age in which Protestant England counted for something in the world. There was much truth in this version of history, which, in the next century, became the touchstone by which James I and Charles I were assayed.

8

Stir Up Your Fame:
A New Breed of
Noblemen

A new breed of aristocrat appeared in the seventeenth century. He was a child of the Renaissance and, through it, heir to the wisdom, experience and intellectual curiosity of ancient Greece and Rome. His mind was agile and his horizons open; he composed and performed music, wrote verses and was a connoisseur of all the arts. He was susceptible to all and was improved by each, as Edmund Spenser observed in one of his dedicatory sonnets at the beginning of his *Faerie Queene* (1590):

> *The sacred Muses have always made claim*
> *To be the nurses of nobility.*

New accomplishments were grafted on to older qualities. The modern aristocrat shared with his ancestors the conviction that virtue was genetically transmitted, was proud of his ancestry and believed that leadership in war and peace was his birthright.

The Renaissance nobleman aspired to a perfect equipoise between mind and body. According to Sir Thomas Elyot's highly influential *The Book Named the Governor*, his overriding aim was service to 'the public weal', that is the public good. Its achievement required a prolonged and intensive study of Greek and Roman philosophy, literature and history in their original languages. This was drudgery for some and so printed translations and glosses were soon on the market. These texts contained wisdom for the public man and led the private towards an interior equanimity which made great men proofs against irresolution and mischance. The deeds of ancient statesmen and heroes inspired their modern successors. Elyot directed readers towards the final books of the *Aeneid* where he promised them examples of 'audacity [and] valiant courage' that would inspire them 'to take and sustain noble enterprises'.

Study cultivated inherent virtue. This was comforting for the nobility, which had been discountenanced by Henry VIII's promotion of humble men of learning to the highest offices of state, most famously the Chancellor Thomas Wolsey and Henry VIII's secretary, Thomas Cromwell. In 1546, Henry Howard, Earl of Surrey (a poet and translator of two books of the *Aeneid*), railed against 'those men of vile birth' whom the King had cherished to the shame and injury of the nobility.[1] The answer was to beat the upstarts at their own game and, as the century progressed, more and more young noblemen flocked to Oxford and Cambridge. Between 1570 and 1639, 146 sons of peers matriculated at the two universities and eighty-eight were admitted to the Inns of Court.[2] A smattering of law was invaluable for peers since it offered some protection against fly lawyers who baffled their clients with arcane terminology before fleecing them. For younger sons, a legal education was a springboard for a career at the Bar.

According to temperament, some young noblemen found intellectual stimulation at university and others were happy to revel with fellows like themselves (the forerunners of the Bullingdon Club), but all believed that they would somehow benefit from contact with academia. Fathers understood this. Robert Devereux, the second Earl of Essex, went up to Trinity College, Cambridge, at thirteen with orders from his father to 'employ your tender years in virtuous studies, as you might in the prime of youth become a man well accomplished to serve Her Majesty and your country in war as in peace'.[3]

Whatever erudition young lords absorbed added legitimacy to the aristocracy's claim to superior sensibilities and wisdom. Learning was soon fashionable, and even if he was happiest in his stables, on the tennis court or at the card table, a noblemen now felt obliged to install a library in his house.

All aristocratic libraries contained treatises, mainly classical, on the art of war. Elyot took it for granted that his readers would prove true to their breeding by testing their honour in the pursuit of danger on the battlefield. 'Stir up your fame,' the ninth Earl of Northumberland urged his son in 1595. The times were right for bold enterprises and the boy was pointed towards the current naval war against Spain, which offered the chance of plunder, or the 'discovery of barbarous countries' where 'mountains of gold and silver' awaited the daring.[4] By his own admission, the older Northumberland had been spendthrift and a gambler and no doubt he hoped that a captured galleon or a New World silver mine would restore the family fortunes. Another extravagant peer, the third Earl of Cumberland, maintained his solvency through privateering expeditions against Spanish shipping in the Caribbean.

This was the same spirit which had sent noblemen to France during the fourteenth and fifteenth centuries, but now the

Americas had replaced France as a source of treasure. An embryonic overseas empire was already luring the aristocracy with dreams of profit and honour. War offered other temptations. 'All women delight to him safe in their arms, who has escaped hither through many dangers,' wrote Sir Philip Sidney.[5] A veteran of Elizabeth's Netherlands campaigns, he may have been speaking from experience.

One danger which enhanced the masculinity and sexual attractiveness of young nobles was the duel. Like the battle, the duel was a touchstone of honour for those who survived and of honourable memory for those who did not. The rise of duelling during the second half of the sixteenth century coincided with the slow eclipse of that less risky test of aristocratic honour, the tournament. Unlike the joust, which was a public spectacle, duels between noblemen were hidden from public gaze, although reports of them circulated widely. Like the tournament, the duel had its prescribed punctilio, with formal challenges and responses which blended politeness with insult. 'Be master of your own weapons and time . . . the place where so ever I will wait on you; by doing this you shall shorten revenge and clear the idle opinion the world has of both our worths' ran Lord Bruce of Kinloss's challenge to the fourth Earl of Dorset in 1613.[6] Bruce was killed.

The weapons used in this and other similar encounters were rapiers and, like them, duelling had originated in Italy. Mastering the rapier required long hours of instruction and practice. There were fencing schools in London, the first established by Italians, and swordsmanship could also be studied in Paris or Italy by young noblemen undertaking the Grand Tour of the Continent. Short tempers, real and imagined slights and extremes of touchiness led to an epidemic of duelling amongst the nobility which peaked between 1610 and 1619, when thirty-three duels were reported. Others may have gone unnoticed, for James I had outlawed duelling in 1613.

Paradoxically, what the Crown and Parliament denounced as wanton manslaughter contributed to public order, since peers now settled their differences man to man, rather than mobilising retainers and servants. Affrays between noble retinues still occurred and, as ever, their cause was honour. In 1573 Lord Grey felt he had been dishonoured when a neighbour, John Fortescue, forbade him to hunt on his land. Backed by his servants, Fortescue confronted Grey and his huntsmen. 'Stuff a turd in your teeth,' snarled Grey. 'I will hunt it and it shall be hunted in spite of all you can do.' His followers then pitched into Fortescue's.[7]

Old bad habits lingered despite the Tudor state's concerted efforts to outlaw private feuds and the disorders they generated. Taming the peerage and, for that matter, anyone else who believed that they could bypass the law and settle their differences with swords, bows and cudgels was the task of the royal council, which could sit as a court, and Henry VII's Court of Star Chamber, in which councillors and senior judges arbitrated disputes which had ended in violence. By bringing these cases before tribunal in London, where local magnates were unable to use their influence to pull strings and evade justice, provincial stability was achieved.

Appealing to two earls to cancel their duel over contested lands, the royal council urged them to 'try their controversies in Westminster Hall', in other words the royal courts. By 1600, more and more peers were taking this course and submitting their differences to litigation. They did so with a belligerent spirit. John Smyth, a lawyer and steward of two Lord Berkeleys, drolly observed that during his lifetime the law courts at Westminster had become a 'cock pit of revenge' in which aristocratic litigants settled their quarrels with the same vindictive passion which their ancestors had applied to private feuds.[8]

In the lower courts corruption had replaced coercion. Advising his son Thomas, the future Earl of Strafford, on how to handle his legal affairs, Sir William Wentworth suggested that judges responded well to 'gifts'. Under-sheriffs needed bribes to empanel a sympathetic jury and, if they gave a favourable verdict, they were to be feasted.[9] A long purse was always better than a persuasive argument in the courts of early modern England.

Royal policy towards occasional aristocratic waywardness and a propensity for violence had always to be tempered by the knowledge that instincts which were intolerable in peace time were invaluable in war. Noblemen continued to use their networks of kinsmen and dependants to raise armies, and impetuous and pugnacious young lords led them into battle. The path to martial glory was mapped by the courtier poet Sir Philip Sidney, whose death at the siege of Zutphen in the Netherlands in 1586 transformed him into a Protestant paladin. His heroic example aroused the spirits of the 'green headed youths covered in feathers, gold and silver lace' who rushed to join the second Earl of Essex's Cadiz expedition in 1596. The Earl imagined himself Sidney's heir in honour and he scattered knighthoods among his adoring followers, which displeased the Queen, although as a field commander he was within his rights.

Noblemen remained royal councillors and companions. That athletic hearty, the youthful Henry VIII shared the pleasures of the tiltyard, tennis court, hunting field and dinner table with rowdies like himself. Their counterparts were the muscular but urbane bloods who were beguiled by the charms of Elizabeth I and vied for her favours like lovesick swains. At New Year 1588 Essex presented Elizabeth I with a jewel which showed a naked man within a gold setting to symbolise his dependence on her affection and patronage.[10]

A 'heroic life' required 'a mausoleum of immortal memory', a churchman advised Ludovick Stuart, the first Duke, Richmond and Lennox, when he was contemplating a tomb for his younger brother.[11] The richness and extravagance of Renaissance sculpture made it ideal for the monuments of the nobility. Status-conscious peers patronised immigrant sculptors who were familiar with the most recent Continental styles. This was why, in 1591, the Manners family commissioned Gerard Jansen, a Flemish sculptor, for the carving of the colossal tombs of the third and fourth earls of Rutland. The monuments were made in sections which were transported by ship to Boston in Lincolnshire and by cart to Bottesford in Leicestershire. Jansen supervised their construction in the church, which involved demolishing and rebuilding the wall of the chancel and reinforcing the floor.[12] Painting the profusion of heraldry on the tombs was undertaken under the close eye of the Manners family. The aristocracy was pernickety over such matters and made a fuss when errors were made.[13]

New, imported styles favoured flamboyant, pretentious memorials on a huge scale. In 1628 Sir Charles Morrison demanded that his effigy in armour should be 'royally' carved and that the sculptor clothe him 'in such habiliments, ornaments and jewels'. Additional specifications were made for the depiction of Morrison's children, now universal on all memorials to peers and gentry.[14] The result in Watford church is overwhelming and somewhat pompous, but it satisfied the same need as earlier memorials: the perpetuation of honourable memory.

An oddity appears on the tomb of the second Earl of Rutland at Bottesford: he holds a book in his hand. It is an unusual conceit which, if the volume is a Bible, may indicate his Protestant sympathies. Or else it was a reminder that noblemen were the natural patrons of learning. Knowledge opened minds, disseminated virtue and its fruits accelerated the advance of civilisation. These assumptions were central to Renaissance Humanism which was slowly infiltrating the aristocratic consciousness in

England and Scotland during the sixteenth century. It was absorbed by men and women eager to embellish their public character through the patronage of learning and the arts.

Old responsibilities were given a fresh and powerful imperative. Sir Thomas Elyot appealed to noblemen to promote the general good of the nation through the patronage of scholarship, schools and universities. Even ostentation acquired a moral and instructive purpose. According to Elyot, a felicitous choice of pictures, ornaments and silverware is a reflection of a nobleman's honour, the more so if they reproduced 'histories, fables, or quick and wise sentences, comprehending good doctrines or counsels'.[15] All the arts exercised and elevated the nobleman's mind; Elyot recommended dancing not because it was fun, but because its movements symbolised the ideal harmony between men and women.

Patronage of all the arts was a patriotic duty. The prestige of a Renaissance state was measured by the brilliance of its scholars, writers and artists and those princes and nobles who encouraged their genius. What was to the common advantage added to the pleasures and kudos of the patron thanks to the intellectual and creative reciprocity between him and the luminaries who gathered around him; their reflected glory added lustre to the aristocratic courtier and sharpened his wits. In the early 1630s young noblemen with literary aspirations clustered around the aged and fragile Ben Jonson at various London taverns to drink with him and listen to his epigrams and memories of Shakespeare.

One acolyte Lucius Cary, second Viscount Falkland, hoped to tempt the playwright to his house at Great Tew in Oxfordshire. Falkland was the epitome of the Renaissance nobleman; he had been educated at Oxford and Trinity College, Dublin, briefly played the soldier and then retired to Great Tew where he studied Greek and wrote poetry. He was the open-handed host to a circle of poets, philosophers and theologians who turned his house into a living Pantheon. Falkland was the presiding genius who charmed, stimulated and encouraged with what his friend Edward Hyde, the future Earl of Clarendon, described as 'a flowing delightfulness of language'. Another admirer, the poet Abraham Cowley, hailed him as the 'great *Prince of Knowledge*'.[16]

Falkland loved knowledge and abstract thought for their own sake; Robert Dudley, Earl of Leicester, regarded them as the means to political and religious ends. He was Elizabeth I's beloved 'Robin' (some of her more impudent subjects claimed he was her lover), a soldier and a leading councillor with strong views. These were expressed in various ways in many of the ninety-three books dedicated to him between 1559 and his death in 1588. History and theology predominated (both original works and translations) and all were responses to the urgent political needs of the Elizabethan state. Histories helped to create a flattering national identity by conjuring up a heroic past, populated by patriotic and warlike leaders, and readers were pointed in the direction of an even more glorious future. Religious texts vindicated Protestantism and confounded Catholic doctrines, in particular the supranational authority of the papacy.

Leicester funded a knot of pliant luminaries who prefaced their books with florid, obsequious epistles which praised their patron's discrimination and wisdom. Contemporaries likened the Earl to Maecenas, who had persuaded Horace and Virgil to write in the interests of Augustus and the new imperial Rome. The patronage of the new Maecenas strayed beyond the narrow demands of official political and theological pleading and embraced cosmography, surgery and linguistics. Leicester was one of the patrons of Thomas Cooper, an Oxford academic whose *Thesaurus Linguae Romanas* was published in 1563, and proved a godsend to future generations of translators.

Cooper's sound Anglicanism persuaded Elizabeth I to install him as Bishop of Lincoln. When he came down heavily on one of Leicester's Puritan protégés, the Earl ordered him to desist, hinting that former favours would be withdrawn. Leicester was in turn unfairly rebuked by one of his Puritan polemicists for not using 'your prosperity and high authority' to defend Protestantism from insidious 'Papists'.[17] Aristocratic patrons were expected to do their bit in support of one orthodoxy or another. The long war of the godly books had begun and, for the next hundred and fifty years, sympathetic noblemen were courted by contending theologians keen to publish their sermons and diatribes.

A dedication to one, or better still, several peers added prestige to a book: Spenser's *Faerie Queene* has sixteen and a blanket commendation to 'all the gracious and beautiful ladies of the court'. One hopes they all read the epic. A dedication to an illustrious figure was the equivalent to a glowing review at a time when there were no critical journals and no doubt helped to boost sales. 'Learning, wisdom, beauty, and all other ornaments of nobility . . . seek to approve themselves in thy sight, and get a further seal of felicity from the smiles of thy favour,' declared Thomas Nashe in the dedication of his edition of Sir Philip Sidney's 1591 poem *Astrophel and Stella* to his sister, the Countess of Pembroke. Her imprimatur carried some weight among the literati, for she was a writer herself, eager to preserve her brother's reputation and assist authors who had been members of his intellectual circle.

In all, Lady Pembroke accepted twenty-five dedications by eighteen writers, a tally which reflected generosity of spirit rather than liberality.[18] Tangible rewards for such dedications were meagre: Elizabethan playwrights commonly got two pounds, other authors one, while some patrons accepted dedications but forgot to make any payment at all.[19] A more reliable form of sustenance for writers, scholars and musicians was service in aristocratic households as tutors. In the dedication of his *First Book of Ayres* of 1622 to the Earl and Countess of Bridgewater, John Attey said that its pieces had been composed 'under your roof' while he had been teaching music to their daughters.[20]

On a lower level, peripatetic troupes of musicians and actors were allowed to adopt the name of an aristocrat and received what amounted to passports which protected them from arrest as vagabonds. In 1595 a pair of musicians carried a warrant from Lord Dudley which allowed them to play 'in all cities, towns and corporations' and no doubt they called themselves 'Lord Dudley's Men' to impress provincial audiences.[21] However tenuous and indirect, a aristocratic connection was a highly desirable indicator of respectability and perhaps quality; during 1577 and 1578 the townsfolk of Nottingham were entertained by players and musicians who claimed attachment to six peers.

The English literary renaissance had been facilitated and often driven by an aristocracy which had immersed itself in the Renaissance. Recipients of its abundant patronage were sycophantic, as one would expect. Soured by experience, Dr Johnson later defined a patron as 'a wretch who supports with insolence and is paid with flattery'. Nevertheless, there is no reason beyond cynicism to believe that all patrons were arrogant and that all dedicatory epistles were either insincere, or untruthful. If the numbers attending university and the Inns of Court are anything to go by, the Elizabethan and Jacobean nobility was on the whole better educated then its predecessors and, therefore, more appreciative of learning and the arts.

In 1578, one of Leicester's most distinguished protégés, John Florio, praised his patron as 'the only furtherer, maintainer and supporter of well disposed minds towards any kind of study'.[22] Florio was an Italian Protestant refugee from the Inquisition, a consummate linguist and the first translator of Montaigne. He believed that Leicester's goodwill had shielded him from spiteful critics, and, it went without saying, that the Earl's generosity had allowed him to study and write without the burden of mundane and corrosive anxieties about money.

This pragmatic consideration is highly significant. Quite simply, lordly patrons purchased the time in which talented and imaginative men had the freedom to study, write, think and compose. A happy combination of the wealth of peerage, the intellectual and creative preoccupations of individual lords, and the wider feeling that an intimate association with learning added to a peer's public reputation established a tradition of cultural *noblesse oblige* that would last for over three hundred years. Even more enduring was the honour which attached to the aristocratic patron. A poem was the equal of any tomb, as Shakespeare's sonnet reminded patrons of literature:

> *Not marble, nor the gilded monuments*
> *Of princes, shall outlive this powerful rime.*

PART TWO

EQUILIBRIUM
1603–1815

9

I Honour the King as Much as I Love Parliament: The Road to Civil War

Seventeenth-century Britain and Ireland were hosts to bitter political and religious animosities. They overlapped, proliferated and spawned a series of political crises which were resolved by civil wars. All these conflicts were fundamentally ideological. Men argued and fought over principles of government, equality before the law, individual liberty, where the boundary lay between obedience to the state and private conscience, and which Christian doctrines secured salvation. In Ireland, there were two related issues: whether the country should remain a dependency of England, and whether the Protestant minority should enjoy legal and political paramountcy over the Catholic majority.

At the root of all the controversies were the innovations of James I (1603–25) and his son Charles I (1625–49). They endeavoured to create an autocratic monarchy which dispensed with or neutralised the checks and balances that had been contrived to restrain their predecessors. Both believed in the Divine Right of Kings, Charles more passionately than his father, and each aspired to a Solomonic brand of kingship in which the all-wise monarch was a just and compassionate father of his people. The Church of England was seen by the Crown as a natural ally in this enterprise and its authority was reinforced: the Crown commanded the souls as well as the bodies of its subjects. From the start, this ambitious programme was hampered by a shortage of funds, and a monarchy on the edge of insolvency took enormous risks by embarking on policies which were bound to offend the political and religious sensibilities of its subjects.

The new monarchy advertised itself through art. Rubens depicted the apotheosis of James I on the ceiling of the Banqueting House in Whitehall as a demigod ascending into Heaven accompanied by Justice, Zeal, Religion, Honour and Victory. In *La Roi à Chasse* (now in the Louvre) Charles I's court painter, Anthony van Dyck, portrayed the King with a horse which bows before him in the manner of beasts in conventional paintings of the Nativity. Onlookers could be forgiven for imagining the same reverence due to God was also due to his earthly representative. An anointed King was beyond mere custom and legal precedent. Charles's leading minister, the first Earl of Strafford, insisted that 'the King's little finger should be heavier than the loins of the Law'. As for Parliament, Charles dismissed it in 1629 and for the next eleven years ruled by exclusive use of the royal prerogative.

What Charles's critics called his 'Eleven Years Tyranny' alarmed and divided his subjects. To succeed in establishing royal absolutism, Charles needed a united and passive nation. This was never within his grasp. The aristocracy and the rest of the landowning class were unwilling to forgo their ancient rights as partners in government. Parliament had long been integral to the governance of the kingdom and, whilst not representative in the modern sense, it represented the theory of government by consent.

Alienated peers revived old concepts of aristocratic resistance. The Puritan intellectual Robert, Lord Brooke argued for medieval and Aristotelian notions of nobility when he claimed that men of honour were repositories of civil virtue. They were framed for noble enterprises and it was their duty to challenge overbearing and unjust monarchs. Brooke took his chivalric romanticism to Quixotic lengths; as a Parliamentary commander at Kineton in 1642 he unsuccessfully challenged his Royalist opponent to single combat.[1] Brooke's circle included the Earls of Bedford and Essex, who shared his views on the political respon- sibilities of the nobility. They interpreted these as the restoration of the traditional balance of power between Crown and subjects and the defence of Protestantism at home and abroad.

Anxieties about the future security of Protestantism were the catalyst for the first of the crises which led to the outbreak of war. An Arminian (High Church) Anglican by conviction, Charles I had encouraged Archbishop Laud's programme of infiltrating pseudo-Catholic rituals into the Church of England's services. In 1638 the policy was extended to Presbyterian Scotland, where it provoked a rebellion. A majority of landown- ers rallied to defend the Kirk from the Antichrist in the shape of Laudian rites and virtually took over the country. The rebels raised an army and invaded northern England.

Charles's efforts to repel them were a fiasco and the war simul- taneously exposed his isolation and divisions within the nobility. At York in 1640 Lords Saye and Brooke refused to endorse the royal declaration against the Scottish rebels (with whom they and their fellow Puritans openly sympathised) and declared that to do so was contrary to 'common liberty'. Other peers were sympathetic, alleging that demands to swear specific oaths to the King impugned their honour. In the meantime, Charles's army disintegrated as mutinous and unpaid militiamen stripped churches of Laudian fittings, and he was compelled to stave off insolvency by calling Parliament, from which he vainly attempted to exclude Lords Brooke, Saye and Mandeville.

Parliament contained a formidable and ruthless opposition which, between 1640 and 1642, systematically dismantled the administrative apparatus of the royal 'tyranny'. The Anglican Church took a hammering: Archbishop Laud was gaoled and all the bishops were expelled from the Lords, which reduced support for the King. Strafford was tried and beheaded and legislation was drafted to compel the Crown to consult Parliament at least every three years. During these proceedings, Charles had to make concessions to the Scots, whose forces withdrew homewards. They were soon needed to suppress the Irish insurrection of October 1641, in which Catholics massacred about three thousand Protestant settlers. Lurid reports of the atrocities circulated widely and generated anti-Catholic hysteria across England; the Protestant cause, wavering in Europe, now seemed in jeopardy at home.

Existing religious and political fault lines in England, Scotland and Ireland were being widened to the point where fracture seemed unavoidable and with it a war. Charles made it certain in the spring of 1642 when he obstructed Parliamentary efforts to secure control over the volunteer militia (England's only army) and launched a military putsch in which he unsuccessfully tried to arrest five prominent opposition MPs and one peer. Charles then withdrew to Nottingham, where he raised his standard and proclaimed that he was fighting to save the Church and the Law from fanatics.

The aristocracy had been closely engaged at every stage of the escalation from political confrontation to war. The House of Lords had approved all the measures proposed by the Commons, although over thirty peers had absented themselves from the proceedings against Strafford. Others had been unnerved by the mobs of Londoners who demonstrated outside the Palace of Westminster during the winter and spring of 1641–2. Recalling these events, Sir Edward Hyde (the future Earl of Clarendon) dismissed the anti-royalist peers as 'discontented and factious' troublemakers driven by self-interest. There were no more than twenty anti-royalists, but they kept the initiative within the Lords. Revealingly, Clarendon says little about the activities and influence of royal supporters among the peers. There was no reason beyond blind loyalty why the peers should have backed the King, for, by asserting the rights of Parliament as an institution, the House of Lords was defending the rights of the aristocracy to a share in government. The peers were never entirely altruistic; as Clarendon observed, many were keen to abolish the prerogative courts of Star Chamber and Wards because they had suffered losses at their hands.

During 1641 Parliamentary opposition had coalesced around an alliance between activists in the Lords and Commons. The Earls of Warwick, Essex and Bedford, Viscounts Mandeville and Saye and others cooperated closely with the MPs Hampden, Pym (who owed his Tavistock seat to the patronage of the Earl of Bedford), Haselrig and Cromwell. All were Puritans and conservative, insofar as they were hostile to religious and constitutional novelties, particularly the notion of infallible kingship. They abhorred any idea of upsetting the social hierarchy; as Cromwell later observed: 'a nobleman, a gentleman, a yeoman were the ranks and orders of men whereby England has been known for hundreds of years' and this order had to be preserved.[2]

The more recent past mesmerised Charles's opponents, who repeatedly compared present strife with the glories of Elizabeth's reign. This was now hallowed as a golden age of harmony between a revered monarch and her nobility and an overriding national resolve which had made England the scourge of Catholic Spain and the champion of Protestant Europe. This heroic vision was cherished by middle-aged and elderly landowners with selective memories and understandable prejudices against the uncharismatic James I and his headstrong son. As a rough rule, the younger generation dismissed this mirage of 'Good Queen Bess' and her happy times and tended to favour Charles I.[3]

According to Marxist analyses, seismic economic forces were also active in deciding men's loyalties. Methodology and results depended on the premise that all landowners were an economic 'class', rather than a stratified social order defined by abstractions such as honour and status. Assuming the former, R. H. Tawney concluded that since the mid-sixteenth century the gentry had been prospering at the expense of the aristocracy. Professor Hugh Trevor-Roper demurred and claimed that in general the gentry were suffering hard times and were looking for royal patronage to bail them out. It was denied thanks to a corrupt court's monopoly of offices, grants and pensions. This is hard to swallow, for it suggests that the ideologies of the Crown's opponents were superficial and could have been neutralised by the redirection of patronage. The fortunes of the aristocracy were also going through a rough patch, concluded Professor Lawrence Stone, and they too needed the Crown's assistance. Yet he provides abundant evidence to show that thanks to flexible and efficient land management and investment policies nearly all peers were keeping afloat and many were getting richer.

According to Stone, long-term cash flow crises eroded the respect and deference hitherto shown to the aristocracy, which underwent a 'crisis of confidence' immediately before and during the first phase of the civil war. This explained why a knot of peers colluded with the Commons in the campaign against absolutism and, in the process, allied themselves with the enemies of their clerical counterparts, the bishops, and the Crown.[4] For Stone, this was an oblique assault on the general principle of hierarchy and its keystone, the monarchy, and, therefore, was contrary to the interests of the nobility. Perhaps so, but those lords opposed to Charles I would have answered that it was their historic duty to correct wayward monarchs. And they were confident that they would do so again.

Whatever their financial status, the aristocracy continued to expect slavish deference and the law gave them comfort. After a brawl in Dundee in 1606 in which John Scrimgeour, a knight's son, assaulted a merchant who had refused to raise his hat to him, the Scottish Privy Council upheld his right to punish such insolence. 'All cairlie [i.e. churlish] and inferior men ought [to] honour noblemen and ought to be compelled if they will not do it wilfully,' declared the Earl of Angus.[5] The rhetoric of flattery remained and, if anything, became more fulsome. Here is Sir John Suckling awaiting the arrival of the Duke of Newcastle in 1640: 'I will as men do wait – my lord – your coming and in the meantime promise my good hours without the help of an astrologer, since I suddenly hope to see the noblest planet of our orb in conjunction with your lordship.'[6]

Quantifying the comparative incomes of the gentry and the aristocracy reveals the obvious: that for a variety of reasons (often temperamental) some families flourished and others floundered. As for flagging aristocratic confidence, Stone vividly describes the extravagant expenditure of the nobility on the often novel trappings of 'magnificence' such as houses, paintings, sculpture and jewellery. Conspicuous consumption on an unparalleled scale suggests a degree of self-assurance.

In terms of Stuart politics, the rapid expansion of the gentry and nobility after 1560 was more important. Between then and 1639 over 3,700 families received grants of arms and gentle status; most were successful lawyers and merchants and there was one playwright/impresario, William Shakespeare. Most of these arrivistes purchased rural property to give substance to their new rank and as security for their progeny.

Knighthoods proliferated among old and new gentry in the early years of James I's reign, when the King discovered to his profit that status-conscious recipients would pay for the honour. In 1611 he began marketing a newly invented honour, baronetcies (which were hereditary knighthoods), initially to fund garrisons in Ireland. James was forever strapped for cash and his attitude to his subjects' desire for status was refreshingly flippant. Unable to pronounce the name of a Scottish knight, he announced: 'Prithee rise up and call thyself Sir what thou wilt.'

New peerages and promotions were also for sale, either through courtiers, or directly from the Crown. During the next thirteen years the total of peers rose from eighty-one to one hundred and twenty-six with the number of earls more than doubling. There was blatant racketeering: in four years the royal favourite George Villiers, first Duke of Buckingham, pocketed over £24,000 from the sale of nine Irish peerages, eleven baronetcies, four knighthoods and the Lord Chancellorship of Ireland. Arrangements were made for buyers to pay by instalments, which must have galled purchasers once prices began to plummet in response to the Crown's growing liabilities. Baronies fell from £10,000 in 1621 to £4,000 in 1628 and Buckingham was always glad to arrange bargains for his toadies. Charles I halted the sale of titles in 1629, but opened shop again in 1643 to finance the royalist war effort.

Trafficking in titles was (and still is) a murky and venal business, but a thriving one thanks to customer demand. The Stuarts enjoyed, initially, a seller's market, for the enlargement of the landowning order had made its members more conscious than ever of rank. The purchasing of peerages and baronetcies was one symptom of a wider mania which gripped the Jacobean and Caroline gentry and aristocracy. Others included faked pedigrees and the erection of massive memorials lavishly adorned with shields with multiple quarterings, which announced that here were no parvenus, but families of ancient and honourable blood. As Francis Bacon suggested, the advancement of many caused consternation among the occupants of Olympus, who feared the dilution of their prestige. This did not occur, although arriviste gentry were ridiculed by contemporary playwrights.

There is no reason to believe that James I's trade in peerages had any permanent effect on the status of the nobility within society, or that it devalued the mystique of titles. Its political consequence was to give colour and substance to the widespread perception of the court as profoundly corrupt. The court comprised the great offices of state and the households of the King and Queen, and it attracted sycophants, string-pullers and tricksters who enriched themselves through bribery and clandestine dealing in offices and titles. Bureaucrats, particularly in the legal administration, collected fees for their services and every office was a potential goldmine. Those in the right place and with the right friends could make easy fortunes: in 1607 Sir Simonds D'Ewes paid £5,000 for a chancery clerkship and during the next twenty-three years made £32,500 from fees.[7]

Antipathy to James I's court focused on two royal favourites, his Scottish toyboy Robert Carr, Earl of Somerset, and his successor, George Villiers, who engrossed royal patronage for himself and his cronies and bullied the aristocracy. In 1626 the Earl of Bristol told the Lords that Buckingham's 'power is such that I cannot get leave for any message to be delivered to the King'. The eighteenth Earl of Oxford refused to be browbeaten and Buckingham warned him that he would 'do him all the mischief he could'.[8] Buckingham's assassination in 1628 was welcomed by all outside the court; he was the last in a line of amoral and rapacious royal favourites which stretched back through the Duke of Suffolk to Piers Gaveston.

*

The tone of Charles I's court was marginally more honest and certainly more decorous than his father's. Nonetheless, it continued to attract censure from landowners of all ranks. Collectively they were known as the Country Party, which suggests backwoodsmen who blamed the court's malfeasance for all that was going wrong with the country. This was certainly true before 1640, but afterwards the Country Party was primarily concerned with the curtailment of the royal prerogative and the recovery of the old balance of power between Crown and Parliament. Recalling those times, Cromwell's son-in-law Henry Ireton believed that what had been at stake was whether or not the 'supreme magistracy' of the nation rested with the King alone.

Clarendon thought Puritanism cemented Parliamentary opposition to Charles. He was correct insofar as the King's opponents were as much exercised by the future of Protestantism as they were with the division of executive authority. By 1642 they had reached the conclusion that Charles had forfeited his right to be regarded as the defender of Protestantism. The Country Party was, therefore, engaged in a mission to save the nation's faith as well as its subjects' right of consent in government. Both causes were represented as the Lord's work by Puritan preachers and pamphleteers, many of whom were funded by landowners. Robert Rich, second Earl of Warwick, instructed his preacher Samuel Marshall to persuade the voters of Essex that by plumping for Country Party candidates they were fulfilling God's purpose.[9]

Extremes of paranoia and fractiousness characterised the religious life of Charles's three kingdoms. In England and Scotland Protestants (of various creeds) were in the overwhelming majority, but in Ireland they were outnumbered three to one by Catholics. Each faith claimed a monopoly of the only truth and with it the means of salvation and, with varying degrees of sectarian passion, they denounced their rivals as perverse and beyond divine grace.

Confessional differences were routinely settled by battle, massacre and assassination; since the 1540s the Continent had
endured intermittent holy wars between Catholics and
Protestants. In England small groups of Catholic gentry had
plotted to murder Elizabeth I and, in 1605, overthrow the
Church and state at a stroke. The discovery of the Gunpowder
Plot confirmed the need for the coercive recusancy laws which
excluded all Catholic landowners from political life and public
office. For Protestant patriots, Catholics were a fifth column
dedicated to a malevolent Pope and his French and Spanish
allies. Among those tainted was Queen Henrietta Maria, whose
Catholic court was seen as a viper's nest of real and crypto-
Papists. Her co-religionists made up between 1 and 2 per cent of
the English and Scottish populations, but their enemies believed
they possessed a superhuman capacity for subversion and
mayhem.

United in their fear and loathing of Catholicism, Protestants
were divided over theology and the perfect formula for Church
government. Doctrinal quibbling strayed into the world of political theory, in particular the nature of the social hierarchy.
Defenders of episcopacy in England and Scotland justified it as
an integral part of the overall, divinely ordained hierarchy, so that
attacks on the bishops were indirect threats to the secular order.
Theoretically, power flowed upwards in the Scottish Presbyterian
Church where congregations chose their ministers and were
represented in the Church's general assembly. The Kirk's national
structure made it a theocracy in waiting with the potential to
supersede the power of the landowning order traditionally exercised through Parliament.

In 1638 the Kirk needed Scotland's landowners to take on
Charles I and neuter local episcopalians. Within a few years, radical Presbyterians were arguing that a general assembly whose

members were distinguished by their godliness should have a greater authority than a Parliament whose members were distinguished by ancestry and wealth. According to the Calvinist dogma of predestination, God chose his elect randomly and without reference to earthly status. This spiritual elite was identified by its members' exemplary piety, continence and evangelical fervour.

The Calvinist spiritual elect included noblemen and squires who used their social authority to promote their creed, directing a propaganda machine whose agents declared that Parliament was being guided by the hand of God and whipped up London mobs in its support. Royalists were horrified; a section of landowning order was breaking ranks and flirting with dangerous and fissile forces which might easily turn on them. In the process, noblemen devalued themselves. Lord Brooke attracted royalist sneers by his contacts with a 'synod' of tinkers, cobblers and millers with whom, as a devout Puritan, he discussed theology.[10]

Early in 1642 Brooke was distracted by other matters. Parliament had proposed him as one of a new batch of lords lieutenants, each with control over their county militia. The post of lord lieutenant was an Elizabethan invention devised to coordinate national defence and was always filled by a senior peer with local influence. As relations between Charles and Parliament deteriorated, the latter sought the insurance of control over the future raising of troops. In areas where sympathetic noblemen were scarce, Parliament appointed men of lesser rank including a judge.

Charles prevaricated in the face of a blatant encroachment on his prerogative and, once it was clear that his traditional military powers had slipped from his grasp, he resorted to a medieval prerogative, commissions of array, which ordered landowners to muster able-bodied men for the royal army. It was too late, for during the summer of 1642 men like Brooke were using their powers to muster an army for Parliament. Or, as their propaganda and some of their banners claimed, 'For King and Parliament'; the two were still inseparable.

Aristocrats had to choose sides during the summer of 1642. Thirty peers backed Parliament, between fifty and sixty were royalists and thirty were neutral, either by conviction, infirmity or absence abroad.[11] The rest of the landowning class was divided in similar proportions. The intellectual Lord Falkland chose the King out of emotional attachment, although royal policies had dismayed him. Francis, Lord Dacre, had opposed the King before the war, but shrank from fighting against him. He retired to his house on the Pevensey marches and his yacht anchored offshore. Dacre was left undisturbed in his neutrality and entertained friends of all political complexions. His calculated indifference was shared by many of his Sussex neighbours.[12] In the Midlands zealous royalists discovered a large body of knights and gentlemen who wished only to be left alone, or were sincerely perplexed by the rival causes. Sir John Hotham, the governor of Hull, feared that civil war might lead to social revolution once the masses had been drilled and taught how to fight. 'I honour the King as much as I love Parliament,' he declared, but, after judging their cases, he plumped for the latter.[13]

Hotham had predicted that the civil war would bring massive upheaval and suffering. News-sheets and pamphlets had given lurid accounts of the destruction caused on the Continent by the Thirty Years War of 1618–48 and similar miseries were expected in Britain. The pessimists were right. During the summer of 1642, the hungry Parliamentarian garrison of Coventry invaded Lord Dunsmore's park and killed all the deer. Royalist soldiers slaughtered most of Bulstrode Whitelock's herd at Fawley in Buckinghamshire and stole his hounds, which they presented to that noted dog lover, Prince Rupert. Whitelock also lost his carriage, horses and household goods, and he later discovered that his books and manuscripts had been torn up to make spills for the soldiers to light their pipes.[14] Hundreds of landowners of all ranks shared his misfortunes. They endured private plundering by soldiers and official theft committed by their leaders who commandeered cash, food and fodder to sustain their respective war efforts.

10

A Circular Motion: Revolution and Restoration 1642–60

What is now called the War of the Three Kingdoms was a human catastrophe. It lasted from 1642 until 1652 and modern calculations suggest that in England, Wales and Scotland a quarter of a million people died out of a population of about six million. Losses were higher in Ireland, where some 618,000 died, two-fifths of the population.[1] Famine and plague were the biggest killers and more than half the casualties were civilians. Some were massacred: Montrose's Royalists slaughtered the inhabitants of Aberdeen in 1644, Prince Rupert's cavaliers did the same in Leicester in 1645 and Cromwell's New Model Army followed suit at Drogheda and Wexford in 1650. Cities and towns were pummelled by siege artillery, houses were demolished or burned, livestock and crops were commandeered, women raped and looting was endemic. There was nothing romantic in the war between Roundheads and Cavaliers.

Destruction and depredation were inevitable given the nature of the war. At every stage it was a contest for resources with each side often desperately endeavouring to pay, feed and equip permanent field armies and garrisons. The fighting, therefore, resolved itself into a series of sieges and campaigns designed to gain strategic control of a region and extract whatever matériel it could yield. Parliament held a trump card in London and with it the machinery of government, and it was strongest in the rich and well-populated South and East. The royalists predominated in the poorer and less populous North, South-West and Wales. This territorial base was gradually chipped away and the royalist war effort collapsed after reverses at Marston Moor in 1644 and Naseby in 1645. Parliamentary mopping-up operations continued into the following year.

Each side had courted allies, principally to acquire manpower. Presbyterian Scotland provided Parliament with troops in 1644 in the mistaken belief that a thankful England would adopt Presbyterianism. Charles secured Catholic and Episcopalian Scotland through James Graham, Marquess of Montrose, whose Irish and Highland army played havoc with the Kirk's levies during 1644 and 1645. The King also negotiated with Irish Catholics and Protestants, but got only a trickle of soldiers who were too late to affect the outcome of the conflict. Gaelic royalists used the war as an opportunity to revive old clan feuds: Campbell levies murdered Macdonnell's in Ulster and Montrose's MacDonald clansmen massacred Campbells in Scotland. The 'civilising' policies of Charles's predecessors collapsed under the pressure of military necessity.

In 1647 the fugitive King snatched at another Caledonian straw by an accommodation with the Kirk in which he compromised his Anglicanism by pledging the introduction of

Presbyterianism in England in return for an army. It was trounced at Preston in 1648 by Cromwell, who attributed his victory to 'the hand of God'. Charles fell into Parliamentarian hands and, at the army's insistence, was tried with making war on his subjects, found guilty and publicly executed in Whitehall in January 1649. The past died with him: the monarchy, the House of Lords and the Anglican Church were abolished and a republic established.

Cromwell, now commander-in-chief of the republic's army, proceeded to extirpate royalist resistance in Ireland and Scotland. In 1651, he again thanked God for a further and decisive victory over the Scots at Worcester, who were fighting to restore Charles, Prince of Wales (the future Charles II), to his father's throne. Royalist outposts in Virginia and the Barbados hung on until 1652, the last surrendering after being threatened with an amphibious landing and the sort of treatment that had been meted out in Ireland.[2]

By then, the three-year-old British republic was firmly established and winning respect and fear abroad, and so it could afford to be magnanimous even to stubborn royalists. Francis, Lord Wylloughby, the governor of the Barbados, was allowed to keep his sugar plantations there and elsewhere in the West Indies, which had been given to him by the Prince of Wales. They were a reward for his defection: until 1647 he had been an active Parliamentarian on the battlefield and in the House of Lords, but had switched sides after falling foul of the Presbyterian faction in the Commons. His religious sympathies were also Cromwell's, which may explain why Wylloughby was permitted to return to England.[3] In spirit he remained loyal to the exiled Prince of Wales, but he tempered his behaviour to the times and survived. Other peers followed his prudent example.

Wylloughby came home to a nation undergoing an experiment in government. By a majority of fifteen votes the Rump Parliament created a new polity which was called a 'Commonwealth or Free State' and embraced England, Scotland and

Ireland. Executive power was held by 'the people in parliament' and whomever they chose to be ministers in a council of state. The House of Lords had ceased to function, although peers were allowed to keep their titles, and, if they were considered trustworthy, to continue to exercise limited power in their localities. This sidelining of the aristocracy was in large part a security measure: about half the nobility had been active royalists and many were unreconciled to the new regime at a time when the Prince of Wales was at large and conspiring with the Scots to restore the monarchy. Public safety as much as republican ideology dictated that the monarchy and House of Lords perished together.

Where did this leave those aristocrats who had either been Parliamentarians or, like Wylloughby, made terms with the republic to save what they could of their estates? Their prestige was intact, but their influence over public affairs had been severely curtailed. Their local powers were largely taken over by Cromwell's dozen major-generals, satraps who took over the supervision of provincial government in 1655. This further pruning of the traditional political power of the aristocracy was possibly a manifestation of Cromwell's dictum: 'I know what I would not, not what I would.'

Marginalising the aristocracy in national politics may also have been an attempt to defuse the dangerous popular discontent that had been recently expressed by Levellers and other radicals, which is discussed later. Or, notwithstanding the fact that the aristocracy had played a significant part in the original rebellion against the King, the nobility was again identified with the Crown, and, therefore had to be kept in a political limbo. Given the royalist plots of the 1650s, this was a sensible precaution.

Yet republican polemicists spared the aristocracy the vituperation that was levelled at hereditary monarchy. Peers continued to receive the deference due to their rank in a society in which the traditional hierarchy was maintained. In Scotland, Cromwell continued James VI's modernisation policies by paring down but not abolishing the nobility's ancient feudal powers, including hereditary jurisdictions and the right to demand armed service from tenants.

A now ornamental aristocracy existed in a society which still revered the outward shows and tokens of status. The republic's rulers remained deeply attached to those principles of personal honour which bound together its upper ranks. When the successful Parliamentarian general Lord Fairfax was rewarded with the lordship of the Isle of Man, it was publicly declared that he deserved it as a man whose honour equalled that of the Stanley earls of Derby, its previous owners, who had been royalists. Gentlemen dominated the government of the republic and expected to be treated as such. When Cromwell dissolved the Rump Parliament in 1653, Sir Arthur Haselrig complained that his escort of musketeers had insolently refused to remove their hats in the presence of their superiors. The republican elite dressed richly, rode in coaches with outriders and sat for fashionable portraitists as if they had been noblemen.[4]

Such ostentation must have dismayed many rank and file Parliamentary soldiers who had welcomed the republic and had once briefly hoped that the war would be a catalyst for a remodelling of the social as well the political order. Their voices were loudest during 1646 and 1647, when the Leveller movement won over sections of the army. Its pervasiveness disturbed the high command, which arranged a sequence of debates in Putney church between agitators and senior officers, including Cromwell's son-in-law Henry Ireton. At the centre of the wrangling was the Leveller proposal for a broader electoral franchise that would embrace 'free-born' yeomen, craftsmen and retailers, who would offset the influence of the aristocracy and gentry.

Such a political counterweight was pointless, argued Ireton, who defended the continued paramountcy of landowners like himself. Their wealth gave them a stake in the kingdom and, therefore, a natural concern for its stability and welfare which benefited everyone. It was an argument that would be repeated during the late eighteenth and nineteenth centuries, when the political dispensation was again challenged from below.

Ireton's case obviously extended to the aristocracy, whose legislative powers the Levellers wished to abrogate for purely historical reasons. They were rooted in ancient injustice, for the nobility were merely the descendants of the fortune-hunting soldiers led by William the Conqueror, who colluded in his suffocation of fictitious Anglo-Saxon liberties. The Leveller concept of the 'Norman Yoke' lacked historical validity, but was attractive because it hinted at a lost golden age of liberty and equality that had been brutally terminated by the ancestors of the rich and powerful. Its modern manifestations included types of tenure which, the Levellers protested, were unfairly balanced in favour of landlords. The Norman Yoke theory lived on as part of radical mythology until the twentieth century.

The Leveller movement was easily squashed by Cromwell backed by loyal troops. Its significance has been overstated by left-inclined historians (particularly in the late 1960s when parallels were made between the Levellers and contemporary student agitation in America and Europe; the only connection was that both movements came to nothing, although the radical left still celebrates the anniversary of the execution of a trio of Levellers at Burford). Nevertheless, former Levellers had the satisfaction of seeing the end of the Lords, although they had to wait until the Restoration for the abolition of archaic feudal tenure.

A far greater threat to landowners of all ranks came from the millenarian sects which flourished briefly in the unsettled late 1640s and early 1650s. The Diggers wanted all land to be held in common, and the Ranters preached universal equality. According to one, 'honour, nobility, gentility [and] propriety' would disappear when the new Zion was established in

England.[5] Both movements were shallowly rooted and suppressed by a republic determined to preserve the social status quo. More formidable, insofar that its adherents had a disproportionate say in the short-lived 1653 'Barebones' Parliament, was the Fifth Monarchy movement, who had a vision of the republic as an embryonic new Israel. The new Zion would see the extinction of an aristocracy based upon land and ancestry to be replaced by an elite based upon individual purity, religious zeal and orthodoxy. The theocracy of Puritan 'saints' never emerged, for Cromwell dissolved the Barebones Parliament.

The brief phenomena of social revolutionary movements of the Interregnum scared all landowners and Anglican clergymen. The antics and fancies of Levellers, Ranters, Diggers and Fifth Monarchy men became implanted in the historic memory of conservatives. Here was a baleful warning: madcap sectarianism and egalitarian subversion were inseparable and the inevitable outcome of defying the Crown and its Church. Perhaps so, but what is fascinating about the movements which disturbed the mid-seventeenth century is that their impact on the population as a whole was transitory. As Jonathan Clark's *English Society 1688–1832* reminds us, submission to authority and the social order remained ingrained in the psyches of the greater part of the population for the next hundred and fifty years. Yes, there were intermittent disorders during this period, but they tended to be spontaneous, violent reactions to injustices such as the enforcement of militia quotas, food shortages, or the expression of demotic, visceral anti-Catholicism. The mob was physically frightening, but it never threatened to overturn the social order.

At every stage of the conflict, royalist propaganda had accused Parliament of fomenting the social antipathy; whatever their rank, all roundheads were levellers at heart. A satirical ballad of 1642 has apprentices joyfully predicting the end of deference and courtesy:

We'll teach the nobles how to stoop,
And keep the gentry down:
Good manners have an ill report
And turn to pride, we see,
We'll therefore pull good manners down,
And hey, then up go we.

Faced with defeat in 1645, the royalist mood became bitter:

And the scum of the land
Are the men that command.
And our slaves have become our masters.[6]

By their own estimation, the royalists were aristocrats in spirit: after all, 'Cavalier' was derived from the Continental term for a gentleman horseman trained in arms. According to a definition of 1644: 'A complete cavalier is a child of honour, a gentleman well born and bred; that loves his King for conscience sake, of a clean countenance and bolder look than other men, because of a more loyal heart.' He was the true heir of the chivalric tradition of 'English gentility and ancient valour'.[7]

But ancestral courage had not prevailed and, after 1646, Parliament found itself governing a country in which at least half the peerage and the gentry had fought against it and could no longer be trusted as agents of the state. It was, therefore, driven to appoint sympathetic men to local offices whose status would have disqualified them before the outbreak of the war. In Gloucestershire the lesser gentry were promoted and in Somerset 'new made gentlemen' found themselves in posts once held by their superiors, and were derided.[8]

Many of the intruders were Parliamentary army officers, often of humble origins, who had been promoted because of a dearth of gentlemen and their outstanding religious fervour. Some relished the turn of fortune which had elevated them, and did all they could to make life unpleasant for their former adversaries. Major George Purefoy, who commanded the garrison in the Earl of Northampton's house at Compton Wynyates in Warwickshire, was a bully and extortioner whom the royalist press revealingly likened to Wat Tyler. Like many others in similar positions, Purefoy was corrupt and, it seems, vain, for he owned a hat embellished with diamonds.[9]

The trouble for the royalist aristocracy and gentry was that men of Purefoy's stamp were often responsible for the sequestration of resources and cash for the Parliamentary war effort, and, when hostilities were over, for the assessment of punitive imposts levied on 'delinquents', as former royalists were called. The fleecing began in the first weeks of the war when Parliamentary and royalist officials began cataloguing the assets of the nobility and gentry and making demands accordingly. In 1643 Parliament voted for £4,000 to be levied from royalist estates in Gloucestershire to pay for the county's garrisons.

Paradoxically, those hit hardest were peers who contrived to keep a foot in both camps. Thomas, Viscount Savile, claimed that royalist forces stole £8,000 in coin and plate from his estates after he had deserted the King in 1643. Reinstated in royal favour and given the earldom of Sussex, Savile abandoned Charles in 1645, and Parliament, doubting his sincerity, locked him in the Tower, where he suffered a bout of bladder stones. He was released and fined £4,000.[10] Savile put his own and his family's interests before those of King or Parliament and got off quite lightly, given his record. Another self-interested trimmer was John Tufton, second Earl of Thanet, who had loyally attended Charles at York in 1639 for the campaign against the Scots with a thousand pounds in cash and a doctor's certificate excusing him from service in the field. Clearly allergic to or unfit for soldiering, he endured a brief spell of it with royalist forces and departed for France in 1643.

On his return a year later, he alleged that livestock, silverware, timber and property with a total value of £54,000 had been seized by Parliament. Charges that he supplied Charles with cash and plate earned Thanet a further fine of £20,000. Soldiers from both armies despoiled his manor at Wiston in Sussex and he suffered further losses when his London house was commandeered for army quarters in 1650. By 1654 he had made his peace with the republic, was appointed sheriff of Kent and helped thwart a royalist conspiracy there. For this reason his still unpaid fine was reduced to £9,000.[11]

This was painful, but not beyond Thanet's means, for his annual revenues were estimated at £10,000. John Strange, Lord Rivers, a Catholic and colonel of a royalist regiment of foot, was less lucky. At the end of the war, he was tottering on the edge of insolvency. He admitted a 'weakness' in his estates and was heavily in debt, despite having sold property to the value of £11,000. It was insufficient, for he died in 1654 while in gaol for debt. His £1,400 delinquency fine was suspended when he swore an oath of allegiance to the republic, not that he could have paid it.[12]

The 'weakness' in Strange's estates may have been the result of mismanagement, or the cumulative fiscal demands and depredations of the war. Losers had no choice but to accept their fate stoically. In 1650 the royalist fourth Earl of Dorset wrote that: 'it has pleased Divine Providence to lay his heavy hand on me (which I acknowledge my sins justly deserved) by making me less able in my earthly fortune by 40 thousand pounds'.[13] Land values slumped and tenants quarrelled with landlords as to which should pay military levies. Some tenants took advantage of economic disruption and their landlords' distraction to demand fresh terms which favoured their interests. The insubordinate spirit of the times may have emboldened the 'proud fellow' who, in 1654, led the resistance of tenants in Drayton in Staffordshire against their landlord's plan to replace their leases with less secure and more onerous tenancies.[14]

Hardship could be mitigated. Delinquents used legal legerdemain to sidestep the complex official machinery for the assessment and collection of charges on their estates. If these were confiscated, then the owners covertly bought back their property: the Marquess of Winchester recovered thirteen or fifteen of his manors. Significantly, Cromwell turned a blind eye to such manouevres.[15] The republic was striving to achieve stability and unity and neither was advanced by the overzealous persecution of royalists. Some sought assistance from kinsmen who had fought for Parliament. The second Earl of Denbigh pulled strings in London for his royalist cousin George Villiers, the second Duke of Buckingham, in the matter of negotiating the fines imposed against him by Parliament. Denbigh also vainly sought a pardon for his brother-in-law James, Duke of Hamilton, who was executed in 1649.[16] Differences of conscience did not erase family ties.

Sales of estates previously owned by the Crown, the Church and royalists who failed to compound their debts attracted purchasers from all social backgrounds, although the gentry predominated.[17] Senior army officers used their influence to secure the choicest pickings: Colonel Thomas Pride, a former brewer, installed himself and his family in the royal palace of Nonsuch. The scale and briskness of the post-war land market persuaded some contemporaries that a revolution in the distribution of land was underway and the gentry were gaining in terms of acreage over the aristocracy.[18] This was not so, and the balance was fundamentally unaltered.

In Ireland, however, the war dramatically changed the pattern of land ownership. Here Parliament treated the conflict not just as pacification, but as a golden opportunity to pursue earlier policies of forcibly replacing Catholic with Protestant landowners. From the beginning, the Irish war had a distinctly colonial flavour. In 1643 Parliament invited English investors (mainly businessmen) to contribute funds for the campaign in return for dividends in the form of lands confiscated from Irish rebels. When the payout came in 1653, over a million acres were available, to which were added the properties of Irish royalists.

All Catholic gentry, whatever their previous loyalties, forfeited a third of the estates and exchanged the remainder for lands in Clare and western Connaught. Over three thousand families were relocated.[19] Catholic landowners with supple consciences and a sense of timing evaded these penalties through collaboration. Piers Butler, first Viscount Ikerrin, fought with the royalists in the 1640s and turned his sword on the 'Tories' (Irish royalists) in the 1650s, for which he secured Cromwell's goodwill and 'some proportion' of his Tipperary estates.[20]

In the short term there was a bonanza in which many speculators sold their holdings, often to officers in the army of occupation. Among them was Captain Robert Godkin, whose troop of cavalry had fought the Tories in West Cork and who had built a fort at Rosscarberry, which he garrisoned with a hundred men. His efforts were repaid with two thousand acres of nearby land in which he invested five hundred pounds. By 1657 Godkin had attracted three hundred settlers to his domain, who lived within 'musket shot' (a revealing phrase) of his stronghold. It was the counterpart of many frontier outposts then being constructed and defended against the natives in North America. After the Restoration, Godkin was pardoned and confirmed in his estate.[21]

Unscrupulous chancers did well out of the Irish land grab. Sir John Clotworthy, an Antrim landowner and kinsman by marriage to the leading Parliamentarian Pym, hitched himself to the Parliamentary cause in the 1640s, proving his zeal by taunting Laud on the scaffold. He acted as an agent for London speculators in Irish lands and was ideally placed to make a killing, dealing in debentures and buying up land cheaply to enlarge and consolidate his Ulster holdings. After the Restoration, Charles II ennobled Clotworthy as Viscount Massereene.[22]

Massereene and the soldier-colonist gentry of Ireland retained most of their gains. Charles II did what he could to compensate his father's Irish supporters, but he dared not risk upsetting the new landowners, who were vital props to the Protestant ascendancy. The brittle public peace of Ireland came before equity.[23] Charles II's accommodations with his father's enemies left the dispossessed Catholic gentry bitter. The war had achieved the objective of the Elizabethan and Jacobean plantations: the creation of a dominant, imported Protestant nobility and gentry who could be relied upon to enforce the political and religious status quo in Ireland. The distance in outlook, sympathies and culture between them and their Catholic-Gaelic tenants was as great as that between a Virginian frontiersman and his Indian neighbours. No such gulf existed in the rest of Britain.

The narrative of the implosion of the British republic in 1658–9 and the negotiations which paved the way for Charles II's restoration has no place here, for the aristocracy played little part in either. After over a decade of unsatisfactory constitutional experiments and rule by army officers, a return to the familiar and tested political order had become increasingly attractive. Disillusioned Parliamentarians began to appreciate the value of abandoned traditions: Robert Beake, MP for Coventry, reminded the Commons in 1659 that 'usage is a good right' and the House of Lords had been a valuable institution.[24]

It was a common sentiment of the time. Abolishing the House of Lords had not significantly devalued the dignity and prestige of the nobility, although whether the respect in which it was held would have decayed if the republic had survived is an imponderable of history. A bonus for the aristocracy in terms of its popularity was the widespread resentment against the agents of the republic who imposed Puritan morality on every aspect of human life. Fun was outlawed, theatres were closed, Christmas was abolished and adulterers faced the gallows; it was a happy time for busybodies and philistines.

The republic did not weaken the general acceptance of the aristocracy as an integral and useful part of society, and the feeling that, individually and collectively, its members had contributed to the overall order and stability of the country.[25] The peerage (and the bishops) regained their legislative powers in 1660 as part of what Thomas Hobbes concluded was the final stage of a revolution. It had been 'a circular motion of sovereign power through two usurpers [Cromwell and his son Richard], from the late King to his son . . . where long may it remain'.[26]

The aristocracy had been buffeted during this topsy-turvy time. Its traumas had been greater than those of the Wars of the Roses, which, despite high aristocratic casualties, had not witnessed the political eclipse of the peerage. The restoration of the House of Lords in 1660 raised morale and there was limited compensation for former royalists, although royal gratitude often fell short of expectations. The psychological impact of the war and its sequel is difficult to measure: some peers' lives had been blighted by financial losses, privation and humiliation by the republic's low-born officials; other peers mastered the arts of survival and flourished. The household accounts of Henry Bourchier, fifth Earl of Bath, show that between 1648 and 1650 he maintained a household of thirty-six servants at Tawstock in Devon. He ate and drank well, smoked large quantities of tobacco, travelled to London in his coach attended by outriders and treated himself to expensive drinking glasses.

Outwardly, the nobility's political power in the post–1660 world was as it had always been, and its official and semi-official functions remained the same. New roles were created, paradoxically, by Cromwell's proto-imperial expansion, which gathered pace in the next century and provided opportunities for the younger sons of noblemen to serve as proconsuls and commanders of fleets and armies.

The old aristocratic sense of inherited distinction and responsibilities remained. Algernon Sydney, second son of the Earl of Leicester, declared: 'Though I am not a peer, yet I am of the wood of which they are made.' It was sound timber with Percy and Sydney roots, but some contemporaries would have detected a canker, for Sydney's father had been a Parliamentarian commander. His defiance of the Crown was, for his son, a vindication of the aristocracy's historic role as sentinels who guarded the rights of property and the liberties of the nation. According to the younger Sydney, men of high birth and ancestry had a unique moral duty and were subject to 'a higher law' which obliged them to challenge arbitrary kingship. In 1642 and, for that matter, in 1399 the nobility had performed its ancestral responsibilites. This was the thesis of Sydney's *Discourses Concerning Government,* written before his execution for treason (he plotted against Charles II) in 1683:

> No better defence has been found against the encroachments of ill kings than by setting up an order of men who, by holding large territories and having great numbers of tenants and dependents, might be able to restrain the exhorbitancies that either the King or the Commons might run into.

Sydney had been unchastened by the aristocracy's recent misfortunes. Other peers had been and favoured quietism. Submission to the will of a strong monarch alone prevented the fragmentation of society into myriads of atoms perpetually contending with each other. This had been the lesson of the wars as understood by Hobbes in his *Leviathan*, published in 1651, in which he argued that benevolent autocracy was the only way of constraining the primal and raptorial instincts of mankind.

The old dilemma remained for the aristocracy: where did its duties lie? Did it serve the Crown, or the nation as a whole as Sydney had suggested. The issues raised in 1642 had not gone away and pessimists wondered whether the Restoration marked a truce, rather than a termination of the civil wars.

11

———•———

Signal Deliverances: Restoration 1660–85

Samuel Pepys was impressed by 'the gallantry of the horsemen, citizens, and noblemen of all sorts' who greeted Charles II as he came ashore at Dover on 25 May 1660. The jubilation (and relief) seemed universal, for the wars and experiments in government were finally over. A future of tranquillity and harmony beckoned, since before embarking from Holland, Charles had promised to defend the 'just, ancient and fundamental rights of his subjects' and to be guided by his Parliaments. The House of Lords and the Church of England were restored with the King and, superficially, at least, it seemed that the clock had been turned back to 1642.

The old social order had not been changed by wars and experiments in government. It remained a layered hierarchy with the aristocracy at the top. Noblemen and their wives could still command deference and submission from inferiors and they continued to fill the great offices of state and supervise the government of their localities. The nobility remained an open elite: families died out for lack of heirs and new titles were created by the Crown, particularly for men who had stayed loyal to Charles II during his exile. Yet, society was changing, slowly and inexorably. The central section of the pyramid was broadening as the 'middling' orders of professional and business- and what were then called 'money' men expanded. Pepys belonged to this body – he was a civil servant – and to prosper he had to show extremes of respect to the peers to whom he looked for promotion. He had accompanied Charles on his voyage across the North Sea and had come ashore in the boat which contained the favourite royal dog, 'which shit in the boat, which made us laugh and me think that a King and all that belong to him are just as others are'. A seditious thought, but a reminder that the ideas which had broken surface before and during the civil wars had not been forgotten.

The revived House of Lords, complete with bishops and peers created by Charles I during the war, reassembled in its somewhat shabby chamber in the Palace of Westminster overlooked by a huge tapestry depicting the defeat of the Armada. One of the Lords' first and most agreeable tasks was to approve an act to liberate all landowners from the Crown's residual feudal powers, which had become 'burdensome, grievous and prejudicial to the kingdom'.[1] Among this legal lumber was the royal right to the wardship of underage heirs.

The hereditary principle had been confirmed and reinforced. Henceforward, a peer was free to arrange for the maintenance of his offspring (and their property) by creating trusts and entails which prevented the fragmentation of estates. These legal formulae confirmed land as the prime and safest form of investment. Even though many noblemen invested in overseas enterprises, including the new Africa Company, which dealt in slaves, land remained the bedrock of their power and independence. A valuable gain could be offset by a small loss when in 1676 peers lost the right to assess their own taxes.

A contented, loyal and active aristocracy was vital for Charles II's survival and the stability of his three kingdoms. His propaganda eulogised him as a deliverer who 'new borne and raised from the dead' had rescued his subjects from the 'late deplorable confusions'.[2] This allusion to Christ's resurrection comes from the preamble to a law which established an annual service to celebrate the King's birthday on 29 May. Further loyal observances were added to the Anglican liturgy: on 31 January parsons remembered the 'martyrdom' of Charles I, and on 5 November prayers were offered in thanksgiving for that divine providence which had saved a Protestant nation from the Gunpowder Plot of 1605. These rites affirmed a royalist, Anglican version of national destiny in which the monarchy was an agent for the fulfilment of divine will.

Charles II needed God's imprimatur to convince his subjects that obedience was in their own as well as his interests. He ruled kingdoms in which recent political and religious antagonisms were barely quiescent and periodically surfaced in the form of sedition, conspiracies and, in Scotland, a small-scale insurrection and terrorist campaign by the extreme Presbyterian Covenanters. Seen in retrospect, Charles's reign was a brittle armistice during which an affable, concupiscent and flexible monarch with an overriding instinct for self-preservation strove to control his fractious and volatile subjects. Their passivity was the key to stability, prosperity and the survival of the Stuart dynasty.

The aristocracy cooperated, for it too wanted peace. Charles could rely upon the House of Lords, his predominantly aristocratic ministers and, most importantly, those peers whom he appointed as Lords Lieutenants in the provinces. They and their deputies spied on and chivvied religious nonconformists (the confessional heirs of the Puritans), twisted arms to secure the election of pliant MPs and vetted potential magistrates. In 1676 Viscount Yarmouth, Lord Lieutenant of Norfolk, forwarded to Charles a list of tractable justices with a note saying that he had chosen them 'for the King's immediate service and strengthening of my own interest in a greater capacity to service the crown'.[3] The traditional reciprocity between Crown and peerage had been restored: the King made Yarmouth the first man in his county (he was made an earl in 1679), in return for which Yarmouth zealously prosecuted royal interests, though he managed his own badly and eventually slid into bankrupty.

In Scotland Charles relied upon the influence and military muscle of the peerage and gentry to contain the Covenanters. Private detachments supplemented units from the small royal standing army which Charles had established in 1660 under young, loyal and largely aristocratic officers. Significantly, he allowed the mobilisation of Catholic and Episcopalian clansmen for operations against the Lowland Covenanters.[4] Noblemen and lairds did their bit in rooting out sedition: the wonderfully named Cromwell Lockhart mustered his tenants to fight the Covenanters, and William, Marquess of Hamilton, pursued 'skulking' fugitives on his estates.[5]

The Scottish Presbyterian rebels were called 'Whiggamores' and its derivative 'Whig' was the title given to Parliamentary opponents of Charles during the late 1670s. Whigs retaliated in kind by calling their adversaries Tories, the name given to Irish Catholic rebels thirty years before. An exchange of insults appropriately marked the infancy of British party politics, although neither faction resembled a modern political party with its ideological discipline and administrative apparatus. Rather, Whig and Tory represented states of mind which had been shaped by recent events and the ideas they had generated.

The Whigs were the successors of the Roundheads who had regrouped and, their enemies alleged, were prepared to start another civil war in pursuit of their theories of government. In 1682 a Tory reviled them as the men 'whose fathers have sucked on the poison of rebellion in the last age', and who, behind the 'mask of Liberty, Property and Religion endeavour the destruction and ruin of the King and kingdom'.[6] There was an element of truth in this, since many prominent Whigs had been in arms against Charles I. Philip, the fourth Lord Wharton, had commanded a regiment at Edgehill in 1642 (it ran away) and afterwards immersed himself in less hazardous administrative duties for Parliament and the republic.

The Tories had inherited the Cavalier mindset. They believed in quietism, loathed religious dissent and upheld the King and the Church of England in Parliament and the countryside. Cohesion and tranquillity could be achieved only through the supremacy of the Crown and acceptance of the Anglican doctrine of submission to authority. The quintessence of Toryism was explained by Edward Stillingfleet, the Dean of St Pauls, in a sermon of 1682. He conjured up a vision of society as an 'orderly communion', a Christian brotherhood which made it possible for people to 'abide where they were called by God, [and] keep their ranks and places where right Reason [and] Religion have fixed them'. Those who questioned or, worse still, spurned this dispensation were, like Cain, 'rebels against God'.[7]

A model for the regulation of Stillingfleet's perfect society was provided by a Cavalier, Sir Robert Filmer, whose *Patriarcha, or that Natural Power of Kings Asserte* was posthumously published in 1680. Universal peace and harmony were the fruits of abject submission. It was the product of a chain of command that stretched from monarchs downwards to masters of households. Greater and lesser patriarchs were wise, benevolent and guided by the knowledge that their authority came from God. This was not an original thesis: Filmer had elaborated on what was an essentially medieval view of society and, because of fears of a renewed civil war, it was accepted by conservatives.

Participation in government rather than unconditional submission was the Whig response to Tory theories of natural obedience. With the approval of his master Anthony Ashley Cooper, first Earl of Shaftesbury, John Locke proposed in 1663 that the new colony of Carolina should have buildings set aside for public meetings and that deputies elected by freeholders should make laws. There would also be religious toleration and, unlike in England and Scotland, no established Church with powers of social correction.

Behind the constitution for Carolina lay the Whig assumption that popular consent should limit royal executive power. Tories argued that it was infinite because it derived ultimately from God. 'It is better to obey God than a man,' insisted a Tory journalist, Sir Roger L'Estrange, in 1680, rather than submit to the Whig conceit that 'sovereign power is in the people'.[8] It was absurd, he continued, to imagine that the Lords and Commons were somehow 'two thirds of the King of England'. The clash of ideas which had been the prelude to the civil war was still underway and old convictions were as strongly held as ever by Whigs and Tories.

Divergent views on the nature of kingship translated into political factions within the Lords and Commons. Yet, in 1710, one pamphleteer considered that 'Whig' and 'Tory' were terms which described the political affiliations of the lower orders. 'Persons of the first rank, who either by their birth or abilities are entitled to govern others' adopted these labels to win electoral support.[9] This was cynical, but it was a reminder that legislators who ignored public feeling risked their careers. Watermen who rowed peers to Westminster talked to the passengers about public affairs as taxi drivers do today.[10]

Public opinion was easily moulded alleged one Whig polemicist in 1667, when he accused Jesuits of 'mingling with gentlemen to poison the Clubs and Coffee houses with fanatic disorders'.[11] It seems that even the educated political elite could be beguiled by subtle political spin. Political debate raged at all levels, and at the lowest was heard most frequently in ale houses. In 1678 a Yorkshire labourer told fellow drinkers that 'the King had thrown up his crown to the Parliament', presumably in response to accounts of the Commons's demands for new oaths of allegiance from Catholics.[12]

Political discussion whether by gentlemen in the new, fashionable coffee houses or artisans in inns had been made possible by the rapidly expanding popular literature of politics. Reports of what passed in Westminster were printed in newspapers and journals, which were conveyed to the provinces by the new postal system. Interpretation and insights into the characters and motives of the nation's rulers were provided by a mass of partisan and vitriolic pamphlets which transmitted the antipathies of Whigs and Tories to the country at large.

The explosion of the press meant that it was now possible to speak of 'national' politics since issues were more widely aired than ever. The phenomenon of nascent popular politics coincided with an increase in the number of voters as a result of more and more men qualifying for the forty-shilling freeholder franchise. This had been set in 1429, confining the right to vote in county elections to all adults who owned freehold land worth forty shillings. It has been calculated that there were at least 250,000 voters in 1714, just under 5 per cent of the population. Despite bribery and coercion by candidates and their paymasters, the proportion of voters who turned up to the polls fluctuated from over a half to less than a fifth in county elections.[13] Boredom with and indifference to politics have had a long history.

Polling was done in public in the county town. The aristocracy had always taken a keen and active interest in Parliamentary elections; the ability to get his man in was a token of a nobleman's influence over his locality. He could rely on deference to sway squires and tenant farmers, and if this did not work, then bribery and bullying were applied. In 1661 William Cavendish, third Earl of Devonshire, veteran royalist and Lord Lieutenant of Derbyshire, rhetorically asked the gentry of that county whether his son would be 'acceptable' as a knight of the shire.[14] No one was bold enough to invite the Lord Lieutenant's disfavour and so William Cavendish was elected.

He later abandoned his father's Toryism and became a prominent Whig. While there was an element of family tradition in attachment to political factions, it never prevented peers from making independent judgements, or, more commonly, trimming their sails to the prevailing wind. The growth of faction was one reason why peers considered it imperative to fortify their influence by placing their offspring in the lower house. Stepping up the infiltration of the Commons was both a political stratagem and, more significantly, an admission by the peerage that it needed trustworthy allies in a body which represented the nation as a whole. Between 1660 and 1690 just over two hundred heirs or younger sons of peers sat in the Commons.[15]

Winning an election was an expensive and, for young patricians, an occasionally demeaning business. In 1679 the Whig Henry Sydney, a younger son of the second Earl of Leicester, complained of the embarrassment he and the rival candidate, the Tory Henry Goring, suffered when they endeared themselves to the thirty voters of Bramber in Sussex. They 'made us spend much more than we should to keep our party firm . . . You should have laughed to see how pleased I seemed in kissing old women and drinking wine with handfulls of sugar, and great glasses of burnt brandy, three things much against the stomach.'[16] The flattered electors agreed to let Sydney and Goring share the two-member borough. Head-to-head contests, particularly for county seats, were far more demanding in terms of entertainment and bribes.

*

Charles II could not change the minds of the Whig nobility and gentry, but he could isolate their potential supporters, the Nonconformists. During the 1660s laws were passed which made active Anglicanism a qualification for all public offices from parish constable and juryman upwards. Additional hurdles were constructed in the form of oaths of allegiance whose wordings were repugnant to all Nonconformists. All royal servants had to swear that it was 'not lawful upon any pretence whatsoever to take arms against the King' and pledge never to 'endeavour any alteration in government either in Church or State'.[17] Dissenters were, however, still permitted to vote. When they did, they favoured the Whigs, whose attitude to religious conformity was more flexible than the Tories.

Both parties united in their loathing and distrust of Catholics, who had lost none of their capacity to make Protestant flesh creep. Anti-Catholic paranoia took on a new lease of life in the late 1670s: the King was flirting with his cousin Louis XIV of France (and receiving secret subsidies from him) and there was unease about Catholic and crypto-Catholic influence within the court.

The conditions were right for a fresh spasm of anti-Catholic hysteria. It was triggered in 1678 by the ravings of Titus Oates, who claimed to have uncovered plans for a violent coup which would place the King's brother, James, Duke of York, on the throne (he had converted to Catholicism five years before) with the assistance of a French army and English Catholics. Oates was a nasty creature, physically and morally akin to another self-appointed purifier of public life, the American Senator Joseph McCarthy. Both understood the psychology of their audiences and exploited their neuroses with lurid revelations of a hidden enemy whose duplicity was surpassed only by its ruthlessness. No matter that Catholics, like American communists, were a tiny minority; what they lacked in numbers they made up for in determination and cunning.

Critical disbelief was suspended and the aristocracy shared the general alarm which followed Oates's disclosures, which implicated several Catholic peers. They were detained and the Commons and Lords immediately joined forces and compelled Catholic peers and MPs to swear an oath in which they denied the doctrine of the mass and declare that prayers to the Virgin Mary and the saints were 'superstitious and idolatrous'.[18] Seventeen of the nineteen Catholics lords refused to comply and were expelled from the Lords.

The 1679 election favoured the Whigs, who were determined to take the purge of Catholics to its natural conclusion and transfer the succession from Charles's brother James to James, Duke of Monmouth, Charles's illegitimate son by his mistress Lucy Walter. The King was appalled, as were the Tories, who objected on pragmatic and religious grounds. They convinced themselves that James's private faith was no impediment to his governing his two Protestant kingdoms, and that human interference with the natural succession flouted the will of God. Moreover, and this ran harshly against the grain of Tory principles, the proposed Whig Exclusion Bill implied that Parliament reserved the right to decide who should wear the crown.

On this Charles was adamant. His minister George Savile, Earl of Halifax, warned the peers that, if he were denied the succession, then York would in all likelihood raise his fellow Catholics in Ireland and Scotland and civil war would follow. The Lords rejected the Exclusion Bill and the King called a second election at the end of 1679, in which he instructed his Lords Lieutenant to do all in their power to hinder Whig candidates.[19]

Taking the analogy of chess, Charles had deployed his bishops, castles and knights to check his opponents. Yet it was a deceptive victory, for the Lords, having preserved the right of succession, gave signal proof of its belief in a Catholic conspiracy by finding an aged Catholic peer, William Howard, fifth Viscount Stafford, guilty of treason. Eighty-six peers attended the trial and fifty-five judged him guilty, including several of his kinsmen. John Evelyn, the diarist and secretary of the Royal Society (of which Stafford was a member), was among the spectators and was impressed by the solemn theatre of the proceedings and disgusted by their blatant injustice. Oates's 'testimony', he thought, 'should not have been taken against the life of a dog'. Evelyn also picked up some gossip which indicated that Stafford was disliked by members of his family, and had indulged 'of a vice in Germany, which need not be named'.[20] It was a perverse verdict in so far as the Lords had acquiesced to the prospect of a Catholic monarch, but, nevertheless, were ready to treat all Catholics as a threat to national security.

Among the supporters of the Exclusion Bill had been Robert Spencer, second Earl of Sunderland, hitherto the King's man. Charles called his defection 'the Kiss of Judas', but the Countess of Sunderland declared that her husband had 'gained immortal fame'. The King's disfavour consigned Sunderland to the political wilderness, from where he soon returned. Halifax later remarked that the King 'lived with his ministers as he did his mistresses; he used them, but he was not in love with them'. Charles was easily bored by lengthy 'serious discourse' which led some 'of the graver sort' to lace their accounts of matters of state with 'the coarsest kind of youthful talk'.[21]

Charles preferred young, witty and aristocratic hedonists who made him laugh and supplied him with concubines whose offspring considerably enlarged the aristocracy. The King did well by his bastards, and their mothers. Lady Castlemaine's son, Charles Fitzroy, was made Earl of Southampton and later first Duke of Cleveland, and his brother Henry Fitzroy, first Duke of Grafton; Nell Gwynn's son Charles became first Duke of St Albans and Louise de Kerouaille's Charles, first Duke of Richmond. All these boys were provided with revenues appropriate to their status Richmond and his descendants got a portion of the impost levied on Newcastle coal shipped to London (which proved very lucrative) and good marriages were arranged for Charles's illegitimate daughters.

A sensualist monarch and his pack of dissipated favourites delighted in shocking the world. In 1663 the playwright Sir Charles Sedley appeared on the balcony of a house in Covent Garden 'acting all the postures of lust and buggery that could be imagined' and delivered a 'mountebank sermon' in praise of an aphrodisiac that would 'make all the cunts in London run after him'. He ended this piece of street theatre by ordering a glass of wine, 'washed his prick in it', drank it and then called for another with which he drank the King's health. Samuel Pepys heard this tale and a report that 'buggery is now almost grown so common among our gallants as in Italy and that the very pages begin to complain of it'. Some years later he noted that Charles had been greatly amused when Sedley and Charles Sackville, the sixth Earl of Dorset, ran through the streets of London 'with their arses bare' and assaulted the city watch. Dorset was present with the King in Thetford when he asked the local 'fiddlers' to play all the 'bawdy songs' in their repertoire.[22]

More sedate aristocrats like Halifax and Sunderland guided the King in the humdrum affairs of state. Sunderland was universally regarded as a political pendulum whose controlling mechanism was ambition and a sometimes desperate need to stay solvent. His royalist credentials were excellent (his father had been fatally wounded at Newbury), he had friends at court who obtained him the post of Gentleman of the Bedchamber and he scraped together £6,000 to buy the office of Secretary of State for the Northern Department in 1679. His principal duties were foreign affairs, as were those of his equally influential partner, the Secretary of State for the Southern Department, which also handled colonial matters.

The secretaryship was Sunderland's entrée into the King's council and the springboard for a career in which, in the space of fifteen years, he successively served and abandoned Charles II and James II and somehow managed to ingratiate himself into the favour of William III. Extravagant, addicted to gambling, dismissive of those with whom he disagreed, Sunderland's aloofness was accentuated by his languid drawl ('whaat maaters who saarves his Majesty') known as the 'court tone'. By contrast, another of Charles's ministers, John Hamilton, Duke of Lauderdale, had a tongue too large for his mouth, 'which made him bedew all that he talked to'.[23] Sunderland was an effective, if not always assiduous administrator, who sometimes signed state letters unread while at the card table. He shunned close attachment to any faction and relied upon his knack of providing his masters with what they wanted: the implementation of policy. In the process of making himself useful Sunderland paid off his debts.

Another indispensable creature, Sir George Jeffreys who was ennobled as a reward for services to the Crown, was one of Sunderland's protégés. He was a pushy and ambitious lawyer in his mid-thirties who was appointed Lord Chief Justice in 1683. Jeffreys came from Shropshire gentry stock, had a sharp legal brain and a waspish wit which he frequently exercised to frighten jurymen, witnesses and defendants. Like Sunderland, he was a chameleon whose views were tempered to the times and, consequently, he quickly moved onwards and upwards. In so far as he had any creed, it was that judiciary was the highly partial enforcing arm of a benevolent royal autocracy. Presiding over the trial of the Whig Lord William Russell for treason in 1683, Jeffreys pointedly reminded the court of the connections between the Whigs and those responsible for the martyrdom of Charles I, adding an oblique warning that they might again provoke a civil war.[24] Sir Francis Bacon had once likened judges to 'lions under the throne', and in Jeffreys, Charles II and James II had one who was prepared to snarl and bite at his master's bidding. He did and in 1685 became Lord Jeffreys of Wem.

Sunderland and Jeffreys were making their way upwards in a political world that was being rapidly transformed to the advantage of the aristocracy, old and new. Old government departments were expanded and new were created to regulate Britain's growing overseas trade and colonies. The Navy Office (where Samuel Pepys worked), the Board of Trade, the Post Office and the Plantation Office were agencies of a centralised state in which more and more power was being concentrated in London. Enlarged bureaucracies extended the patronage of the Crown and its predominantly aristocratic ministers. They controlled appointments at every level, decided the awards of government contracts and approved army commissions.

New sources of patronage had an immense impact on political life by creating a network of reciprocity which extended across the country. An influential peer in London could procure an army commission for a younger son of a country squire in return for the father's vote in the county election, or secure an excise post for a proven supporter in a coastal borough. The pattern extended to the legislature, with ministers offering favours to peers and MPs in return for their votes. Such deals were not new: what had changed was the amount of patronage available and its concentration in the hands of aristocratic ministers.

Looking back on Charles II's reign and justifying his part in its politics, Halifax characterised it as a period of 'general discontent' which was to outright rebellion what a 'spotted fever' was to 'plague'. He had slipped in and out of royal confidence and the twists and turns of his ministerial career earned him the nickname of 'Trimmer', although it could easily have been applied to Sunderland and others. Halifax was guided by the principle of *salus populi*, the safety of the people, which overrode party politics, which he deplored as 'engines of dissension'. Public affairs contaminated a patrician of sensitivity and intellect: 'The government of the world is a great thing, but it is a very coarse one, too, compared with the fineness of speculative knowledge.'

Halifax disdained faction for its own sake and saw himself as a patriot. He loved liberty, believed that the King was not above the law and that Parliament was vital for good government. Halifax's ideals were firmly within the aristocratic ministerial tradition of pragmatism, dispassion and a devotion to the national welfare.[25] For this, he was admired and listened to during the upheavals of James II's reign.

———— ◆ ————

The People Assembled
and Freely Chose
Them: The Glorious
Revolution and After

During the winter of 1688–9 the English and Scottish aristocracy reasserted its right to make and unmake kings. A large majority deserted James II, welcomed his son-in-law William of Orange, and participated in the Parliamentary proceedings which made William and his wife Mary joint monarchs. Peers and people were broadly of one mind. When the Duke of Norfolk entered King's Lynn at the head of the Norfolk militia, 'the tradesmen, seamen and inferior sort, put orange ribbons in their hats, shouting and echoing huzzas for the Prince of Orange and the Duke of Norfolk'.[1] In Edinburgh, Colin Lindsay, third Earl of Balcarres, was horrified by the encouragement given to anti-Catholic mobs by his fellow peers.[2] The Edinburgh riots were part of a vast carnival of disorder across the country in which bonfires were lit, windows were broken, Catholic chapels were looted and sometimes burned, and supporters of James maltreated. Lord Jeffreys, now Lord Chancellor, was nearly lynched by the London mob.

This wave of hooliganism and vandalism was an expression of anger against a dying regime that had upset the constitutional equilibrium and ridden roughshod over ancient liberties. There was also relief that the country was about to be rescued from a King whose ultimate goal appeared to be an absolutist, Catholic state of the sort ruled by his ally and secret paymaster, Louis XIV.

James II had inherited a favourable situation. The aristocracy and the rest of the country were reconciled to a Catholic monarch in his mid-fifties whose heir was his Protestant daughter, Mary. It was assumed by many experienced politicians such as Halifax that James would have the sense to play by the rules, accept the political and religious status quo and never allow his Catholicism to impinge on decisions of policy. Inactivity and dispassion ran against the grain of James's character and he refused to let convention stand in his way. He was a deeply pious Catholic, wilful, stolid and oblivious to the feelings (and prejudices) of his subjects. His overriding aim was to integrate his fellow Catholics into national life by repealing the laws which had excluded them from public offices. Royal toleration extended to dissenters, but they suspected a decoy and their response was lukewarm and wary. As Halifax warned them in his *Letter to a Dissenter* of 1687, 'You are therefore to be hugged now only that you may be squeezed later.'

Both the English and Scottish Parliaments blocked James's plans. Eighty-five English peers voted against the repeal of the penal statutes against Catholics, fifty-seven (including twenty Catholics) voted in favour and nineteen wavered. It was a warning shot to which the King responded by imposing toleration by decree through Declarations of Indulgence in 1687 and 1688 which granted complete religious freedom. Whether his will alone could nullify statutes in this manner was a moot point, but what mattered was that James had signalled that he would govern without the aristocracy. Many of his subjects rightly detected a lurch towards absolutism.

The King's rejection of the will of Parliament agitated an aristocracy already disconcerted by the rapid advancement of Catholics in public life. Five Catholic peers sat in James's council, Catholics were being granted commissions in an enlarged army and were being appointed as judges, sheriffs and magistrates. In 1687, the Lord Lieutenants of twenty-one counties were sacked for suspected disloyalty and replaced by yes-men, including Jeffreys and thirteen inexperienced Catholic peers. Catholic gentry supplanted unsympathetic deputy lieutenants.[3] The Anglican nobility was being hustled out of power in central and local government, and tampering with the Lord Lieutenancies had sinister implications, for it placed county militias under Catholic command.

James's policies were hopelessly impractical. There were never enough Catholics (who made up a fifth of the hundred or so peers) available to fill the vacant posts at both national and local levels. Nonetheless, devout Anglican peers faced a crisis of conscience. In May 1688 the second Earl of Clarendon (son of Charles I's Lord Chancellor) explained his moral dilemma to Princess Mary: 'I had the happiness to be born a Protestant . . . I could much more willingly go to the stake in defence of it than live the greatest man in the world.' Now he was faced with a choice between his faith and his allegiance to a monarch who was delivering control of the nation into the hands of Catholics. 'I cannot in conscience give those men leave . . . to come into employments of the state, who, by their mistaken consciences, are bound to destroy the religion I profess.'[4] Clarendon gave vent to his feelings by refusing to sit in a council which now included the royal confessor Edward Petre, a Jesuit.

Anglican peers were also disconcerted by James's efforts to subordinate the Church of England. This culminated in an unsuccessful attempt to prosecute seven bishops for seditious libel in the summer of 1688. Twenty-one peers (including Clarendon) volunteered to stand bail for the clerics and the trial became a public test of the King's popularity. When his Secretary of State Sunderland entered Westminster Hall at the beginning of the trial, he was kicked in the backside and threatened with a clenched fist.[5] On his departure, someone shouted 'Kill the new Popish dog.' True to form, the protean Sunderland had converted to Rome the day before (and would revert to Anglicanism after James's downfall). The bishops were acquitted and even James's soldiers joined in the street celebrations in London and across the country.

Cheers for the bishops drowned those for the birth of the King's son James in June. Assuming that the infant Prince of Wales grew to manhood, England and Scotland were henceforward to be ruled by a Catholic dynasty. The King was already acquiring the muscle to secure a Catholic monarchy by enlisting his co-religionists in Ireland. He had begun to dismantle the Protestant ascendancy and was raising a Catholic army under Catholic officers. Its future employment was predicted in the ballad 'Lilliburlero', written in a mock brogue by the Whig peer Thomas, Lord Wharton. In one verse, the Irish hailed their new Deputy Lieutenant, the Catholic Richard Talbot, Earl of Tyrconnel:

> *Ho, by my shoul, it is a Talbot*
> *And he will cut de Englishman's troat . . .*
> *Now, now de heretics all go down,*
> *By Chreist and St Patrick, the nation's our own!*

Published in October 1688 and set to a jaunty traditional air, 'Lilliburlero' caught the public mood and became the Glorious Revolution's equivalent of the 'Marseillaise'.

*

The birth of James's son was the catalyst for a revolution. Its instigators were the Tory Earl of Danby, the Whig Earl of Devonshire, the Bishop of London, the Earl of Shrewsbury, Lord Lumley, Edward Russell and Henry Sydney. Peers and cleric spoke for the people and the last three for the army and navy. Together these men claimed to be the authentic voice of a nation seeking rescue from tyranny and turmoil, and, it was they who invited William of Orange to invade England at the head of a Dutch army and promised him massive support. 'Much the greatest part of the nobility and gentry' would rally to the Prince when he landed. William agreed to the enterprise and secret approaches were made to disaffected Scottish peers.

At least in its early stages, William's amphibious assault was a gamble. On paper, James's English army outnumbered the invasion force and, once alerted to the threat, the King summoned reinforcements from Ireland and the Scottish Highlands. He was whistling in the dark, for, as events soon revealed, his regime was a fragile structure supported by a tiny minority of his English and Scottish subjects. It buckled and disintegrated within six weeks of William's landing at Torbay on the anniversary of an earlier deliverance from Catholicism, November. Protestants again detected the hand of a benign Providence.

James's generals, including Lord John Churchill, the future Duke of Marlborough, deserted to William and their regiments followed. The aristocracy frustrated attempts to muster the militia by James's Lords Lieutenants. Mounted militiamen from Yorkshire, some in armour, laughed down the Lord Lieutenant the Duke of Newcastle, which may not have unduly troubled him, for he had already been won over for William by Danby.[6] In Scotland, Lord Balcarres had been asked by James to command the Catholic and Episcopalian Highland nobility to mobilise its clansmen and march them to the Borders to intimidate northern England.[7] Fearful that this provocative measure would lead to war, James's Scottish councillors later insisted that they would deploy the Highlanders in the Lowlands only in a dire emergency. Nonetheless, some were stationed at Stirling, alongside clansmen raised by the pro-William Marquess of Atholl and John Campbell, the first Earl of Breadalbane.[8]

Claymores were not drawn. The loyal and neutral Scottish nobility were paralysed by the swiftness of William's success in the south and increasingly anxious about their personal safety and political futures. James offered them no leadership, and, stunned by the spate of defections and the success of his enemies, he lapsed into melancholic resignation. In England and Scotland, the military and political initiative passed to William and the lords who were advising him.

Everywhere, the nobility and gentry took the law into their own hands, formed posses and raided the houses of Catholics in search of arms. In Cheshire, Lord Delamare raised his tenants, local squires and the 'richer tradesmen' and, with a force of two hundred and fifty, rampaged through the county like a 'mad man', seizing arms and horses from Catholics and wrecking their chapels. One Catholic gentleman considered a counter-attack on Delamare's house, but was checked by several thousand local people who rushed to defend it. James ordered the local Lord Lieutenant, the ninth Earl of Derby, to intervene, but after reading the letter, he smiled and remarked that the King ought to have sent his orders earlier. Derby's crafty neutrality made sense in terms of his own safety: William's supporters were gaining the upper hand everywhere and there were rumours that the Earl's house at Knowsley might be attacked by Protestant mobs.[9] A few months later Derby voted in the Lords to accept James's abdication.

While the North-West teetered on the edge of civil war, hair-raising reports circulated of James's Irish troops running amok, and there were rumours that thousands more were on their way from Ireland, thirsting for Protestant blood. Yet the fighting was confined to a handful of skirmishes between William's forces and

Irish detachments. The Irishmen quickly recognised the futility of the royal cause and began to drift away and make for their homes. The King followed their example and set off for France, but was arrested and manhandled by Faversham sailors and brought back from London. His second escape attempt succeeded and James fled to France, but did this represent an abdication?

This question and its corollary – who should replace the King – were resolved by the Convention Parliament that assembled early in 1689. It had been summoned at the very end of 1688 by William after consultation with an assembly of peers which requested him to take charge of the government. The Commons comprised 174 Whigs, 156 Tories and 183 new members whose sympathies were still unclear. Tories narrowly predominated in the Lords, which chose the bipartisan Halifax as its speaker. The Whigs in the Commons made the running: they proposed that James, like Richard II (whose deposition was cited as one justification for the present proceedings), had subverted the nation's fundamental laws and liberties, and by cutting and running had dethroned himself. The crown should, therefore, be presented to his daughter Mary and her husband William.

The peers and bishops found themselves in a quandary. They had been instrumental in James's expulsion, but now had to confront its moral and political consequences. Whigs grasped the chance to affirm the principle that monarchs were subject to Parliament, which, acting for the country, could depose one and choose another without reference to the 'natural' bloodline. The bishops and Tory Anglican peers like Clarendon equivocated. By supporting the coup they had denied the doctrine of submission, and now they were being asked to cancel their oaths of allegiance. Worse still, in terms of impiety, they would allow Parliament to obliterate the rights of the infant Prince of Wales and dictate the succession.

Voting figures indicated a divided and discomposed House of Lords. By a margin of eleven, the peers complied with the Commons' charge that James had been guilty of misrule. Then followed several days of quibbling over terminology: over fifty peers refused to acknowledge that the King had abdicated and that the throne was now 'vacant'. The impasse was broken by William's threat to return to Holland if he was not offered the crown. The issue was now one of security: another civil war appeared imminent as James and his followers in Ireland and Scotland were planning a counter-revolution. To resist it, Britain needed a legitimate government with the authority to mobilise the resources of the state. Pragmatism triumphed over dogma and a number of Tories switched sides and, by the majority of twenty, the Lords agreed to offer the crown to William and Mary. The Scottish Parliament came to the same conclusion in a session held against the noisy background of further anti-Catholic riots in Edinburgh. The Protestant aristocracy had played kingmaker, but with varying degrees of enthusiasm and, in the final phase of the coup, with considerable nudging from a Whig House of Commons.

After they approved the succession of William and Mary, the English and Scottish Parliaments resolved the fundamental issues which had divided both kingdoms for the past sixty years. The upshot was the English Bill of Rights and the Scottish Claim of Right, which defined the legal rights of subjects and imposed restraints on the Crown which were designed to prevent a recurrence of the arbitrary and overbearing use of the royal prerogative.

The decisions taken in 1689 laid the foundations for that political stability and national unity essential for the economic miracles which transformed Britain into a global commercial and industrial power during the eighteenth century. The Whigs sensed this and were quick to claim the Glorious Revolution for themselves. Their views had prevailed (Whig peers and MPs dominated the committee which framed the Bill of Rights) and henceforward the Whigs projected themselves as both the saviours of the nation and the underwriters of its liberties.

Congratulating his fellow peers on their part in the recent revolution, the Marquess of Atholl declared that they had been successful in 'reducing our government to a just temper and balance'.[10] Over one hundred and twenty years later, the Whig Lord John Russell praised the revolutionary settlement as 'the triumph of enlightenment of the few over the bigotry of millions', which, despite the inaccuracy of his mathematics, represented the subsequent Whig version of the event.[11]

Supporters of the revolution emphasised continuity with past. In 1690 the Lord Lieutenant of Leicestershire, the Earl of Stamford, praised the recent settlement in a speech to the local gentry who had gathered for the quarter sessions. Since the distant days of the ancient Britons, England had been a 'limited monarchy' and all who loved liberty and the rights of property should be grateful to William and Mary for preserving and defending both.[12] A radical Whig, Stamford quoted John Locke's recently published *Two Treatises on Government* to argue that 'we are all equal in the state of Nature' and inheritors of natural rights. Squires and jurymen regularly heard variations on this theme delivered by Whig Lords Lieutenants and judges. In 1709 the Norfolk magistrates were reminded that while Saul and David had been made kings by God's will, 'the people assembled and freely chose them'.[13]

Having been the prime movers of the Glorious Revolution, the aristocracy and gentry proclaimed themselves its servants and guardians. The Whig John Hervey, later the first Earl of Bristol, assured the electors of Bury St Edmunds in 1694 that he would forever uphold the balance between 'the just and necessary prerogatives of the crown and the inestimable happy privileges of the people'. Seeking re-election in 1698, Hervey promised that he had and would continue to do all in his power to preserve 'the monarchy and hierarchy in their just legal rights' so that 'the people may be protected in their liberty and property'.[14] The last two were now secure in the hands of men of superior rank and property whose estates gave them a stake in the nation and a permanent interest in its future tranquillity and prosperity.

After over fifty years of turbulence, a new equipose had been established. An aristocracy which had been fragmented by political faction, endured a civil war and, under the republic, a brief expulsion from public life was now secure. It had regained all its former political powers, although the course of events during the winter of 1688–9 indicated that the driving force of the legislature was now the Commons. Given that the Commons contained a growing number of noblemen's sons, there was no significant shift in the balance of political power between the two houses. What did alter was the balance of power between Parliament and the Crown, which now played a subordinate but not impotent role in government. What was most significant of all for the future of the nobility was that it had emerged from an unquiet century as the collective protector of the nation's liberties. On the whole, the country accepted this claim and, with it, the political ascendancy of the aristocracy. For the next century, the nobility enjoyed a near monopoly of all the major offices of state.

13

I'll Share the Fate of
My Prince: Jacobites

Jacobites wanted to reverse the settlement of 1689, placing religion above political expediency, and, over the next fifty-six
years, endeavoured to restore to the throne James II and then his
Catholic son and grandson (the Old and Young Pretenders)
because it was theirs on account of divine, hereditary right.
There were Jacobite insurrections in Scotland and Ireland in
1689, and in Scotland in 1715, 1719 and 1745. All were
crushed, although historians have been mesmerised by what
might have happened if they had achieved success. Such speculation is entertaining, but it overlooks the cold fact that the
Jacobites always lacked recruits, and this deficit in manpower was
never adequately made up by their Spanish or French allies.
Nevertheless, and out of all proportion to their numbers, the
Jacobites possessed a capacity to unnerve the politico-economic
establishment of Hanoverian Britain.

The Jacobite leadership was confined to a tiny section of the

Scottish aristocracy who, like its rank and file, were either Catholics, Episcopalians or High Church Anglicans who believed that the 1689 revolution had been inherently sinful. The English and Scottish Parliaments had usurped God's prerogative to make kings and, after the Union of 1707, the British Parliament repeated this profanity by nominating a Lutheran prince, George, Elector of Hanover, as Queen's Anne's successor. His accession in 1714 was a signal for an outbreak of nominally Jacobite unrest. Analysis suggests that, then and later, those who took to the streets were Jacobites by adoption rather than conviction, and that their gripes were primarily about such domestic matters as high taxation.

In 1715 the Jacobites played their military hand, conjuring up phantom armies in Wales and the South-West and mustering a real one of fourteen thousand in Scotland and another of about a thousand from the Catholic gentry of Northumberland and Lancashire and their servants. A jittery Whig government feared that the restlessness in the remote and economically depressed periphery of the country might prove contagious. The Marquess of Tweeddale, Lord Lieutenant of East Lothian, was warned to keep an eye open for crypto-Jacobites among his militia officers. Only men with the 'greatest and most known zeal' for 'the Protestant succession' were to be trusted with commissions.[1]

The loyalty of the Lothian volunteers was not tested, which was just as well, for Tweeddale judged them a feeble lot. Two inconclusive battles at Preston and Sheriffmuir near Stirling severely shook Jacobite morale and their forces disintegrated. Blame was laid at the door of the Jacobite commander in Scotland, John Erskine, sixth Earl of Mar, but a more plausible explanation was that his army was in a perpetual state of deliquescence with clansmen who had been press-ganged by their chiefs sneaking off to tend and harvest their crops.

Highlanders again deserted during the 1745–6 uprising. It

was led by James II's grandson, Prince Charles Edward, the Young Pretender and 'Bonnie Prince Charlie' of romantic legend. His cause may have thrilled skittish minds in later gen-erations, but when he landed in Scotland, Highland lairds and chieftains had to use their customary clan and feudal authority to fill his army. A tenant of the seventy-five-year-old dowager Lady Nairne was warned that if he refused to take up arms, his live-stock would be impounded. He later deserted, as did many others who been enlisted under physical and moral duress. Alan Cameron, an officer in Donald Cameron of Lochiel's regiment, explained to an English jury that he had joined the uprising because 'the right of [the superior] is always absolute'. So too were the ancient obligations of blood feud, which was why Camerons used the rebellion as an opportunity to sack and burn Campbell farms.[2] The events of 1745 revealed that, despite two hundred years of official sanctions, the residual bonds of clan kinship and feudal obligation remained strong in the Highlands. Without them, the Jacobite aristocracy and its allies would have been powerless.

Jacobite peers were outcasts. Defeats drove diehards into exile in France and a life of tedium, mulling over what might have been and dreaming of what might be. The third Earl of Balcarres, who had joined the Earl of Dundee's failed rebellion in 1690, found émigré existence unbearable. After ten years of it, he returned home, lured by an annual pension of £500, and, in return, publicly declared that the revolution had been in 'the interest of the country'.[3] William Mackenzie, Lord Seaforth, was a hardier spirit. He raised three thousand clansmen in 1715, went into exile, returned to Scotland in 1719 for a brief uprising (backed by Spanish infantry) and again fled to France to continue his hand-to-mouth existence. His lands had been forfeit and his attempts to get cash secretly from his loyal tenants resulted in a corrective and predatory tour of his estates by General Wade's redcoats in 1725. Rather than remain in penniless exile, Seaforth renounced Jacobitism in exchange for permission to reoccupy his lands.

Inducing Jacobite peers like Seaforth to rejoin political society was the best way of neutering the movement. This policy succeeded, for Seaforth's heir Kenneth Mackenzie stayed loyal in 1745 and was rewarded with an earldom the following year. In 1771 he raised the 78th Regiment from his clansmen for service in the colonies. He was following the example of previous generations of Scottish peers who, after the Union, had increasingly gravitated towards London for pleasure, politicking and, most tempting of all, patronage. In 1733 the Jacobite-inclining Tory James Erskine grumbled that 'our peerage . . . [have] fallen into universal contempt for their low and slavish compliances to whatever was in power'. The independent spirit of the Scottish peerage had withered and its typical, modern representative was 'a giddy, prating fellow . . . [a] self seeker and faction monger'.[4] But he was making his way in the world and getting richer, while Jacobites had only fantasies for nourishment.

Loyalty to the Crown gave Scottish peers what they craved: preferment and rewards. This was why the majority distanced themselves from Jacobitism and, in 1745, backed the government. On the eve of Prince Charles Edward's return, the seventeenth Earl of Sutherland promised to have his servants 'look out sharply' for signs of a Franco-Jacobite landing on the Caithness coast. He also ran a voluntary intelligence network, which included two 'gentlemen' who used the pretext of visiting their kinsfolk to probe the sympathies of chieftain Donald Cameron of Lochiel, a suspected Jacobite. Sutherland's agents augmented those employed by the Marquess of Tweeddale, now Secretary of State for Scotland. They included a spy who had once been employed by the Duke of Argyll and had a 'great affection for our present happy establishment'. This supporter of the Glorious Revolution and the Hanoverian succession was a mole in the household of the Jacobite Drummonds in Perth.[5]

Sutherland's agents may have found Cameron of Lochiel a lukewarm Jacobite, but he was also the heir in spirit to the culture and customs of his forebears. When Prince Charles Edward landed, Cameron spoke with the authentic voice of a clan chieftain: 'I'll share the fate of my prince; and so shall every man over whom nature or fortune have given me any power.' Ancient concepts of honour overrode political and strategic common sense and propelled Cameron into the Jacobite army. He joined exiled noblemen like James Drummond, self-styled Duke of Perth, Lord George Murray, William Murray, Earl of Tullibardine, and James Drummond, Viscount Strathallan. Like the Prince, they were snatching at a chance to recover titles, prestige and power.

What followed has often be written up as a romantic adventure. Rather, it was a desperate gamble undertaken by a band of filibusters with delusions of hidden popular support. Prince Charles Edward's army of four and a half thousand Highlanders and about two hundred Lancashire volunteers reached Derby and gave the government a nasty turn, but it had had a dusty reception during its advance southwards, was suffering chronic logistical problems, and was outnumbered by approaching royal forces. Two fluke victories at Prestonpans in September and Falkirk in January did not influence the outcome of a campaign which ended decisively at Culloden in April 1746. Artillery and the disciplined firepower of a modern army destroyed a feudal host of axe- and swordsmen who charged in the obsolete, heroic manner of the clan warrior.

His leaders suffered forfeiture and four peers were beheaded, the last aristocrats to suffer this punishment for treason. A government which now had fourteen thousand soldiers (including many Lowlanders) and a squadron of warships at its disposal systematically hammered the Highlands, using, paradoxically, that combination of fire and sword which had characterised ancient clan warfare. New laws finally completed the long-drawn-out process of cultural and political deracination which had been started by James VI. The clans were forcibly disarmed, Highland dress was outlawed and landowners were stripped for ever of their remaining military powers and private jurisdictions. Yet, ironically, the clan spirit of obligation survived and was profitably exploited by chieftains who proved their loyalty by raising regiments for the Crown.

These soldiers were clothed in a version of the traditional costume of clansmen and their feats on the battlefield were blended into a highly romantic, alternative version of the history of the Highlands and the Jacobite movement in general. Jacobitism may have won over few minds, but, thanks to Sir Walter Scott's Waverley novels, it seduced many hearts. Among them were those of the Scottish noblemen and their wives who congregated in exotic, and often invented, varieties of Highland dress to greet George IV when he visited Edinburgh in 1822. Scott acted as master of ceremonies and devised a spectacle which simultaneously celebrated the patriotism of Scotland's aristocracy and its picturesque and stirring past. He urged noblemen to parade in pseudo-feudal splendour with trains of armed clansmen in tartans often contrived for the occasion. The King entered into the mood of the pageant by wearing Highland dress with pink tights under his kilt and drinking tumblers of Glenlivet whisky, which he found much to his taste.

The old bogey of Jacobitism was a distant memory and lords and ladies whose ancestors had spurned the Stuart pretenders now masqueraded as the followers of Bonnie Prince Charlie. He had died in 1788, an alcoholic and wife-beater, unaware of his imminent metamorphosis. Thanks to Scott's imagination, he and his followers had become central to a new self-image of the Scottish aristocracy, who were soon building mock Gothic castles, commissioning clan histories and wearing tartan fancy dress. Queen Victoria and Prince Albert would be manic converts to the cult of the Highlands and Balmoral became one of its most impressive shrines.

Irish Jacobitism was never posthumously glamourised. It left sour memories which embittered the country's history for the next two hundred years. In the spring of 1689 James had crossed from France to Dublin, where he called a parliament with which he hoped to undo the political and economic settlement established by Cromwell and Charles II. Down would come the Protestant ascendancy and up would go a Catholic one. Irish Protestants resisted, most famously holding out in Londonderry, and were rescued by an army led by William III. It decisively defeated James's forces at the Boyne in July 1690, a victory which is still annually celebrated by Orange lodges in Ulster and parts of Scotland.

The Protestant ascendancy was then upheld and reinforced by an exclusively Protestant parliament, militia, judiciary and administration, prayed for by clergy of the Anglican Church of Ireland and defended by a garrison of twelve thousand royal troops distributed in over one hundred and fifty barracks. Catholic clergymen were virtually outlawed, and Catholic landowners were elbowed off their lands by laws framed to expedite their extinction. When one died, his estates had to be divided among all his sons, unless the eldest converted to Protestantism, which qualified him to enjoy the right of primogeniture that applied to landowners in England and Scotland. In 1703 Catholics had owned 14 per cent of the land, by the 1770s 5 per cent. One particularly spiteful statute left the Irish squireen worse mounted than his Protestant neighbour, for Catholics were banned from owning a horse worth more than five pounds. No wonder Catholics called the Glorious Revolution the 'Woeful Revolution'.

Cultural, linguistic and religious barriers continued to divide the Anglo-Irish aristocracy from its tenantry. Irish peers were never tempted to dress up as Celtic chieftains, or entertain perceptions of themselves as inheritors of a Gaelic culture, genuine or fabricated. Distance provided a further gulf as an Anglocentric nobility copied its Scottish counterpart and headed for London. It was here that all the crucial decisions for Ireland's future were made, for in 1720 the Irish Parliament was demoted by a Declaratory Act which placed ultimate authority over the island in Westminster.

—— •——

14

Magnificence: Grand Houses and Grand Tours

Great houses built between the sixteenth and the nineteenth centuries are the familiar, enduring face of aristocratic power. Some, like Hardwick Hall, built in the 1570s by the formidable Elizabeth, Countess of Shrewsbury, are landmarks deliberately sited to dominate the countryside as castles once had. Later architects strove for the same effect. Their plans and contemporary paintings show the great house at its most impressive, square-on. Vast landscapes were contrived with driveways and avenues of tree which drew the onlooker's gaze towards the often distant but imposing building. A Tudor physician advised builders of a new house to consider first the 'prospect' and choose a site that was 'pleasant, fair and good to the eye'.[1] A perfect house was, he claimed, a jewel whose colour and brilliance were enhanced by its settings.

By 1700 these settings were becoming increasingly elaborate

and extravagant: there were disciplined lines of trees planted in geometric patterns, woodlands arranged so as to provide charming views, and artificial lakes. In the next century and in response to fashionable fancies, statues and mock temples were added, so that a nobleman might imagine himself as a Roman senator enjoying a carefree retreat from public duties in his Tuscan villa. Later, Romantic-Gothic themes were introduced with grottos (some with live hermits) and bogus ruins.

Always the aristocracy were straining after the sublime. It was achieved through the satisfaction of the senses and the engagement of the intellect. Beyond the house, the eye and the mind were pleased by prospects of nature brought under human control to provide agreeable walks and idyllic vistas. Inside were paintings, sculpture, ornaments and collections of rarities and curios which aroused the imagination and stimulated conversation. The ensemble of house, contents and grounds were the highest expression of a civilisation which promised to surpass its Greek and Roman prototypes.

The great house and its surroundings were statements of political and economic power. They represented stability, the security of property, dynastic continuity and dominance of the landed interest. All were underpinned by the Glorious Revolution of 1688–9, which had ended fifty years of political discord and uncertainty to discourage building on a grand scale. Aristocratic confidence returned and expressed itself in a grandiose manner; Chatsworth, Castle Howard and Blenheim celebrated tranquillity restored and the Whig ascendancy. Baroque exuberance suited this triumphalist mood, but within fifty years it had been discarded by the Whig aristocracy because it smacked of Continental and Stuart absolutism. August, Palladian restraint now reflected the temper of the times and cognoscenti sneered at the tastes of their fathers and grandfathers. Horace Walpole, fourth Earl of Orford, dismissed the work of Sir John Vanbrugh, the architect of Castle Howard and Blenheim, as 'execrable within, without and almost all round'.[2]

The evolution of architectural fashion styles is not relevant to this narrative beyond the fact that the speed with which they gained popularity was a measure of the aristocracy's infatuation with whatever was new. In any case, general terms such as 'Baroque' and 'Palladian' are simplifications which ignore the overlap and fusion of styles. What is beyond question is that in the early 1600s there was an architectural revolution which had far-reaching consequences for the aristocracy: the adoption of the Italianate style. Its sources were Greek and Roman and it was promoted by Inigo Jones and patronised by James I and Charles I and the nobility of their courts. For the next two hundred years the aristocracy took its architectural taste from antiquity as interpreted by Italian artists and designers.

Understanding the Italian schools of architecture and the Classical examples which inspired them required the first-hand experience of the Grand Tour. Inigo Jones had travelled to Italy in the entourage of William Herbert, third Earl of Pembroke, and sketched what he had seen there, giving his designs the authenticity his patrons wanted. Noblemen and architects unacquainted with the originals resorted to the text and engravings of Sebastiano Serli's *Architettura*, published in 1584 and translated in 1611. Other architectural handbooks followed and their engravings and texts were pored over by patrons and architects who wished to keep abreast of the Italian innovations which were the touchstone of all that was fashionable.

Aristocrats also looked to each others' houses for inspiration. In the 1570s William Cecil, Lord Burghley, was overwhelmed by the 'largeness and lightness' of Holdenby House, then being built by his fellow councillor Sir Christopher Hatton. Hatton, too, was impressed by Burghley's Hertfordshire seat, Theobolds. Its scale and design also caught the imagination of Henry Percy, ninth Earl of Northumberland, as he began to construct his new house at Syon in Middlesex. 'I must borrow of my knowledge of Theobalds,' he told Burghley's son in 1603. Northumberland also consulted illustrated books on European architecture and called in the maestro, Inigo Jones.[3]

Illustrated guides were poor substitutes for experience, which was why every young nobleman with cultural pretensions and a desire to be ahead of fashion (the two were virtually inseparable) had to make his way southwards and undertake the Grand Tour of the Continent. It was a journey of discovery in which the traveller inspected classical architecture in its original and recent forms and examined paintings and statuary in the galleries of foreign princes and noblemen. At the same time, the tourist learnt foreign languages and acquired that social finesse and swordmanship for which the French aristocracy was famous. He returned home acquainted with both Raphael and the rapier, and an urge to surround himself with Classical grandeur. During his expedition, what he saw was explained and interpreted by his tutor. The philosopher Thomas Hobbes accompanied his pupil, the future second Earl of Devonshire, during extended peregrinations between 1634 and 1637 and purchased books for his master's library.

It would be impossible to overstate the importance of the aristocratic Grand Tour to the cultural history of Britain. It was a conduit which irrigated all the arts and kept the country in constant and fruitful contact with the artistic and intellectual movements of Europe. Look around any country house and there are mementos of the Grand Tours undertaken by previous owners. There are books, Old Masters (genuine and 'attributed'), the busts of Greek and Roman worthies, cabinets of coins, medallions and cameos and walls hung with almost massproduced canvasses of scenes from classical mythology, or Italian landscapes with picturesque ruins. Like all forms of tourism, the

Grand Tour generated a market in souvenirs, many of them hack work, or fakes.

There are plenty of narratives of individual Grand Tours and an excellent analysis of the phenomenon in John Stoye's *English Travellers Abroad* which deals with the seventeenth century. After the signing of a peace with Spain in 1604, a steady flow of aristocrats and their trains of companions and servants proceeded through France towards Italy, which was always the magnet; letters of introduction and safe conducts were always carried. Tutors sent intermittent reports to fathers with details of their sons' activities and welfare and accounts of incidents they considered pertinent or diverting. Letters written by John Schau to the seventh Earl of Mar between 1617 and 1619 revealed that one of the party had died from the 'pox' (syphilis) at Bourges and that his sons Henry and Alexander Erskine were making progress. The Earl was reassured that 'There is very little time spent idly,' and that Alexander 'dances very properly' and 'plays prettily well upon the lute'. Tennis lessons were arranged, but proficiency in French was hindered by the pupils' unwillingness to speak the language.

Italy was full of potential snags for the stiff Presbyterian Schau and his charges. There was 'no more danger of any Inquisition', but fears remained that the boys could be seduced by cunning Jesuits. On returning to Paris early in 1619, Schau was relieved to tell the Earl that the 'abominations' of Rome had 'confirmed your Lordship's sons in [the] only truth of the reformed church. A detour followed through the Low Countries in which Schau promised 'I will not be prodigal in nothing except buying books.'[4]

Schau hints at those persistent anxieties that the Grand Tour, or any excursion on the Continent, had the potential for corruption and apostasy. Foreign perils were listed by Thomas Nashe in 1594 and repeated in various forms during the next two hundred years. Italy exposed a young gentleman to 'the art of atheism, the art of epicuring, the art of whoring, the art of poisoning, [and] the art of sodomy'. In Paris he would learn only 'to distinguish the true Bordeaux grape, and know a cup of neat Gascon wine from the wine of Orléans: yea, and peradventure this also, to esteem the pox as a pimple, to wear a velvet patch on their face, and walk melancholy with their arms folded'.[5]

Henry and Alexander Erskine returned home untainted and unpimpled and were presented to James I, who remarked that their father 'should be pleased with them'.[6] This was a gratifying return on Lord Mar's investment: his sons were now fit to move easily among the sophisticated and fashionable lords and ladies of the court and, if they had persevered with their French and Italian, were qualified to serve the Crown on diplomatic missions. The Grand Tour was a passport to a court where finesse, wit and cleverness counted as never before. Insularity was ignorance: the stay-at-home peer was ridiculed as a bumpkin whose horizons were his boundary markers and whose company was confined to rustic ignoramuses.[7]

The Grand Tour was wholly beneficial for aristocrats. It served, in Sir Francis Bacon's words, to 'entertain minds with variety and delight' and satisfied a natural and desirable curiosity.[8] The diary of Charles Bertie, son of the second Earl of Lindsey, who travelled through France in 1660 is a catalogue of places and things observed, written for the most part without comment. He saw the royal apartments at St-Germain-en-Laye, inspected dog kennels and art galleries and recorded the height of steeples. He was particularly struck by the 'rarest' Italian paintings and 'two women naked excellently painted' in the Palais du Luxembourg.[9]

Bertie was undertaking a reconnaissance. Noblemen on the Grand Tour rarely purchased what pleased their eye or captivated their imaginations. Rather, they were acquiring a corpus of knowledge that would be employed later when they embarked on collecting paintings and sculpture.[10] Window shopping was the prelude to buying through agents based in Italy of whom one of the busiest and most obliging was Sir Henry Wotton, several times ambassador to Venice between 1604 and 1624.

The aristocracy had first become addicted to collecting paintings in the mid-sixteenth century and at first showed a preference for portraits. According to the herald and portraitist Sir William Segar, they preserved for ever the memory of the 'excellent actions' of those who had 'lived honourably and died virtuously'.[11] Likenesses of 'honourable friends' hung in the gallery of Lord Howard of Bindon and it delighted him to stroll through it and contemplate them.[12] Elizabethan statesmen acquired pictures of foreign princes, both allies and enemies. Their portraits hung in Lord Burghley's gallery at Theobalds, and in the Earl of Leicester's at Kenilworth, alongside likenesses of himself in full armour and his friends and family.[13] These records of honour were comparatively inexpensive, for portraits cost between three and nine pounds, which was the cost of a hogshead of claret.[14]

Elizabethan portrait painters knew what their patrons wanted. Honour and status were emphasised by the meticulous rendering of rich textiles, lace, embroidery, jewels and the insignia of office and heraldry. There were also private and allegorical images which were often enigmatic and intelligible only to the sitter or members of his intimate circle.

The nature of aristocratic art patronage and collecting was changed radically by the Grand Tour and the examples set by the Stuart court. James I's Queen Anne of Denmark, her sons Henry, Prince of Wales, and Charles I set the pace and course of picture buying. Britain entered the mainstream of Continental princely culture and the aristocracy was happy to be swept along by its currents. First among the cognoscenti was Thomas Howard, second Earl of Arundel, an austere and dignified figure whom some of his equals believed was the complete embodiment of aristocratic virtue. 'Here comes the Earl of Arundel', one remarked, 'in his plain stuff and trunk hose, and his beard in his teeth, that looks more a noble man than any of us.'[15]

This is confirmed by Daniel Mystens's portrait of the Earl. He sits in his dark, fur-trimmed gown and holding his Earl Marshal's baton at the entrance of his gallery lined with classical statues. He acquired thirty-seven of these, and over a hundred busts as well as Greek and Roman inscriptions, altars and sarcophagi, coins, medals and gems, and eight hundred paintings. Arundel had representatives active in Italy, Asia Minor and the Levant and had excavations undertaken in Rome to uncover sculptures. His collection rivalled Charles I's, with whom he shared a critical aesthetic judgement that was often absent in other aristocratic collectors.[16] Some were jealous; the third Marquess of Hamilton suspected that Arundel's obsession had bred arrogance, rating him a 'proud man who lived always within himself, and to himself'.

Hamilton for his part confessed himself 'much in love with pictures', a romance that had started in 1620 when he was fourteen and first saw his father's collection in his Whitehall lodgings, which included works by Caravaggio and Rubens. Young Hamilton preferred the Venetian school, and during the 1630s he retained Sir Basil Feilding, later the second Earl of Denbigh, the ambassador to Venice, as his agent. They agreed a scale for grading potential purchases and Feilding sent details of the titles, sizes and 'stories' (i.e. subjects) of the paintings he had found.[17] Like all noble collectors, Hamilton had to show deference to Charles I, who assumed the right to choose items from consignments in return for suspending customs duties. (It was a latitude which in modern times extended to Queen Mary and her granddaughter Princess Margaret. Whenever they expressed admiration for an object in a private collection, its owner felt a deferential obligation to offer it as a gift.)

By 1643 Hamilton had bought six hundred paintings, half of them Venetian. Why he and so many contemporary peers were willing to spend so much effort and cash on imported works of art was explained by William Cecil, the second Earl of Exeter. He had made two expeditions to Italy and considered himself' qualified to advise fellow peers on what to buy and where. In 1609 he told the seventh Earl of Shrewsbury that the purchase of a major work by the Venetian Jacopo Negretti Palma il Giovane would 'increase your magnificence'. This artist specialised in 'large pictures' of Classical subjects and one would be ideal for Shrewsbury's 'great chamber'. At the same time, Shrewsbury might consider a bronze made by a 'little old man' called John Bolognia, 'who is not inferior much to Michaelangelo'.[18] This was Giovanni Bologna, who had cast the equestrian statue of Cosimo I in Florence; unfortunately for Shrewsbury he had died the year before.

Magnificence was the mirror of status and wealth. Of course the aristocracy had already been mentally conditioned to absorb the concept of magnificence: it had been present in the courts of the medieval and Tudor monarchs. There is a familiar ring to the analysis of magnificence written in 1614 by Wotton, the diplomat and purveyor of art to the aristocracy. Prudently, he cited James I's favourite George Villiers, first Duke of Buckingham, as the greatest exemplar of magnificence. He had 'a fine and unaffected politeness' and had the capacity 'to sift a question well, and supply his own defects by drawing unto him the best interests of experience and knowledge'. He was, Wotton thought, 'more magnificent' than Elizabeth's favourite Essex, who, revealingly, had never built or adorned a great house of his own.[19]

Buckingham did both. His London seat, York House, possessed a gallery which contained the Duke's recently acquired art collection, which included del Sartos, Titians, Raphaels and Tintorettos. All were status symbols, a quick fix of magnificence for an arriviste aristocrat who wanted instant recognition as a collector. He was no cognoscenti, for, unlike Charles I or

Arundel, Buckingham knew little if anything about the nuances of style and techniques of the painters he collected.[20]

Even if he placed rarity and its concomitant cost above all else, Buckingham was helping to establish an aristocratic tradition of collecting works of art which lasted until the late nineteenth century, when the money for such luxuries began to run out. The international culture of the aristocracy survived too, although its presence in the courts of James I and Charles I had provoked criticism. Xenophobia and religious bigotry combined in allegations that the aristocracy had become effete and unwarlike (this would be disproved in 1642) and that its taste in art was subversively Popish.[21] Malevolent Puritan philistinism combined with the poverty of exiled royalist peers led to the sale and dispersal of several large collections, including Charles I's. (Some of Arundel's sculpture found its way into the Ashmolean Museum and many of Hamilton's paintings passed via the Habsburg collections to the Kunsthistoriches Museum in Vienna.)

The Grand Tour was thus established as an aristocratic rite of passage. The fruits of breeding needed watering and care and it provided both. In 1693 John Locke likened the Grand Tour to the careful polishing which transformed the uncut diamond (virtue) into the perfect jewel, and for that reason it was the only proper conclusion to a humanistic education.[22] Italy remained the ultimate goal, but more and more time was spent in France learning what was considered the purest form of French in the Loire valley towns, and testing fluency in the salons of the noblesse in Paris, where the acolyte was introduced to the arts of polite and witty conversation. Instruction in riding and swordsmanship balanced intellectual fine tuning with muscular accomplishments.

The love affair between the aristocracy and the classical and

Renaissance imagination continued to be consummated in Italy. Old aesthetic preferences remained strong, with eighteenth-century noblemen favouring 'history' (i.e. narrative) paintings that depicted historical and mythological scenes which illustrated moral and philosophic themes. Hercules's choice between virtue and vice was popular, so too were dramatic deaths like that of Cleopatra. Copies of celebrated works were acceptable: Houghton Hall in Norfolk has a bronze of the Vatican *Laocoön* that was purchased by Sir Robert Walpole, first Earl of Orford.

Tastes confirmed by the Grand Tour were catered for in London's art market, which expanded swiftly after the 1680s. It supplied what its patrons wanted: material imported from the Continent. Native artists were dismayed and complained. In 1737 the painter and satirist William Hogarth grumbled about the arrival of shiploads of 'dead Christs, Holy Families, Madonnas and other dismal subjects' on which the names of Italian masters had been written. Gullible buyers were beguiled by the dealer's patter. 'Sir, I find you are no connoisseur – That picture, I assure you, is in Alesso Boldovinetto's second best manner, boldly painted and truly sublime, the contour gracious; the air of the head in the high Greek taste, and a most divine idea it is.'[23]

Hogarth was making a case for British artists whose work, portraits apart, were then despised by noble patrons. There were other criticisms of the aristocracy's mania for foreign tastes and manners, and these increased in intensity as notions of British nationalism began to infiltrate the general consciousness. In the 1770s the Macaroni Club, whose young members had all made the Grand Tour, attracted satirists who denounced them as un-English and unmanly, two attributes which were synonymous in the patriotic imagination. In one lampoon a macaroni declares that he is distinguished in society by the odour of his face powder, a French concoction to which he has added a strong hint of violet.[24] Vapid dandies with mincing gestures were widely suspected of homosexuality, still, in the popular imagination, an Italian pastime.

Questions as to whether the nobility somehow lost their Englishness by two- to five- year excursions across Europe belong in the next chapter. What is certain is that the prolonged contacts with the Continent were an antidote to insularity and facilitated a flow of ideas between Britain and Europe and confirmed the aristocracy as part of an international culture. The classical preferences of the nobility permeated the middling orders (or, as they were known by 1800, the middle class) since the great houses and the artwork they housed were open to middle-class inspection whenever their owners were absent. The visitors liked what they saw and were eager to buy copies. Paintings were reproduced by printmakers for general sale and Josiah Wedgwood's potteries provided fine copies of the medallions and basalt work whose originals could be seen in country houses. Eighteenth-century middle-class consumerism rested on the assumption that aristocratic taste was infallible.

Magnificence remained desirable. In his influential anatomy of the sublime and beautiful, first published in 1757, Edmund Burke insisted that the 'great of dimension' was an element of the sublime in architecture. 'A great profusion of things which are splendid or valuable in themselves, is magnificence,' he concluded, vindicating past and present aristocratic taste.[25] It was reproduced in the façades of the grand terraces which were constructed in cities and larger towns to house the richer members of the middle class. In London, Bath, Bristol and Leeds lawyers, bankers and merchants occupied houses with collonaded parapets and decorative Corinthian columns and set in rows. Their collective frontage resembled a nobleman's country house, and sometimes they were set around grassy squares planted with trees which were suggestive of rural parks. Magnificence had been adapted for those rising up the social ladder.

15

Public Character: The
Aristocratic Century
1714–1815

Selecting a single phrase to sum up a hundred years of diverse human achievements is a tricky business and the result can never be wholly satisfactory. One recent historian plumped for 'aristocratic century' and another characterised the period as Britain's '*ancien régime*', which links it with the absolutist monarchies of Europe.[1] These titles seem apt for a book about the nobility, although it should be remembered that the British *ancien régime* emerged in 1815 as secure and confident, in contrast to its Continental counterparts, which had been severely shaken by the French Revolution and the wars it spawned.

There are valid alternatives. It can be called the age of revolutions (agricultural, industrial, American and French), or of wars (too many to list), or of intellectual and scientific enlightenment, all choices that remind us just how much happened and changed during this century. The age might also be named after the trio of Hanoverian Georges whose reigns it almost spans. Unlike that of their predecessors, their freedom of action was confined by the Glorious Revolution, which left them passive if not always contented bystanders rather than active makers of history. This was left to their aristocratic ministers and Parliaments.

What is beyond doubt is that the aristocracy did enjoy an astonishing ascendancy in public life thanks to those networks of obligation and reciprocity, which, together with adroit Parliamentary and electoral management, kept it in power. Equally remarkable was the capacity of the nobility to convince people that its monopoly of power was indispensable, that the aristocracy was the keystone of the nation. 'How long do you think the Constitution and liberties of the country would survive the loss of public character in the aristocracy?' the MP Thomas Creevey asked his patron the Duke of Norfolk in 1818. The Irish writer Thomas Moore compared the peerage to 'a break-water between the people and the throne, in a state of double responsibility – to liberty on one side, and authority, on the other'.[2]

Moreover, and this seemed an impregnable argument for its champions, the system worked to the nation's advantage. This was why, in 1791, the new Constitution for Upper and Lower Canada included provisions for governors to appoint life members to the upper chambers of the legislature, making them in effect the counterpart of the House of Lords. It was even suggested that the King might confer 'Hereditary Titles of Honour' on these lawmakers.[3] An aristocracy was integral to what, in 1830, Wellington praised as the 'most efficient legislative body in the world', which, for all its eccentricities, had presided over unprecedented prosperity and Britain's emergence as the first global superpower.[4]

All this was true. Aristocratic politicians had overseen the transformation of Britain into a commercial, industrial and maritime power and contrived and implemented the strategies which facilitated imperial expansion in the Caribbean, North America (where Canada was kept and the future United States lost), India, Australasia and South Africa. A landowning nobility was glad to do all within its power to promote the enrichment of the nation and encourage the capitalist enterprises that made this possible. The aristocracy also accommodated the interests of commercial lobbyists, of whom the most influential were investors in the East India Company and the West Indies plantocracy and its accomplices in the slave trade. Other lesser pressure groups whose voices were heard and heeded in Parliament pleaded for private bills for new canals, turnpikes, docks and agricultural enclosures.

Between 1688 and 1815 Parliament passed over fourteen thousand laws framed to facilitate and regulate investment, manufacturing and shipping. The generation of wealth occupied the greater part of Parliament's time; in 1784 parliamentary committees were investigating petitions from, among others, Nottingham shopkeepers seeking legislation to enforce the collection of small debts, ropemakers seeking closer supervision of their trade and licensed peddlars and hawkers from Staffordshire seeking protection from outsiders. Unlike its French counterpart, the British *ancien régime* took very good care of entrepreneurs and manufacturers.

Aristocratic ministers were also concerned with the health of money markets. These were now inextricably linked with the state through the Bank of England, founded in 1693, which controlled the money supply, and the National Debt, which had been launched in 1696 to finance what turned out to be over a hundred years of intermittent wars. Investors loaned money to the government which guaranteed the value of the stock (consols) and paid annual dividends. The soundness of public credit became a yardstick for the economic health of the country; political mischances and crises shook money markets, as they did in 1797 when consols briefly plummetted. As governors of an industrious and flourishing nation, the nobility were like a self-perpetuating board of a company who were expected to listen to the shareholders and deliver the dividends.

Noblemen and their sons were actively engaged in British commercial and colonial enterprises. They commanded the fleets and armies which secured markets, saw off French, Dutch and Spanish interlopers and conquered territories in North America and India. Their courage and tenacity gave a lustre of martial glory and kudos to the aristocracy, for victorious generals and admirals were ennobled. Sometimes, as with Lord St Vincent or Lord Nelson of the Nile, their titles incorporated their triumphs. Such men formed a new, heroic branch of the nobility, which was exalted as a collective example of a new national spirit.[5] It was a compound of pugnacity, resolve and fortitude. All were shown in different ways by George Anson, who earned his barony commanding fleets in the Caribbean and Pacific (taking one around the world), and George Brydges, who was created Lord Rodney after he had restored British naval supremacy in the Caribbean at the Battle of the Saintes in 1782.

Nelson had dreamed of joining this *noblesse d'épée*: on the eve of his attack on the French fleet in Abukir Bay in 1798, he declared: 'Before this time tomorrow I shall have gained a peerage or Westminster Abbey.' By then, what had started life as a royal mausoleum was being colonised by the marble statues of aristocratic admirals and generals, often accompanied by lively carvings of their victories. There were other forms of immortality. Patriotic landlords named their inns after national heroes such as John Manners, Marquess of Granby, a dashing eighteenth-century cavalry general always portrayed bare-headed on inn signs since he had once lost his wig galloping at the French.

Comparisons were made between these heroes and their Roman counterparts, who, like them, held that service to the state was the highest expression of the virtue latent in men of honour and birth. George III (1760–1820) was displeased when Benjamin West chose to portray General Wolfe and his soldiers in contemporary uniforms rather than Roman armour. Nonetheless, *The Death of General Wolfe* (he died fighting the French in Canada in 1759) appealed to patriots who purchased prints of the scene, as they did the portraits of victorious generals and admirals. Reports of their exploits helped kindle that sense of unity and national pride which were the key components of a new and intoxicating abstraction, Britishness.

There was a paradox in all this. An amazingly successful proto-modern commercial and industrial state and its sophisticated military and naval resources were controlled by a landed aristocracy which owed its dominance to a mastery of the old political arts of power-broking and wire-pulling. The complex system and its components of patronage, kinship and bribery have been dissected by Sir Lewis Namier, who concluded that they alone explain the maintenance of aristocratic power. Walpoles, Townshends, Pelhams, Stanhopes, Cavendishes, Russells, Campbells and Yorkes intrigued, made and broke promises, flattered and politely bullied kings and scattered largesse to win elections and secure majorities in Parliament. The terms 'Whig' and 'Tory' became meaningless; all that now mattered was distributing rewards to the right people at the right time. As the first de facto Prime Minister, Sir Robert Walpole, who held the office from 1721 till 1742, cynically remarked, every man had his price.

In fact it was never so neat and tidy. Modern reassessments of eighteenth-century politics indicate a significant, residual attachment to traditional loyalties and habits of mind. In Henry Fielding's *Tom Jones*, published in 1749, Squire Western damned his sister for a Whig and mocked her metropolitan pretensions, and she responded with contempt for his bucolic boorishness.

These caricatures and their comic exchanges were not inventions and must have struck some chords with Fielding's readers. The backwoodsman Western was clearly a Tory at home in a new Country Party, a loose combination united by its distrust of court venality and Whig chicanery. If he had chosen to enter Parliament, Western might have sat alongside 'independent' country squires, a small but influential body that grandee power-brokers ignored at their peril.

The politically engaged aristocracy formed a close-knit circle whose members were connected by blood, upbringing and education. Of the twenty-six prime ministers who held office between 1714 and 1832, seventeen had been to either Eton or Westminster. Their reputations as the kindergartens of successful politicians attracted aristocratic parents who now preferred public schools to private tutors. By 1800 over two-thirds of the nobility was sending its sons to these establishments, with Eton far and away the favourite choice.[6] For the past fifty years, it had become the custom for Eton's most promising alumni to present portraits of themselves to hang in the provost's lodgings. Among the likenesses were one Whig politico (Charles James Fox) and a Tory governor-general of Bengal (Richard Wellesley, Earl of Mornington).

Hard knocks accompanied hard study. Public schools were disorderly, virtually self-governing republics in which the masters exercised a spasmodic and often brutal authority that their pupils sometimes violently resisted. A bloody-minded spirit flourished alongside respect for public duty, and during the latter part of the eighteenth and first of the nineteenth centuries there was a spate of public school insurrections, including three at Eton. George Nugent-Grenville, the future Marquess of Buckingham and a cabinet minister, and Viscount Petersham were among the rebels in 1768. Petersham's father Lord Harrington ordered his son to submit. 'Sir, I shall be damned if I do,' responded the boy. 'And I will be damned if you don't,' answered Harrington. 'Yes, my lord,' riposted his son, 'but you will be damned whether I do or not.' This was true enough, for Harrington was a celebrated rake who preferred 'the lowest amusement in the lowest brothels' to his domestic and public duties.[7] A year after, he purchased his son a commission in the Coldstream Guards.

The hurly-burly of the public school life fostered independence and self-assurance, qualities which distinguished Lord Palmerston, whose ministerial career began in 1809 and ended in 1865, when he was at the start of his third term as Prime Minister. Soon after leaving Harrow in 1800, 'Pam' praised the public schools as 'a nation in miniature' where the boy who took the lead in games and 'enterprises . . . for mischief or amusement' was the one destined to 'distinguish himself at the head of an army or a council'. Over forty years later he confided to his brother that a minister's peevishness was the outcome of his never having had 'the wholesome buffeting of a public school'.[8] 'I owe my spirit of enterprise to the tricks I used to play in this garden,' Wellington told Etonians during his visit to the school in 1818.

Boys learned how to survive in a robust, competitive world, while their parents fretted about their intellectual progress and the likelihood that idle sons would drift into the sexual vices for which public schools had become notorious. In 1784, Charles Jenkinson, first Earl of Liverpool, urged his fourteen-year-old son Robert, the second Earl and a future Prime Minister, to stick at his Homer and Virgil and 'apply yourself to algebra and mathematics' so as to 'acquire a habit of reasoning closely and correctly on every subject'. The Jenkinsons were in the foothills of the political world and hoped to ascend higher, and so Charles reminded his son that his family 'look forward with anxiety to the figure you will hereafter make in the world . . . and in the character you bear'.[9]

At sixteen Robert Jenkinson undertook the next aristocratic rite of passage and proceeded to Christ Church, Oxford, the college of choice for noblemen's sons, where they wore a distinctive gold-laced nobleman's gown and dined with the college fellows as of right. He left after the usual two years, having shown what his tutor considered an alarming preference for 'general ideas' rather than close textual analysis. Jenkinson was already immersed in the world of politics, challenging his father's support for the slave trade. He also cultivated what he called 'a few particular people' whom he liked and whose political sympathies he shared, and his companions included future ministerial colleagues and an adversary, George Canning.

Attachments and sometimes antipathies made at school and university bound together the often overlapping aristocratic networks which dominated political life. Jenkinson also acquired his nickname 'Jenky', which has a schoolboy or undergraduate ring to it, as did those of other contemporary grandees. The Prince Regent called the Duke of Norfolk 'Jockey', while Henry Addington, the first Lord Sidmouth, was 'Doctor' on account of his father's profession, and Lord Grenville was inexplicably 'Bogy'.[10]

Nicknames were a novelty in the everyday discourse of politics. They could be heard at court levees, balls, masquerades, over card tables, at race meetings, cricket matches and in coffee houses, in fact anywhere where the rich and powerful enjoyed themselves. In his diary for October 1731, John Perceval, first Earl of Egmond, recorded coffee house discussions which ranged over religion, metaphysics, ancient statutes, the 'antiquity of Parliament', and a recently published gloss on Newton's *Mathematical Principles of Natural Philosophy*.[11] Over seventy years after, Creevey described an evening's conversation with the Duke of Norfolk which wandered 'from the bawdy to the depths of politics'.

Political conversation encompassed persiflage, anecdote, rumour and speculation as well as hard-nosed horse-trading over the dispersal of power and patronage. Ultimately, all political activity focused on the crucial business of persuading men how to vote, either in Parliament or at provincial polling booths. Astute electoral management at both levels explained both the progress and durability of Thomas Pelham-Holles, first Duke of Newcastle, who was a Secretary of State between 1724 and 1754 and Prime Minister between 1754 and 1756, and, with William Pitt the Elder, between 1756 and 1762.

Newcastle was a maestro who exploited the avarice, vanity and ambition of those whom he persuaded to beef up the Whigs in the Commons and Lords. Survival depended on strings pulled in London and in the provinces, where indifferent or uncommitted voters had to be petted. Newcastle worked in tandem with Charles Lennox, second Duke of Richmond, whom he counted 'his best and dearest friend in all the world'. Together, they seduced the voters of Sussex, where both owned substantial estates.

Every social occasion was turned to political advantage. In 1733 Newcastle urged his friend to sound out the feelings of the Sussex gentry whenever they gathered for the assizes and races at Lewes. Personal contact was vital and so, in 1737, Richmond attended the Lewes races in person to charm the electors. Meanwhile, his steward spied on the Tories, who were using a race meeting at Steyning to select their candidate for Chichester. Another of Richmond's agents strolled among spectators at cricket matches, testing opinion. But it was Richmond's presence which won hearts: squires, substantial farmers and anyone who had a forty-shilling freehold were flattered by the personal attention of the first man in the county and a celebrated sportsman.

Patience, good humour and a resilient liver were vital for canvassing. Newcastle once shrank from attendance at the Lewes races and assizes, for he was 'not at all fond of a week's drunkenness'. Nevertheless he had to abase himself, show warmth and affability towards social inferiors and heartily join in the alcoholic revels which Hogarth portrayed in his sequence of election paintings. Sussex Whigs sang:

> *Then fill your glass. Full let it be*
> *Newcastle drink while you can see*
> *With heart and voice, all voters sing*
> *Long live great Holles – Sussex king.*[12]

Voters expected bribes as well as beanfeasts. Richmond described the borough of New Shoreham as 'a new whore that is anybody's for their money', and a place where, thankfully, 'that ugly word conscience is not known'. New Shoreham succumbed to sweeters, and excise posts procured from Whitehall were scattered among leading townsmen. Tom Baker, a Chichester chandler and 'chief pillar of the dissenters', understood the game when he pledged his vote and powers of persuasion in return for Richmond's pressure on the trustees of St Thomas's Hospital to secure his son a position as a surgeon there.[13] Small men did favours for great and vice versa. In 1754 Newcastle gave the novelist Laurence Sterne the archdeaconry of York in return for his costly endeavours in expelling 'Popish seminaries' from the city.[14] The political nexus demanded that grandees in Westminster helped and were helped by chandlers, schoolmasters, farmers and the growing number of urban businessmen who had acquired a forty-shilling freehold.

With so many applicants for favours, clashes were inevitable and ministers had to judge precisely the political consequences of satisfaction or disappointment. In 1759 Newcastle was faced with rival requests for the governorship of Dunbarton Castle. One was from Lord Eglinton, who raised the matter at Lewes races, the other from General Campbell, a kinsman of the fourth Duke of Argyll. Honour was at stake and the Duke became 'very violent' when Newcastle hinted that he favoured Eglinton. He bluntly warned the Prime Minister that a slight to the

Campbells would have bruising repercussions for the Whigs in Scotland.[15] Argyll prevailed, as his family usually did.

Titles and promotions within the peerage were incentives for lobby fodder in both houses. Approving a peerage for one MP, Newcastle noted that he was 'faultless and one of the best supports I can have in the House of Commons'. John, second Viscount Bateman, was an Irish peer who sat for Woodstock in Oxfordshire and deserved the post of Lord of the Admiralty because he was a 'most useful man who does not speak' and had the goodwill of his uncle, the Duke of Marlborough.[16] Bateman's mute services obtained him posts within the royal household, first as Treasurer and then Master of the Buckhounds. He was at home in George III's court, for 'he possessed that mediocrity of talents, which forms the best recommendation to royal favour'.[17] The Tory Bateman was dependable in the Lords where he faithfully supported Lord North's ministry. When it fell in 1782, Bateman forfeited his sinecure, since it was customary for posts in the royal household to be redistributed when governments changed.

Like every other Prime Minister, North had to bargain with an increasing number of peers who, by inheritance or through investment, owned so-called pocket boroughs, constituencies in which the voters were, metaphorically at least, in their landlord's pocket. In many instances there were only a handful of voters and in a few (the rotten boroughs) none at all. Where they existed, voters had to be cherished: at Newark in Nottinghamshire each received half a ton of coal at Christmas and at East Retford in Nottinghamshire each received an annual twenty guineas. Truculence did occur and was stamped on. In Yorkshire in 1807 Malton voters defied Lord Fitzwilliam, who retaliated with evictions and raised rents, which did the trick, for next year they returned his candidate.[18] Alcohol induced compliance and gratitude, and in Westminster, where nearly every adult male had a vote, £2,285 (brandy was two shillings a bottle, beer a penny a pint.) was spent by Newcastle on tavern bills in 1754.[19]

Tractable constituencies were valuable assets and were bought and sold. In 1787 Lord Egremont paid £40,000 for Midhurst in Sussex, and in 1812 the sixth Duke of Bedford paid £32,000 for Camelford.[20] The number of boroughs owned by aristocrats rose sharply from 156 in 1747 to 207 in 1784, which represented nearly 40 per cent of the Commons. The aristocracy was tightening its grip on the legislature in the face of a growing challenge from India and West Indies moneybags who were buying up seats and, by 1790, had a block of forty-five members keeping an eye on the East India Company's interests. They were a force to be reckoned with, for there were enough of them to play havoc with ministerial majorities.

Inflation hit the borough market as more and more colonial Midases sought seats in the Commons. Politics became increasingly expensive; Newcastle was compelled to sell off estates worth £200,000 to meet the debts he had run up sustaining the Whigs in power.[21] Leaders chasing Commons' majorities were forced to haggle with boroughmongers competing in a seller's market. In 1774 Lord Edgecombe demanded £15,000 for his five Cornish seats, but Lord North knocked him down to £12,500, which was the going rate. The Prime Minister considered Viscount Falmouth had been 'rather shabby' by accepting the standard price, but asking for payment in guineas (worth one pound and five pence) for his six Cornish seats, thus slipping an extra 5 per cent onto the final bill.[22]

Hugh Boscawen, second Viscount Falmouth, was notoriously greedy: at a levee he had once asked Pitt the Elder to recommend him for the Garter and was refused. Furious, Falmouth warned the Prime Minister that: 'I bring in five votes who go with the ministry in the House of Commons; and if my application is disregarded, you must take the consequence.' Pitt remained obdurate and quoted a Roman proverb: '*Optat*

Ephippia Bos piger' ('as much as the lazy ox wishes to be saddled'). Ignorant of Latin, Falmouth asked where it came from and what it meant. On hearing it was from Horace, he presumed, to the amusement of everyone present, that the words had been uttered by the contemporary dilettante Sir Horace Walpole.[23]

Falmouth was a dunce, but he was acutely conscious of the immense prestige attached to the pale blue ribbon of the Garter. It and the orders of the Thistle, founded in 1703, and St Patrick, founded in 1783, were tokens of special royal favour which created an elite within the peerage, immediately recognisable by the ribbons and badges worn in the Lords and on public occasions. Like titles, these honours required ministerial recommendation, which made them counters in the political game. George I (1714–27) and his son George II (1727–60) acquiesced, not always graciously, but they had the compensation of the civil list, a payment annually endorsed by Parliament to cover the Crown's private expenses. In 1760 it stood at £800,000.

George III chafed against the constraints that had bound his predecessors. Wilful and dogmatic, he was guided by an atavistic philosophy of kingship and cast himself as the 'patriot King', an honest patriarch dedicated to the welfare of his subjects and above the venality and bickering of partisan politics. George considered Parliamentary debates exercises in fruitless verbosity. Old ideas were briefly brought out of mothballs, and Pitt the Elder was perturbed to hear a royal chaplain preach on the doctrine of non-resistance.[24] Others may have been amused, although there were plenty of MPs and peers who were glad to indulge the royal fancies and harvested the rewards which came the way of the King's 'friends'. An axis of Whigs, Tories, apolitical country squires and officials of the royal household (whom George called his 'household troops') kept the biddable mediocrity of Lord North in power from 1770 to 1782.

The tentative revival of the Crown's executive power foundered because of George's pigheadedness. Its fruits were humiliating reverses in America, the temporary loss of British maritime supremacy in the Atlantic and Caribbean which led to an invasion threat in 1779, and spiralling levels of taxation. George convinced himself it was all the fault of the Whig opposition, whom he accused of fomenting rebellion in America and hampering his ministers at home. The decisive Franco-American victory at Yorktown in 1781 confirmed what was already clear: Britain could not suppress the colonists. A ministry whose justification was to continue fighting collapsed and North resigned.

George III became entangled in serpentine manoeuvres to exclude his old enemies from office, turning in 1783 to the Tory William Pitt the Younger. The patriot King swallowed his disdain for partisan politics and, through flagrant intervention, sustained the minority ministry of Pitt until the general election of 1784. George converted the uncommitted with peerages: Edward Eliot was made Lord St Germains in return for delivering his two Cornish boroughs and their quartet of MPs to Pitt.

George III's excursions into factional politics transformed the aristocracy. Keeping Pitt in office required a steady flow of creations, and between 1780 and 1800 the total of peers soared from 189 to 267. Arrivistes now predominated in the Lords, where four-fifths of its members had titles less than a hundred years old. Old blood was scandalised. 'There are so many Lords made, that I can hardly spit out of my coach without spitting on a Lord,' exclaimed the Duchess of Queensberry in August 1784.[25]

A bandwagon was rolling and the ambitious quickly jumped on to it. Snobbery, vanity and anxieties over status compelled men to beg for titles, often blatantly and sometimes without success. In 1796, Sir James Graham Bt. pleaded with Henry Dundas, the Secretary for War, for a safe government constituency, reminding his friend that 'my sole object for coming into Parliament would be to obtain a peerage'.[26] His hopes were raised in 1798 when, with ministerial backing, he was elected for Ripon in Yorkshire, which he represented for the next nine years. Graham was asthmatic, which may explain why he never spoke in debates, but his silent support for successive ministries did not merit a peerage.

Another loser in the scramble for titles was James Stewart, the seventh Earl of Galloway, a Tory, a Lord of the Bedchamber and Lord Lieutenant of Wigtonshire. Here he enjoyed 'some consequence' as he told Pitt and Dundas, but his kudos had been dimmed in 1793 when his nominee had been beaten in the county election. Only his elevation to an English peerage and with it a guaranteed seat in the Lords would restore his prestige.[27] Over the next two years, he anxiously scanned the annual lists of creations and promotions in the belief that Pitt would heed his pleas. The Prime Minister did not, aware perhaps that this vain nobleman's son had backed the opposition candidate for Kirkcudbright. The disappointed Galloway died in 1806 from gout of the stomach.[28]

Graham and Galloway possessed large estates, but now acreage was beginning to count for less when it came to creating peers. Many new lords, including the naval commander Lord Collingwood and Lord Ellenborough, a former Lord Chief Justice, had little land. Looking back from the 1840s, the romantic Tory Benjamin Disraeli saw the separation of the aristocracy from the land as a blow to its ancient mystique. In his novel *Sybil* (1845), he castigated Pitt for giving titles to 'second-rate squires and fat graziers' and to bankers and businessmen whom 'He caught . . . in the alleys of Lombard Street and clutched . . . from the counting houses of Cornhill.' A few of these 'mushroom' lords were uncomfortable about their lack of the wherewithal to keep up their positions. On the eve of Trafalgar, Thomas Hardy, Nelson's Flag Captain, confided to the Admiral that 'his want of fortune' would make it difficult for him to maintain the baronetcy which, he rightly guessed, he would soon be awarded.[29]

No such embarrassment was allowed to disturb Wellington: after each of his major victories in the Peninsula he leapfrogged up the peerage from Viscount Wellington of Talavera to Duke of Wellington in five years. A financial award was attached to each title, culminating with £400,000 with which to buy estates sufficient to uphold the 'dignity' of his dukedom.[30]

As in previous periods when the aristocracy underwent rapid expansion, there was backbiting about a perceived devaluation of the peerage as a whole. It was already stratified, with English peers taking precedence over Scottish, who were allowed only sixteen representatives in the Lords, and both took precedence over Irish, who had none. The theatre of power required the strictest observation of protocols with everyone in their proper places in public processions, which offered plenty of opportunities for grumbling over slights. In 1733 some English lords believed that Irish peers were no more than commoners, and they were incensed by George III's Queen's kissing the hands of Irish countesses but not those of English viscountesses.[31]

Always fussy about the minutiae of court punctilio, George III protested in 1776 when it was proposed that Irish peers might be given English lord lieutenantcies.[32] When, in 1806, one Irish peer, Lord Mornington, was offered an Irish marquessate for having enlarged British territories in India, he was furious. 'There was nothing *Irish* or *Pinchbeck* in my conduct,' he declared and, therefore, he expected 'nothing *Irish* or *Pinchbeck* in my reward'.[33] His *amour propre* was satisfied with an English title, Marquess Wellesley, but his political ambitions were hampered by his libido. As Foreign Secretary between 1809 and 1812 he devoted more time to his mistresses than to his duties; his younger brother remarked that castration might be the only way to save his career.

Wellesley joined an aristocracy at the apex of its political supremacy. Its future seemed assured, for over the past fifty years it had engrossed more and more political power. The steady acquisition of pocket and rotten boroughs, corruption and private non-aggression pacts were making the nobility less and less answerable to the electorate. In the 1761 election only one-fifth of seats were contested.

Yet mastery of the electoral apparatus did not mean that aristocratic politicians were cocooned from outside pressures, whether from voters or boroughmongers seeking favours, or, on occasions, the masses. Even an ostensibly tame MP could disregard the wishes of his patron. In 1795 William Bontine, who had been elected as member for Dunbartonshire through the influence of the Tory third Duke of Montrose, told his patron that he could no longer 'satisfy' his conscience by voting for Pitt's repressive domestic policies. He resigned and the Duke gracefully accepted, acknowledging Bontine's 'delicate and nice sense of honour'.[34]

The will of the masses expressed itself in various and sometimes unnerving ways. That 'liberty' which the aristocracy boasted was under its protection was also a slogan which could bring noisy and belligerent mobs on to the streets. They regularly appeared throughout the century to protest against genuine and perceived encroachments on 'liberty', which included excise duties, militia drafts and proposals for Catholic emancipation. In the early 1760s Londoners demonstrated on behalf of John Wilkes, a radical journalist and politician, and against high-handed government censorship of the press. Citizens everywhere had the right to petition the Crown and the number and content of their petitions served as a rough barometer of public opinion. Noblemen, and for that matter the Crown, were regularly exposed to often savage criticism and ridicule in newspapers and pamphlets and by cartoonists.

From the 1760s onwards there was evidence of growing disquiet about the glaring faults in the electoral system. It was being reduced to a form of calculus in which party managers totted up the number of seats available, assessed the costs of acquiring them and haggled with their owners. The result was stability and (the loss of America aside) effective government, but the reputation and tone of Parliament were being blighted. This worried Pitt, who, in 1785, proposed a bill concocted, in his own phrase, to secure a 'right balance'. The new equilibrium would require thirty-six rotten boroughs voluntarily to surrender their rights in return for compensation, and their members to be allocated to new seats in areas of expanding population. Privately, Pitt hoped that this measure would keep 'nabobs and peculators of all descriptions' out of the Commons and so, indirectly, reinforce the ascendancy of the landed interest.[35]

Lord North would have none of this. The Constitution was an 'ancient, venerable, substantial fabric' which was about to be vandalised by 'decorating it with modern frippery'. Antiquity was the yardstick of soundness and North was confident that the 'guardians of freedom' would always find their way into the Commons.[36] The old order was saved by 248 votes to 174. What was significant in terms of the future was that North and his allies regarded the present Constitution as immutable and permanent. So too was the ascendancy of the nobility, or so it seemed.

16

A Fair Kingdom: Fame,
Taste and Fashion

The aristocrats who dominated eighteenth- and early nineteenth-
century Britain were highly visible public figures, whose daily
lives and conduct were under constant scrutiny. Forever changing, aristocratic aesthetics offered the middle orders a guide as to
what was desirable, proper and, therefore, worth imitating.
Ordinary people were not only allowed to inspect the houses of
noblemen, they were able to peer into their intimate lives
through the prism of the press. Between about 1680 and 1710 a
highly significant but little noticed revolution occurred in
Britain: the emergence of newspapers as a force in political and
social life. In 1714 2.5 million newspapers were printed in
London and the provinces, and titles and circulations soared
during the next hundred years.

The aristocracy provided journalists with a vast amount of
copy which was avidly read, mostly by men and women of the
middle class. Newspapers printed routine announcements as to

which peers were arriving in London, Bath and later Brighton, and there were lists of aristocratic births, marriages, illnesses and deaths with appropriate details. In January 1758 the London *Public Advertiser* announced the death of the sixth Duke of Hamilton from an 'inflammation of the bowels', and reported a wedding in which the bride was 'a beautiful young lady with a handsome fortune and every other gratification necessary to render the married state happy'.[1] Such material obviously appealed to the bon ton, who were eager to keep abreast of metropolitan gossip.[2]

High-life scandal was soon established as a press staple, although editors always had to be circumspect, or risk a challenge or a horse-whipping. In 1824 the 'Fashionable Herald' column of *Bell's Life in London and Sporting Chronicle* (which relished this kind of story) announced that: 'Lord ++++ is given to understand that Lady ++++ has been called "a person of doubtful character by Sir +++++"'.[3] Sexual innuendo, often coyly written, was very popular, although it was only fully intelligible to a limited circle. Outsiders drew their own conclusions, tutted and enjoyed the frisson of sharing in part the secret lives of their betters.

Aristocratic entertainments were regularly reported, often in a grotesquely obsequious prose. Four hundred guests turned up for a ball held by the Countess of Galloway in June 1800, and readers of *The Oracle* heard how she and her daughters 'displayed all the assiduities of which warm hospitality and good breeding are susceptible in the first rank'. These ladies were all but outshone by the 'youth and beauty' of the Marchioness of Donegal, whose 'elegant' dress was worn with 'much grace and dignity'.[4]

The fictional counterpart of this type of reporting was the 'silver fork' novel mostly written by and for women, which enjoyed a large readership. They were picaresque high-life adventures, and their content and mildly scandalous flavour was caught by a 1785 puff for *Anna, or the Memoirs of a Welsh Heiress*, 'written from real life' by 'a lady' and dedicated to Princess Charlotte, George III's daughter; its chapter headings included 'The Kept Mistress', 'Immaculate Peer' and 'Masquerade Adventure'.[5] Levées, salons and grand balls were the background to Lady Caroline Lamb's *Glenarvon*, which appeared anonymously in 1816. The 'world of fashion', she believed, was 'like a fairy kingdom' whose inhabitants' wit, manners and sophistication had made them perfect. Amusement and an 'incessant hurry after novelty' dominated their lives and relationships.[6] Her readers wanted to enter this magic world and Lady Caroline was a well-qualified guide. She was an earl's daughter who had married Lord Melbourne, the future Whig Prime Minister, was divorced and subsequently became the mistress of Lord Byron and, it was rumoured, the Duke of Wellington.

Those outside this enchanted domain of handsome lords, demure beauties, gossiping peeresses, witty badinage and self-indulgence were drawn towards it like moths to a candle, an illumination provided by the press and silver fork novels. Some writers warned their impressionable younger readers that the world of the bon ton was an amoral hothouse whose pleasures were artificial and unsatisfying. This was the message of *A Sentimental Journey*, written by 'a Lady' and serialised in the *Lady's Magazine* in 1773. Her heroine wisely wonders whether 'politeness' is a poor substitute for 'humanity' and, after an assembly, decides that the 'Trifling elegancies of high life too frequently make us forget what is essential to happiness.'[7]

The real or imagined ambience of society and those eager to break into it brings us close to the familiar modern world of 'celebrity'. In essence, it was an eighteenth-century invention and was then called 'fame'. Fame was the goal of the vain and ambitious outsider, and it was as brittle and transient as modern celebrity. As Dr Johnson tartly observed:

Unnumber'd Suppliants crowd Preferment's Gate
Athirst for wealth and burning to be great,
Delusive Fortune hears th'incessant call,
They mount, they shine, evaporate and fall.

Fame required press coverage and aristocratic patronage. Both were extended to the mistresses of peers, beautiful girls, often from nowhere, who thrived on notoriety. In 1758 the *Public Advertiser* contrived what must have been the first photocall when it arranged for a famous courtesan, Kitty Fisher, to fall from her horse in Hyde Park to reveal her thigh and perhaps more (knickers were then not worn) to watching crowds.[8] A nobleman's mistress attracted press attention and secured status for herself and her keeper. On arriving in Paris, gentlemen undertaking the Grand Tour felt immediately obliged to take one of the 'Filles D'Opera' into their protection.[9]

In the same year, the necessities of the fashionable aristocrat were enumerated as membership of White's Club (celebrated for gambling), horses at Newmarket and 'an actress in keeping'.[10] When ordering his wife's portrait from Joshua Reynolds, the second Lord Bolingbroke instructed the artist 'to give her the eyes of Nelly O'Brien [a well-known courtesan], or it will not do'.[11]

Reynolds would have known what was expected from him. He was a tireless and unashamed self-promoter and a toady to the aristocratic patrons who helped him. Speaking with his Devon burr and having gained the fame he had craved, Reynolds told young painters that they would never succeed as artists unless they secured public fame. 'I never saw so vulgar and so familiar a forward fellow,' sneered one aristocrat, but his fellows were glad to have Reynolds portray themselves, their wives and mistresses.

Reynolds was a member of the Dilettanti Society, which had

been founded in 1734 to distil and define the elements of taste. Aristocratic collectors rubbed shoulders with artists and together they drank wine, examined works of art (chiefly classical) and endeavoured to create and promote a scientific and absolute rationale for connoisseurship.[12] It was synonymous with taste and exclusive to collectors who had studied and discussed shade, colour and form. When the aristocratic connoisseur evaluated a painting, he talked with authority; knowledge separated him from the mere collector who hoarded indiscriminately. His rooms were crammed not just with works of art, but curios and natural history specimens which intrigued or amazed onlookers, but had no aesthetic merit. Typical were the stuffed birds, fossils, shells from the cabinet of 'a gentleman under misfortune' which were auctioned at his creditors' request in 1785.[13]

The informed pursuit of beauty had close affinities with the pursuit and possession of beautiful women. Italian mistresses were among the trophies of the Grand Tour and aristocratic mothers rightly feared that their charms would prepare their sons for lives of vice and indolence.[14] Two leading Dilettanti, the fourth Earl of Sandwich and Sir Francis Dashwood Bt., were infamous rakes and the connection between dissipation and connoisseurship was lampooned by Thomas Rowlandson's *The Connoisseurs*, painted about 1800. Clinical aesthetic judgement and sexual voyeurism are linked by three connoisseurs peering at a painting of a voluptuous Susanna surprised by the peeping elders. The trio clearly desire to possess both the image and the person of Susanna.[15]

Rowlandson's satire on the motives of the connoisseurs was a symptom of a new public attitude towards art which was critical of its dominance by the nobility. The essentially aristocratic absolutism of taste belonged to that *ancien régime* of the mind and spirit which had been overthrown in France in 1789. There, significantly, the royal collection in the Louvre was opened to every citizen in 1793. In Britain art was largely hidden from view in private collections. Artists were under the thumb of the Royal Academy, an exclusive and intensely conservative association of established figures, which had close links with the aristocratic connoisseurs who flocked to its annual exhibition held early in May.

Benjamin Haydon called it a 'despotism' which resembled a 'House of Lords' without a Commons or a King. The Academy's outlook was patrician and haughty as the painter John Henning recalled. As a young artist in 1810 he had asked permission of the seventh Earl of Elgin to draw the marbles from the Parthenon which he purchased from the Turkish government. The Earl refused because Henning had no recommendation from an academician. 'My Lord,' he protested, 'I cannot understand why noblemen or gentlemen should dare not allow an individual to draw or model from the works of art in their possession.' This was the 'popery of art' and a form of slavery. As for the Royal Academy, it represented a 'selfish spirit of exclusion'. Elgin, who had once been blackballed by the Dilettanti, warmed to Henning's spirit and relented.[16]

The 'selfish spirit of exclusion', the rigid orthodoxies of taste and the veneration of the Classical retarded creativity, and private collections hid genius from the public. Hennings's feelings blended with that wider movement for political and institutional reform which was then gathering momentum. The aristocracy's grip on taste and the arts reflected its political dominance and was, as Hennings's choice of the words 'popery' and 'slavery' implied, autocratic and unjust.

Wider questions emerged: was art like a rotten borough, a possession over which the owner had an unqualified right? Did the aristocracy have the same monopoly of wisdom in connoisseurship as it did in politics? These issues were raised in a symbolic contest fought in 1816 over the future of the Elgin Marbles. A mainly Tory Parliamentary committee was appointed to assess the 'merits and value' of the sculpture and it decided in favour of what today would be called 'art for the people'. Its report claimed that Elgin's collection would 'improve our national taste for the Fine Arts and diffuse a more perfect knowledge of them throughout this Kingdom'. *The Times* concurred and hoped the Marbles would both inspire native artists and stimulate the taste of the public once they were in the British Museum, which, since 1810, was legally bound to admit anyone 'of decent appearance'.

This decision was a reverse for the Dilettanti, who wanted the Marbles to have been placed on the market for private collectors. This principle of delivering art to the people was further advanced a few years later, when Lord Liverpool and Sir Robert Peel backed plans for the National Gallery, whose exhibits would include works bought from aristocratic collections. Inviting the people to discover and enjoy art was a Tory concession which did not directly compromise the aristocratic principle. Paintings and sculpture were still private property at the disposal of their owners, but now the state competed with collectors when they came up for sale.

The preferences and influence of aristocratic taste remained. John Constable, who wanted to paint landscapes, complained about commissions for portraits and the tendency of patrons to be swayed by the fashions of France. In 1823 a friend predicted that 'English boobies, who dare not trust their own eyes, will discover your merits when they find you are admired in Paris.' Constable made compromises, but Benjamin Haydon refused to and discovered painfully that potential patrons did not recognise his unique genius. In consequence he spent most of career teetering on the brink of insolvency. In 1829 he wrote enviously of the young Edwin Landseer, whose portraits of animals and children secured abundant commissions, riding on his 'blood horse' (thoroughbred) with the 'airs of a man of fashion'. Haydon consoled himself that he had not surrendered to the 'vices of fashion'.[17]

Haydon's use of the word 'fashion' is instructive: 'a man of fashion' indicates social status and the 'vices of fashion' refers to prevailing, if ephemeral, addictions. The nature and manifestations of eighteenth-century fashion and how and why it changed have been extensively analysed.[18] From the point of view of this history what matters is that the rest of the world was on the whole content to follow whatever found favour with the aristocracy from styles of dress to musical taste. Political ascendancy went hand in hand with cultural ascendancy and both were challenged in the next century.

Aristocratic cultural power was demonstrated in 1728 when only the determined influence and financial backing of the Duchess of Queensberry secured the first production of John Gay's *Beggar's Opera,* which broke with convention and verged on the subversive. A 'prodigious concourse of nobility and gentry' gathered for the first night and applauded generously when the curtain fell. Gay was delighted and confessed to Jonathan Swift his amazement at and gratitude to the Duchess's 'brave spirit' and 'goodness'.[19]

Aristocrats dictated musical taste, although they disagreed passionately over the merits of one composer or style over another. In 1720 half of the twenty directors of the Royal Academy of Music were peers, some of whom, like the first Earl of Egmont, were keen amateur players. He was devoted to Handel's music, the popularity of which was 'convincing proof of our national taste' according to a newspaper of 1754.[20] Over ten years before he had abandoned composing 'Italian' operas which had been favoured by the nobility, but which upset patriots. In 1737 a newspaper deplored the 'vast sums of money' paid to Italian performers for a decadent form of entertainment. 'The ancient Romans . . . did not admit of any effeminate music, singing and dancing on their stage, till luxury had corrupted their morals and the loss of liberty followed soon after.'[21]

Xenophobes of the John Bull tendency feared that noblemen

paying thousands of pounds to hire and listen to famous Italian castrati were a symptom of impending moral collapse. The aristocracy's infatuation with foreign, particularly Italian novelties was unpatriotic: they drained the country of money and encouraged the physical and moral ennervation of the nation's leaders. Solid, British sustenance was scorned by men of fashion, who 'regale on macaroni or piddle with an ortolan' and judge the quality of a meal by its cost rather than its constituents complained a journalist in 1754.[22] Tenants languished while their landlord trifled with alien frivolities. They were spurned by the new squire of Harpswell in Lincolnshire and his tenants were grateful:

> *Their consequence some may presume they advance,*
> *By learning the capers and vapours of France;*
> *Home-bred and home-fed, what we tenants admire,*
> *Is the true English spirit display'd in our Squire.*[23]

This young fellow (reminiscent of Goldsmith's Squire Lumpkin) had clearly not made a Grand Tour.

The xenophobes were mistaken. There is abundant evidence which suggests that many dedicated followers of fashion did not shirk their public duties and were not uncaring landlords. Consider the career and interests of James, seventh Earl of Findlater, a Scottish landowner who took the Grand Tour in the company of the neoclassical painter Colin Morrison. He made several extended visits to Paris and Brussels between 1776 and 1784 and between 1790 and his death wandered across central Europe. During this time and because of financial strains, Findlater worked in Dresden as an architect and had his plans published in *Les Plans et Desseins tirés de la Belle Architecture*, which appeared in Paris in 1798.[24] His medical bills indicate either fragile health or hypochondria, although his payments for food and wine indicate a stalwart appetite. There is the distinct likelihood that he was a homosexual, so that his absences abroad were a means to avoid prosecution for what was then a capital offence.

Findlater was clearly a nobleman of taste attuned to current fashions. During a visit to Bath in 1783 he purchased a 'superfine' blue coat, 'fine ostrich feathers', 'pomade au jasmin', a 'brown Canadian fox muff' and a swansdown puff for applying powder to his face, and, in Paris, he bought quantities of gold and silver silk. In Bath he dined on English food (eel pie) and foreign (an 'Italian' cutlet and chicken fricassee). He subscribed to *British Magazine* and *Les Nouvelles de la République des Lettres et des Artes*.[25]

Findlater also fulfilled his responsibilities as a landowner. He invested in the development of his estates, the construction of a local canal and the rebuilding of the harbour at Banff in Moray. When in Scotland, he gave between seven and eleven shillings a week to the poor. Findlater also funded what was in effect a free health service for his tenants and labourers, paying a local surgeon for their treatment. During 1785 and 1786 the bill came to fifty-three pounds and covered, among other things, quinine, a 'mercurial purge', expectorants and 'extirpating a cancerous tumour'.[26] It was a remarkable and humane service and a signal reminder that the pursuit of fashion did not obliterate the traditional social duties of a nobleman.

In 1782 Findlater paid twelve guineas for a pair of fine duelling pistols.[27] It was a large sum, but it provided protection for the Earl's person (Lord North's carriage had been attacked by a pair of mounted highwaymen near Gunnersbury in 1774) and his honour.[28] Gentlemen of all ranks continued to believe that their honour and public reputation demanded that they submitted to tests of courage if these were in any way slighted. By the mid-eighteenth century pistols had become the commonest weapon. Between 1760 and 1820 there were 170 duels which resulted in sixty-nine deaths, and there was an unknown number of confrontations which ended in apologies.[29] Prosecutions were infrequent, and during this period there were eighteen trials, fourteen convictions for manslaughter and murder, and just two hangings.

The law was broadly tolerant of duelling. The jurymen in the Macnamara case accepted the plea that the duel was the only way in which the accused could have upheld his honour as an officer and gentleman. The prevailing opinion was expressed in a newspaper editorial of 1789, which accepted that the duel was 'a remnant of chivalry', but it was a 'necessary evil which operates to preserve a proper order in that part of society where laws would be ineffectual'. It was impossible for juries and judges to comprehend the nuances of the arcane code of honour in which the 'insult of a frown' or the 'malignity of emphasis' were grounds for a challenge. Moreover, the duel protected 'female innocence' and preserved 'the decorum of familiar intercourse, and the respectability of honour'.[30]

Newspapers and their readers were fascinated by the causes and outcomes of duels. Affronts to honour varied enormously from the trivial to deliberate provocation: 'allegations of effeminacy' led to a challenge in 1731, whilst 'marks of rudeness' including picking teeth and lounging at a table with his feet in the challenger's face led to another in 1777.[31] One duel in 1824 was a consequence of a squabble over billiards and another concerned 'unjustifiable assertions' against a gentleman's sister, which compelled him to travel from Madras to issue the challenge.[32] The voyage was worth it, for his shot shattered the thigh of his sister's traducer.

Reports of the incidents which culminated in duels added to a perception of the world of fashion as amoral and self-indulgent. Gambling for high stakes, adultery, fornication, drunkenness and violence seemed endemic amongst the bon ton. A joke of 1754 alleged that the difference between prostitutes and 'fine ladies' was that the first had a 'trade' and that the second lived by smuggling.[33] At a ball in 1789, two young ladies were admiring the dress of men and one whispered behind her fan, 'I am for the undress – what say you?' 'I see we are certainly sisters,' her companion answered, 'for I was just thinking of the same thing.'[34] The louche and purblind pursuit of pleasure led towards decadence and effeteness. It was epitomised by 'exquisites' like Lord Dallas in Lady Caroline Lamb's *Glenarvon*, who was 'quite thorough bred though full of conceit'. His conversation passed effortlessly from the 'nature of love' to the beauty of the Greek language and the 'insipidity of all English society'.[35]

During the first two decades of the nineteenth century the excesses of the bon ton came under increasing censure and what had once been tolerated or ignored was now being challenged and condemned. During the French wars radicals castigated aristocratic extravagance and found themselves in an alliance of convenience with right-wing patriots. In 1800 the *Anti-Jacobin* railed against the 'depravity of the age', which was manifest in the behaviour of theatre audiences. There were 'horrible outrages of modesty, the most obscene language, and the most indecent conduct' in the lobbies and the boxes, where richer patrons sat.[36]

There were suggestions that the antique codes of honour which sanctioned duelling needed revision to bring them in line with modern reason.[37] What moral or logical justifications were there for one section of society to claim immunity from laws which were framed for the whole community? Furthermore, the aristocracy's resort to duelling set an appalling example to those who looked to it for leadership; in 1810 the *Gentleman's Magazine* was disturbed by reports of duels fought by shopkeepers.[38] Submission to the 'cruel and false principles of his class' drive the gentleman to commit murder argued the Evangelical William Wilberforce in an appeal designed to remind the upper levels of society of their Christian duty.[39]

Better known for his campaigns against the slave trade and slavery, Wilberforce devoted almost as much energy to persuading the landed classes to reform their lives according to Christian doctrines.

For Wilberforce, perceived aristocratic licentiousness and hedonism set a bad example to the rest of society which looked upwards for moral guidance. Traditional duties were neglected: in 1818 the writer and caricaturist George Cruikshank wrote that 'Dame Fashion' was subverting the nobility:

> For one rout – for one year she shuts her gate on the poor,
> Then the box at the opera, shar'd with a few,
> Makes her give up, in church the old family pew.[40]

There were parallels between the criticism of the aristocracy's moral failings and assaults on its political power. Both were integral to the 'old corruption' which reformers wanted to uproot and both were products of middle-class ideologies which rejected the 'wisdom of our ancestors'.

There was a paradox here, for the middle class remained in thrall to aristocratic taste. The eighteenth-century consumer revolution had witnessed an increasingly prosperous middle class spending its disposable income on carriages, clothes, furniture, silver and tableware, and clothes which copied styles then in favour with the nobility. Retailers advertised themselves as suppliers of goods or provisions to the 'nobility and gentry' to tempt middle-class customers. Middle-class women could pore over prints of the latest Paris fashions in the *Lady's Magazine* and instruct the local sempstress to reproduce them. The results could be paraded at social gatherings whose rituals were aristocratic in form, but which had been commercially organised. A new breed of impresarios organised concerts and masquerades which charged for admission. The beau monde was often present at these entertainments and rubbed shoulders with lesser

Chivalry in action: a knight rescues a lady from a wild man of the forest, *c.*1340.

(British Library)

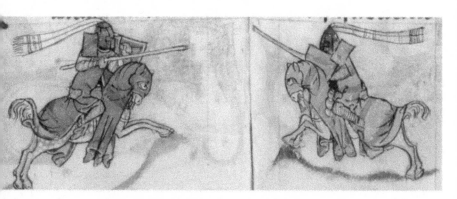

Aristocratic spectacle: knights jousting, *c.*1300.

(British Library)

Aristocratic sport: falconer, *c*.1450; lady archer pots a rabbit, *c*.1340.

(British Library)

Aristocratic patronage: John Hoccleve
presents a volume of verse to Henry
Prince of Wales, *c.*1410.

(British Library/Bridgeman Art Library)

Knightly perfection:
effigy of Richard Beauchamp,
Earl of Warwick, *d.*1439,
St Mary's Church, Warwick.

(Private collection/Bridgeman Art Library)

William Lord Herbert presenting a copy of
Lydgate's *Troy Book* to Edward IV.

(British Library)

Eminence in death: mourners carry heraldic hatchments and banners at the funeral of the Marquess of Huntley, 1636.

(Trustees of the National Museums of Scotland)

William Brooke, 10th Lord Cobham and his family; the children's pets included a parrot and a marmoset.

(Longleat House, Wiltshire/Bridgeman Art Library)

Magnificence: George Villiers, Duke of Buckingham: favourite of James I, collector of Renaissance paintings and trafficker in peerages, painted, *c.*1616.

(National Portrait Gallery)

Fashion models: children's dolls show an elegantly dressed Lord and
Lady Clapham, early eighteenth century.
(Victoria and Albert Museum / Bridgeman Art Library)

The Grand Tour consummated: men of taste gather in Rome, *c.*1750.
(Paul Mellon Collection, USA / Bridgeman Art Library)

Death in the coppice: Freeman, the Earl of Clarendon's gamekeeper with a doe and a hound, c.1800 (George Stubbs). *(Paul Mellon Collection, USA/Bridgeman Art Library)*

A connoisseur and his antiquities: Charles Townley in his gallery (Johann Zoffany). *(Townley Hall Art Gallery and Museum/Bridgeman Art Library)*

From a view to a kill: Thomas Oldaker on 'Pickle' (Ben Marshall).

Britain's ancien regime: the elder sons of peers carry the coronation mantle of George IV.

An aristocracy imagined: fictional Flytes pose outside Castle Howard in a publicity shot for ITV's *Brideshead Revisited*, 1981.

(ITV/Rex Features)

Old splendour and new realities: members of the House of Lords, chiefly life peers and peeresses, attend the state opening of Parliament; their robes differ little from those worn by their medieval predecessors.

(Press Association)

A power over the land: Ralph Lord Cromwell's castle at Tattershall, built mid-fifteenth century.

(National Trust Photographic Library/Andrew Butler/Bridgeman Art Library)

Retainer: Sir Thomas Burton wears the SS collar of his lord, John of Gaunt, Duke of Lancaster, late-fourteenth-century brass, Little Casterton, Rutland.

Jacobean magnificence: Hatfield House, Hertfordshire, built between 1607 and 1612 by Robert Cecil, first Earl of Salisbury.

(Heritage Images)

Palladian splendour and Whig ascendancy: Blenheim Palace, Oxfordshire, built for John Churchill, the first Duke of Marlborough.

(Country Life)

Medieval splendour revived: Belvoir Castle, Leicestershire, rebuilt in the Gothic styl by the fifth Duke of Rutland in the early nineteenth century.

(Country Life)

Contemplating the Classical world: the Temple of Ancient Virtue in the grounds of Stowe, Buckinghamshire, by William Kent, *c*.1735.

The perils of politics: William Hogarth's satirical 'Chairing the Candidate' reflects the realities of a contested election in the mid-eighteenth century.

Guardians of the nation: aristocratic statesmen *(clockwise from top left)*

Charles Lennox, 2nd Duke of Richmond (1701–50).
(Trustees of the Goodwood Collection / Bridgeman Art Library)

Lord North (1732–92).
(Gift of Dr and Mrs Frank C. Winter / Bridgeman Art Library)

Henry Temple, 3rd Viscount Palmerston (1784–1865).
(© Philip Mould Ltd London / Bridgeman Art Library)

Arthur Wellesley, Duke of Wellington (1769–1852).
(Bonhams, London / Bridgeman Art Library)

Eviction: bailiffs with a battering ram take possession of an Irish farmhouse; a British soldier (left) and a Hussar officer (foreground) watch the proceedings, c.1890.

(Corbis)

Landlords fight back: the famous Captain Charles Boycott adopts a fiant stance in a posed photograph of about 1880.

(Corbis)

Domestic servants

Liveried coachman with
Newfoundland dog, *c.*1850.
*(New Walk Museum, Leicester/Bridgeman
Art Library)*

Housemaids, *c.*1900.
(Stapleton Collection/Bridgeman Art Library)

Bicycles for two: the newlywed
Lord Suffolk and his second
wife set out for a ride.
(Tatler)

Kick off: Lord Lonsdale opens
a charity soccer match.
(Tatler)

Shooting party.
(Tatler)

Debutantes arriving at Buckingham Palace, 1954.

(Getty Images)

Dark thoughts: an admirer of Hitler, the Duke of Westminster at the Cheshire Hunt Ball.

(Getty Images)

creatures. Even the 'impures of Marylebone' attended a public masquerade at the Pantheon in 1786, mingling with 'people of fashion' who maintained 'that kind of reserve usual for them at guinea masquerades'.[41]

Commercialisation made art less exclusive and less reclusive. The mushroom growth of the print industry after 1750 meant that the banker or the surgeon could acquire engraved copies of Old Masters and fashionable modern painters such as Reynolds. Living artists got the reproduction fees, which made them less dependent on aristocratic patrons, and the middle-class collector could create his own private gallery.[42] Commercialisation infiltrated the world of music. The fourth Earl of Abingdon had been the patron of Haydn's proposed but later abandoned visit to London in 1782, but it was a professional impresario, Johann Saloman, who organised his concerts during the early 1790s. Their press advertisements carried the usual formula 'For the Nobility Gentry', but many others clearly attended, for Haydn was delighted to find that he had established a 'credit with the common people'.[43]

The nature of musical performances was very gradually changing. They had always been social occasions at which the fashionable gathered to meet and converse with familiar friends, although this did not mean that they were inattentive audiences.[44] This custom had disappeared by the middle years of the nineteenth century, when the aristocracy's attendance at operas and concerts declined. Middle-class listeners replaced them and tended to concentrate solely and intensely on the music.[45]

A different kind of earnestness pervaded the middle class's attitude to visual art, which laid a heavy emphasis on didactic instruction and moral worth. In 1849 the Art Union, which had been formed to mass produce and sell prints to the middle class, was offering *The Death of Boadicea*, *The Fall of Satan* and *Richard II and Bolingbroke*. In the same year, in an analysis of the utilitarian functions of art, a critic referred to its capacity to 'strengthen the bonds of the social order' and its 'moral and social value'.[46] This was a long way from the spirit and vision of the Dilettanti, although their principles still animated an older generation of noblemen. In 1845 Wellington told Benjamin Haydon that the aristocracy did not want 'High Art', rather it desired 'first-rate specimens', by which the Duke meant Old Masters.[47]

The moral ethos of society was being transformed, slowly and in accord with the temper of the middle classes. The new mood was apparent at Queen Victoria's court, and after a stay at Windsor in 1838 Charles Greville disapprovingly noted an absence of 'the sociability which makes agreeableness of an English country house' and a lack of room for 'guests to assemble, sit, lounge and chatter'.[48] Public antipathy to duelling intensified. In 1842, Prime Minister Sir Robert Peel responded by adding clauses to the Articles of War which outlawed it, insisted that officers who fought duels were cashiered and withdrew pension rights from the widows of officers killed in duels.

One stalwart of the anti-duelling movement had been Lord Lovaine MP, who was also a fierce supporter of strict Sabbath observance. Evangelicalism had permeated the aristocracy and with it philistinism. During the 1857 debate on the Obscene Publications Bill, two older peers, Lords Brougham and Lyndhurst, wondered whether many Renaissance paintings might be liable to prosecution. The former Lord Chief Justice, Lord Campbell, was unmoved and horrified by the idea of rich collectors possessing such corrupting material.[49] The bill became law and its passage was a significant token of the loss of aristocracy's influence over matters of social conduct. There was some hankering after the old ways: in 1881 Lord Randolph Churchill challenged Lord Hartington to a duel after he had called him 'vile, contumacious, and lying'. Hartington apologised.[50]

17

We Come for Pheasants: Peers and Poachers

Poaching remained a constant irritant for the aristocracy. It was both theft and an insolent disparagement, for only the aristocracy and gentry were permitted to kill game. This privilege was confirmed by the 1671 Game Act, which restricted the taking of game to landowners with estates valued at over £100 a year (freehold) and £150 (leasehold). Wealth accumulated through trade or investment was conspicuously disregarded, and a lawyer with thousands in government stocks committed a crime if he snared a rabbit or potted a pheasant. This mandate was defended and enforced by the nobility and gentry and resented by the rest of society. The war of attrition between poachers and landowners intensified during the eighteenth century and was punctuated by increasingly bloody skirmishes.

Faced with an upsurge of poaching in 1779, a despairing Wiltshire peer suggested that the culprits, who were 'idle fellows', were corralled, dragged to the nearest recruiting sergeant and drafted as reinforcements for the army in North America.[1] It was a solution typical of the times: crime would be reduced by exporting criminals and putting them to good use. It did not work: America was lost, and, like the rest of the country, Wiltshire continued to be plagued by poachers.

If caught, these poachers would have found themselves fighting Americans, whom a British intelligence report had described as infected by doctrines of 'levellism' which endowed all men with 'equality as to birth, fortune and independence'.[2] There was no hereditary aristocracy in the colonies, which, in 1776, had repudiated George III's sovereignty. American law treated slaves as private property, but not deer, hares, rabbits, partridges and pheasants, while French Game Laws were as exclusive as Britain's and as heartily detested. Welcoming the revolution in France in 1789, a Salisbury newspaper editor noted approvingly that: 'Our Gallic neighbours are about to establish the right of farmers and tenants to kill game on their own grounds. May our landed interest go and do likewise.'[3] Nothing was further from its mind, and during the next twenty years further Game Laws were approved by Parliament with little or no debate. The urgent need to protect game transcended partisan politics and united all but a handful of landowners.

The widespread defiance of the spirit behind the Game Laws is just one of a number of loosely connected forms of resistance to the idea of aristocracy and its social and political manifestations during the last two quarters of the eighteenth and the first of the nineteenth centuries. American and French revolutionaries vilified the aristocratic principle as irrational and unjust, and specifically excluded aristocracies from the new social and political orders they constructed. American and French constitutional experiments appealed to some within that growing section of British society, the middle class.

Denials of the aristocratic principle were rooted in the thinking of the European Enlightenment of the late seventeenth and eighteenth centuries. Its conclusions were invoked in 1776 by the American Declaration of Independence, which employed the laws of 'nature and nature's god' to vindicate the assumption that all men were 'of separate and equal station'. The Constitution of the new republic outlawed the creation of a hereditary, titled elite; talent and endeavour dictated an American's place in the world, not ancestry. An alternative social structure had been born, which won converts in Britain, where its advocates argued that it compared favourably with their own, and was refreshingly free from the corruption which Americans believed irredeemably blighted the old world of hereditary princes and noblemen.

Similar claims were made for the egalitarian and democratic order which emerged (briefly) in republican France after 1792, in which monarchy, aristocracy and the God who sanctioned both were successively abolished. The Rights of Man supplanted the will of God, and this substitution was applauded by British radicals who suspected that the nation's vaunted liberties and Constitution were a fig leaf which barely concealed an aristocratic dictatorship.

Poachers were not inspired by philosophical abstractions. Their impulses were visceral and rested in a belief that every man had a God-given right to catch, eat or sell all wild creatures. The poacher did not want to remake the world, he just wished to be left alone to do as he pleased. Yet he was a subversive with a contempt for the law, the legitimate rights and pleasures of the nobility and gentry, and he went abroad armed and at night. When apprehended, poachers insisted, often truculently, that they were exercising their natural rights. 'My men, what are doing you there?' a Norfolk squire shouted to a band of nocturnal intruders in his plantation. 'You bugger, we come for pheasants and pheasants we'll have them,' was their reply.[4]

The squire was backed by a formidable armoury of legislation. In 1707 trading in game was forbidden and throughout the next century the penalties for poaching increased in severity. Fines spiralled and recidivists faced six months in gaol and a whipping, and further terrifying deterrents appeared after 1770. Mantraps which splintered shin bones and spring guns which discharged grapeshot on interlopers were deployed in fields and woodlands. In 1803 the Ellenborough law made an assault on a gamekeeper a capital crime.

Most intimidating of all was the 1723 Black Act, an emergency measure passed hastily and undebated by landowners on the verge of hysteria. Its cause was the 'Blacks', a name given to loose associations of audacious and well-armed criminals, chiefly poachers of deer, who operated on horseback in the forests of Berkshire and Hampshire. Sir Horace Walpole's Whig ministry detected undercurrents of sedition and with the flimsiest evidence branded this 'lawless, riotous sort of people' as covert Jacobites bent on insurrection.

In fact, the Blacks were concerned with taking deer rather than power and were apolitical, preying on landowners of all persuasions. In 1722 gangs of Blacks made two mass raids on the deer parks of the Whig first Earl of Cadogan. Cadogan was a graceless Irishman who had squeezed a fortune out of his services as quartermaster to Marlborough's army. His fellow victims included the crypto-Jacobite Earl of Arran and Thomas Pitt, the grandfather of the prime minister and an artful nabob who had invested some of his Indian treasure in an estate at Swallowfield in Berkshire.[5]

The impudence and depredations of the Blacks were localised, but Walpole made them the excuse for legislation which extended the coercive power of the state to protect property and its owners everywhere. The Black Act made deer stealing, cattle maiming, illegally cutting down trees, extortion and blackmail hanging offences. More crimes, including arson in coal mines, were later added to this list. All were already criminal, but henceforward property was guarded by the gallows. The law, the panic which had triggered it and the hugger-mugger manner of its journey through Parliament are uncannily reminiscent of recent anti-terrorist legislation. Those whom the Black Act protected sometimes found its implementation distasteful, and in 1734 Thomas Paget, the son of a peer and a keen sportsman, wrote:

> Poor rogues in chains but dangle to the wind,
> While rich ones live the terror of mankind.[6]

The Black Act was an ineffective deterrent against poachers. Anecdotal evidence indicated that poaching and the clandestine trade in game were rising. Paget's kinsman and scourge of Staffordshire's poachers, Henry Paget, the ninth Earl of Uxbridge, calculated from his local intelligence sources that his estates, including Cannock Chase, harboured at least eight hundred who could be named, and twice that number who were anonymous. Among those who came within his keepers' view were two labourers who had killed three deer and were hanged in 1744 under the terms of the Black Act.

It was easier to measure the extent of poaching in the next century when the state's bureaucracies compiled statistics on just about every form of human activity. The results were chilling for landowners. In 1817 over a thousand poachers were gaoled, and, thirty years later, one-seventh of all convictions were for offences against the Game Laws and the tally of imprisoned poachers had nearly trebled. Forty-two keepers had been murdered between 1833 and 1842 and others suffered terrible injuries.[7] On one December's evening in 1843 a keeper patrolling near Speckley in Oxfordshire accosted a well-known poacher and set his bulldog Spring on the man after he produced a gun barrel from beneath his jacket.. Spring mistook his target and attacked the poacher's dog, leaving its owner free to bludgeon the keeper with the gun barrel, breaking his arm and cracking his skull. He was later arrested, tried and sentenced to twenty years transportation.[8]

Just about every landowner joined the offensive against poachers. In 1756 the Society of Noblemen and Gentlemen for the Preservation of Game was formed with the aim of prosecuting poachers and closing the black market in game. The society retained the sharpest lawyers, including a former Attorney-General, Sir Fletcher Norton ('Sir Bull-Face-Double-Fee'), and announced its successes in the press.[9] Individual noblemen adopted their own measures, not all of them coercive. In 1756 Lord Weymouth employed an agent to procure the enlistment of a notorious poacher, and, in 1776, the fourth Duke of Queensberry accepted a bond of one hundred pounds from an obviously prosperous gang who promised to keep off his lands.[10] Presumably this immunity did not extend to his neighbours' coverts. The sixth Duke of Bedford, a radical Whig, was lenient towards a poacher from his own household since he 'had been a good servant and . . . very zealous in the discharge of his duty'.[11] This exemplary devotion did not extend to the Duke's rabbits.

Magistrates adjusted sentences according to the youth and previous character of the accused, so that a callow novice might escape with a five-shilling fine. Exile and hard labour in Australia awaited poachers who resisted arrest. Three were transported for seven years in 1820 after an exchange of shots and cudgel blows when a gang of seventeen poachers had been ambushed by nineteen keepers in Cainhoe Park near Ampthill in Bedfordshire.

That county's coverts were then in a virtual state of siege. The sixth Duke of Bedford took the lead and attempted to reassert

the authority of the law (and landowners like himself) by offering rewards of one hundred pounds to informers and recruiting
'active and intelligent' local constables to track down suspects.
They undertook their sleuthing in a carefree manner, treating
suspects in pubs and charging the bills (one of fifty pounds) to
the Duke. Excusing this extravagance, the constables alleged that
they were securing the goodwill of the locals, which was essential if they were to identify poachers and uncover their plans.[12]

·Regular keepers, who could earn as much as forty pounds a
year, were by reason of their occupation unloved and isolated
figures within their communities. Some took backhanders,
others turned a blind eye to poaching, and all took precautions.
Giving evidence in the 1847 trial of a man who had murdered
his colleague, a Northumberland gamekeeper told the jury: 'My
dog is between a Newfoundland and bloodhound; he is very
large, but I do not know how savage he is ... he has been
trained to scent a man.'[13]

In all likelihood, the quarry tracked by this fearsome hybrid
would have been a professional or semi-professional poacher. He
was a businessman (one gang of Suffolk poachers had a bank
account) dealing in a contraband commodity which always commanded a good price. In the 1820s a hare fetched two shillings
and a brace of pheasants three shillings and sixpence. These were
tempting sums when farm labourers seldom earned more than
seven shillings a week; a night's poaching could bring in the
equivalent of a month's earnings. Forget the sentimental image
of the poacher as a poor man risking his freedom to find food for
his starving family. He was more likely to have been (and still is)
a ruthless entrepreneur working the black market and making a
better living than he could in regular employment. John Banks,
indicted at Chester in 1859 as accessory to the slaying of a
keeper, had a criminal record which stretched back twenty-
seven years and included charges of poaching, assaults on keepers
and attempted murder. He was one of a gang armed with guns

and cutlasses, and two of his partners were found guilty of murdering a keeper and hanged.[14] There no was romance in the world of poaching.

For the aristocracy and gentry, the enforcement of the Game Laws was the defence of their legitimate property rights, their prestige in the countryside and the sovereignty of the law. On a personal level, they were protecting what gave them infinite pleasure: hunting was still the aristocracy's prime source of diversion. It was enjoyed to the full by Joseph Addison's country squire Sir Roger de Coverley, who, in the pages of *The Spectator*, chased hares at least twice a week. Addison found the exercise invigorating:

> I must confess the brightness of the weather, the cheerfulness of everything around me, the chiding of the hounds, which was returned upon us in a double echo, from the neighbouring hills, with hallowing of the sportsmen and the sounding of the horn, lifted my spirits into a most lively pleasure, which I freely indulged because I was sure it was innocent.[15]

Sir Roger's mental vigour was the consequence of his hunting, which was an antidote to over-indulgence at the table and the sedentary inertia of public duty. Although heavily engaged in politics, the second Duke of Richmond was always reluctant to go to London during the hunting season. Rather, he preferred the sheer joy of a day's ride across the downs and was indifferent to how the chase ended. He once confessed to the pleasure of having been thwarted by 'a true gallant Sussex fox'.[16]

It must have been a resourceful animal, for Richmond's Charlton Hunt was celebrated and attracted a galaxy of huntsmen; seventeen peers attended one meet in 1743. Hunting of all kinds was an opportunity for fellowship and the quality of sport provided was a measure of a nobleman's standing among his equals. From the mid-eighteenth century greater resources than ever were concentrated on game preservation and it became common to supplement stocks with hand-reared and semi-tame pheasants and partridges. An artificial abundance of game was essential for the now fashionable 'battues' in which beaters flushed out birds which were shot by lines of guns. In 1800 a day's bag of eighty pheasants and forty partridges and hares was considered excellent; a hundred years later tallies were in the hundreds, even thousands. Colonel Thomas Wood, MP for Brecon and a sportsman of the old school, thought these mas- sacres deplorable. They were, he told the Commons in 1819, 'as different from English hunting as French gentlemen were from English gentlemen'.[17]

Maintaining stocks of pheasants, which the Colonel claimed were 'as tame as chickens', was expensive for landowners and burdensome for their tenants. Calculations based on about four hundred acres of the Duke of Rutland's estates revealed an annual loss of £916.[18] Tenant farmers bore the brunt of these depredations by creatures that the law forbade them to kill. Yet game preservation served an economic function, or so its sup- porters alleged. They repeatedly argued that while in essence the Game Laws were selfish, they were invaluable to the rural econ- omy since the persecution of poachers helped drive the poor towards lawful and productive employment.

By the early nineteenth century, the harsh pragmatism and the harsher realities of the implementation of the Game Laws were stirring consciences. The moral and intellectual climate was changing; Evangelicalism emphasised an active, compassionate Christianity which expressed itself in concern for the weak and poor, and there were strands in Romanticism which attributed sentience to animals. In his 1794 poem 'To a Young Ass', Coleridge addresses the creature as one of 'an oppressed race', and, like Rousseau, Shelley advocated vegetarianism as a positive way of reducing the cruel exploitation of animals.

An equivocal reflection on this theme appears on George Stubbs's *Freeman, the Earl of Clarendon's gamekeeper, with a dying doe and hound*, painted in 1800 towards the end of a life in which he had painted many stirring hunting scenes. Against a sombre woodland background, the keeper is poised to cut the throat of a wounded and wide-eyed doe, while his hound seems about to intercede. We do not know whether the creature is the victim of a poacher or of a cull. The dapper keeper stares impassively at the onlooker as he performs his duty to his master, who commissioned the picture.[19] Yet, there is a disconcerting quality to what otherwise might be another celebration of the world of hunting, for our sympathies (and perhaps those of the hound) are directed towards the stricken doe. And yet contemporary sportsmen would have seen merely a very minor, everyday episode in the perpetuation of their pleasure.

It was concern for the human victims of game preservation that led to a Parliamentary challenge to the Game Laws in 1819; it was delivered by Thomas Brand, a Whig MP and landowner. He wanted to jettison the underlying principle of the legislation so that all species of game would be treated as 'the property of the person on whose lands it was found'. Henceforward, tenant farmers would be permitted to kill game on their own property. While Brand's supporters condemned the present laws as 'vicious and tyrannical' and 'odious', others rushed to their defence. Thomas Bankes, possessor of sixty thousand acres in Dorset and MP for the rotten borough of Corfe, warned that a relaxation of the Game Laws would lead to a free-for-all and the extinction of all the game in the country, which is what had happened in France after the Revolution. Sir John Shelley, a Corinthian dandy and gambler, predicted that if gentlemen were denied their sport, Bonaparte would be vindicated and Britain would indeed become 'a nation of shopkeepers'.

William Wilberforce was in a quandary. As a Tory he was bound to uphold the law, although he feared that sending poachers to county gaols or flogging them compromised the moral standing of the magistracy, 'who constituted the glory and honour of our domestic government'. Wilberforce the Evangelical humanitarian was further distressed by oppressive statutes which punished poachers for merely following the natural, economic laws of supply and demand.[20] The bill passed two readings, which says something for the strength of disquiet about the Game Laws in a predominantly landowning and Tory Commons, but it died during its committee stage. It is highly unlikely that the Lords would have agreed to forfeit a legal privilege at a time when their monopoly of political power was under attack. Amelioration came slowly and in the teeth of opposition from the beneficiaries of the Game Laws. In 1827 spring guns were banned, and in 1831 dealing in game under licence was permitted. Rural opinion was turning against the Game Laws. After the murder of a keeper by poachers on the Earl of Coventry's estate at Croome in Worcestershire in 1844, the coroner's jury protested against 'the continuation of laws so immoral in their tendency, so fruitful in crime and so destructive of human life'.[21]

18

A Gang of Ruffians:
Americans and
Aristocracy

'No kind of government is so mischievous as aristocracy,' Benjamin Towne warned readers of the *Pennsylvania Evening Press* in November 1776. He advised citizens of the fledgling American republic to reject a model for a state legislature that included a chamber 'something like a House of Lords' where, it was hoped, 'wisdom will forever reign'. History suggested the opposite; British peers, once the militant 'guardians of liberty', had had their freewill and nerve sapped by corruption. The guard dogs of liberty in 1688, the aristocracy was now the lap dog of George III. Why else had the House of Lords consistently voted to deny Americans their rightful liberties as Britons?[1] In fact, roughly a third of the Lords had been sympathetic towards the colonists' grievances, but what mattered was that in the rebel imagination the aristocracy had been and was an accessory to George III's despotism.

Aristocratic distrust of the masses was ingrained according to another Philadelphia journalist, Thomas Paine. A former Suffolk corsetmaker, he had drifted through various occupations, emigrated and in America discovered an audience for his pent-up grievances. He also found a knack of addressing artisans and labourers in a language they understood. Paine gave a pungent form to sentiments which they felt, but could rarely articulate. His polemic pamphlet *Common Sense* first appeared early in 1776 and went through twenty-five editions in a few years. It was a caustic denunciation of monarchy with sideswipes at aristocracy.

Paine attacked his enemies where they were weakest. He stripped kings and the noblemen of their ancient mystique. He probed history to expose its flawed foundations: the modern peer was merely the descendant of the 'principal ruffian of a gang of ruffians' who had clawed his way to authority over his fellows; while George III owed his throne to a 'French bastard' who had conquered England with 'an armed banditti'. Overlordship, gained disreputably, perverted its inheritors: 'Men who look upon themselves born to reign, and others to obey, soon grow insolent.'[2]

Paine's readers included many humble rank-and-file soldiers who were then risking their lives in a war against George III's armies, and who hoped that a political revolution might mutate into a social one. Everyone knew that there was no hereditary aristocracy in America, but there was a groundswell of apprehension that the rich planters, merchants and lawyers who had orchestrated the opposition to George III's taxes and framed the Declaration of Independence were aristocrats at heart. 'Men of rank', warned a Paineite convert, secretly desired to impose 'the system of Lord and Vassal . . . common in Europe'.[3]

This was partly true. Many 'men of rank' had convinced themselves that it was in the best interests of the republic to preserve the colonial hierarchy based upon property and general esteem. The representatives of the colonies who assembled in the Continental Congress had no wish to upset the existing social fabric. In 1776 it decreed that all officers in the American army were to be addressed as 'esquire' or 'gentleman' and were legally bound to uphold the 'character of an officer and gentleman' and could be dismissed if they did not.[4] Early in 1777, and after defeats around New York, Congress proposed to invest officers with an 'Order of Independency' with a green riband for 'knight companions' as 'a spur' to their efforts in the field.[5] General Washington was addressed as 'Your Excellency', and the Marquis de la Fayette, the commander-in-chief of French forces in America, was amused to find that senior American commanders soaked up flattery and expected 'more respect' than an emperor.[6] Americans were susceptible to aristocratic charm; in 1780 Philadelphians were struck by 'the politeness and manners' of blue-blooded French and German officers serving as advisers to the Continental army.[7]

There had always been an ambivalence towards rank in American society. On one hand, there was a faith in abstract equality, and on the other, a wish to live within an orderly, stratified world in which outstanding talent and industry were publicly honoured. Colonial society had always been layered, and there was an abundance of rich men who expected deference and believed that their property and success gave them the wisdom to rule others. The poorer colonists would have recognised a de facto aristocracy, and subsequent historians have treated the wealthiest planters in the southern colonies and the commercial elites of the northern as a functioning aristocracy in terms of their political sway and social dominance.

A visitor to Virginia in the 1740s was impressed by the 'dignity and decorum' of the Williamsburg court sessions, where gentlemen justices assembled in a court room decorated with portraits of the royal family and former governors.[8] There were acute social tensions in North Carolina in the 1760s when poor, backcountry farmers clashed with the planters, lawyers and businessmen who had a stranglehold on the legislature. These murmurings echoed the protests against the English aristocracy and gentry in the sixteenth and seventeenth centuries, and, like them, were silenced by force.[9] The egalitarianism implicit in the Declaration of Independence did not change attitudes; a patrician Philadelphian reviled the soldiers of the republic as 'in general damned riff-raff – dirty mutineers and disaffected'.[10] In Maryland, the architects of the state's new constitution laid down stiff property qualifications for electors and office-holders.

Colonial America was proof that a hierarchy could exist without a hereditary aristocracy at its apex. British noblemen did visit the colonies, but they were birds of passage like the colonial governors who departed when their term of office ended. There was no point whatsoever in a peer settling in the colonies; he was cut off from London and the sources of political power in the Lords and royal patronage. Those aristocrats to whom the Crown had granted swathes of the American wilderness preferred to stay at home and leave the management of their windfalls to agents, or sell up to residents.

Domiciled aristocrats would have been tolerated in America, but they would not have received the automatic respect they had grown accustomed to at home, and they would have had virtually no political clout, for the colonial assemblies had no provision for hereditary legislators. The political and social ethos that was developing in North America diverged from that in Britain. The differences were already clear by 1768, when General Guy Carleton, the Governor-General of Canada, predicted that: 'The British form of government will never produce the same fruits as at home, chiefly because it is impossible for the dignity of the throne, *or the peerage* [my italics] to be represented in the American forests.' Where land was plentiful and cheap, it could not have the same prestige as in Britain. Moreover, those who settled it adopted an egalitarian mentality. Carleton also noted that elected local assemblies inclined towards 'a strong bias to republican principles' and the people's 'independent spirit of democracy' was incompatible with 'submission to the Crown'.[11]

For most immigrants, the process of colonisation was one of liberation. In 1786, Anna Gillis, a Gaelic poetess lately arrived in Canada, celebrated her new freedom and that of her fellow colonists from Knoydart on the west coast of Scotland.

> *We got farms of our own*
> *with proprietary rights from the king,*
> *and landlords will no more oppress us.*[12]

The final line says it all: North America offered prospects of economic independence and with it chances of individual advancement that were lacking at home. Since the early seventeenth century, the colonies had been populated by fortune seekers, refugees from Anglican intolerance and smaller numbers of debtors, petty criminals, vagrants, prostitutes and royalists and Jacobite prisoners of war. The ambitious, discontented and unwanted coalesced into a society which evolved its own values and rules appropriate to a fiercely competitive world in which individuals were free to find their own level in society. Advancement depended solely upon enterprise, intelligence and hard graft.

These qualities bestowed dignity and commanded respect. Yet the social superiority and pretensions of, say, a Virginian tobacco planter were the consequence of his own industry rather than his birth. Unlike the British nobleman, he owed his place in the world to his achievements, not his ancestry. The Virginian called himself 'esquire', but his standing in the world was gauged by the number of slaves he owned, rather than a dependent tenantry. Nor did the planter, or, for that matter, any other rich colonial feel bound by custom or family obligation to pass his estate intact to his eldest son. On the whole, Americans had no truck with primogeniture and entails, those legal contrivances essential for a permanent aristocracy.

Both were considered unjust and were abolished by the Continental Congress in 1779. This act had been strongly urged by Thomas Jefferson, one of the founding fathers and a future president. He believed with equal passion in the rights of property (he was a well-to-do planter and slave owner) and in the right of everyone to be fairly rewarded for their labour and the application of natural talents. Primogeniture and entails prevented this; they enriched the eldest at the expense of his siblings, and reduced their capacity to progress upwards in the world. American law encouraged the continual fragmentation of estates and discouraged drones, whom Jefferson saw as harmful to the republic. In 1786, when serving as ambassador in France, he was outraged by the way in which the aristocracy allowed so much land to be 'idle in the pursuit of game'.[13] Visiting America in the 1830s, the French aristocrat Alexis de Tocqueville observed that the absence of primogeniture allowed wealth to circulate 'with inconceivable rapidity' and that 'it is rare to find two succeeding generations in full enjoyment of it'.

The American spiritual frame of mind was never conducive to the idea of aristocracy. A large proportion of immigrants, particularly in New England, were dissenters who preserved their traditional antipathy towards Anglicanism and its hierarchy. Neither put down deep roots in the colonies; there were no bishops and few parsons to preach obedience and non-resistance. In 1717 Lord Baltimore, the proprietor of Maryland, attempted to instal Anglican ministers in the colony, but was frustrated by the colonial assembly. A Whig lawyer remarked in the 1750s that 'the body of the people are for an equal toleration of protestants and utterly averse to any kind of ecclesiastical establishment'.[14]

During the 1775–6 campaigns, Colonel Lord Rawdon Hastings disdainfully noted the prevalence of dissenters in the American army. They were 'ignorant bigots', he told his uncle, the Earl of Huntingdon, and he found the 'godly twang' of the 'Yankees' discordant.[15] Moreover, Americans were purblind to the niceties of war as waged by gentlemen. In 1775 General Sir Thomas Gage complained to Washington about the maltreatment of prisoners of war forced to work 'like Negro slaves'. Such brutality diminished 'the glory of civilised nations' which had endeavoured to make 'humanity and war . . . compatible'.[16] American officers cared little for this accommodation of opposites and, in 1780, General Lord Cornwallis again appealed for kinder usage of prisoners. 'I have always endeavoured to soften the horrors of war,' he added, reflecting a view common among senior British commanders.[17] There were dissidents, including Hastings, who convinced themselves that the amateur soldiers of Congress and their civilian supporters would quickly throw in the sponge if treated with the utmost severity. Some aristocrats quietly sympathised with the rebels; Richard Fitzpatrick, the son of an Irish peer and officer in the Guards, regretted having to fight a war against men who had 'justice and truth on their side'.[18]

While some of their brothers-in-arms ignored the proprieties which theoretically restrained British generals, American officers quickly adopted the essentially aristocratic codes of personal honour of their British and French counterparts. Duelling was one result, and it became embedded in the culture of the revolutionary and then the regular army of the United States. Gentlemanly honour was consonant with individual equality, a point made by Albert Johnson, a future Confederate general, in 1845 after he had vindicated his reputation with his troops by fighting a fellow officer. 'Manly virtue was integral to democracy,' he declared.'[19]

After having beaten the British, former American officers attempted to preserve their elevated wartime status by banding together in the Order of Cincinnati. Membership was confined to former officers, their sons and collateral male heirs who would wear a blue riband and medal.[20] This was later superseded by a more impressive gold eagle which resembled the insignia of a European order of knighthood. These proposals stirred up press hysteria: the republic was about to be subverted by a crypto-aristocracy. One New England journalist predicted that each member of the Order would think himself 'a peer of the realm' and another was shocked that Americans could be so easily ensnared by the 'ostentatious' trappings of nobility. A third denounced the Order as 'contrary to the spirit of free government' and several states outlawed it.[21]

The squall of protests which followed the formation of the Order of Cincinnati suggests that some Americans feared that their new republican culture needed protection from insidious notions of aristocracy. In 1788 this apprehension was expressed in the federal constitution, which placed a perpetual veto on the introduction of hereditary privileges and titles. They were un-American insofar as they denied the ideals of nominal equality for white males and limited democracy (property ownership alone defined the politically active citizen) embodied in the Declaration of Independence. Alexis de Tocqueville concluded that the 'aristocratic element' had always been weak in America and, fifty years after independence, had virtually no influence in the politics of the republic.[22]

Had de Tocqueville toured America in the 1850s, he would have detected an atavistic inclination towards distinctively aristocratic fancies among the plantocracy of the southern, slave-owning states. Its members of both sexes read the medieval novels of Sir Walter Scott and aped the romantic world he had depicted. The southern gentleman was a man of exquisite manners; he possessed the honour of a knight; fought duels to defend his own and any lady's reputation; he carried a sword at assemblies; and rode well. Southern pseudo-chivalry was a cultural expression of a growing political and economic rift between the North and South. The northerners were bourgeois moneybags who cared for nothing but profit and were numb to the finer feelings which animated gentlemen.

Defeat in America had tarnished the prestige of the British political establishment. George III, his ministers and generals had blundered and their ineptitude had deprived the nation of a valuable commercial asset and lowered its international standing. Americans had lost faith in monarchy and constitution, and reformers at home were sympathetic since, like the rebels, they were denied representation. After the war, conservatives argued that American democracy was shallow and transient. Aristocracies were indispensable for a sophisticated state and so, as the economy of the United States expanded, an aristocracy would naturally emerge.[23]

It did not. The minority of Americans who had repudiated monarchy and the aristocratic principle in 1776 were also rejecting the doctrines which for so long had justified them as the best way for states to be governed. The rebels were not only at war with an obdurate King, but with that historic wisdom stretching back to Aristotle which justified the authority of all kings and aristocrats. They and the accumulated dogma which justified them were incubi which had to be exorcised.

This was the opinion of Jefferson, whose vision of the ordering of the new republic profoundly influenced its early development. He believed that the United States represented a fundamental break with the past and its dusty ideologies, which were stumbling blocks to human progress and happiness. The truth of this was self-evident since in Europe (and Britain) the veneration of ancient ideas and forms had produced infirm, corrupt and unfair societies. America would be different since reason had liberated its people from the oppression of history, leaving them free to evolve in dynamic and wholly new ways.

The infancy of the American republic proved that a nation

could flourish without an aristocracy and do so spectacularly. Its progress inspired British reformers; the United States was a beacon for radicals and an example of what could be achieved if a country discarded the lumber of the past which conservatives venerated as 'the wisdom of our ancestors'. 'America offers a glorious instance of a successful democratic rebellion,' declared the radical journal *The Gorgon* in 1819, which every 'aristocrat would gladly blot from the memory of mankind'.[24]

In the same year, Percy Shelley wrote admiringly that, unlike Britain, the United States 'constitutionally acknowledges the progress of human improvement'. Americans had turned their backs on what Shelley considered the mistakes of history and made themselves 'a free, happy and strong people'. Their condition contrasted favourably with that of the bulk of his countrymen suffering under a heartless and antiquated system.[25]

19

The Aristocrat to
Quell: Peers, Patriots
and Paineites
1789–1815

The events between the fall of the Bastille in July 1789 and the creation of the French Republic in November 1792 had a shattering impact on the nobility of Europe. They were vilified as idle parasites, the principles which upheld their pre-eminence were denied and derided, and revolutionary ideologues predicted their impending and violent extinction. It was already underway in France, where aristocrats lost their titles, legislative powers, legal and fiscal privileges and often their lands and lives. All this was reported in the British press and the anecdotes of aristocratic émigrés provided often lurid evidence of the malice and cruelty of the revolutionary mob. Sans-culottes may not have feasted on the corpses of aristocrats, as some alleged, but it seemed that all which was noble, gracious and honourable in France was being trampled under the 'hoofs of the swinish multitude'.

These were the words of an Irishman, Edmund Burke, a Whig MP and one-time Parliamentary proponent of American liberties. He had followed events in France with growing dismay and was disturbed by the purblind and, he believed, dangerous acceptance of revolutionary doctrines in Britain. In November 1790 he published his *Reflections on the Revolution in France*, which was intended as a warning to those naive spirits who had talked themselves into believing that the Revolution was the first stage in a humane and rational remaking of the world. Rather, Burke contended that it was a concentrated, vindictive and sacrilegious offensive against civilisation. Parallels then being drawn between conditions in pre-revolutionary France and Britain were false and mischievous, as were direct comparisons between the French *noblesse* and the British aristocracy.

Embedded in Burke's political and philosophical analysis was a heartfelt, eloquent obituary for the French aristocracy. Marie Antoinette's mistreatment by the Paris mob was proof of the terminal decay of the chivalric spirit that had once animated generations of noblemen. No French peer had drawn his sword for his Queen, leaving Burke to conclude that 'Never, never more, shall we behold that generous loyalty to rank and sex, that proud submission, that dignified obedience' which had been the quintessence of chivalry. Nevertheless, Burke's encounters with individual French noblemen had revealed 'men of a high spirit' and 'a delicate sense of honour' who were 'tolerably well bred . . . humane, and hospitable'. Their behaviour towards the 'inferior classes' was affable and more familiar than that of their British counterparts, and, as landlords, they were no worse than Britain's landowners.[1]

The value of the aristocracy was simple and inestimable. 'Nobility is a graceful ornament to the civil order. It is the Corinthian capital of polished society.' It was also, Burke believed, a living expression of the historic continuity of society, that thread which bound the present to the past. 'Nobility,' Burke argued, 'forms the chain that connects the ages of a nation.' Later, he expanded on this theme when he praised the benefits of the uninterrupted ownership of land. 'The idea of inheritance furnishes a sure principle of conservation and . . . of transmission; without at all excluding a principle of improvement.' History and the advance of civilisation were processes of organic and natural growth; whatever survived and flourished did so because it had grown out of what had gone before and had been tested by time. The existence of an aristocracy both illustrated and validated Burke's theory of history.

There were pragmatic reasons for the preservation of aristocracy. In Britain, it was the sheet anchor of a legislature that contrasted favourably with the new French National Assembly. On one hand, there was a Parliament 'filled with everything illustrious in rank, in descent, in hereditary and acquired opulence, in cultivated talents, in civil, naval and political distinction'. On the other, was a body dominated by 'obscure provincial advocates' and, most frightening of all, ignorant men often 'immersed in hopeless poverty' who regarded 'all property, whether secular or ecclesiastical with no other eye than that of envy'.

Burke's *Reflections* sold nineteen thousand copies in England within a year. It was a seminal vindication of those ancient truths and customs which had always been a 'compass to govern us'. Burke's conclusions were also prophetic, for he had diagnosed France as infected by an uncontrollable collective lunacy. Its symptoms were soon self-evident: the declaration of a republic, the trial and execution of Louis XVI, massive confiscations of aristocratic and church lands, and the abolition of God. Expansionist war was integral to the new French order (as it was to Nazi Germany) and Revolutionary armies invaded the Low Countries and the Rhineland, where they established republics on the French model.

Revolutionary sympathisers in Britain answered Burke

robustly. The proto-feminist Mary Wollstonecraft was among the first with, in 1790, her *Vindication of the Rights of Men* and set the tone for much of what followed. Aristocrats were 'petty tyrants' who oppressed the weak (she cited the Game Laws) and Burke had disregarded the 'silent majority of misery' in his account of the condition of the French people.[2] Perhaps the most trenchant and certainly the most widely read riposte to Burke was Thomas Paine's *The Rights of Man* which appeared in two parts in 1791 and 1792, the second appearing shortly before the author's indictment for treason.

Paine's counterblast elaborated on the themes of his shorter pamphlet, *Common Sense*, of sixteen years before. Its lengthier successor denounced monarchy, aristocracy, the Constitution and the Church of England as fraudulent and oppressive. Paine urged his readers to purge their minds of the accretions of mumbo-jumbo which had justified these institutions and look to America and France to learn how a nation could be fairly and honestly governed in the interests of all. At various stages, he engaged Burke head-on. The 'Quixotic age of chivalry nonsense' and the aristocracy were about to perish, victims of a preordained sequence of governments. The age of 'priestcraft' had vanished, that of 'conquerors' was passing and that of 'reason' was imminent.

The British aristocracy and the French *noblesse* were the same species with the same selfish instincts and habits. Paine dismissed the notion of a hereditary lawmaker 'as absurd as an hereditary mathematician, or a hereditary wise man; and as ridiculous as an hereditary poet-laureate'.[3] (This gibe was resurrected by Jack Straw, the New Labour Home Secretary, during the debate on the future of the Lords in 1998. Echoes of Burke were heard in the Lords when the life peer Lord Cobbold praised the 'traditions, pageantry and mystique of a seven-hundred-year-old institution that is part of the fabric of the country'.)[4]

Burke and Paine had opened a still unresolved debate on the legitimacy and usefulness of the aristocracy. Both writers deployed reason to powerful effect, but Burke laced his arguments with emotional appeals to the imagination. Paine's mindset was that of a man utterly convinced of his own rectitude, and his tone was often captious and doctrinaire. He loved statistics and used them to reveal how taxes were syphoned into royal and aristocratic pockets.

Most important of all in terms of the future nature and course of British politics, Paine had compiled a text that gave a rational coherence to a hitherto inchoate sense of frustration and injustice felt by humble men and women. They were dissatisfied by the status quo and now they knew exactly why, and what needed to be changed. Mentally armed by Paine, his readers were ready to repudiate the past and their superiors' veneration of a wisdom which had been contrived to keep them in perpetual subordination. Paine's historical process was not evolutionary in the Burkean sense, but revolutionary. Its goal was that liberation of mankind which, he imagined, had been accomplished in the United States and was underway in France.

Paine won converts, but he lost the debate. It was halted by Pitt's emergency wartime legislation passed between 1794 and 1799, which silenced political debate and drove Paineites underground. The establishment remained physically secure, although prone to occasional spasms of bad nerves brought on by rumours of phantom revolutionary conspiracies. Burke had provided intellectual security through an ideology which reinforced the status quo and confounded its enemies. Yet Paine's ideas had not been extinguished; they survived to provide ammunition for future generations of radicals and, in time, socialists. Moderates harnessed Paine's logic to arguments for franchise reform and extremists worked to fulfil his vision of democratic republic. All shared his rejection of the aristocratic principle as bogus and moribund.

*

The Rights of Men and Reflections on the Revolution in France were the opening salvos in a war of pamphlets and speeches. It became increasingly one-sided after George III's proclamation against sedition in May 1792 and the French Republic's declaration of war on Britain the following February. The war was more than another Anglo-French military contest of the kind that had been fought for the past hundred years. It was a struggle for national survival in which Britain was defending its Constitution and liberties from an ideological offensive. Addressing the Commons in 1794, George Canning reminded his listeners that defeat would mean their replacement by a 'Corresponding Society or a Scotch Convention' and submission to the will of some satrap of the French Committee of Public Safety.[5] This was happening on the Continent where indigenous quislings were assisting French armies of occupation.

War transformed Paine's followers into a potential fifth column. Their corresponding societies (there were about ninety in 1795) and the Edinburgh convention of radicals referred to by Canning were placed under intelligence surveillance. Henry Dundas told Canning that it was his duty as a Secretary of State to spy on anyone 'meditating mischief and sedition' and so his agents had penetrated corresponding societies and kept him fore-warned of their plans. Some of the intelligence gathered was used for prosecutions under the new anti-sedition laws.

Moderate government supporters in Parliament wondered whether the legislation was too severe and if the threat of sub-version had been deliberately inflated by ministers. Perhaps so, but domestic economic problems, including poor harvests and food shortages, generated outbreaks of restlessness which could easily have been exploited by Paineite agitators.

Occasionally, the hidden enemy broke cover. Paineite par-tisans appeared among the sailors tried after the Spithead and Nore mutinies of 1797. One, a member of the London Corresponding Society, told his shipmates that 'he had traced history and could not discover any one good quality belonging to him [George III]'. A ringleader at the Nore had foretold that the mutiny 'shouldn't end until the head is off King George and Billy Pitt'. 'Damn and bugger the King! We want no king!' declared another mutineer.[6] Posters appeared in Lewes in 1795 calling upon militiamen to defy their officers and 'join the Rage, the Aristocrat to quell'.[7] In 1812 an anonymous Huddersfield Luddite warned a local mill owner that his fellow machine-breakers would overthrow the 'Hanover tyrant' with the help of Napoleon and create 'a just republic'.[8]

Had all these angry men read Paine? Some clearly had, for court martial evidence indicated that agitators discussed his ideas with their illiterate shipmates, not all of whom were sympathetic. The Huddersfield Luddite knew his Paine, but were his comrades driven by an urge to remake the nation? The answer is 'No'. Like the sailors, the Luddites and nearly everyone who protested at this time were denouncing (and sometimes punishing) scapegoats rather than declaring war on the political system from which their authority was derived. Their targets were sadistic officers, heartless Poor Law bureaucrats, modernising industrialists who substituted machines for men in the name of efficiency and farmers and grain merchants who added to the miseries of the poor by playing the market in times of shortage. Lords were more likely to be troubled by burglars and highwaymen than protesting mobs.

They did, however, suffer defamation by Paineite polemicists, whose pamphlets depicted the nobility as rapacious, overbearing and extravagant. These enemies of the people built 'elegant dog kennels' and turned arable land into pasture for their hunters, while 'the honest and labouring poor' endured privation. The nobility was also decadent; one strait-laced Paineite (and many were) castigated the aristocracy as 'the detestable patrons of boxers and strumpets'.[9]

Open Paineites were a fragmented minority united only by

their exclusion from conventional politic life; they embraced intellectuals like Mary Wollstonecraft and her circle; they were urban professional men, shopkeepers, craftsmen and artisans, in short the kind of people Burke had identified as the malign impetus behind the French Assembly and its levelling policies. There were also nonconformists, but their enthusiasm for radicalism was shaken by the militant atheism of the French Republic. Most Paineites favoured political reform through persuasion, although a minority called for an armed revolution. Internal disagreements, lack of an efficient national organisation, and, after 1793, official persecution combined with popular, patriotic hostility combined to neuter the radical movement. Nonetheless, a handful of covert Paineites from Burke's 'swinish multitude' revealed their existence through isolated acts of individual defiance to authority, either by public outbursts or through clandestine handbills.

But the aristocracy was in no immediate danger. Its political authority was unshaken; of the fifty-two men who held ministerial office between 1783 and 1815, forty were peers. Paradoxically, the threat from below actually strengthened the power of the aristocracy, the Crown and the Anglican Church. Each was a beneficiary of a deluge of propaganda written to convince Britons that their Constitution gave them freedom, wealth and domestic harmony. As Lord Mulgrave reminded the Lords in 1794: 'This war which has been declared against us is not an ordinary war, it is a war for the annihilation of our laws, our liberties, our prosperity, our civilisation and our religion.'[10]

What had more or less been taken for granted in the past now had to be vindicated through reason coupled with appeals to old-fashioned patriotism, including Francophobia. Paine's comparison of the French and British aristocracies were invidious, claimed one loyalist pamphleteer, for the French *noblesse* had been 'ignorant, proud and tyrannical'. By contrast, the Lords was filled with the 'best men' in a nation who were not, as Paine had alleged, effeminate, degenerate 'drones'.[11] The peerage was manly and athletic (witness their prowess in the hunting field) and many lords had reached their eminence through their intelligence and industry.

A considerable effort was made to portray the nobility as an elite of ability, rather than birth. Loyalist literature insisted that the word 'aristocracy' did not describe a system of government in which power was held exclusively by a rich minority. Rather, the aristocracy was just one, admittedly very important element in a Constitution that was of universal benefit. A few loyalist hacks edged towards the idea that the peerage represented a meritocracy, and attempted to redefine the aristocracy as a broad elite which contained everyone who created wealth, including traders and manufacturers.

Arguments along these lines were made to win over the middle classes, who had to understand that any assault against the aristocracy and their lands was a general attack on property as a whole.[12] Revolution endangered factory owners, farmers and shopkeepers as well as noblemen. The anti-sedition laws supplemented the work of government propagandists; any slander or libel directed against the aristocracy was criticism of the Constitution and liable for prosecution.

Loyalism prevailed. By 1800 that stout-hearted curmudgeon John Bull had been persuaded that the House of Lords was an essential part of that bulwark which protected him, his family, his home, his tankard of ale and plate of roast beef from Gallic predators and their homegrown accomplices. Furthermore, Burke's prognosis as to the final outcome of the revolution had been correct. Frenchmen had lapsed into a prolonged madness and placed themselves in the hands of a gang of demagogues and atheists without education, honour or possessions of their own; the elevation of the jealous had been accompanied by a slide into depravity. In 1799, the *Anti-Jacobin* described Paris under the Consulate as 'the most filthy place in Europe' and its rulers as slaves to 'luxury, dissipation and debauchery'.[13] Ultra-loyalists argued that France could only be brought to its senses by the full restoration of its *ancien régime*.[14]

Its political ascendancy secured, a confident aristocracy threw itself into the war effort with varying degrees of enthusiasm. An overwhelming majority of peers backed the Tory-dominated coalitions which ran the country between 1793 and 1815. Noblemen commanded armies and fleets and represented Britain at the courts of the Continental powers, cajoling emperors, kings and princes into alliances, usually with pledges of subsidies. Diplomacy was traditionally an aristocratic art practised by men of breeding and fine manners who understood the protocols of courts and spoke French fluently with men of their own caste.

Not all peers marched in time to the strident drum of patriotism. A rump of seventy or so Whig followers of Charles James Fox remained on the opposition benches and undertook a guerrilla campaign against soaring wartime taxation and strategic miscalculations. Foxite Whig peers stayed true to their party's libertarian traditions and condemned Pitt's sedition laws as encroachments on the liberties of Britons. The watchdogs of liberty barked loudly during the Lords debate on the 1795 Treasonous Practices and Seditious Meetings Bill. The fifth Duke of Bedford echoed Paine by invoking the long history of 'oppression' imposed by the aristocracy on the people of France, and reminded peers of the 'profligacy and extravagancy' of the Bourbon court. Crushing legitimate and lawful protests under the colour of national security was a 'remedy worse than the disease' argued the eleventh Duke of Norfolk. The bill was carried by a huge majority, but Bedford and Norfolk joined with eleven like-minded lords to issue a formal statement that ancient rights were now in jeopardy.[15]

Bedford may have made surreptitious approaches to populist radical groups, a flirtation with treason which might explain why his private papers were burned after his death in 1802.[16] Norfolk's proclaimed his views boldly. At a party celebrating Fox's birthday in 1798, he proposed a toast to 'Our sovereign, the Majesty of the People', which prompted his immediate sacking as Lord Lieutenant of the West Riding. In a perverse way (which neither they or he would have appreciated), these peers were justifying Burke's faith in the independence of the aristocracy.

Meanwhile, the rest of the nobility were zealously promoting the war effort in the provinces. Everywhere they took the lead in coaxing their countrymen to fight to preserve their freedom and immersed themselves in every form of activity contrived to boost national morale. Aristocrats financed and attended public celebrations of unity which were orchestrated to prove that patriotism transcended social divisions. After the naval victory of the Glorious First of June in 1794, the Earl of Aberdeen headed the list of subscribers to a fund for the widows and orphans of men killed in the battle with a gift of ten guineas. Below were the names of Aberdonian lawyers, merchants and shopkeepers who subscribed between two guineas and five shillings each. A few months later, the local newspaper reported that Aberdeen's leading citizens were 'vying' with local lairds in their efforts to raise a regiment of volunteers.[17] What better proof could there be that the aristocracy and the middle class were of the same spirit and resolve.

On the ideological front, aristocrats joined forces with Anglican clergymen to beef up loyalist organisations, of which the largest and most boisterous was the Association for the Preservation of Liberty and Property against Republicans and Levellers, founded in 1792. Some of its members sponsored drunken, popular street parties in which patriots burned effigies of Paine (he had successively fled to France and the United

States), smashed the windows of radicals and sometimes man-handled them.

Noblemen also patronised more sedate festivities. At one, held at Frogmore, near Windsor Castle, on a sunny day in July 1800, George III and Queen Charlotte together with lords and ladies attended a grand *fête champêtre* devised by Princess Elizabeth. She wanted her father's subjects to have a jolly time and, as they did so, reveal to the world that here was a truly united kingdom in which there was harmony between Crown, peers and people. Guests were entertained by a tightrope walker, dancers dressed as gypsies, and musicians. Many of the performers were men from the Staffordshire militia, one of whom sang a riposte to Paine:

> *When republic doctrines are everywhere found, Sir*
> *And levelling principles so much abound, Sir*
> *Let each son of Liberty, joyfully sing, Sir*
> *Long to reign over us, God save the King, Sir.*

As evening approached, the royal party and the peers and peeresses withdrew for dinner and a ball held in a converted barn.[18] These and similar events were reported in the local and national press.

Many of the younger noblemen at Frogmore would have been in uniform. They were fulfilling the historic duty of all gentlemen, irrespective of their rank. Its nature and manifestations were outlined by Captain James Macnamara RN in his trial at the Old Bailey in 1803. He was accused of murdering a cavalry officer whom he had fatally wounded in duel which his personal honour and public reputation as an officer had compelled him to fight. 'When called upon to lead others into honourable danger,' he told the jury, 'I must not be supposed to be a man who had sought safety by submitting to what custom has taught others to consider a disgrace.' Macnamara's innate courage and leadership was in his blood, instinctive and beyond analysis. 'It is impossible to define . . . the proper feelings of a gentleman; but their existence has supported this happy country for many ages, and she might perish if they were lost.' Two famous titled admirals, Hood and Nelson, testified to Macnamara's character, which was evident to the journalists covering the case, who were impressed by his confident bearing and 'manly' appearance. He was acquitted.[19]

Throughout the war the British people learned as never before of how men of Macnamara's stamp conducted themselves in battle. The London and provincial press reprinted official despatches which vividly described acts of heroism by individual, named officers. One, which appeared in 1814, may attest for hundreds of others. During the capture of the French frigate *Clorinde*, Lieutenant Foord of the Marines had been mortally wounded in the thigh by grapeshot, 'gallantly leading his men'.[20]

If Macnamara was to be believed, and on the whole the nation accepted his analysis of the ingredients of leadership, Foord's men followed him because they respected him as a gentleman and, therefore, a man of courage and honour. So too was Nelson, whose death and funeral saw an outpouring of national grief more heartfelt and intense than that later expressed at the obsequies of Princess Diana. Nelson was joined in the national pantheon of heroes by another equally audacious commander, Lord Thomas Cochrane, the eldest son of the tenth Earl of Dundonald (and the historic model for Patrick O'Brian's Jack Aubrey). Differences in status did not matter unduly – Nelson was the son of a parson – what really counted was that they were both gentlemen.

Gentlemen of all ranks were kept busy at home. In July 1792 France had called for the *levée-en-masse*, which transformed every able-bodied male citizen into a soldier of the Republic. War was democratised and huge armies materialised, full of volunteers whose idealism compensated for their lack of training and discipline. Between 1797 and 1798 and 1803 and 1805 these mass French armies threatened to invade Britain. The response was a carefully controlled form of the revolutionary *levée*, which involved mobilising, arming and training about a quarter of a million men. It was a potentially risky enterprise, given the groundswell of sedition and recurrent economic distress, which was why Pitt's government turned to the nation's landowners, who could be relied upon to be loyal and uphold the political and social status quo.

Lord Lieutenants supervised the enlargement of the county militias and appointed their officers. In a signal display of its faith in the aristocracy's loyalty and influence, the state licensed individual peers to raise volunteer regiments of infantry (fencibles) and troops of light cavalry (yeomanry) and nominate their officers. This devolution of military power meant that a large section of the nobility took responsibility for the deployment of troops for external and internal security and the creation of a reservoir of soldiers for service overseas. Political animosities were suspended; at least one yeomanry troop was raised by a Whig nobleman who objected strongly to Pitt's obduracy and wartime taxation.[21]

Paradoxically, an outwardly modern state was adapting an essentially medieval expedient. The local prestige of the nobility, its networks of kinsmen and dependants, and ingrained habits of deference combined with the new popular affection for George III and the cash bounties provided by the Treasury produced a formidable army. In 1804 it was calculated that there were about four hundred thousand men under arms, two-thirds of them volunteers and militia.[22]

In Scotland, the ancient bonds of blood and customary obligation to clan and chieftain were thoroughly and sometimes cynically exploited. Of the twenty-nine officers of the Duke of Sutherland's Fencibles, twelve were from his extended kin. In 1800 a supplicant for the promotion of Alexander Cameron in

Lord Seaforth's volunteers listed his qualification as experience of soldiering, his 'genteel' demeanour and the fact that he was a 'cousin once removed' to Seaforth.[23]

Cameron was seeking advancement in what could easily have been mistaken for a feudal host, had it not been for the cut of its uniforms and its modern weapons. In 1797 the government had authorised the Dukes of Atholl, Montrose and Argyll and the Earls of Aberdeen and Gower to raise sixteen thousand volunteers organised into nine brigades, each commanded by a nobleman or some other figure high in the clan hierarchy. Below them were Highlanders recruited from the circle of clans and septs traditionally attached to their colonel. Macnabs, MacGrigors and Menzies served under Atholl's command, as their ancestors had under his ancestors.[24] All shared the atavistic bonds of common ancestry and inherited obligations.

There were limits to the Highlanders' patriotism and endurance. Reports of colossal losses of soldiers in the West Indies from indigenous fevers had a baleful effect on recruitment and triggered a spate of mutinies among Highland militiamen and volunteers. All involved fears of posting abroad and the defiance of local figures of authority, noblemen, lairds and ministers of the Kirk.[25] Revealingly, they were accused of having betrayed their paternal responsibilities by deceiving the clansmen. Elsewhere in the country, men refused to join the militia because service was an intrusion into their time or out of indifference to the threat of invasion.

Lassitude was strongest in districts, often urban and industrial, where the influence of landowners and parsons was weakest. This was unsurprising thought one ultra-conservative commentator. The 'proprietors of the soil', their tenant farmers and labourers were natural patriots and monarchists. Their loyalty was unshakeable, unlike that of manufacturers, tradesmen and artisans, who were rootless creatures with no real stake in the kingdom.[26]

At every level, command was entrusted only to those with a 'real stake' in the nation. All volunteer officers had to be gentlemen with a landed income of at least fifty pounds a year. Exceptions were allowed in the case of militia officers. Faced with a dearth of qualified candidates, the third Duke of Richmond grudgingly agreed to give a commission in the Sussex militia to a keen Lewes ironmonger, although he would have preferred 'an independent gentleman'. Necessity also persuaded the nobility to admit poachers to their units on the pragmatic grounds that they would prove excellent skirmishers.[27]

Sussex poachers-turned-sharpshooters joined detachments raised from the tenants and servants of the county's five leading peers. Units included a battery of horse artillery partly funded by Richmond, and the Petworth Yeomanry recruited and commanded by the third Earl of Egremont, who was more interested in the arts and agriculture than amateur soldiering. Nonetheless, he performed his public duty and, like so many aristocratic yeomanry commanders, simultaneously upheld his prestige and satisfied his vanity by designing and paying for the uniforms of his troops. The Petworth yeomanrymen wore green jackets, white waistcoats, blue cloaks trimmed with scarlet and Tarleton helmets with bearskin crests; Egremont's was distinguished by a large scarlet feather. Basic funding and arms came from the government; muskets, bayonets, sabres and pistols supplied to the Leicestershire militia and yeomanry are now attached to the walls of Belvoir Castle.

In 1804 Egremont's dashing horsemen were ready to repel Napoleon's Grande Armée, which was mustering at Boulogne for a seaborne invasion of the south coast. The nature of the war against France had changed dramatically. Napoleon Bonaparte had made himself Emperor of France and, like Hitler, he believed that conflict was natural to the human condition. Again like Hitler, Bonaparte intended to create a subordinate Europe of cowed monarchs and puppet kingdoms kept in line by the threat of force, ruthlessly applied. Britain's new adversary was a godsend for official propaganda; Britons were repeatedly told, and on the whole believed, that they were fighting not only to save their own liberties, but to rescue Europe from the grip of a bloodthirsty tyrant who was indifferent to the suffering he inflicted.

Bonaparte's invasion of the Iberian peninsula in 1808 gave a welcome substance to this view of the conflict. British forces under Wellington were the liberators of Spain and Portugal, nations which had been overrun by Bonaparte's military machine but retained their spirit of independence. By the close of 1813, the French were expelled from Spain and the poet laureate Robert Southey celebrated a victory for freedom that would inspire the rest of the world.

> *Now, Britain, now thy brows with laurels bind;*
> *Raise the song of joy for rescued Spain!*
> *And Europe, take thou up the awakening strain . . .*
> *Glory to God! Deliverance for Mankind!*

Within months, British, Russian, Prussian and Austrian armies were sweeping across France and at home patriots were awash with self-congratulation. In the Lords, a peer declared that Britain had fought tirelessly 'for the sake of justice, for the sake of loyalty, for the sake of insulted and tortured humanity'.[28] Soon after, 'Boney' was on his way to Elba and the Bourbon Louis XVIII was king of France. His restoration was depicted as a flattering moral triumph for the British Constitution. A jubilant *Times* announced that the allied sovereigns had compelled the new king to accept a constitution based on Britain's, which gave France the equivalent of Magna Carta and the Bill of Rights.[29] Moreover, the new French senate contained hereditary aristocrats, including diehard émigrés, peers who had been reconciled to Napoleon and some of the marshals he had ennobled, such as Ney and Soult.

In his coup of March 1815 Napoleon, who had escaped from Elba, reinvented himself as the true heir of the Revolution and offered himself to France as a democrat and reformer. Exhausted by war, the French people were largely lukewarm or hostile, and the Emperor reverted to type and attempted to consolidate his power in the only way he knew, by an aggressive war. He was decisively defeated at Waterloo by an allied army commanded by Wellington, who famously remarked that, for all his martial talents, Boney was not and never could be a gentleman.

Waterloo confirmed Wellington as a national hero. His victories were a spectacular vindication of the aristocratic principle in which he fervently believed. Approaching eighty, he explained his philosophy of war:

> The British army is what it is because it is officered by gentlemen; men who would scorn to do a dishonourable thing and would have something more at stake before the world than a reputation for military smartness. Now the French piqued themselves on their 'esprit militaire', and their 'honneur militaire', and what was the consequence? Why, I kicked their 'honneur' and 'esprit militaire' to the devil.[30]

It had never been as simple as that. The principle worked because of the sheer force of Wellington's character. He understood the mind of a gentleman and, when necessary, he used this knowledge to appeal, often caustically, to the consciences of his officers. After the 18th Hussars had been castigated by the Duke for looting and threatened with being sent home in disgrace, one of its officers, Lieutenant Woodberry, was cut to the quick. 'I want language to express the grief I feel on this occasion,' he wrote in his journal. He had been a Corinthian dandy who had dreamed of returning to England as a hero and boasting to his Brighton cronies that he was no longer the 'puppy' they had once known.[31] The 18th Hussars continued to serve in Spain and the chastened Woodberry fulfilled his responsibilities as an officer and a gentleman. The second Earl of Portarlington had no second chance. After a distinguished career in the 23rd Light Dragoons, he somehow failed to join his regiment on the morning of Waterloo. He hastily attached himself to a Hussar regiment, fought in the battle and had a horse killed under him. His gallantry did not expiate what men of honour considered a default of duty: he had abandoned his men. Ostracised, he led a life of gambling and debauchery and died in poverty in 1845.[32]

The aristocratic principle worked for Wellington because he was a nobleman of remarkable intellect and energy, and a brilliant strategist who had mastered the mechanisms of war. This was why he devoted so much time to logistics and the collection and analysis of intelligence, and favoured officers who shared his sense of public duty and cared for the welfare of their men. Yet Wellington was often hampered by the aristocratic principle. Many times he was driven to protest to his superiors in London about the networks of patronage which promoted officers far beyond their competence and filled administrative departments with negligent drones. In a political career which lasted from 1818 to his death in 1852, Wellington resolutely upheld the aristocratic principle which he embodied in the public imagination. If it appeared to fail, the fault always lay with individuals and never the ideal.

The defeat of France left an imprint on Tory thinking. Britain's *ancien régime* with its intricate constitutional and legal checks and balances had been assayed and emerged victorious and stronger than ever. Crown, altar and aristocracy had survived the ideological brickbats of Paine and his adherents. Their perfect state–revolutionary France – had dissolved into anarchy and, in its mutated form under Napoleon, had been trounced. Whigs did not interpret recent events in such uncompromising, triumphalist terms. As the liberal *Edinburgh Review* argued in 1814, the world and how individuals saw their place in it had been transformed forever by the French Revolution and its aftermath.[33] Moreover, popular wartime patriotism was not necessarily a national endorsement of the political or social status quo.

PART THREE

DECLINE

1815–

20

Rats: Crisis and Compromise

Gilbert Elliot, second Earl of Minto, was proud to be a modern man who understood the nature and potential of the new world that was emerging after the French wars. The temper of the times seemed unfavourable to the aristocratic ideal, but he was certain that it remained valid. Men of his birth and outlook would remain the natural leaders of the nation, so long as they were flexible, imaginative and attentive to the opinions and needs of every section of society. Minto was a Whig peer and heir to the pragmatism and libertarian philosophy of his party, which, he believed, offered the best compass to steer the country through difficult and mutable times. Once, after a conversation with two like-minded noblemen, he approvingly remarked that the pair were 'very decidedly men of the nineteenth century'.[1]

Yet Minto's political activities followed a traditional pattern. Like an eighteenth-century aristocrat he straddled and connected two worlds, one provincial and the other metropolitan. He regularly visited the Borders, where he owned vast estates, and used his prestige to promote the Whig cause among lairds and farmers. He also listened to their views, as well as chatter about livestock prices and hunting prospects. Conversation was very different in his other base, London, where he attended the salons held by Whig grandees and their wives. The discourse was witty, sometimes racy and concerned ideas, literature, policy, Parliamentary strategy and high-life scandal. Like others in political circles, Minto indulged in the fashion for asperity, making terse and spiteful summaries of the faults of eminent acquaintances. After meeting the second Lord Ellenborough at the Travellers Club in 1819, Minto observed that he had inherited the 'coarseness' of his father and that his 'intellectual rigour' was bogus and so a 'commonplace vulgarity and shallow intolerance' marked his political opinions.[2] These shortcomings did not prevent Ellenborough from following a career as a proconsul, although it ended under a shadow when he was recalled as Governor-General of India after the blunders of the First Afghan War of 1838–42. Perhaps Minto had been right about his qualities.

Since Waterloo, the political discourse of men like Minto and Ellenborough had been about reform. We are inclined to think that the word referred only to the reform of Parliament, which is partially true, but at the time reform embraced every area of national life. It was applied to all institutions which were being choked by the deadwood of venality, lassitude and an irrational veneration of the past. The Anglican Church, civil and criminal law, medicine, universities, the civil service, the arts and public morality needed overhaul and regeneration. Ossified institutions handicapped a country which portrayed itself as innovative and modern.

Britain was being transformed by what were later recognised as the agricultural and industrial revolutions. They were slow and uneven processes that would continue until 1860 with the completion of the national rail networks which would remain in situ for the next hundred years. Economic change was the father to social and demographic revolutions. There was a gradual shift in population away from the countryside to towns and cities which owed their existence to mining, manufacturing and ship-building. These enterprises swelled the numbers of the urban working class and the middle class. The middle class embraced everyone engaged in the professions, commerce at all levels from shopkeepers to financiers, the proprietors and managers of industrial plants and clerks who, like Bob Cratchit, were the foot soldiers of capitalist enterprise.

Capitalism required efficiency, which could be achieved only through the dispassionate application of reason to human relationships and the management of public affairs. Old accretions of privilege in public bodies, arcane professional practices, monopolies such as the East India Company and arthritic administrative machinery frustrated efficiency. They also, and this angered many of the middle class, held back ambitious, talented men who lacked the personal connections to facilitate the advancement they deserved. The self-perpetuating and self-satisfied elites who upheld the status quo were united by a horror of change. In 1832, the Whig Lord Althorpe denounced the mandarins of the Royal Academy as the 'Borough Mongers of Art', who, like the peers then opposing Parliamentary reform, were 'interested men who are fearful of their supremacy'.[3]

The concept of reform contained elements which denied the aristocratic principle. Wellington, who sometimes treated his countrymen as an awkward squad which needed to be knocked into shape by doses of firm discipline, believed that all demands for reform reflected a 'contempt for authority'. In the vocabulary of the more radical reformers, the word 'aristocracy' became synonymous with any exclusive body whose power rested upon ancient custom, birthright or connections, or a combination of all three. Antiquity and custom were replaced as touchstones for future survival by public utility. The passionate reformer Shelley insisted in 1819 that 'A man has no right to be a King or a Lord or a Bishop but so long as it is to the benefit of the People and so long as the People judge that it is for their benefit.'[4]

Minto believed that the nobility would pass the assay of usefulness, but he was disturbed by the implications of such thinking. As a Whig peer, he was broadly sympathetic to the principles of reform and hoped that his party would implement them in such a way as to satisfy public feeling without compromising the influence of the aristocracy. Committed to what would prove a very tricky balancing act, the Whigs made alliances of convenience with nonconformists, moderate reformers and radical populists, many of whom wanted to diminish the influence of the nobility. Another equally dangerous threat to the aristocracy were the diehard Tory and Anglican enemies of reform, whose intransigence inflamed social and political tensions.

Minto was exposed to visceral Toryism in the Borders at the end of 1819, when reluctantly (he would have preferred to be chasing foxes) he attended meetings at which local landowners drafted addresses to the Prince Regent. The matter at issue was the Tory government's reaction to the 'Peterloo massacre', an incident in Manchester earlier in the year in which cavalrymen had knocked down and trampled to death a dozen demonstrators at an open-air reform meeting. And quite right too, thought the lairds and farmers who gladly endorsed new laws which clamped down on sedition. Nevertheless, and to Minto's secret pleasure, his neighbours shared his revulsion at the 'violent and intemperate' language of that Tory ultra Sir Walter Scott, who had had experience of dealing with mobs as a yeomanryman over twenty years ago. Minto's suggestion that the conduct of the Manchester magistrates ought to be thoroughly investigated was also rejected.[5]

Back in London at a meeting in Burlington House, Minto heard the Whig leader Lord Gray reiterate his party's old support for popular liberty: 'the privileges of the people' were not to be 'violated with impunity'. However, Lord Liverpool's Tory ministry placed order before liberty and succumbed to the same neurosis which had infected Pitt nearly thirty years before. New laws were passed which treated calls for reform as subversion. One justification was the Cato Street Conspiracy of 1820, in which the half-crazed Arthur Thistlewood planned to murder the Cabinet and declare a republic, although there were rumours that the plotters had been egged on by government agents.

In the same year, reformers of all kinds united behind Princess Caroline, the estranged wife of the profoundly unloved George IV (1820–30) who wanted to divorce her. She demanded to be crowned alongside her husband and fellow adulterer, and across the country petitions were drawn up and mobs assembled to defend her legal rights. London rioters cornered Wellington and asked him to give a hurrah for Caroline, which he did, adding, 'May all your wives be like her.' His security measures, including a guard of champion prizefighters, kept Caroline out of Westminster Abbey and this 'people's princess' died soon afterwards.

A wronged, pitiable and slightly mad woman had briefly become the symbol for a wronged nation. Its rights and aspirations, like hers, had been trampled on by an oppressive government and an ultra-reactionary monarch, who incidentally embodied the dissipation that Paineites had once attributed to the aristocracy. Minto was worried by the tone and language of radicals who lumped aristocracy and gentry together as 'a corrupt and [self-] interested oppressor' of the people. The response of the landowners was panic, which was why so many welcomed the 'arbitrary and violent' measures introduced by the Tories. During 1821 he was troubled by the 'revolutionary spirit' among the Whigs of the Borders.[6] All this fed Minto's pessimism; a rift was widening between the upper and lower classes and the aristocracy seemed to have lost its way and its capacity for steady leadership.

Political passion and tumults were reduced after 1822 thanks to an upturn in the economy. From 1815 until the mid-Victorian boom, Britain's economy oscillated between good and bad times. Their features were described in a survey of the past decade compiled in the *Economist* early in 1845. 'In 1835 commerce was prosperous, manufactures flourished, labour was in great demand with ample wages. In 1839 all was the reverse – ruin, discredit, and sinking finances.'[7] These were accompanied by chronic unemployment and an upsurge in popular political violence in the northern and Midlands industrial areas. All this had occurred during the post-Waterloo years.

There was no consensus as how to escape from the cycle of booms and slumps, or how to ameliorate the consequences of the latter. One view, known as laissez-faire, which was gaining ground during this period, insisted that the economy possessed its own dynamic and operated under the laws of the market, and should be trusted to do so in the general interest. Correcting mechanisms existed and, if allowed to function freely, would provide the remedies for recession; state intervention hindered natural processes and distorted the market. In particular, the Corn Laws passed in 1815 to limit the imports of grain from the Continent drove up the price of bread and, with it, wages. High labour costs reduced competitiveness and profit margins, as businessmen repeatedly told successive governments.

Against the iron laws of economics were the older considerations of the moral responsibility of the rich for the poor and their modern offshoot, the Christian humanitarianism of the Evangelical movement. The nature of philanthropy was being transformed; traditional charity was supplemented by political action, which involved the conversion of the public and then mass lobbying and petitioning of Parliament. This form of campaigning had secured the abolition of the slave trade in 1807 and was being adopted by movements against slavery and the abuse and exploitation of men, women and children in mines and factories. Laissez-faire dogmatists, chiefly plantation and factory owners, insisted that philanthropists were endangering profits. Humanitarian sentiments transcended partisan politics. In 1832 the anti-reform Tories Lord Eldon and the Bishop of London joined forces with a self-proclaimed 'liberal' Whig, the third Lord Suffield, to present a bill against child labour in the Lords. Suffield was also an opponent of slavery and the game laws and he backed measures to reduce cruelty to animals; he died after a fall from his horse while riding on Constitution Hill.[8]

The slave trade had been abolished by an unreformed Parliament. How long it remained in that condition depended upon the capacity of the Tory Party to keep the monopoly of power it had secured in 1794. The Tory mind was not wholly indisposed to reform. Between 1780 and 1825 successive ministries had cut the number of state sinecures from two hundred to ten, and the amount doled out in civil list pensions had fallen from £200,000 in 1810 to £75,000 in 1830.[9] Nonetheless, substantial perks remained: as Prime Minister, Lord Liverpool had received £4,100 a year as Constable of Dover Castle and the Marquess Wellesley nearly £5,000 as remembrancer of the Irish Exchequer. Chipping away at what was called the 'old corruption' was not really a concession to the spirit of reform, but part of the reduction of government expenditure in response to pressure from landowning taxpayers.

The Tory ascendancy was shattered between 1829 and 1830. The cause had been a major reform – the political emancipation of Catholics – taken with great reluctance by the Prime Minister Wellington and against a background of rancorous bickering within his own party, which split. Wellington was a humane man and a pragmatist who believed that this concession would forestall an insurrection and possibly a civil war in Ireland. His opponents disinterred atavistic anti-Popery and alleged that, in the interests of expediency, he had jeopardized the spiritual prestige and authority of that sturdy prop to Toryism, the Church of England. Tempers snapped. George IV wailed that he had been 'deserted by the aristocracy' and Wellington was forced to fight a duel with another bigot, the tenth Earl of Winchilsea. Both men fired wide. The Duchess of Richmond, who had been hostess to the famous ball in Brussels before Waterloo, reviled the peers who had voted for emancipation as 'rats' and placed stuffed rats in glass cases on a table in her drawing room, each labelled with the name of an apostate lord. It was rumoured that a mischievous peer had released a live rat during the Lords debate.[10]

Disunited Tories turned on each other. There were already signs that the party was losing its hitherto tractable supporters in the shires; in recent Cornish elections farmers had refused their landlords' bidding and rejected ultra candidates.[11] Loyal Oxfordshire defected in the 1830 general election, an early symptom of what turned out to be a general defiance of the Tory aristocracy and the electoral machinery it controlled.[12] Early in 1831, when the Whigs introduced the first Reform Bill, two Tory grandees, the Duke of Buccleuch and the Earl of Lothian, faced a 'mutiny' by Borders' voters, much to Minto's delight. He also noticed that many MPs were suddenly taking the trouble to consult their constituents as to how they should vote. In previously docile pocket boroughs tenants risked and sometimes suffered eviction to vote for pro-reform candidates.[13]

The will of the nation was clear. The Tories disregarded it and, as Minto told his wife in March 1831, were bent on 'wrecking' the bill in the Lords. A clash was unavoidable, for 'the people certainly would not allow itself turned out by a vote in the Lords'.[14] The Tory peers rejected the bill and their mulishness transformed its passage into a prolonged and bitter contest between the Lords and the people.

Tensions increased and, during the winter of 1831–2, there were large-scale riots in Nottingham and Bristol, where a combination of arson, looting and cavalry charges led to heavy casualties. In October Minto feared a proliferation of popular violence and his pessimism was widely shared. The painter Benjamin Haydon sensed that popular feeling went far deeper than his Tory friends thought, and he gloomily wondered whether Britain was about to undergo a revolution of the sort that had occurred in America. The monarchy, the aristocracy and the Commons would all be extinguished. Some fearful Tories, including the poet laureate Robert Southey, contemplated flight from what seemed an imminent and inevitable revolution by emigrating to the United States.[15]

There is something bizarre about the exaggerated reactions to a measure designed to redistribute Parliamentary constituencies and create an extended and theoretically uniform franchise in Britain and Ireland. In common with other Whig lords, Minto imagined that the bill would simultaneously rescue Parliament from 'the mischievous influence of the great boroughmongers' and revive the influence of the aristocracy in general.[16] He was right insofar that fewer and fewer seats were being contested in general elections and more and more were being settled by private compacts made to spare contestants' money. The value of pocket boroughs had soared, and in 1820 Gatton in Surrey had changed hands for £180,000. After Parliamentary reform, Minto predicted a return to elections which would be won not by high spenders, but by peers asserting their influence over boroughs close to their estates. The Prime Minister, now Lord Grey, attempted to calm the Tory peers by arguing that the enfranchisement of 'large, wealthy and populous towns' in no way encroached on the 'privileges' of the aristocracy, or the 'prerogatives' of the Crown.[17]

Why then did the Tory peers resist so tenaciously? Speeches made during the last-ditch resistance to the bill in April and May 1832 reverberated with fury, hyperbole and predictions of impending revolution. There were also expressions of a deep and sincere veneration for the past. The Bishop of Durham described the bill as a 'dangerous example of destruction and annihilation' and merely 'change . . . for the sake of change'. He dismissed the so-called 'march of intellect' as a 'restless disposition' which sought to erase everything that was 'ancient'. Innovations would accumulate until all the institutions 'on which our ancestors had prided themselves' had disappeared. Some peers protested that the abolition of their pocket boroughs was an assault on the rights of property. The Earl of Malmesbury correctly predicted that the landed interest for which the peers spoke would eventually become subservient to that industry.[18]

There was rage too about the public clamour for reform. The sometime duellist Lord Winchilsea denounced all political unions as 'illegal combinations', and Lord Haddington was infuriated by the way in which the Lords was excoriated in the press and on public platforms. Lord Wynford, a former judge, melodramatically declared that he would vote against the bill even if it meant that he would be hanged from 'the nearest lamp iron' the moment he walked into the street.[19] (He died in his bed in 1845.) Outside the Lords, there was braggadocio; Haydon heard tales that some younger and wilder spirits hoped for a violent showdown. Some 'dandies' were 'longing for a fight' and Lord John Churchill, brother to the fifth Duke of Marlborough, was looking forward to a civil war. 'It will come to blood [which will] do 'em good.'[20] The spirit of 1642 was evident among a few Whigs, some of whom resigned their yeomanry commissions rather than suppress protests against the House of Lords.

Wellington and William IV (1830–7) resolved the impasse. The Duke, who believed that a good general always knew when to retreat, persuaded the hardline peers to stay away from the Lords rather than vote, scupper the bill and provoke a confrontation with the Commons. It would lead to disorders which might easily be beyond the capacity of the government to control. The King reminded the Lords that, if necessary, he would create as many peers as were needed to secure the bill's passage. The diehards submitted with a bad grace. A handful fired a Parthian shot after the Reform Act was passed, proclaimmg that the country and the throne were imperilled and all ancient institutions were now in jeopardy.[21]

Tory anguish was a product of a genuine fear that any tampering with the old order would bring about its demolition, which suggests unspoken anxieties about its fragility. There was also sullen puzzlement, for the Tory peers had misjudged the temper of the country and overestimated the residual loyalty of their traditional supporters. They had defected in droves, but, unchastened, the Tory peers imagined that the will of the Commons (and the nation) could be frustrated by a show of aristocratic solidarity. Wellington and William IV brought them to their senses by reminding that they could not flout the will of the nation and the Crown.

But were the lamentations and dire prophecies of Tory peers the swansong of the aristocracy? Historians agree that the Reform Act was pivotal insofar as it opened the way towards a fuller democracy. This had not been the aim of the Whig aristocracy. Rather they saw themselves as fulfilling the ancient function of the nobility: national leadership. Men like Minto, Lord John Russell and Earl Grey had accepted the popular will, directed it in a sober and moderate manner and through compromise preserved some of the political power of the aristocracy. Reform in the wider sense had triumphed: the Whig ministry elected in 1832 proceeded to abolish slavery within the British empire, reorganised local government and passed a national Poor Law.

In broad terms the character of political life had been changed. There were more voters, most of them from the middle classes. The United Kingdom electorate increased from 290,000 to 495,000 with a rise from 5,000 to 60,000 in Scotland. The newly enfranchised voted for a House of Commons which was now supreme, for the events of 1832 had proved beyond question that the Lords veto could not override the will of the Commons.[22]

With hindsight, the Reform Act was a turning point in the history of the aristocracy. It set a constitutional precedent, and henceforward the predominantly Tory peers could only camel trade with the lower house by amending legislation or sending back bills for further consideration. Aristocratic power was on the wane, but the pace of its deterioration was halting and often barely perceptible to contemporaries. Early in 1833, an army officer angling for promotion tried to secure the patronage of Lord Seafield on the grounds that 'Lord Palmerston is an old college friend of yours'. He added: 'I suppose even in this reformed Parliament, private friendship has something to do with these appointments.'[23] Businessmen in the big cities agreed in principle and preferred MPs whose aristocratic connections made them more effective as lobbyists.

Members of Parliament were still expected to pull strings for their supporters in the old style. Minto's eldest son, Lord Melgund, who was MP for Hythe between 1837 and 1841, was bombarded with requests for patronage from Whig voters. David

Page, whose straitened circumstances could be offset by a minor administrative post, reminded Melgund that 'my brothers, my sons and myself have invariably supported your lordship's interest and that of the present government both in the borough and the county' and that he had never before asked for the 'favour of any Parliamentary gentleman'. Ten electors backed Edward Thomas's application for the pursership on HMS *Ocean* on the grounds that he was about to settle in Hythe and 'is likely to be politically useful'.[24]

The Reform Act had not outlawed electoral corruption. Aristocratic pressure continued to be vigorously applied during election campaigns, particularly in small and middle-sized boroughs in the shadow of great houses. In 1832 Lord Dimsdale told the seven hundred voters of Hertford that he expected 'all my tenants and friends' to vote for his favoured candidate, the Tory Lord Ingestre. Samuel Sedgewick, a draper, disobeyed, allowed the Whig candidate to address a crowd from a window above his shop, and was evicted. 'Bullies' wandered on the streets during polling and voters were invited to the 'Rat's Castle' inn where there was free beer, bread, cheese, onions and gallons of port. The reckoning was sent to Lord Salisbury at Hatfield, or so the Whigs alleged. Not surprisingly, the defeated Whigs challenged the result and the election was scrutinised by a Common's committee. This legal procedure cost the plaintiffs two hundred and fifty pounds a day; only rich men could hope to expose electoral corruption.[25]

There were occasional attempts to escape the stranglehold imposed by peers. In 1852 the electors of Peterborough rebelled against Earl Fitzwilliam, whose family had controlled the city since the 1790s in the Whig interest. A populist Tory prevailed, but the result was overturned after charges of corruption.[26] The following year the *Edinburgh Review* regretted the venality of the newly enfranchised urban middle classes who treated the vote as a marketable asset to be sold to the highest bidder. During the

1866 election the price of a householder's vote varied from seven pounds in Lancaster to sixty pounds in Totnes.[27] Worse still was widespread political apathy; in the 1859 election well over two hundred constituencies were uncontested.[28]

These included many of the fifty-nine constituencies at the beck and call of forty-four peers.[29] Some were handed to younger sons in the old fashion. In Disraeli's *Sybil* (1845) the Countess of Marney resolves that her younger son Lord Egremont will have the borough of Marney with the help of his elder brother's cash and a thousand pounds from her. For her it was a matter of 'regaining the family influence and letting us hold up our heads again'.

Seen from the perspectives of a provincial shopkeeper with brandy in his belly and the nobleman who had paid for it to get the man's vote, the Reform Act seemed to have changed very little. Intransigent Tory peers had had a pyschological shock in 1832 when they had been isolated and reviled, but they quickly recovered their confidence under a new leader, Sir Robert Peel. He was the son of a textile manufacturer (one of the first non-landed millionaires) and a shrewd pragmatist. Peel made it clear to the new electorate that his party was no longer hostile to the spirit of reform. A fictional Conservative in Trollope's *The Prime Minister*, set in the 1870s, remarks:

> You' can't have tests and qualification, rotten boroughs and the divine right of kings, back again. But as the glorious institutions of the country are made to perish, one after another, it is better they should receive the coup de grâce tenderly from loving hands than be roughly throttled by radicals.

The clock could not be turned back and it was electoral suicide to imagine otherwise. The Conservatives wanted power and Peel understood that it could only be secured if his party compromised with the spirit of reform. There were exceptions, most famously Colonel Charles de Laet Waldo Sibthorp, the Tory MP for Lincoln, who, until his death in 1855, upheld the old aristocratic principle and denounced every manifestation of the modern age from railways to the Great Exhibition. A tall, striking figure dressed in the fashion of the Regency and with bushy dragoon's whiskers, he entertained the Commons with his tirades. In Lincoln, he courted voters in the old style and they gratefully sang:

> Come then, Freemen, let us sing,
> 'God save Sibthorp, Church and King'
> Bacchus sure will mirthful fling
> Round us wreathes of jollity: . . .

Sibthorp diverted a House of Commons that was a more balanced body in terms of the range of interests represented than it had been when he had been first elected in 1826. The supremacy of the landed interest was over; it now stood on equal footing with those of the City, manufacturing, railways and shipping, which were now generating more and more of the nation's wealth.

21

Thoroughbred: Sport and Manliness

While the aristocracy's political ascendancy declined, its domination of the nation's sporting life remained strong. Noblemen financed and gave tone to British sport. It has always been integral to British culture, and its contribution to the national self-image and character has been enormous. We are proud to be a sporting nation, although now winning has become subordinate to participation. Yet, until recently, the word 'sportsman' signified more than a mere participant; it implied that a player adhered to the rules, practised self-control, was indifferent to adversity and was guided by a personal code of honour which prized fairness. Sportsmanship was a distillation of old chivalric ideals.

Nerve and tenacity mattered as much, if not more than technical skill. A 'game' (another revealing word) gentleman amateur was worthier of admiration than the professional who trained rigorously and in the process may have absorbed some of the ungentlemanly techniques of 'gamesmanship'. This was why, in

1803, the patrician MCC (Marylebone Cricket Club) insisted on the distinction between 'gentlemen' and 'players' (i.e. professionals) which was perpetuated in changing rooms and on team lists until 1963. The tension between these two approaches to sport and the spirit which animated them was a theme of the 1981 film *Chariots of Fire*, which follows the training of British athletes before the 1924 Olympics. The hurdler Lord Burghley represents the amateur tradition, while the sprinter Harold Abrahams seeks professional coaching, which the old guard (two Cambridge dons) find distasteful.

Burghley, who became sixth Marquess of Exeter in 1956, later entered public life as a Conservative MP and was Governor of Bermuda between 1943 and 1946. Shortly before, he had represented the Ministry of Aircraft Production in Australia where he won many hearts, according to George VI's private secretary, Sir Alan Lascelles. 'A lord, an MP, an MFH [Master of Foxhounds] and an Olympic hurdler – worked wonders.'[1] Sporting aristocrats had always won popular affection, mostly masculine. They possessed a dash and verve, and, in their earlier incarnations as Regency Corinthians and early Victorian plungers, had a taste for devilment and fast living. They aroused a more or less suppressed envy among those constrained by prevailing moral conventions.

Sport transcended social barriers and sporting peers mixed freely and cheerfully among inferiors who shared their passions. The sporting journalist Charles Apperley, who wrote as 'Nimrod', overheard the following exchange at Newmarket during the 1820s.

> 'What do you bet on this race, my lord?' says a vulgar-looking man, on a shabby hack . . . 'I want to back the field,' cries my lord. 'So do I,' says the leg [turf swindler]. 'I'll bet five hundred to two hundred that you don't name the winner,' cries my lord. 'I take six,' exclaims the leg. 'I'll bet it you,' roars my lord.

The stake was then doubled and the pair agreed the wager.[2] In 1851 the fourteenth Earl of Derby and future Conservative Prime Minister was seen at another racetrack 'in the midst of a crowd of blacklegs, betting men and loose characters of every description, in uproarious spirits, chaffing, rowing and shouting with laughter and joking . . . as completely at his ease in contemplating the racecourse as in championing the cause of Altar & Throne'.[3] Tories were always well represented among the sporting aristocracy.

The traditions, conventions and philosophy of the sporting world did not spring into existence ready-made. They had evolved during the eighteenth century under the influence of the aristocracy and, from the mid-nineteenth century onwards, that version of the aristocratic ideal as practised in the post-Arnoldian public schools. The latter catered for the Victorian upper middle class which joined forces with the aristocracy to impose discipline and regulations on the often anarchic and unruly culture of many sports and bring them within the pale of respectability.

The upshot was the creation of voluntary national bodies like the Football Association, founded in 1863, and the formulation of rules that were universally imposed. These new authorities were modelled on the aristocratic MCC and Jockey Club, founded in 1787 and 1750 respectively. The reorganisation of the sporting world was a prelude to its commercialisation, which was underway by the 1880s.

The 'reform' of sport during the middle years of the nineteenth century was to a great extent a reaction to the drunken commotions which marked many sporting events. Every form of contest was a source of gambling, which made sport a magnet for the criminal underworld. Sport may have provided fun for all classes, but it was a seedbed for moral licence. This was how it was portrayed from the pulpit with the most vigorous denunciations coming from plebeian and middle-class nonconformists, for whom just about every form of entertainment was a form of depravity. Lawmakers took a purely pragmatic line, treating sport (particularly bare-knuckle prizefighting) and its murky peripheries as a mainspring of crime and a constant threat to public order.

The aristocracy could find itself in very bad company, not that this troubled many sporting peers. In 1842 the sixth Viscount Chetwynd was charged with organising a prize fight in rural Bedfordshire and obstructing a local magistrate who vainly attempted to halt it. Among Chetwynd's twelve co-defendants was a former champion of England, 'Blind Burke'. Each was fined forty pounds.[4]

Boxing had become fashionable among the nobility during the second half of the eighteenth century, and bouts between champions and contenders attracted huge unruly audiences. A 'large contingent of the rabble' joined the two thousand who had paid half a guinea each to watch 'Big Ben' thrash Johnson in a field near Wrotham in Kent in 1791. There were smaller 'bye-battles' in which the boxers discarded any rules and were judged by 'cognoscenti' to be mere 'violent, straightforward brawls with much bloodshed and very little skill'.[5]

Railways increased the numbers of spectators and opportunities for mayhem. In November 1855 the 'staunchest Corinthian supporters of pugilism' gathered with humbler fans at Fenchurch Street and Shoreditch Stations for trains which took them to Birmingham and a bout between Morris Roberts and 'Young Harrington'. They slugged it out in a fight that went to 142 rounds and lasted for just over three hours. By the end, Roberts was blinded by blood and Harrington was unconscious, but many 'gentlemen' were impressed by his 'plucky' performance and gave him money. The match had been illegal and the arrangements for it clandestine. Three weeks before, the police had stopped a fight between George Baker and the 'New Black' held on a hillside near Tilbury in Essex.[6]

Defenders of boxing claimed that it was demotic and distinctly

British. In 1818 the sporting journalist Pierce Egan noted that 'distinction of rank' was ignored by followers of the 'fancy'. It was 'congenial to the soil of liberty' and a bulwark against incipient decadence, particularly among a nobility which seemed to be sliding into wimpish foppery. 'The English character may get too refined, and the thorough-bred bulldog degenerate into the whining puppy,' warned Egan. There was no chance of this so long as royal princes and peers not only sponsored prizefighters, but regularly took exercise in the new boxing academies and sparred with the veteran pugs who ran them.[7]

This was broadly the view of Lord Palmerston, who, in 1860, described the recent Sayers–Heenan championship fight as an exhibition of British manliness and tenacity which had made a favourable impression on the French. Perhaps so, but the Evangelical MP Lord Lovaine spoke for many others when he characterised the bout as a barbaric spectacle which had shamed a progressive Christian nation and attracted the most depraved sections of society. This was, of course, essentially a high-minded middle-class perspective on prizefighting, but it was one that modern Corinthians had to acknowledge. It was left to one, the volatile eighth Marquess of Queensberry, to initiate reform from within and above, and so bring boxing within the compass of public tolerance. The result was the Queensberry rules of 1867, which, among other things, introduced gloves, and they became the universal regulations for modern boxing.

Horse racing faced similar problems. They were gradually overcome by the efforts of a handful of noblemen working through the Jockey Club. By the 1870s it had secured control over the day-to-day governance of racing. (It still does; in 1998, and following a precedent first set over a hundred and seventy years before, the Jockey Club 'warned off' [i.e. exiled from 'the Turf'] two figures judged to have brought racing into disrepute. Peers still have a powerful say in the Club; in the 1990s they made up two-fifths of its 112 members.[8])

There had always been a close psychological affinity between the aristocracy and the successful breeding of horses. The thoroughbred racehorse was a perfect expression of the aristocratic principle; its superiority was the consequence of the transmission of ability and virtue through bloodlines. Heredity was everything: an ideal horse and an ideal peer were the products of their ancestry. In an age which discounts or even rejects such genetic theories, they remain entrenched in the world of racing. Interestingly, a modern anthropological dissection of this world indicates that it is inhabited at all levels from owners to stable lads by people who feel that racing is somehow 'in their blood', and that there are, as in the aristocracy, interlinked dynasties of trainers and breeders whose expertise is hereditary.[9] Modern racing remains a detached universe which preserves elements of deference and respect for rank that are rarely found elsewhere.

Racing was inseparable from gambling. It had been an aristocratic pastime since the Middle Ages and there are account books which record peers' winnings and losses among regular daily expenditure.[10] Games of hazard killed boredom and offered aristocrats and anyone else who played them the opportunity to make a favourable impression on the beau monde by acquiring a reputation for audacity, indifference to risk and a disdainful nonchalance in the face of often crushing adversity. The same qualities which marked out the gentleman on the battlefield distinguished him at the gaming tables. All gamblers were subject to the gentleman's code of honour; accusations of cheating and non-payment of gambling debts were among the commonest causes of duels.

In the 1790s one illegal London gaming hall had a shooting range attached at which card-sharps daily practised their marksmanship with pistols. Its purpose was explained to rich young men who had been lured into playing by free food, wine and brandy, lost heavily to the sharps and then contemplated welshing.[11] Gambling strongly appealed to callow young aristocrats anxious to acquire the image of a devil-may-care Corinthian and many came a cropper. In 1816 the sixteen-year-old Lord Beauchamp was inveigled into the quarters of the Honourable Augustus Stanhope of the 12th Light Dragoons, who then took £8,000 from him in an evening's play. Stanhope's superiors judged fleecing the naive to be ungentlemanly conduct and he was court-martialled and cashiered.[12]

Racing peers gambled on and off the track. During the prosecution of the proprietors of a London gaming hall (and brothel) in 1844, the third Marquess of Conyngham, a twenty-four-year-old officer in the Life Guards and racehorse breeder, confessed to twice losing £500 in an evening's play. He did not mention any winnings, but these losses may have shocked his Irish tenantry. Their rents contributed to his annual income of £50,000, and so his bad luck at the tables was a bagatelle.[13]

Conyngham died solvent, so he presumably knew when to stop. Others did not and the complementary addictions to betting and bloodstock could prove ruinous. They did for the fourth Marquess of Hastings, whose short life reads like the scenario for a contemporary Christian novel written to warn the young of what God has in store for reprobates. At Eton, Hastings was feckless, idle and irresponsible: he once released a sackful of rats in a ballroom, which created a horror-struck panic among ladies in crinolines. Hastings later eloped with Lady Florence Paget after her engagement to Henry Chaplin, a landowner and breeder of crack thoroughbreds. The two men became racing rivals, and in the 1867 Derby, Chaplin's Hermit beat Hastings's horse and lost its owner £102,000. His attempt to recoup his deficit in the next year's Derby failed and Hastings faced bankruptcy. He died, aged twenty-six, and his final words epitomise the sang-froid of the true plunger: 'Hermit's Derby broke my heart. But I didn't show it, did I?'[14] He was the last of his line.

There had been a strong suspicion of chicanery about the fixing of the odds for Hastings's horse. Scandals had bedevilled the early nineteenth century Turf and, indirectly, they tainted its aristocratic patrons. The principal cause was money: the proliferation of betting and the sums involved had led to various forms of race-fixing, including the poisoning of several horses in 1812, for which a groom was hanged. 'Unprincipled miscreants', all connected with betting, were contaminating the Turf, according to Charles Apperley. The remedy, he thought, lay in the hands of 'Noblemen and gentlemen of fortune and integrity', who had a duty to 'elbow' the intruders from 'ground which ought to be their own'.[15] The same solution was suggested by Judge Alderson when he presided over the case which followed the substitution of a horse which had won the 1843 Derby. The ploy of substituting horses (common enough at the time) was exposed, but Alderson blamed its success on the inertia of men who ought to have known better: 'If gentlemen would associate with gentlemen, and race with gentlemen, we should have no such practises. But, if gentlemen will condescend to race with blackguards, they must expect to be cheated.'[16]

Matters were already in hand thanks to the intervention of Lord George Bentinck, a strong-willed Jockey Club member, bloodstock breeder, amateur jockey and duellist. A protectionist Tory in politics, Bentinck was a radical on the racetrack, where he introduced numerous reforms, including the strict supervision of starts and a fair system of handicapping. Bentinck also waged war against illicit bookmakers and their accomplices and introduced measures to charge spectators and control crowds. Losing ground in the political world, the aristocracy retained and exercised its authority on the Turf. The law assisted: the 1853 Betting Act cracked down on betting houses and opened the way for the modern licensed bookmakers who strove for a respectability which was embodied in the later euphemism 'turf accountant'.

It was not just the honour and prestige of the racing aristocracy that had been compromised by criminality; their livelihoods had been threatened by systematic deception. Bentinck had pocketed £100,000 from betting, over five times the amount he had received in prize-money.[17] When the thirteenth Earl of Eglinton retired from breeding horses in 1855, it was calculated that they had netted him an average of £4,000 annually over twenty years.[18] Between 1873 and 1883 Lord Falmouth made £212,000 and sold his stud for £150,000.[19]

These were returns on investments in bloodstock, premises and staff which only the richest peers could afford, although during the second half of the century there was a growing number of businessmen and industrialists who took up racing. James Merry, a Scottish ironmaster, was one who had Derby winners in 1860 and 1873. Nevertheless, the capital and the prestige of the aristocracy remained vital to the Turf. In 1911, *The Tatler* announced that, after a few wins, the ninth Duke of Devonshire was rekindling his interest in racing, which was welcome news since 'men of the stamp of the duke are badly wanted'.[20]

There was a chilly disdain for the Turf among early Victorian hunting men. After a brief membership of the Jockey Club, the famous sportsman Thomas Assheton Smith resigned. 'He loved the straightforward honesty of a fox hunt, but observed that the chicanery of racing was uncongenial to him.'[21] 'Racing is for rogues,' declared R. S. Surtees's hero Jorrocks, a common and understandable view of the Turf before its reform.

Fox hunting had been an eighteenth-century craze which quickly captured the imagination of landowners of all ranks. It both demanded and cultivated qualities to which gentlemen aspired: fearlessness, nerve and audacious horsemanship. In 'stiff country', observed Charles Apperley, 'a man has nothing to do but to throw his head over and follow it'.[22] Admiration and honour were bestowed on the rider who kept ahead and took his jumps, come what may. Impetuosity and insouciance marked out the heroes of the chase: the third Marquess of Waterford rode his horse into the Kilkenny Club House, guided it upstairs, jumped the dining room table and then returned to the street. He was killed by a fall in the field in 1859.[23] Masters of Foxhounds enjoyed immense local prestige and many went to great lengths to put on lavish entertainments at meets. In the 1820s the Goodwood pack was said to have cost £19,000 a year to maintain. The 'splendour' of Lord Sefton's 'establishment gave spectators more the idea of an imperial hunting party in a foreign country than that of an English pack of foxhounds' noted Apperley.[24]

As with racing, there was a distinctly aristocratic obsession with bloodlines, both of hunters and hounds, whose potential in the field was determined by their ancestry. There was a delight-ful poetry in their names; Juliet, Jingle, Jollity and Jealousy were among Sir Bellingham Graham's pack in the 1820s. They ran ahead of a field which included a Shrewsbury surgeon and lawyer, who, Apperley noted approvingly, 'will charge as large a fence as most people'. In Leicestershire, Apperley was impressed by that 'capital sportsman Mr George Marriot, the draper', whose broken bones testified to his pluckiness.[25] Hunting was aristocratic in tone, but enthusiasm transcended social barriers and it was always open to anyone who could ride and afford to keep, or hire, their mounts. By the 1870s ladies were joining the chase, thanks to the three-pommelled side-saddle and the 'safety skirt'. They soon proved they could equal or surpass men in stamina and pace.

Horse racing, hunting and shooting confirmed the aristocracy's traditional image of itself as fit, tough, adventurous and jauntily indifferent to risks. These were manly qualities, invaluable in war, and worth cultivating among the young of all classes in an imperial nation conscious of its need to keep ahead in a com-petitive world. The second half of the nineteenth century saw the promotion of the cult of manliness through sport and the revival of chivalry. Schoolmasters, clergymen and social reformers led the way, and, with some moral amendment and a strong injection of notion of knightly self-sacrifice and duty, the values of the sporting aristocracy became models for the nation's youth. Living examples littered schoolboy literature: there were resourceful subalterns thrusting forward imperial frontiers and daring gentlemen sportsmen stalked big game in Asia and Africa.

One celebrated big-game hunter imagined, with some accuracy, the upper-middle class lad returning home from his public school:

> The first thing he does . . . is to rush off to his own den to see if his fishing-rod or stuffed birds are all right; then he goes to his kennel to see his spaniel and ferrets. His first question will be whether there are lots of rabbits and trout about, and whether the rats have come back to the hayloft . . .[26]

Moving upwards in the scales of age and social status, these preoccupations parallel those of a sporting peer, who, on returning from London to the country, immediately inspects his stables and kennels and questions his keepers and huntsmen about pheasant numbers or the whereabouts of local foxes.

In all likelihood, the sporting lad would have been exposed at school to indoctrination in the rules of the new chivalry. The young Victorian knight was strong, courageous, courteous, just and, like Sir Galahad, he was pure in heart and mind. What was taught in the public schools was disseminated to the lower-middle and working classes through the Boys Brigade and, in the early 1900s, the Boy Scouts. There was a paradox here: the Gothic moral revival was resuscitating and elevating the values of the medieval aristocracy at a time when its successors were gradually forfeiting their political and social eminence.

The Victorian adoration of chivalric virtues was selective and never an endorsement of the excesses of some of the contemporary sporting peerage. Some of their activities were judged incompatible with spiritual regeneration. Dr Arnold banned sporting guns and dogs from Rugby in the 1830s, and at Marlborough in the 1850s illicit ratting and poaching were replaced by football and cricket. Team games demanded the suppression of the individualism of the hunting field, even if footballers and cricketers were likened to knights.[27] This extended to horse racing: figures of knights were chosen for the silver trophies designed in 1852 and 1853 for the Ascot Queen's Cup and the Doncaster Race Cup.

The reinvention of chivalry was an offshoot of the Romantic Gothic movement which had emerged at the close of the eighteenth century. Its prophet and guide had been Sir Walter Scott, whose Toryism coloured his historical novels and appealed to aristocratic ultras. They found themselves immersed in a world favourable to their kind at a time when their old power was being challenged and eroded. The England of *Ivanhoe* (1819) was a rural country united by the human ties of feudalism: vassals obeyed lords who cared for their welfare. It was much the same in the Scotland of the Waverley novels, where the bonds between chieftains and clans held society together. There was reverence for the hierarchy of Crown, aristocracy and Church, and, so it was imagined, happiness for all in a universe in which everyone knew their duties and their place.

Industrial Britain had discarded ancient certainties and modern economists focused on profit had little truck with theories of social reciprocity, or paternalism. The Gothic past was, therefore, an attractive country for conservative noblemen, who, unable to preserve its spirit, resorted to restoring its outward trappings. Peers rebuilt and altered their houses in the Gothic style and filled them with collections of genuine and fabricated armour. One nobleman, the thirteenth Earl of Eglinton, went a step further and, in 1838, announced that he would hold a tournament at his castle in Ayrshire in the August of the following year.

Eglinton was a Tory and a celebrated racing peer who, like many of his kind, had been dismayed by the way in which the cheapskate and prosaic Whigs had stripped the Queen's coronation of its medieval splendour. Out had gone the banquet in Westminster Hall and the challenge made by the mounted and armoured royal champion, and the high officers of the royal household were denied their ornamental functions. Eglinton offered to make amends with a Gothic extravaganza to which he invited 2,690 guests; Whigs and radicals were banned.

The Eglinton tournament was a splendid fiasco. Thirteen armoured knights (including six peers) turned up to cross lances and swords, visitors wore medieval dress and there was an unfunny jester. All were soaked by heavy rain and the jousting field became a quagmire. There was some compensation for the Gothic-minded aristocracy in 1842, when Queen Victoria held a medieval *bal costumé* at Buckingham Palace in which she appeared as the fourteenth-century Queen Phillipa and Prince Albert as her husband Edward III. Another less celebrated (or notorious) tournament was held in 1912 at Earl's Court before a blue-blooded audience. Lady Curzon was the 'Queen of Beauty' and five peers jousted for her favour. The winner was the first Lord Ashby St Ledgers, whose family had made its fortune in steel.[28] At the same time, General Baden-Powell was persuading his scouts to think of themselves as young knights dedicated to chivalry. A few years later, images of medieval knights and St George were used extensively to promote Britain's war effort.[29] Many appeared on the war memorials of the 1920s.

*

Pseudo-Gothicism had been grafted on to the traditions of sport. The aristocratic principle of leadership remained strong and was justified by A. G. Steel, the captain of England's Test XI in 1904. 'Amateurs have always made, and always will make, the best captains; and this is only natural. An educated mind, with the logical power of reasoning, will always treat every subject better than one untaught.' The seventh Lord Hawke, who captained Yorkshire between 1880 and 1910 and led teams on several Empire tours, believed that it would be a 'black day' for national prestige if a professional ever captained a touring team.[30]

Lord Hawke was one of the heroes of a nation that had become infected by a sports mania to which the aristocracy succumbed with energy and enthusiasm, which was not surprising given its muscular traditions. While peers squared up to the political challenges of 1910 and 1911, many found abundant time to engage in sport and be photographed doing so for the aristocracy's house magazine, *The Tatler*. The diehard Lord Willoughby de Broke ('a very skilful game shot') poses with his shotgun and the fifth Marquess of Conyngham ('the best-known sportsman in West Ireland') maintains his family tradition by wading thigh deep in a river with his stick in hand in pursuit of otters. The marriage of the eighty-one-year-old Lord Suffield ('a famous cross-country rider [who] once won every race on the card at an Irish point-to-point') to a colonel's widow is celebrated by a picture of the pair standing with their bicycles. The fifth Earl Lonsdale, a racing peer and master of the Cottesmore Hunt, kicks off a charity football match and elsewhere are pictures of peers and peeresses at race meetings, hunts, shooting parties, the Henley regatta and Cowes week. *The Tatler's* regular 'Varsity Notes' are wholly devoted to the achievements of Oxford and Cambridge sportsmen. The overall impression is that undergraduates spent all of their time in pursuit of blues, which many did.

Looking at these images, one could be forgiven for conclud-
ing that the sporting life was now the only one for a large swathe
of the nobility. Of course, peers had always engaged in sport,
often fanatically and for a valid reason. Since the Renaissance,
they had been urged to achieve a balance between the athletic
and the intellectual which was vital for men destined by birth
and custom to lead in peace and command in war. The latter
prerogative had survived into the twentieth century, the former
had not. Yet the new dispensation and the depleted chances of
attaining the highest offices had not deterred young peers from
embarking on political careers. In these circumstances, pre-eminence in the world of sport offered a compensation, insofar as
the aristocracy remained integrated within the fabric of national
life and enjoyed a degree of popularity. Of course, there were
political peers who had a sporting reputation; Lord Rosebery's
three Derby winners and Arthur Balfour's enjoyment of golf
and motoring did them no harm.

At the same time, the early twentieth century's aristocracy's
passion for sport was an indication that the decline in its public
responsibilities allowed its members greater time for leisure. As
always, field sports loomed large; the trio of 'huntin', shootin'
and fishin'' which appear so often in *Who's Who* entries became
synonymous with the aristocracy and gentry and also retired
officers, diplomats and colonial officials. During the political
crises of 1910 and 1911 *Punch* cartoonists depicted peers as
ermined and coronetted figures incongruously wielding shot-
guns on grouse moors.

Then and afterwards, field sports defined the aristocracy, in
particular, its most conservative elements. An addiction to field
sports emphasised the nobility's isolation from the middle classes
who watched cricket and played tennis, golf and rugby, although
these had a strong aristocratic following, and the working classes
who were addicted to football. By the second half of the century,
all were subject to increasing commercialisation and became

'products' to be marketed to the masses through television. The pass once defended by Lord Hawke and those of his mind was finally and symbolically sold in 1963 when the MCC abolished the distinctions between 'gentlemen' and 'players' and agreed to the razor manufacturer Gillette's sponsorship of the novel one-day cricket tournament.

Yet, ironically, since the early nineteenth century, the Scottish aristocracy had been perfectly happy to rent out its shooting estates, often for large sums.[31] Economic survival came first, although, on the eve of grouse-shooting season in 1911, *The Tatler* was saddened by the fate of 'some of the Scotch landowners' who had been 'turned out of their castles to make room for the shooting tenants'. There was, however, consolation, since the Dukes of Richmond, Atholl, Sutherland and Buccleuch could still afford to maintain their 'great shootings' for themselves and their guests. Economic forces intruded and, within seventy years, the owners of just about every Scottish shooting estate had become entrepreneurs selling the right to shoot their game to the highest bidder, who was often a moneybags who had made money in the City. It was revealing that the new rich of the late twentieth century wished briefly to enjoy the pleasures of the Edwardian aristocrat, but then new money has always adopted the spending habits of old.

22

The Surrender of Feudalism to Industry: The Mid-Victorian Peerage 1846–87

Henry Manners, fifth Duke of Rutland, believed that the Reform Act had been a calamitous break with the past. Unable to reverse the course of history, he could comfort himself by re-creating the distant glory of an aristocracy whose future now seemed uncertain. He rebuilt Belvoir Castle in a self-consciously backward-looking style, Regency Gothic. The result was an enchanting piece of romantic medievalism in the same spirit as Scott's novels and border ballads. Turrets, crenellations and vaulted passages remind us that the Manners were an ancient family of the kind Scott venerated. In 1815 he had confessed that his 'aristocratic prejudices are much hurt by the decay of the ancient nobility of Britain'.[1]

Belvoir's architecture and Scott's imagination idealised the Middle Ages. Each evoked a world of chivalry in which a gallant and humane aristocracy had exercised a benevolent power over a happy and grateful peasantry. There was a political element in this atavism which forms the theme of Benjamin Disraeli's Young England novels, *Coningsby*, *Sybil*, and *Tancred* (1844–47). Each was an appeal to the younger generation of noblemen to revive feudal paternalism and rescue the nation from a cold-hearted and rapacious plutocracy, which, he believed, was the beneficiary of the Reform Act. Bonds of feudal obligation and mutual respect between aristocracy and people would replace the inhuman cash nexus of capitalism. An alliance between the nobility and the masses would politically marginalise the middle class and its arid philosophies of profit and usefulness. Rutland's eldest son, Lord John Manners MP, was converted to Disraeli's vision, but his level-headed father and most other peers thought it fanciful.

The Duke was, however, a paternalist of the old school when it came to hospitality. Every year, Belvoir was the setting for lavish and exuberant celebrations of Rutland's birthday on 4 January. Charles Greville was a regular guest and in 1838 he slipped away from the main party to watch the festivities in the servants' hall, now used for wedding receptions and conferences. A duke's grandson and a stiff Tory, Greville was heartened by what he saw. There were nearly a hundred of his host's servants full of bounce and food, raising their glasses to their master. He was most struck by a toast made by the head coachman, a man 'of great abdominal dignity' in the flaxen wig which denoted his office. Greville wished that this spectacle could have been seen by 'the surly radical' who ranted about 'the selfish aristocracy who have no sympathies with the people'.

Would, he wondered, the middle-class, Benthamite creed of 'the greatest happiness for the greatest number' be advanced by the 'destruction of all the feudality' represented by this merriment? Or would 'abstract political rights' compensate for 'all the beef and ale and music' which gave the servants such joy, even for a short time? Greville thought not and the following day he was delighted to witness a ball to which over two hundred 'tenants, shopkeepers, valets and abigails' had been invited.[2]

Greville had witnessed the reality of what would become the Arcadia of romantic Tory imagination and, for that matter, later romantic novelists in which buxom milkmaids curtseyed and apple-cheeked yokels touched their forelocks to kind-hearted squires. This rural world and its essentially hierarchical patterns of human relations was familiar to the aristocracy and it survived. In 1880, Earl Percy, heir to the sixth Duke of Northumberland and MP for North Northumberland, assured the Commons that the old rustic order was alive (as his election proved) and deserved their admiration. 'Country gentlemen were the most respected and respectable class in the country,' he claimed, for they had 'the interests of the people at heart, took part in sports and directed the local affairs of their districts, thus showing they were of use and influence'.[3] This was, of course, a view from the top, uttered in opposition to a drastic revision of the Game Laws, but it should not be forgotten that social change in Victorian Britain was a slow and uneven process in which the rural universe lagged behind the urban.

Victorian noblemen continued to perform the same duties as their ancestors had. Greville thought his host Rutland addicted to the common vices of his kind: selfishness and hedonism. Nevertheless, the Duke yielded to 'duty and inclination' and took seriously his responsibilities as a guardian of the local Poor Law Union, which collected and dispensed the rates levied to relieve the poor. Every fortnight he visited workhouses, listened to the paupers' grievances and took them up with his fellow guardians. Henry Fitzroy, fifth Duke of Grafton, visited cottagers on his Suffolk estates, enquired as to their wants, distributed gifts (including blankets) and had a reputation as a lenient magistrate. He was also a staunch Anglican and made sure that all his tenants were as well.[4]

Aristocratic vices coexisted with virtues in a society whose tone had become more restrained, godly and earnest. In 1838 Greville was dismayed by the tedium and joylessness of the young Victoria's court at Windsor. Older peers stuck to the free-and-easy codes of their youth. Greville observed that the sixth Duke of Bedford was a 'complete sensualist' who 'thinks nothing but his personal enjoyments; and it has long been part of his system not to allow himself to be disturbed by the necessities of others'.[5] The life of the seventh Earl of Waldegrave, who died aged thirty in 1845, was summarised by an obituarist as one of 'wild excesses', details of which 'adorn the records of the police courts'.[6] Other peers succumbed to the new moral severity. The eighth Duke of Argyll was president of the Society for the Encouragement of Purity in Literature, and Lord Robert Grosvenor MP was a notorious killjoy who was hooted by London mobs for his championship of strict observance of the Sabbath.

Aristocratic eccentricity remained inventive. Alexander, tenth Duke of Hamilton, wore a frogged military jacket, skin-tight trousers and hessian boots and had his hair in a pigtail, which had been the fashion when he had been a young diplomat at the court of Catherine the Great. He was extremely haughty and imagined that he was the rightful King of Scotland, which may explain why he ordered his executors to have his body placed in an ancient sarcophagus imported from Egypt and buried under a huge mausoleum.[7]

Hamilton's quirks were trifling when set alongside the crankiness of the fifth Duke of Portland, who died in 1879. Whether because of a fixation with privacy or manic shyness, he withdrew from the world into a vast network of tunnels excavated in and around his house at Welbeck in Nottinghamshire. The largest was over a mile long, wide enough to allow two carriages to pass and lit by skylights in daytime and gas at night. The crepuscular Duke was generous to the workmen who burrowed for him, giving them umbrellas in wet weather and providing donkeys to carry them to and from their labours. His servants were ordered to treat him as if he were invisible and not to look at him as they performed their duties.

Noblemen were the heroes of the largely male, working and lower-middle class sporting public. One of its heroes, the fifth Earl of Glasgow (1792-1869) was the ideal Corinthian peer, a devil-may-care extrovert who spoke his mind freely and was 'a liberal supporter of all manly exercises'. His jockeys' colours of white and red always attracted bets, for Glasgow had a knack of matching suitable bloodlines. Sadly, he failed in his ambition to win the Derby and St Leger, but, as a true sportsman, he always 'sank all memories of his losses in the sunshine of the next victory'.

Glasgow was also a 'plunger' who lived hard and dangerously. His 'boon companions' were the Marquess of Queensberry, Lord Kennedy, Sir James Boswell and Sir John Heron Maxwell who were 'as rollicking a quintet as ever drained a bottle and drank a toast'. During one bout, Glasgow wagered five-hundred pounds on a midnight coach race between himself and Kennedy and won. The Earl's interest in the world beyond the stable and covert was negligible, although he did break ranks from the majority of peers by voting to repeal the Corn Laws, perhaps more out of mischief than conviction.[8]

Historians tend to overlook peers like Glasgow, preferring to concentrate on more august figures who filled ministries and regularly declaimed in the Lords. Contemporaries were not so dismissive. In 1868, the Tory *Saturday Review* noted approvingly that a considerable section of society warmed to the aristocracy simply because so many were dashing sportsmen. Men who read 'sporting journals' and bet on 'dark horses' loved peers, whom they associated with 'a "jolly" enjoyment of life' and a 'reckless prodigality of money'.[9]

This goodwill offset the animosity towards the aristocracy expressed by 'disappointed doctrinaires and unsuccessful politicians'. The author had in mind predominantly middle-class liberals and radicals impatient with the hesitant pace of reform under Palmerston, who served twice as Prime Minister and dominated mid-century political life. 'Pam' believed that the nation was prospering as never before because it had achieved social unity and a political equilibrium in which the aristocracy was a vital makeweight.

Radical Liberals disagreed. They wanted to extend the franchise to include the better off working classes and to remove the influence of the aristocracy over appointments to the civil service and army, which they considered unjust and an encouragement to inefficiency. Ample proof of this was provided during the winter of 1854–5, when the logistics and medical services of the army in the Crimea fell apart. Radicals blamed aristocratic commanders, notably Lords Raglan, Cardigan and Lucan who owed their rank to purchase, connections and nepotism. Cardigan was said to have paid £10,000 for command of the 11th Hussars and spent a similar sum annually on their gorgeous uniforms. He was a reactionary Tory, a duellist, a magnet for a scandal and showed a swaggering contempt for social inferiors and middle-class morality. His qualities made him an aristocratic hate figure in the press, not that he gave a damn.[10] Battlefield blunders of men of Cardigan's stamp were compounded by bureaucrats who owed their posts to patronage.

Early in 1855 Palmerston praised Cardigan and the system he had come to embody. 'Talk to me of the aristocracy of England,' he challenged the Commons. 'Why, look at that glorious charge of cavalry at Balaklava – look to that charge, where the noblest and wealthiest of the land rode foremost, followed by heroic men from the lowest classes in the community, each rivalling the other in bravery.'[11] The Charge of the Light Brigade had taught Britain a lesson in social cohesion and the value of the aristocracy. This was already understood by the middle classes; throughout the war, the newspapers had been full of stirring reports of the exploits, wounds and heroic deaths of well-born young officers who set their men examples of selfless courage.

Palmerston had bought time for the aristocracy. His death in 1865 marked the beginning of a cascade of electoral reforms over the next twenty years which transformed the political landscape. Reform and redistribution acts, the introduction of a secret ballot and the 1883 Corrupt Practices Act created a democracy in which nearly two-thirds of adult males had the vote and were theoretically free to use it without external pressure. Democratic politics required the tightening of party discipline within and beyond Parliament and nationwide party machines whose local agencies registered voters, managed elections and helped choose candidates who would dance to the party's tune.

Where did this leave the Lords? It remained integral to public life; it was a watchdog which could bark and, in exceptional circumstances, bite, although it preferred not to. Biting meant throwing out laws passed by the Commons and, in theory, approved by the electorate. This impotence disturbed Lord Robert Gascoyne-Cecil MP, the younger son of the second Marquess of Salisbury, who succeeded his father in 1868. He was the rising star of the Tories, a pessimistic intellectual and a mordant political journalist who believed that the aristocratic principle was central to Conservatism. Mass politics frightened him: 'Whatever happens will be for the worse,' he once said, 'and therefore it is in our interest that as little should happen as possible.' In the same vein, he observed that 'The use of Conservatism was to delay changes till they become harmless'.[12] Scientific innovation was another matter; during the 1870s Salisbury was one of the first peers to have his house lit by electricity and possess a telephone.

In 1868, the year he entered the Lords, Salisbury was anxious about its future. He regretted its 'slavery' to the Commons, feared that it might wither away from disuse, and wanted to revitalise it by ennobling men from diverse but not necessarily landed backgrounds, something he achieved as Prime Minister after 1886. A regenerated Lords could enlarge its influence by 'interpreting the deliberate wishes of the nation'.[13]

The 1880 election confirmed Salisbury's pessimism. The Liberals won and showed signs of lurching towards the left, although the new generation of radical MPs were restrained by the Whig peers who dominated William Gladstone's cabinet. This situation offered advantages to the Tories, and an opportunity for the Lords to reclaim their old reputation for independence despite the inbuilt majority of Conservative peers. They and their party were now what one journalist called 'a safeguard against the fatal rashness of popular movements, and against the disregard of justice which popular excitement would sometimes, in haste, drive us'.[14] 'Justice' embraced the abstract rights of property which some radicals and Irish Home Rulers were bent on eroding. All property owners could look with confidence to the Lords as their natural allies.

As the Lords contemplated a new political role, most peers were beginning to feel the pinch. Land had remained the prime source of wealth for the mid-Victorian aristocracy; in the 1870s nine out of ten British millionaires were landowners, with 180 peers owning estates of over 10,000 acres. These statistics did not mask the facts that the overall wealth generated by industry and commerce had outstripped that produced by agriculture and that land was no longer a stable asset.

This seismic shift in the British economy had been politically confirmed in 1846 by the repeal of the Corn Laws. This had been a bitter experience for the aristocracy, for it both confirmed the constitutional demotion of the Lords and hurt their pocket books. Superficially, the debate over whether to continue to impose duties on imported wheat was about economics, but the arguments of the protagonists transformed it into a symbolic struggle between industrial and agricultural interests. Town and factory were ranged against countryside and farm. Early in 1846 the Sussex branch of the Agricultural Protection Society assembled at Brighton (there were two dukes and three earls present) to hear the fifth Duke of Richmond call upon landowners, farmers and labourers to unite. He spoke 'as a landowner, as a farmer and a member of the aristocracy' and warned that if the Corn Laws were repealed, then estates would fall 'under the hammer' and rural communities would become destitute.[15]

As in 1832, the aristocracy was isolated and divided. Whigs and Liberals favoured repeal, as did the Conservative Prime Minister Sir Robert Peel and his personal supporters. Adherents of the Anti-Corn Law League believed that the country was behind them. Since 1839 it had waged a large-scale, national campaign in the press and through public meetings and pamphlets, all of which were lavishly funded by northern and Midlands businessmen and manufacturers. They hoped that without the Corn Laws bread prices would stabilise at a low level which would keep down wages. The League also opened a second front against the Game Laws.

Using their Lords majority, the Tory peers resisted. Lord Gage predicted that agricultural revenues would plummet. More than money was at stake, he continued, for the opponents of the Corn Laws included Quakers, Baptists and Unitarians, whom Gage identified as 'known and suspected' enemies of the Crown, the aristocracy and the state.[16] Jeremiads and hyperbole were the Tory lords' only weapons in a rearguard action which was discreetly terminated by the Duke of Wellington. He persuaded the Lords not to provoke a constitutional crisis by blocking a measure which was backed by the Commons, Queen Victoria and the vast majority of her subjects. The Duke's prestige prevailed, and the Conservative Party disintegrated, with the Peelites trooping off towards the Whig benches and the protectionist rump under the fourteenth Earl of Derby and Disraeli wandering off into the political outback. The Conservatives did not win another general election until 1874.

The inability of the aristocracy to save agriculture led to minor tremors in the countryside. In 1851, the Tory Lord Newark, the heir of Earl Manvers, had a rough time contesting South Nottinghamshire against a local solicitor, W. H. Barrow, who called himself the farmers' candidate. His platform was 'a good price for the farmer and cheap food' and local landowners treated him as a direct challenge to their traditional influence. 'We are opposed by four Dukes, six other peers, nearly the entire body of the squirearchy and most of the clergy,' boasted Barrow, 'but we can win.' And he did.[17]

Barrow's balance of cheap food and fair prices was impossible to achieve. Agricultural profit margins had always been narrow, although, thanks to the Corn Laws, the economic future for farming had seemed bright. Between 1815 and 1846 the Dukes of Northumberland and Newcastle had invested over half a million pounds in the extension and improvement of their estates. Like every other landowner, they were cushioned against periodic poor harvests by the Corn Laws, which inflated the price of home-grown grain whenever a dearth occurred. Even so, their rent rolls were never wholly protected; whenever yields fell below par, landlords were driven to make rent reductions.

The Corn Laws had provided a safety net. The foreboding expressed during the debate on repeal proved correct, but premature. There were rough times; between 1850 and 1852 poor harvests did not drive up bread prices (thanks to imported wheat), but landlords were forced to make rent concessions of up to 10 per cent.[18] The problem then and later was that while a landlord had to accept a lower rent, he could not fend off his creditors or suspend mortgage payments and allowances to his dependants.

Agriculture did undergo a recovery, guided and financed by the larger aristocratic proprietors who had the resources to fund investment and adjust their land-management policies. Extended leases, the weeding out of incompetent tenants, investments in modern techniques, the exploitation of new chemical fertilisers and diversification alleviated short-term problems. Surveying the state of farming in 1866, the *Edinburgh Review* was optimistic; modernisation was working and the great aristocratic landlords were praised for financing improvement schemes which were raising yields.[19]

Yet progress required ambitious investment programmes which were beyond the resources of most of the nobility. Returns on capital were disappointing, hovering between 1 and 4 per cent, figures that ruled out borrowing on the money markets, which charged annual interest rates of between 3 and 4 per cent. Agriculture was being starved of capital and the symptoms of stagnation began to appear.

There were some areas untouched by scientific husbandry, where farmers stuck to the old ways and went to the wall. In parts of north Wales, tenants were sinking to the level of subsistence farming.[20] As ever, there were the natural hazards of agriculture. During 1865 and early 1866 a cattle plague spread across the country and thousands of beasts had to be destroyed. A royal commission investigated the outbreak, chaired by the fifth Earl Spencer; the nobility continued to undertake those unpaid, useful public duties which the state had always expected from them.

The cattle pandemic was a prelude for a series of poor harvests in 1873, 1875, 1876 and, worst of all, 1879. Landlords were driven to remit between 10 and 20 per cent of their rents, and agriculture was plunged into a recession which lasted until the Great War. Corn from the American and Canadian prairies fed the nation, which, by the mid-1880s, was also eating canned and frozen meat from the Argentine and New Zealand. Meanwhile, the aristocracy faced the severest economic crisis in its history with serious liquidity problems and plummeting land values. The value of arable land in south-eastern England fell by nearly 40 per cent and pasture in Scotland and the North-West by 20 and 12 per cent respectively.[21] A former asset had become an encumbrance. In Oscar Wilde's *The Importance of Being Earnest* (1895), Lady Bracknell cruelly summed up the predicament (and embarrassment) of the aristocracy: 'Land has ceased to be either a profit or a pleasure. It gives one a position, and prevents one from keeping it up.'

Some peers possessed non-agricultural assets. For the past four hundred years, noblemen had exploited mineral deposits on their lands and urban property, particularly in London and its suburbs. During the eighteenth century, aristocrats had invested in canals, turnpikes and harbour developments which facilitated the distribution of foodstuffs, coal and iron ore.

Railway expansion in the 1830s and 1840s attracted aristocratic capital and lobbying. In 1844, the fifth Earl Fitzwilliam endeavoured to have the London-Edinburgh line routed through Lincoln so that crops grown in his estates could secure fast access to markets in London and the North-East. He also purchased shares in the South Yorkshire Railway which carried coal from his mines.[22] Profit was not allowed to interfere with pleasure and Fitzwilliam demanded a small detour in the London-Edinburgh line near Peterborough so that trains would not disturb the foxes in one of his best coverts. Edward Littleton, created Lord Hatherton in 1835, was a Midlands landowner with extensive interests in local canals and railway promotion. Landownership never blinded peers to the potential returns offered by industrial expansion. Four millionaire peers who died between 1830 and 1880 had mineral, transport and urban real-estate interests.[23]

Nor were aristocrats snobbishly averse to new forms of moneymaking. Hampered by debts, Lord Robert Cecil agreed in 1867 to become executive chairman of the very wobbly Great

Eastern Railway for seven hundred pounds a year. It was less than half of what he had been offered, but, unlike so many of his modern counterparts, he had admirably high moral standards. 'A highly paid chairman', he told his employers, 'is a luxury which should be reserved for the return of a good shareholders' dividend.' Within a year and after some intensive and rigorous reorganisation, he had turned round the Great Eastern.[24]

Hitherto, the aristocratic principle had rested on landowner-ship, which, in theory, had given the nobility its political independence. But by 1880 land had been superseded in terms of its gross value by the assets amassed by those engaged in manufacturing and trade. As early as 1856 The Times had suggested that the peerage should be extended to include rich men whose fortunes did not rest on land. Celebrating the peerage given to Edward Strutt, a radical MP with an industrial background, it endorsed a Manchester newspaper's comment that the Lords should now reflect current economic reality, which was the consequence of 'the surrender of feudalism to industry'.[25] This suggestion was not taken up for thirty years, largely thanks to a lack of political will.

In discussing the expansion of the Lords, The Times insisted that the aristocratic principle 'corresponds to sentiments so long cherished in the bosoms of Englishmen that they have become part of our nature'. Affection for the nobility did not override deeply felt resentments against the old methods of patronage which the aristocracy continued to practise. They offended the sensibilities and ambitions of the middle class, who believed in the sovereignty of talent and perseverance. These qualities rather than birth or connections had secured the middle class its place in the world. In 1870 Gladstone's government introduced competitive examinations for the civil service and abolished the purchase of army commissions. The latter provoked some rumblings from the Lords but they subsided when the measure was passed by a royal warrant.

The aristocracy had suffered a limited setback. Vestiges of patronage remained. Ministers retained the right to choose their secretaries, while proconsuls chose their immediate staff and some other appointments. In 1878 Lord Malmesbury invoked 'old friendship' when he wrote to the seventh Duke of Marlborough, then Viceroy of Ireland, asking him to secure a resident magistracy for his nephew, who had been invalided out of the Indian civil service. The request was approved.[26]

Significantly, the Foreign Office was exempt from the new system of recruitment. Upholding the dignity and prestige of Britain abroad was best entrusted to noblemen and gentlemen and their sons, whose manners and bearing enabled them to move confidently among their own kind at foreign courts. As Lord Robert Cecil cynically commented, all that was required of junior attachés was fluent French and the ability to 'dangle about at parties and balls'.[27]

Ornamental diplomats moved up the ladder and, in time, would become responsible for the conduct of Britain's relations with foreign countries and the governance of its dominions and colonies. In 1883 all ambassadorships (Paris, Vienna, Berlin, Rome, Constantinople and St Petersburg) were held by peers, and there was a large scattering of baronets and younger sons among the secretaries, attachés, consul-generals and legation staff. The Viceroy of India, the Governor-General of Canada and the Governors of Victoria and New South Wales were peers. Whether as an ambassador in Vienna or as Governor-General in Sydney, a nobleman knew how to behave tactfully and with grace, observe the punctilio of precedence and play host at receptions in which he represented the person of the Queen. In 1891 an Australian parliamentarian insisted that his countrymen 'want English gentlemen to lead society instead of some broken-down or disappointed local politician'.[28]

While the aristocracy manned the nation's outposts, its domestic prestige suffered a hard although not unexpected knock. Within weeks of winning the 1880 election, the Liberals introduced the Ground Game Bill which finally overturned the old Game Laws and permitted tenants to hunt hares and rabbits on their own land. Supporters of the measure argued that it was now imperative, given the chronic agricultural recession, although despite this there were sporting landlords who preferred granting 'large reductions of rent' to forfeiting their game rights.

These were fiercely upheld by most peers, many of whom were angry that the state should introduce a law that interfered with the essentially private relationship between landlord and tenant. This was 'outrageous' thought Lord Elcho, another peer believed that the bill would encourage poachers, and Lord Balfour of Burghleigh feared that it would foster rural idleness, since young men with sporting proclivities would abandon work to shoot hares and rabbits. In support of the bill, the fifth Marquess of Ailesbury argued that it was intolerable for a labourer and his family to go hungry while 'half-tamed pheasants' wandered about near his cottage.[29] Ninety-four peers voted for the bill, fifty-nine against.

The loss of game rights appeared to be the thin end of a wedge that would be driven into the rights of property in general. An Irish peer, Lord Oranmore and Brown denounced the game legislation as arbitrary confiscation which transferred to tenant farmers 'the property of another class'.[30] Equally disturbing was the Irish Land Act of 1881, which allowed the state to dictate rents. Landlords faced further vexation (and possible losses) from the radical 'Three-Acres-and-a-Cow' agitation which proposed creating smallholdings for labourers with land taken from rural estates. This movement sank without trace, but Liberal crofting laws confirmed the widespread fear that landlords' legal rights were in jeopardy. The 1885 election saw a severe jolt to rural deference when newly enfranchised farm-workers swung to the Liberals.

Aristocratic morale sagged in the early 1880s, although Gladstone reassured Queen Victoria (1837–1901) of his unwavering faith in the 'hereditary principle'. Some peers were unconvinced. The otherwise taciturn fourth Earl of Carnarvon got the jitters and invested in lands in Canada and Australia in case the 'times should grow bad', so that his family could 'make a new home across the seas'.[31] Lord Salisbury's reaction to uncertain times was aggressive, for he recognised that the new tenor of Liberalism gave Conservatives and the aristocracy an opportunity to find friends. When Gladstone had described his Irish land statutes as measures to appease the 'land hunger' of the Irish peasantry, Salisbury responded tartly. If land hunger justified what was tantamount to confiscation of aristocratic estates, would 'house hunger', 'consols hunger' and 'silver plate hunger' be used to justify the expropriation of middle-class property?[32] It was a telling point and was not lost on the middle-class owners of villas in the expanding suburbs of London and other large cities; their property meant as much to them as mansions and acres of the aristocracy meant to their owners.

The charismatic, bold and pugnacious Lord Randolph Churchill MP, the second son of the seventh Duke of Marlborough and father of Winston, was prepared to go further. In the Commons he mercilessly harried Gladstone (it was said that he treated him as a telescope, drawing him out, seeing through him and shutting him up), and at public meetings across the country he preached his new creed of Tory Democracy. 'Give it 'em hot, Randy,' shouted one listener, and Churchill did.[33] His Conservatism was patriotic, populist and sympathetic to reform. In the words of Churchill's admirer Lord Charles Beresford MP, the Tories 'must go with the people . . . organise and guide the masses and not treat them as scum as the Tories had so often have done'.[34] The aristocracy was at the heart of Lord Randolph's vision; in 1884 he portrayed the Lords as a 'bulwark of liberty and civil order' which rendered invaluable services to the nation. There were distinct echoes of Disraeli's Young England idealism of forty years before with its dream of peers leading the people.

Churchill's friend the Liberal Lord Rosebery saw in him a fusion of the aristocratic and the bohemian who brought to politics the 'keen enjoyment of an undergraduate on the fifth of November'.[35] This was about right, but the qualities which endeared Churchill to Rosebery disturbed Salisbury, who instinctively despised demagoguery, even the Tory brand. Nevertheless, he had to admit Lord Randolph to his Cabinet as Chancellor of the Exchequer, but in 1887 a quarrel over naval estimates led to his resignation. It was a flourish which failed, and Lord Randolph drifted into the political wilderness. The Conservative succession was open to Salisbury's nephew, Arthur Balfour, whom Churchill had once nicknamed 'Posslethwaite' on account of his diffidence.

The career of Lord Randolph Churchill is one of the great might-have-beens in the history of the aristocracy. In just over five years he had attempted to revitalise Conservatism as a positive rather than negative political force, and proved that an aristocrat could master the new demotic politics and inspire the masses. He scared the Liberals and the stuffier elements in the Conservatives, who were always uncomfortable with genius, particularly if it was wayward. Salisbury and the spirit of 'safety first' prevailed; he won elections in 1886, 1895 and 1900, which, among other things, confirmed the resilience of the aristocratic principle in which he had so much faith.

It is a commonplace that the mid-Victorian period witnessed the 'triumph' of the middle classes. This is true up to a point, but their new eminence also allowed the nobility plenty of scope to exercise the very considerable remains of its old influence. The British aristocracy had adapted well to a new world, unlike the Irish, which found itself increasingly detested and isolated.

——◆——

Revolvers Prominently Displayed: The Downfall of the Irish Aristocracy

The Irish aristocracy failed to stay afloat in the nineteenth century. A far less sturdy craft than its British counterpart, it drifted, capsized and finally sank under the weight of its own debts. Its fate drew few tears from the mass of the Irish people. They lived in a predominantly agricultural country which staggered from one economic crisis to another, each caused by demography, primitive husbandry, low investment and landowners largely concerned with preserving a fragile solvency.

It was calculated in 1841 that a thousand Irish men and women produced enough food for fourteen hundred, including themselves. In England the same number fed four thousand.[1]

Given the rapid rise in Ireland's population (over 8 million according to the 1841 census) and the absence of manufacturing industries to absorb the surplus, a Malthusian catastrophe was a matter of time. It occurred between 1846 and 1849, when successive failures of the potato crop led to a famine and epidemics of typhus and dysentery. One and a quarter million died and during the next thirty years a further 2.75 million emigrated. Amazingly, this demographic upheaval made very little difference to Ireland's economic problems.

Aristocratic reactions to stagnant agriculture varied. There was a sense of resignation mingled with despair, such as that expressed by Lord Dufferin, who, in 1874, complained to a fellow peer that 'An Irish estate is like a sponge, and an Irish landlord is never so sick as when he is sick of his property.' Dufferin's cure was to sell out and simultaneously rid himself of a liability and wipe out the huge debts he had run up in his glittering career as diplomat and proconsul.[2] By the last two decades of the century other noblemen were doing the same. A few aristocrats were cushioned against unreliable Irish revenues by their mainland estates. Mineral rights from Durham coal mines provided ballast for the Marquesses of Londonderry who owned over 27,000 acres, mostly in Ulster.

Investment offered landowners an opportunity to escape from a precarious existence, but few possessed the necessary reserves of capital. For those who did the results were disheartening. In 1823 James Hamilton, a young, idealist Scotsman with a taste for Protestant theology, inherited 20,000 acres in Donegal. Appalled by the backwardness of his farms (many tenants had neither ploughs nor carts), he invested £20,000 in improvements which yielded him an extra £200 in rents, a paltry 1 per cent return.[3] At all levels, landlords were constrained by tight budgets and were always in danger of sliding into insolvency because of accumulated, long-term debts known as 'encumbrances'. These encompassed mortgages, marriage settlements and allowances to widows, children and outlying relations. Over generations,

encumbrances spiralled to alarming levels; in 1852 one nobleman with £6,500 a year in rents had obligations that totalled
£106,000. When he disposed of his Irish lands for £676,000 in
1887, the sixth Duke of Leinster had encumbrances of
£292,000, including annuities of £154,000 to his offspring.[4]

A landlord's outgoings were fixed and unavoidable. To meet
them, he could remortgage his property, which, of course, compounded his long-term difficulties. Or, and this was the
commonest alternative, he could jack up rents, squeeze tenants
in arrears and evict those who could not pay. There was never a
shortage of potential tenants. They faced the same problems as
their landlords, but on a smaller scale. Farms varied in size from
eight to twenty or more acres, their leases were short-term and
could be terminated by their landlords at will. There was no
incentive for improvements, for, until the 1870 Land Act, farmers were never compensated for any investment they might have
made. Subsistence farming was common, and, for those who
rose above it, margins were tight. Inevitably, there were rancorous disagreements as to what was a 'fair' (i.e. affordable) rent,
and tempers flared and violence often followed.

In 1843 W. S. Trench, the land agent for the Marquess of
Bath, was beaten up by a mob at Carrickfoss after he had refused
to lower rents on his master's estates to levels agreed by neighbouring landlords. He got away with bruises, but, a few years
before, a landlord had been shot by an assassin who had been
hired by one of his tenants with a grudge. Trench found the
corpse in a field and noticed the looks of 'triumphant satisfaction' on the faces of the 'peasants' working nearby. A reward of
£1,500 tempted an informer to name the murderer, but the jury
ignored his evidence, and the accused was acquitted. Solidarity
was already a weapon which could frustrate the laws upon which
landlords depended.[5]

*

Trench's employer the Marquess of Bath occupied the upper reaches of the hierarchy of Irish landowners. According to a survey of 1873, he possessed 23,000 acres which were valued at nearly £20,000. Bath was one of the sharks, but there plenty of minnows, squireens with properties worth £500 or less, who just qualified for the status of 'landed gentry'. Trench, who had properties of his own, fell into this category. En masse, he and the rest of Ireland's landowners have been demonised in the raw version of subsequent nationalist history as outsiders who were rapacious, heartless and absentee, a gibe made by Sir Robert Peel and repeated by Disraeli.

This last was untrue: the 1873 survey shows that absentees and birds of passage made up less than 20 per cent (517) of Irish landowners and that the rest (2,439) were residents, either on their own estates or elsewhere in the country. The exiles included peers who were public servants in England or abroad. Nearly all Irish landlords were native-born and 42 per cent were Protestant and 43 were Catholic.[6]

Headcounts may scotch the myth of an absentee aristocracy, but they give no indication of where the loyalties of the Irish nobility lay, or, more importantly, the extent to which Irish peers engaged in the life of the nation beyond collecting rents, hunting foxes and attending functions at the court of the Viceroy in Dublin. Some did serve as non-executive servants of the administration as Lords Lieutenant, Poor Law guardians and justices. There were never enough landowners to fill rural benches, and so in many districts the government had to appoint stipendaries, mostly former officers and lawyers. Watching one of these resident magistrates in action in 1881, a journalist thought them abrupt and lacking the gentle paternalism of the English squire.[7]

Relations between peers and the people were inevitably soured by the continual war of attrition between tenants and landlords. By vigorously enforcing their legal rights, landowners became predators in the popular imagination, symbols of Ireland's subjugation and the impotence of its people. During the 1893 Commons debate on Home Rule, a Tory MP predicted that Irish self-government would lead to all landowners being treated as 'robbers'. A nationalist MP riposted that 'it did not lie with the Irish landlords to speak of robbery', drawing cheers from his colleagues.[8]

The antecedents of the Irish aristocracy remained an impediment to its assimilation. Its members were Protestants, the descendants of outsiders who had secured their lands by force. The eighteenth-century 'ascendancy' had been preserved by garrisons of British troops who upheld laws passed in Dublin by a Parliament filled with Protestant gentry and peers. In 1798 the old polity nearly disintegrated under the pressure of a popular nationalist insurrection which received French assistance. As in the 1640s and 1690s, the Irish landowning elite was rescued by the British army.

In return for its survival, the aristocracy forfeited its old political power. In 1801 it agreed to the Act of Union, which dissolved the Dublin Parliament and transferred its legislative powers to Westminster. Self-emasculation was made less painful by the anaesthetic of bribery: Ireland's former lawmakers were given titles, promotions to English peerages and a million pounds in backhanders. Prestige remained attached to the ownership of land, but not political power.

Catholic emancipation had been promised in 1801, but the offer was withdrawn when George III announced that it would compromise his coronation oath. Catholics got what they wanted in 1829, in the form of the Catholic Relief Act, not as a favour from Westminster, but as a result of mass agitation which threatened to make Ireland ungovernable. This success was a signal lesson for the Irish people which was applied throughout the rest of the century: disciplined and directed, the collective will of the Catholic majority could gain concessions.

Insurrections in the 1798 style were tried in 1848 and by the revolutionary Fenian movement of the 1860s, but they were contained by the police and the army. Yet old fears of mass insurgency remained strong. In the spring of 1878, when a war with Russia seemed imminent, the Chief Secretary to the Dublin government warned that the outbreak of hostilities would be a signal for popular insurrection.[9]

Irish causes found no champions among the aristocracy. Home-grown, charismatic leaders took command of populist movements. Daniel O'Connell, a Catholic barrister, led the agitation for Catholic emancipation in the 1820s and, afterwards, the repeal of the union. A Protestant squire, Charles Stewart Parnell, did the same for land reform and Home Rule. Popular pressure for self-government, which gained momentum in the 1870s, unnerved the peerage and for good reason, for it was expected that an independent Irish Parliament would set the interests of tenants over those of landlords. Moreover, there would be no place for an aristocracy in this assembly in which the Lords would be replaced by an elected senate. For thirty years a mere tenth of its members would be peers sitting as of right, but this concession could mask the reality that Home Rule equalled extinction for the Irish peerage, a fact often overlooked.

A handful of landowners backed the restoration of the Irish Parliament. Sir Rowland Blennerhassett Bt. and his cousin Rowland Ponsonby Blennerhassett sat as Home Rule Members for Kerry, where they were returned unopposed in 1880. Sir Rowland owned a middle-sized estate and spoke up for tenant farmers during the 1881 Land Act debate, locking horns with Viscount Castlereagh, an Ulster Tory who defended the right of landlords to negotiate rents without interference from the government.[10]

Castlereagh was the eldest son of the fifth Marquess of Londonderry and represented a recent shift in Irish political alignments which favoured the aristocracy, at least in Ulster. The province's farmers had far greater legal protection than their counterparts in the south, and the Protestant majority there had become disturbed by the growth of the Home Rule Party, which by 1880 had eighty MPs. In the simple language of the famous slogan, 'Home Rule' would be 'Rome Rule', an equation which united Ulster's peers and people. Aristocrats like Londonderry allied themselves to the working- and lower-middle-class Orange lodges to create Unionism, a potent political cocktail whose ingredients were Toryism, anti-Catholicism and a readiness to fight a civil war to prevent home rule.[11] Interestingly, some conservative Catholics led by the Duke of Norfolk were worried that self-government would inflict godless 'Jacobinism' on Ireland.[12]

Like Irish Protestants, the Irish aristocracy was convinced that it would be thrown to the wolves when Ireland obtained self-government. Recurrent economic and political crises had driven the Irish nobility into the protective arms of the British state and its administration in Dublin. This controlled a formidable apparatus of coercion. In the front line was the Royal Irish Constabulary, a gendarmerie armed with carbines, bayonets and swords which grew in numbers after every outbreak of disorder and terrorism. By 1880 it totalled 12,600. No statistic better illustrates the scale of Irish disaffection than the proportion of policemen to the rest of the population: in England this was 1 to 455, in Ireland 1 to 194.[13]

Even so, the police frequently had to be stiffened by troops and naval landing parties. During the 1852 County Clare election, troops were needed to escort a party of farmers who had pledged their votes to their landlord. The procession was ambushed at Sixmilebridge and several of the assailants were shot. This incident was soon commemorated in a ballad which revealingly compared Queen Victoria's redcoats to Cromwell's Ironsides.[14] Both shared a common purpose: the perpetuation of a political and economic system that was forever tilted in favour of England, Protestantism and all landowners. Just as there was a continuity of injustice, there was another of resistance. At Kildare early in 1881 tenants of the Duke of Leinster publicly burned one of his landlord's new leases on the blade of a pike that had been brandished during the 1798 uprising.[15]

This gesture of defiance was performed in the presence of soldiers summoned to forestall a riot. In the same year, soldiers were guarding landlords' agents enforcing warrants on defaulting tenants, and sailors and marines were landed at Castletown to protect bailiffs carrying out evictions.[16] Landowners and their representatives travelled armed. Robert Eyre White, a cousin of the Earl of Bantry and owner of 16,000 acres in Cork, rode abroad with 'two or three revolvers prominently displayed in his belt', dared his tenants to shoot him and compelled some to give three cheers for the Queen. Similar bravado was shown by another land agent, Townsend Trench, a keen cyclist (and inventor of a tubeless tyre), who practised his marksmanship by freewheeling downhill, throwing plates in the air and firing at them with his revolver.[17]

Such precautions were very wise. In 1878 the third Earl of Leitrim was ambushed by a gang who shot his secretary and coachman and fatally wounded him before beating him about the head; the murderers fled and may have found their way to America. Leitrim was a wayward and tough landlord who, shortly before his death, was in the process of throwing out eighty tenants. Once, he had ordered the massacre of his tenants' goats after they had chewed his recently planted saplings, and when some tenants mistakenly ploughed up some pasture, he forced them to replace it sod by sod. Despite his seventy-two years and white whiskers, he was rumoured to be a virile lecher who seduced innocent Catholic servant girls. A 'mob of the lowest type' congregated at his funeral, cursed him as 'an old ruffian and heretic' and tried to seize his coffin.[18] Folk legend claimed that Leitrim's assassin had been the father of one of the girls he had led astray, a tale which was repeated in a doggerel ballad of his last hours:

> *It being the 2nd of April this old debauchee left his den*
> *He left bailiffs, bums and harlots in the castle of*
> *   Lough Rynn –*
> *To Makem and Kincaid [his servants] he gave a*
> *   hellish bawl*
> *Saying we'll tumble down the cabins in County Donegal.*

Leitrim was the moustachio-twirling demon-king of landlords. His assassination and that of Viscount Mountmorres in September 1880 were spectacular coups in the terrorist campaign which followed a sequence of disastrous harvests in the 1870s. The statistics reveal the scale of the crisis: between 1879 and 1882 evictions rose fourfold to over five thousand a year and writs for the recovery of rents to over twenty thousand.[19] What police files described as 'agrarian outrages' increased from 863 in 1879 to 2,590 in 1881.[20] Many of these crimes were directed against landlords or tenants who had taken over the holdings of evicted farmers, but some were the upshot of familial antipathies and inter-family feuds of the sort which Zola described in his bleak novel on contemporary French peasant life, *La Terre*.[21]

What was most terrifying about the agrarian crisis of the 1870s was the mass resistance led and coordinated by the Land League, which had been founded in 1879. Roughly half its members were farmers and their sons, while the rest were labourers and the proprietors of small businesses in country towns who were victims of the knock-on effect of the recession. The League's clandestine activities were arson, cattle maiming and intimidation, most famously the ostracism of Captain Charles Boycott, a landlord and agent for Lord Erne. No local man or woman would have any dealings with Boycott and no

labourers could be found to tend his land and livestock. League
solidarity was matched by official muscle: Protestant labourers
from Ulster guarded by troops and police harvested his crops.

The League's legitimate activities were tiding over evicted
tenants with handouts, and paralysing the legal system by hampering the auctions of goods distrained by landlords for
non-payment of rent.[22] Criminal prosecutions were hampered
by obstruction and the 'canvassing' of jurors, who were sometimes seen carousing with the accused before his trial.[23] The
Irish aristocracy was under siege and, viewed from the terrace of
the country house and from London, Ireland seemed to be
lurching into anarchy.

The Irish aristocracy had no firm friends beyond the Protestant
voters of Ulster. Before the 1870 Ballot Act, landlords had been
able to win limited popular support at elections through threats
and bribes. Now they had to stand by and watch Parnell's Home
Rule Party sweep the polls with backing from the Land League.
All that was left for landowners of all ranks was to fall back on a
traditional expedient and appeal for help from Westminster in
the form of fresh coercion laws and reinforced garrisons.

Gladstone preferred placebos to more astringents. He fervently believed that God had called upon him to bring peace to
Ireland by eliminating two historic Irish grievances: the status of
the Protestant Church of Ireland and the system of land tenure.
Neither measure was to the taste of the Irish or the British aristocracy. The 1869 Irish Church Disestablishment Act, which
removed the privileges and some of the estates of the Irish
Anglican Church, was denounced in the Lords as confiscatory
and, therefore, a threat to every form of property. Many peers
faced personal losses, for Irish livings provided employment for
younger sons and many were well paid. Alarm bells rang and 325
peers attended the debate, the greatest number present since the

repeal of the Corn Laws. A spirit of defiance flared and then was dampened by Lord Salisbury, who argued that however outrageous in principle, the bill did reflect the sentiments of voters in the recent election. Paradoxically, some of the cash paid in compensation for the Church of Ireland's assets was placed in a fund that issued mortgages to straitened Irish landowners.[24]

The 1870 and 1881 Land Acts were bitterly contested within the Lords as official intrusions into the freedom of landlord and tenant to make agreements, and, in the case of the second law, the imposition of official tribunals with the authority both to define and enforce a 'fair' rent. Landlords complained that they were the victims, and some were. The perhaps crazily optimistic land agent Samuel Hussey, who had paid £80,000 for an estate in 1879 (the year of a calamitous harvest), later alleged that the 1881 Land Act reduced his rents by a third. It was too much and he soon sold out at an overall loss.[25]

Others followed his example and received official encouragement. Between 1885 and 1903 successive Liberal and Conservative governments passed laws which made it easier for landowners to sell out by providing loans for Irish tenant farmers to buy their holdings. Critics cynically but reasonably concluded that the state was subsidising inefficient husbandry and that taxes were being delivered straight into the pockets of peers who had manifestly failed to manage their estates competently. The all-but-holy doctrines of free-market competition had been suspended in Ireland, while in the rest of the country landowners and farmers were left to face the agricultural recession alone. Yet, by seemingly rewarding failure, the British government had ended the land war and secured comparative peace in Ireland.

Moreover, the policy of financing a transfer of land had helped the Irish aristocracy to shed its estates relatively painlessly. As the *Spectator* perceptively commented in 1893, 'the immense majority' of British and Irish peers 'would be just as well off without

Ireland, as with it'.[26] Nonetheless, Irish peers and their Unionist sympathisers in the Lords were dismayed by the cold indifference of the Conservatives, who seemed as willing as the Liberals to satisfy the demands of the Irish tenantry at the expense of their landlords. After the 1887 Land Act, the Marquess of Waterford had told Prime Minister Lord Salisbury that he would rather be 'killed by my enemies than tortured slowly by my friends'.[27] His friends gave a further twist to the thumbscrew in 1898, when the Irish Local Government Act terminated aristocratic influence in the countryside and delivered it to Ireland's middle classes. There were no objections from the House of Lords.

Opposition to Home Rule united Irish and British peers. They had been denied the chance to make their feelings known in 1886 when a mass defection of Liberals scuppered Gladstone's first Home Rule Bill. In 1893 he tried again, and the measure was debated at tedious length in the Commons before being passed only with the support of Home Rule MPs. Old, aristocratic Ireland was represented by David Plunket QC, third son of Lord Plunket, kinsman of several senior Protestant clerics and Unionist MP for that stronghold of Protestantism, Trinity College, Dublin. He prophesied that self-government would mean the 'certain doom' of all Irish landlords and the 'speedy and complete ruin of their country'.[28]

His fears were echoed in the Lords. The prospect of Home Rule had aroused aristocratic passions to a pitch equal in intensity to those generated by Parliamentary reform and the Corn Laws. Then, the numbers attending the Lords had soared, with backwoodsmen flocking to London to uphold the immediate interests of all their kind. This phenomenon was repeated at the end of August 1893 when grouse moors, yachts and race meetings were abandoned and, in the words of Herbert Asquith, Gladstone's Home Secretary, 'strange and unfamiliar figures' appeared at Westminster.[29] Out of the 545 peers eligible to vote, 460 turned up to kill Home Rule.[30]

They did so in a brief, one-sided and intemperate debate watched from a crowded gallery. One after another the Irish representative peers denounced the measure, some quoting opinions they had heard in their homeland. Lord Muskerry, who proudly claimed that he was a resident landlord, alleged that everyone with a stake in Ireland opposed self-government. Others predicted economic stagnation and a nation variously enslaved to 'American-Irish Fenians', the 'mob', the Catholic clergy, or the 'illiterate voters of Kerry or Clare'. There was anger that the proposed Irish legislature would lack a hereditary and, therefore, 'independent' element.[31] Forty-one peers voted for the bill and 419 against, including more than half the peers ennobled by Gladstone.

The rejection of Home Rule was the greatest victory secured by the Lords that century, and the last in its history. It was a signal vindication of Lord Salisbury's doctrine that the constitutional duty of the peers was to reject laws which enjoyed limited public support, even when they had been passed by the Commons. British voters were bored by Irish issues and resentful of Irish clamour and terrorism.

Peers and people had been in accord over Home Rule. Having saved the Union and justified its function as a mirror of mainland opinion, the Lords left the Irish peerage to languish, for, like Irish nationalism, their interests had no appeal for voters. Irish landowners either took advantage of government funds and disposed of their estates, or soldiered on as best they could under a legal system which operated against them. Their history during the nineteenth century was a reminder of what they had been and remained: a colonial elite whose roots were shallow and who never entirely secured the goodwill of the natives.

There were pockets of affection for devil-may-care sporting peers who rode hard. Nearly twenty years ago I had a drink in a village pub in Meath which was decorated with photographs of the lords (including Field-Marshal Lord Roberts), ladies and squires of local hunts of the early 1900s. I was told that each had been a fine horseman, that the hunt had never known better and that the memory deserved to be preserved. Yet British peers never rode to hounds with revolvers in their pockets or visited their tenants armed to the teeth.

24

Like Chaff Before Us: Hanging on 1887–1914

We tend to view the world of the late Victorian and Edwardian aristocracy through the prism of the First World War, which both illuminates and distorts. It reveals the super extravagance of a privileged elite which flaunted its wealth in a most flamboyant manner, just as it had done in earlier ages. What makes this period different was the nemesis of 1914; this was a doomed universe. The horrors of the war gave an intensity to the nostalgia of those who survived and, when they recorded their memories, they chose metaphors which suggested an extended, exciting and innocent childhood. Its summers were always warm, its amusements always enthralling and its colours always bright.

'It is difficult to recall the power and riches of the aristocracy in those days,' wrote Lord Chandos in 1960. He had come down from Cambridge in June 1914 and joined in the tribal rituals of the London season. He watched the yellow carriages of Lords Londonderry and Lansdowne 'sweep up to Ascot' with their liveried postillions, and listened to the 'ripple of elegant conversations' at balls, and dinner parties in which guests enjoyed ten courses beginning with clear turtle soup and ending with savouries.[1] The diplomat Duff Cooper looked back to that year's season as 'that last gay summer of a dying age', while future Prime Minister Harold Macmillan recalled '*la douceur de vivre*' of his pre-war youth.[2]

Those who had tasted its pleasures contributed to the legend of a golden age which is now part of the national historic consciousness alongside Arthur's Camelot and the 'Merry England' that supposedly existed in the pre-industrial age. Fiction enhanced personal memories of the pre-war idyll. There is Noel Coward's moving 1931 play *Cavalcade*, which provided the inspiration for the 1970s television series *Upstairs Downstairs*, which traces the parallel fortunes of a peer and his family and those of his servants. The visually seductive 1971 film version of E. P. Hartley's 1953 novel *The Go-Between* reveals both the charm of the aristocracy and its chilling private codes as seen through the eyes of a young boy during the fabulously hot summer of 1900. 'Queen's weather' it was called by Nanny in Alan Bennett's *Forty Years On*, which opened in 1968 and affectionately parodies the reminiscences of those who had lived through this period.

As we all know, the balls, dinners, shooting parties and carefree badinage abruptly stopped in 1914. The diversions of 'Society' reappeared in 1919, but, for a time, their tone was muted by a pervading awareness of wartime losses, which was strongest and most poignant among those who had survived the slaughter. The casualty lists intruded everywhere; as the guns gathered on the moors for the 'Glorious Twelfth' in 1919, one sportsman mourned the absence of 'familiar faces'. There was, he felt, 'a peculiar charm surrounding one's recollections of the last ·Twelfth of 1913 . . . we shall never quite get back to those days – worst luck in many ways'.[3] Others who looked back shared this sentiment, which blended with selective memory to create the lost wonderland of the pre-war aristocracy.

For the aristocracy, 'those days' had been a time of carefree and expensive indulgence in the face of a world consumed by intermittent outbreaks of social discontent and acrimonious political strife. Both contributed to an animus against the rich in general and a prodigal nobility in particular. By 1900 modern class warfare had arrived, and the aristocracy no longer seemed as well integrated into public life as it had been in previous generations. Moreover, by its own, if not everyone else's estimate it was getting poorer.

Watching the peers arrive at Westminster in 1893 to scupper the Home Rule Bill, the Liberal Home Secretary Herbert Asquith remarked that their sole qualification to change the course of history was their birth, or, as he expressed it, 'the accident of an accident'.[4] It was a point which could have been made at any time during the past five hundred years, but the fact that the House of Lords was now a satellite of the Tory Party gave Asquith's gibe a fresh sharpness. Accident combined with a political realignment had turned the second chamber into a partisan assembly which, if its members so wished, could frustrate the will of the electorate and the Commons. Not surprisingly, an increasingly left-wing Liberal Party and, after 1900, the new Labour Party were uncomfortable with this anomaly. In the 1906 election over 3 million men had voted for the Liberal, Labour and Home Rule parties, but at any time their wishes could be overridden by five hundred titled Tories. The aristocracy found itself walking a political tightrope; one misplaced or overconfident step would provide its enemies with the chance either to slice away its remaining constitutional powers, or even abolish them altogether.

Yet, if the numbers of rich men seeking titles was anything to go by, the prestige of the aristocracy was as high as ever. Between 1837 and 1911 nearly five hundred families were ennobled, more than balancing losses from natural wastage. Since 1886 possessors of non-landed wealth had been crowding into the Lords with one-third of all new titles being awarded to commercial and industrial tycoons. There were financiers (Lord Rothschild), brewers Edward Guinness (Lord Iveagh) and Sir Michael Bass (Lord Burton), newspaper proprietors (Lords Northcliffe and Glenesk), railway and shipping magnates (Lords Brassey, Inverclyde and Nunburnholme), mine owners and industrialists (Lords Swansea, Overtown, Airedale, Ashby St Ledgers and Glenconner), and the armaments manufacturer, Lord Armstrong. By its own desire the plutocracy was merging with the aristocracy.

The impetus behind this remaking of the Lords was Lord Salisbury. Above all, he wanted to keep the power of the Lords intact so that it could, in an emergency, rein in the Commons as it had done in 1893 over Home Rule. This was a risky stratagem, and Salisbury believed that it could be employed only when the peers were absolutely certain that they reflected national rather than partisan interests. Modern political parties had to be highly sensitive to the wishes of minority lobby groups, such as the temperance movement, which then had a stranglehold on the Liberals. In theory, the peers were a counterweight to what the right dismissed as 'faddism', but to be effective they had to be representative and reflect interests other than landowning. The new equilibrium between landed and non-landed wealth was already apparent within the Commons. In the 1910 election the Conservatives and Liberals fielded 147 candidates with landed connections and 883 who were either professionals or businessmen.[5] The numbers of MPs who were the heirs or younger sons of noblemen continued to fall; there were sixty-seven in 1910 and thirty-three in 1940.[6]

Land values and revenues continued to fall. In 1893 a Suffolk squire complained that over the past three years his annual rent roll had fallen from £2,500 to £1,900 and that half his income was consumed by taxes, tithes and interest charges.[7] His difficulties with liquidity were multiplied many times and at many levels. Quite simply, British agriculture could not compete in the new global market for food. By 1914 landowners made up just one-third of British millionaires.

The plight of the aristocracy aroused very little sympathy in the rest of the country. Governments and voters were concerned with more important matters such as the strength of the Royal Navy and the need for tentative welfare legislation. Both demanded increased public expenditure, and if the aristocracy was as rich as appearances suggested, then the time had come to tap its resources, particularly land. In 1894 the Liberal Chancellor of the Exchequer, Sir William Harcourt, whose family had owned estates in Oxfordshire since the Middle Ages, introduced death duties. This levy was the brainchild of a late Victorian Widmerpool, Alfred Milner, a bureaucrat whose twin deities were efficiency and the British Empire, and who wished to rationalise the complicated system of inheritance taxes. They were superseded by death duties of 8 per cent which were charged on all estates with a sale value of over 1 million pounds with payments to be spread over several years.

What Milner and Harcourt treated as a purely administrative adjustment was revealingly seen by Gladstone as the 'most radical' measure of his lifetime (he was eighty-five). His successor as Prime Minister, the liberal Lord Rosebery, disapproved of a tax which, he imagined, was a direct assault against the landed order.[8] Other peers agreed and, in 1895, asked the new Conservative government to abolish death duties. Lord Salisbury, Prime Minister for the third and final time, refused because, while his party was favourable to the aristocracy as an institution, over-generosity towards its members was an electoral handicap. Middle- and working-class voters would never be moved by the sufferings of hard-up peers.

Pessimistic landowners remained bitter about a tax which, they convinced themselves, had been deliberately designed to harry them to extinction. In 1913 the editor of *Burke's Landed Gentry* fulminated against the 'vicious and crushing burden of taxation' which had been 'dictated by a hatred of landowners rather than the necessities of imperial finance'. As a result, ancient families were being driven off their estates and land had ceased to be 'the criterion of social status'.[9] Death duties then stood at 15 per cent, and, by 1919, they had doubled. This increase prompted the ninth Duke of Marlborough to protest that they were a 'social and political' stick whose sole purpose was to chastise the aristocracy. Death duties contributed what he amazingly considered to be mere bagatelle (£33.5 million, or the cost of five battleships) to a national revenue of £1,213 million.[10] The Duke had missed the point. The prodigious costs of the war effort had driven up all forms of taxation and simultaneously caused inflation; everyone was paying more and the richest simply paid most. In 1918 the eighth Duke of Northumberland netted £23,890 from mineral revenues of £82,450.[11]

Impositions placed on an already devalued resource, land, were bound to erode aristocratic capital and incomes. In 1930 the eleventh Duke of Leeds sold off lands to cover the death duties on his father's estates, and further sales were needed to fund divorce settlements in 1948 and 1955.[12] Divorces were unpredictable hazards, unlike the agricultural recession or death duties, which could be overcome through shrewd financial management, economy and exploitation of alternative sources of income through investment in stocks and the acquisition of directorships. Peers on the Board added lustre to a company and enhanced its trustworthiness.

Prestige could be marketed in other ways. Peers chased the affections of American heiresses whose fathers were hungry for the glamour and status which foreign titles gave to new money. On the marriage of his daughter Jennie to Lord Randolph Churchill in 1873, her father Leonard Jerome, a New York financier, gave the couple funds which provided an annual income of £3,000.[13] Churchill's cousin, the ninth Duke of Marlborough, steered his dynasty out of insolvency through his marriage in 1895 to Consuelo Vanderbilt, the daughter of the American shipping tycoon William Vanderbilt. Even without transfusions of American capital, the flexible, imaginative and prudent could stay afloat; the eleventh Duke of Bedford increased his annual revenues from £264,000 to £320,000 between 1895 and 1910.[14]

Other peers survived, flourished and, for all their croaking about imminent beggary, seemed to have plenty of spare cash for the upkeep of their houses and to pay for lavish entertainments, the wages of legions of servants, that novel and highly popular luxury the motor car, and the indulgence of whimsies. The sixth Duke of Portland owned eight seats scattered across England and Scotland and a house in Grosvenor Square, and at Welbeck Abbey in Nottinghamshire he arranged to have several tennis courts dispersed in the grounds so that he could play at any time of day without having to endure the glare of the sun. In 1901, retrievers with good pedigrees were being sold for between thirty and forty guineas with exceptional dogs fetching a hundred or more, the average annual salary for a junior clerk or schoolteacher.[15] After the 1909 budget, the eighth Earl of Harrington indignantly declared that its new taxes would so impoverish him that he was having to contemplate selling his hounds. Press reports of this sacrifice drew laughter from Liberal and Labour voters.

*

Lord Harrington's dilemma also drew a chuckle from 'Charlie' Carrington, first Lord Carrington and future Earl of Lincolnshire. An affable and witty peer, he was something of a rarity for his times: a Liberal aristocrat. His career as an administrator, courtier and politician illustrate a strange paradox of this period. While the constitutional powers of the House of Lords were being called into question, individual peers with a political vocation were still making easy entrées into the world of high politics and diplomacy assisted by their families and friends. Aristocratic patronage had receded, but not completely disappeared.

Carrington's life had parallels which stretched back to the earliest history of the aristocracy. His birth gave him the responsibility to serve the nation for the general good. As to what form this good might take, Carrington was an open-minded man, sympathetic to the spirit of change and willing to work with it, even when it ran counter to the private interests of his fellow peers. In 1909, when Lloyd George's 'People's Budget' reduced the Tory aristocracy to a mass apoplexy, Carrington praised it in his diary as 'a bold, liberal and humane' measure.[16]

For a man who later developed a strong independence of mind and faith in the future, Carrington's upbringing had been conventional and predictable. Born in 1843, he proceeded through Eton to Trinity College, Cambridge, to a commission in the Royal Horse Guards and, when he was twenty-two, a seat in the Commons as MP for Wycombe, which was next door to his family seat. Carrington inherited his title in 1869. Soon afterwards, he accosted a newspaper editor who had insulted his late father and horsewhipped him outside the Conservative Club in St James's. This 'scoundrel' was an illegitimate son of the Duke of Buckingham, and he unsuccessfully attempted to prosecute Carrington in a case which ended in a courtroom brawl from which counsel and witnesses emerged bruised and bleeding.[17]

A young officer of honour and spirit, Carrington was chosen

as an aide-de-camp to the Prince of Wales during his tour of India in 1875–6, and, in 1885, he was appointed Governor of New South Wales. In 1890 he returned home, held several offices in the royal household and in 1905 joined the Liberal Cabinet as President of the Board of Agriculture.

Carrington was a member of a small, self-selected group for whom politics remained a legitimate and honourable activity for men of his birth and education. Time and money were at the disposal of the political peer and he began his career well supplied with patrons and potential allies. School and university had thrown him into the company of other young men with identical backgrounds who were also hosts to dreams of power. All had been raised in houses where they overheard the everyday chatter of politics, and afterwards they ritually passed through Eton to Oxford or Cambridge. These were the kindergartens for a nobleman with a political vocation, where he made those contacts and cultivated the friendships that would accelerate his progress. The sixth Marquess of Londonderry, the leader of Ulster's Unionists, was Arthur Balfour's fag at Eton and twenty years later was Viceroy of Ireland working in harness with Balfour, the Secretary of State for Ireland.

At university, the athletic life was usually preferred to the intellectual. William Palmer, the heir of the first Lord Selborne hunted, played tennis and cricket and 'ragged'. Ragging fine-tuned by intoxication distinguished the predominantly aristocratic university dining clubs. What Lord Rosebery called the 'unifying quality' of Oxford's Bullingdon Club was the catalyst for his lifelong intimacy with fellow Etonian Lord Randolph Churchill.[18] Churchill was also a member of the Merton Myrmidons who, like the Bullingdon men, dined well, got drunk and afterwards broke windows and bottles. Once he smashed some windows in the Randolph Hotel and, since precedent always mattered to the aristocracy, future generations continued this tradition of drunken vandalism.

It flourished in the Oxford of the 1920s and was described by Evelyn Waugh in *Decline and Fall* in 1928:

> A shriller note could now be heard rising from Sir Alisdair's rooms; any who have heard that sound will shrink at the recollection of it; it is the sound of English county families baying for broken glass. Soon they would all be tumbling out into the quad, crimson and roaring in their bottle-green evening coats, for the real romp of the evening.

Such hearty rituals of youthful aristocratic rebellion stretched back to the eighteenth century and beyond, and they helped to engender a powerful sense of belonging to an exclusive and self-confident caste.

On coming down from university, the Bacchantes calmed down and glided into their political apprenticeships. Kinsmen and family friends provided unpaid posts as private secretaries to ministers, and there was an admittedly dwindling number of constituencies which were still susceptible to pressure from neighbouring landowners. Selborne influence secured the eastern division of Hampshire for William Palmer in 1885. After his father's death in 1890, he entered the Lords, but very reluctantly because the Commons was now regarded as a more certain route to the highest offices.[19] Nevertheless, Selborne held ministerial posts between 1900 and 1905 and between 1915 and 1916.

Dynastic as well as personal ambitions continued to propel young aristocrats into politics. Edward Wood, fourth son and eventual heir of the second Viscount Halifax, was told by his father at the age of eleven: 'You are to get a first class at History at Oxford and do all sorts of grand things.' At Eton a malformed left hand restricted Edward's athletic activities to tennis, fives and bicycling, and at Oxford he followed the beagles, caroused with the Bullingdon and managed to get his first. Well satisfied, his father set him new goals: 'I am quite determined that you are to be Prime Minister and reunite England with the Holy See.' A seat, Ripon, was procured in 1910 with the assistance of his in-laws, but the reserved and bookish Wood found the rough and tumble of the Commons disconcerting.[20]

The parental ambitions of the sixth Marquess of London-derry and his wife were less grandiose than Halifax's. They wanted their only son and heir, Viscount Castlereagh, to enter the Commons, where he could oppose Irish self-government and keep an eye on the economic interests of the peerage. He had had a career as an ornamental soldier in the Royal Horse Guards (his parents had refused to allow him to serve in the Boer War because his death would terminate the direct Londonderry line) and had undertaken a two-year imperial grand tour. Young noblemen armed with letters of introduction and sporting rifles were now regularly traversing the dominions and colonies to inspect at first-hand the lands they might even-tually govern and to absorb the wisdom of their present rulers. An imperial peregrination was also an opportunity for hunting, and so tiger skins and the heads and horns of tropical animals were steadily added to domestic trophies on the floors and walls of country houses.

Castlereagh came home in 1905, and, after some wire pulling, his mama secured him a Parliamentary seat, Maidstone in Kent. It had been 'a very near thing' he told her, but the local con-stituency party 'like a lord'.[21] They got one, and the twenty-six-year-old Castlereagh was elected, despite rumours of chicanery. In the Commons, he banged an Orange drum for his parents and protected Londonderry mineral revenues by opposing the reduction of working hours for miners. These, he warned, would drive up coal prices and were unnecessary since modern conditions made working underground healthier than ever.[22]

What is fascinating and instructive about the political careers of Carrington, Selborne, Edward Wood and Viscount Castlereagh is how closely they followed the old aristocratic tradition. In the opening years of the twentieth century, a young nobleman could still choose a political career as of right and expect to find himself a few rungs up the ladder of advancement. Thereafter, ascent depended upon experience, hard work and a reputation for steadiness. Too much passion was dangerous, as Lord Randolph Churchill and, for that matter his son Winston, discovered.

Wood inherited his father's title as Viscount Halifax and between the wars successively served in various junior ministries, as Viceroy of India and then as Foreign Secretary. After Chamberlain's fall in 1940, he was seriously considered by ultra-Conservatives as an alternative to Churchill as Prime Minister. Castlereagh inherited the Londonderry title and, between 1931 and 1935, held that most modern of Cabinet posts, Minister for Air. He also took an active, and some would have argued sinister part in promoting friendship between Britain and Nazi Germany, which involved fawning over Hitler at the 1936 Berlin Olympics.

The aristocratic political novice was now almost bound to be a Conservative. Since the 1880s the aristocracy as a whole had swung to the right and remained there. The Whig peerage, which had done so much to urge reform and temper the extremes of radicalism, became increasingly distanced from the new Liberalism. Radicals were moving from the fringes to the mainstream of the party and their ideological baggage included programmes for the redistribution of wealth. Some nursed a vindictive animosity against an aristocracy which had become synonymous with the Conservatives. David Lloyd George, a Welsh solicitor first returned to the Commons in 1890, later admitted to having been animated by an 'elementary revolutionary feeling'. Its strands included a childhood memory of Tory landlords evicting labourers who had voted Liberal.[23] Liberal support for Irish and Scottish land redistribution and Home Rule were the last straws, and provided the impetus for the mass defection of the Whig nobility. A rump, including Lord Carrington, remained in the Lords, where there was a permanent Conservative majority of at least two hundred peers.

Aristocratic support was both an advantage and liability for the Conservatives. Lord Salisbury was committed to preserving the power of the Lords as a bulwark against demotic Liberalism, militant trade unionism and the politics of envy. As the poet and novelist Charles Kingsley had once prophesied, the aristocracy would survive because the middle classes would see them as the defenders of 'every silver fork' in the country.[24] The silverware of the Pooters was safe, Kingsley believed, since the aristocracy was financially independent and, therefore, immune to the sometimes purblind and transient obsessions of 'public opinion'. This was an argument that had been heard in 1832, and Salisbury believed it still held true.

At the same time, Salisbury needed to deflect criticism of the nobility as an inherently idle and hedonistic elite. The public had to see the peerage as an energetic body of men, working tirelessly and selflessly for the nation. Between six and ten peers served in Salisbury's Cabinets and that of his nephew and successor Arthur Balfour, and there was a steady flow of lords to embassies and imperial governorships. The 'new' imperialism of the 1890s was capturing the public imagination and the aristocracy was working hard to protect and secure an empire which defined Britain as a global superpower. High-minded peers like Lord Curzon, who was Viceroy of India between 1898 and 1904 and 1904 and 1905, were agents of the benevolent paternalism which, so its defenders claimed, defined and justified British imperialism.

The peerage offered the Conservatives practical help. Tory lords contributed to party funds, donations rising from £20,000 in 1880 to £44,000 in 1892.[25] In the countryside, the nobility rallied support for the party through its patronage and leadership of the Primrose League (named after Disraeli's favourite flower), which had been founded in 1883 to promote working- and middle-class Toryism. Within four years, it had attracted half a million members, most enticed by jamborees and summer fêtes held in the grounds of country houses and guided tours of their interiors for weekend excursion parties. Visitors included families from the suburban working and lower-middle classes who were flattered by being entertained by their 'betters'.

Popular Toryism benefited from the sporting nobility, particularly the owners of racehorses, who enjoyed the goodwill and admiration of the vast numbers of working men who followed the Turf. Moreover, the aristocracy was closely associated with the enjoyment of life; the lord drank his champagne and whisky (one advertisement of the 1890s showed a Highland laird sipping his Dewars in his great hall) and the working man his beer. Liberal, teetotal chapelgoers wanted to deprive both of their pleasures.

Yet the aristocracy gained little in return for its loyalty to Conservatism, beyond the knowledge that the Party would uphold the constitutional rights of the Lords and block Irish self-government. Irish landlords got cold comfort from Tory legislation, death duties were continued and, in 1888, the Local Government Act loosened the centuries-old grip of the aristocracy and gentry on the administration of the countryside through the establishment of common councils.

Rural democracy made slow inroads into old, deferential voting habits. The new county councils elected in 1889 contained 137 peers, twenty-five of whom were chairmen and vice-chairmen. One, Lord Carnarvon, Chairman of Hampshire

County Council, was happy to find that the '"outsiders" behaved well and showed no disposition to give trouble'. The 'outsiders' soon acquired confidence; by 1914 the number of aristocratic county councillors had fallen to ninety-eight, of whom nineteen were chairmen or vice-chairmen.[26]

The crushing landslide election victory of the Liberals and their Labour allies early in 1906 ended what had effectively been a twenty-year Conservative and Unionist ascendancy. The left was on the march and some peers took fright. According to the fourth Marquess of Salisbury, son of the Prime Minister, the country had suffered 'a mild attack of the revolutionary malady in Russia and the socialist complaint in Germany and Austria'.[27] Tory peers wondered whether this distemper would turn out to be incurable and, if so, what might they expect from a government whose Commons majority included 130 MPs who were members of the Land Nationalisation Society?

Yet despite their misgivings, the Tory peers stuck with the Salisbury doctrine and acquiesced to unpalatable legislation only because it reflected the will of the country. Nicknamed 'Mr Balfour's poodle', the Lords cavilled at, but finally let through child benefits, old-age pensions and, in 1906, the Trade Disputes Act, which gave astoundingly generous legal immunities to trade unions. A Licensing Bill was rejected in 1908 to remind the Liberals that the poodle had teeth.

These teeth were drawn, painfully, after a protracted war of political and constitutional attrition which began in the spring of 1909 and ended in the summer of 1911. The dramatic events of the conflict have been vividly described in George Dangerfield's *The Strange Death of Liberal England*, which interprets the behaviour of the most reactionary peers as the fulfilment of a kind of death wish. Certainly, during the final phase of the struggle several lords adopted the metaphors of the battlefield, calling themselves 'diehards', the nickname of the 57th Regiment, which chose to continue fighting the French at the Battle of Albuera in 1811 when the odds were heavily against them. Stubbornness paid off and the French were beaten.

The war consisted of two interconnected campaigns; the first against the new taxes proposed in Lloyd George's 1909 budget, and the second against the 1910 Parliament Bill, which effectively abolished the Lords' right to veto legislation. In both contests, the Lords presented itself to the country as its only defence against what Lord Selborne called a 'single-Chamber tyranny' and the first victims of confiscatory 'socialism'. 'Except for the protection of your Lordships' House', declared Lord Knaresborough, 'property is far safer in Turkey than it is in the United Kingdom.'[28] There was nothing novel about these claims, save that now they were put to the test of public opinion in the elections of January and December 1910.

The People's Budget of 1909 followed an old fiscal principle which stretched back to the land taxes of the eighteenth century and beyond: the extraction of the largest sums from those who could afford to pay them. Lloyd George faced an emergency: he needed £13.5 million to cover new welfare benefits and additional battleships to keep Britain ahead of Germany in the naval race. Duties on tobacco, alcohol and petrol went up and there were rises in income tax and death duties. There were also contentious innovations. A supertax of sixpence in the pound was introduced for the twelve thousand taxpayers with annual incomes of over £5,000, which raised £1 million, or the cost of one Dreadnought. New impositions were levied on the current capital value of undeveloped land and, where applicable, the unmined minerals which lay underneath.

The rich were squeezed, not as severely as they would be during the war, but hard enough to raise an outcry from sections of the aristocracy as intense in its fury as those which had greeted the Reform Bill and the repeal of the Corn Laws. Why?

Certainly, individuals ended up paying more, including, ironically, those peers who had been demanding more battleships. To judge by the histrionics and bouts of hysteria which punctuated debates over the budget and the future of the Lords, more was at stake than higher tax bills, galling though these were. For the past eighty years the peerage had seen its political powers whittled away and had, on the whole, been content to cooperate in the governance of a democratic state. Now the aristocracy had been ordered to be an accomplice in what pessimists believed was its deliberate impoverishment, contrived by socialists and their Liberal fellow-travellers. Then, to cap it all, the peers were asked to assist in their political suicide by surrendering the remnants of their old legislative influence. Henceforward, titles would be devalued and their owners exiled to the periphery of politics.

Paradoxically, many of the peers who made the most noise were backwoodsmen who had rarely, if ever, attended the Lords and had, through their extended absences, voluntarily confined themselves to the margins of politics. Nevertheless, they would fight for the ancient, defining privilege of their caste. The diehards were able to do so for there was no counterpart of the Duke of Wellington or Salisbury, who had died in 1903, on hand to deploy their authority and prestige in the interests of caution and pragmatism. The Tories had split in 1904 over whether to abandon free trade in favour of taxing foreign imports and allowing imperial products to enter the country duty-free. Balfour had wavered and his influence over the party was fragile. Lord Lansdowne, the party's leader in the Lords, carried little weight with his fellow peers, although he was a wise man who, in 1916, would have the courage to question whether Britain's losses in the First World War would ever be offset by gains.

This lack of leadership was soon apparent. Immediately after the budget peers moaned about imminent poverty in silly ways which suggested how far they were isolated from the rest of the

world. The sixth Duke of Buccleuch publicly announced a programme of retrenchment by withdrawing his annual payment of
a guinea to Dunfermline Football Club. The sixth Duke of
Portland declared that his new tax bill would compel him to sack
a thousand servants and so save a thousand pounds a week. Lord
Carrington thought this an 'idiotic' gesture which showed how
miserably Portland paid his servants. Liberal propaganda made
much of such asinine pleading.[29]

Among the beneficiaries was Lloyd George, whose contempt
for the peerage was well known and passionate. In 1908 he had
told a meeting in Liverpool that the Lords were 'stuff bottled in
the Dark Ages . . . not fit to drink, cobwebby, dusty, muddy,
sour'.[30] When, by the summer of 1909, it was clear that his
budget would be rejected by the Lords, he allowed his invective
a free run. In July, he addressed a meeting of working men at
Limehouse in the East End. Ignoring barracking by suffragettes,
he reminded his listeners of how the seventh Duke of
Northumberland had sold a plot of land needed for a school for
over eight hundred times its current rateable valuable. 'If it is
worth £900, then let him pay taxes on £900!'

The money was desperately needed, he continued:

> . . . when the Prime Minister [Asquith] and I knock at
> the doors of these great landlords and say to them:
> 'Here, you know these poor fellows who have been
> digging up royalties at the risk of their lives, some of
> them are old, they have survived the perils of their
> lives, they are broken, they can earn no more. Won't
> you give something towards keeping them out of the
> workhouse?' They scowl at us. 'We say only a half-
> penny, just a copper'. They retort: 'You thieves!'

'With your help,' he concluded, 'we can brush the Lords like
chaff before us.'[31]

Lord Curzon hit back. At Oldham, lecturing in a monotone, as he usually did to any audience, he praised the ancient virtues of 'illustrious dynasties such as the Cavendishes and Cecils', and repeated the French historian Ernest Renan's conclusion that 'all civilisations [have] been the work of aristocracies'.[32] Catcalls suggested that his middle- and working-class listeners were unconvinced. Soon afterwards, Winston Churchill, then President of the Board of Trade, riposted that it been the upkeep of aristocracies that had been the chief work of all civilisations. Lacking comparable wits in their own camp, peers resorted to mindless rage. The ninth Duke of Beaufort dreamed of placing Lloyd George and Churchill 'in the middle of twenty couple of doghounds'.[33]

Tempers flared and civilities were suspended. In January 1910 Carrington's wife Lily found herself seated next to a Tory admiral, who said to her: 'How can you allow your husband to be a member of this blackguard government?' 'Don't be an ass and go on eating your dinner,' was her reply.[34] Her husband noted that Churchill and Lloyd George were 'much abused in society'. 'Look at those wicked Cabinet Ministers!' Lady Londonderry declared at one of her receptions. 'We can turn them out.'[35] Similar expressions of pique were heard in clubs, messes, salons, parties and wherever else diehard Tories congregated.

Passions intensified once it was clear that the Lords would lose. The two elections of 1910 confirmed the Liberals in power, although their majority depended on the support of Labour and Home Rulers. Liberal losses had been heaviest in the predominantly middle-class seats in London and the South-East, which suggests that Tory arguments about the safety of property had disturbed those sections of the electorate which had something to lose. Nevertheless, Lloyd George believed that he had the mandate of the middle classes, whom, he was confident, shared his resentment against all landowners.[36]

The January 1910 election compelled the Lords to back down

and pass the budget, that of December 1910 indicated that the country would accept limitations on their power. As the Conservative MP Austen Chamberlain concluded, the electorate had voted 'against the Lords and also against all landlords'.[37] Liberal election posters portrayed the peers as ermined and coroneted dotards, plutocrats hugging moneybags labelled 'unearned increment', and young boobies.

Tory realists, including Balfour and Lord Lansdowne, began searching for a compromise as an alternative to a fight in which the odds were against the peers. A series of inter-party meetings discussed various formulae, including referendums for contentious bills and restricting the automatic right of a hereditary peer to a seat in the Lords. Nothing emerged and the Parliament Bill went ahead in the spring of 1911. Fearing that it would be defeated in the Lords, Asquith had already sought an insurance policy from Edward VII (1901–10) who, driven by a sense of constitutional duty rather than conviction, pledged himself to create enough peers to offset any majority the diehard Tories could muster. A similar undertaking had been made by William IV in 1832. After Edward VII's death in May 1910, his son George V (1910–36) unenthusiastically agreed to confirm this guarantee, but only as a measure of last resort, and a list of five hundred potential Liberal peers was drawn up which was said to have included the writer Thomas Hardy. The King was extremely unhappy about having to nearly double the number of peers, but he placed duty before his private sympathies. These were with the diehards; as Lloyd George and Carrington separately discovered, George V was surrounded by courtiers who openly supported the reactionaries in the Lords.[38]

The final engagement was marked by all the savagery of a desperate rearguard action. In the Commons, Tories jeered Prime Minister Asquith mercilessly with Lord Hugh Cecil alternating between extremes of clownishness and discourtesy. The latter's cousin Balfour, sadly observed that: 'Fragments of the Unionist party seem to have gone temporarily crazy . . . As usual the leading lunatics are my own kith and kin.'[39]

This madness infected the Lords, where the ultras were commanded by a blunt-spoken racing peer, Lord Wylloughby de Broke, and a former chancellor, Lord Halsbury. Born in 1823, the son of a Tory newspaper editor, Halsbury was a former Lord Chancellor who sincerely believed that the Crown, Constitution and Union would be endangered if the Lords lost any of its historic powers. A jaunty, pugnacious figure with old-fashioned white side-whiskers, Carrington thought him 'simply splendid, a rugged, red-faced little Tory'.[40] Behind him were the backwoods peers who approached the issues in the spirit of the hunting field. They were all-or-nothing, hard-riding men with no truck for compromise; they were fighting to preserve their hereditary rights even it they seldom chose to exercise them. Nor would they ever meekly surrender the profits of their acres to radicals and socialists.

After a dramatic fortnight of emotional speeches, threats and a steady haemorrhage of supporters, Halsbury's diehards went down with their faces to the enemy and the Parliament Bill was passed by a narrow margin. There were vinegary recriminations; Lady Halsbury hissed at renegades from the gallery of the Lords and one defecting peer was hooted and booed as he left the Carlton Club. In the ultra-right-wing *National Review*, Lord Robert Cecil blamed the 'Great Betrayal' on the 'Whig habit of compromise' and railed against 'salaried peers, Radical snobs, Unionist renegades, two time-serving Archbishops and thirteen Bishops – an unlucky number'.[41] Lord Selborne thought the Commons was now the 'tool of a tipsy tyrant', a reference to Asquith's drinking, a peccadillo which had been raised by Tory hecklers during the Commons debate on the Parliament Bill.[42]

The rump of Tory peers had gambled and lost. With hindsight, they had been defeated in a battle that had been inevitable since the Lords' rejection of Home Rule eighteen years before. With no Wellington or Salisbury to curb them, the Lords had chosen to fight on unfavourable ground. Their protests against the budget struck voters as mere selfishness. In 1918 Lord Henry Cavendish suggested that all the diehards had really wanted was pleasure and not power. They wanted to retain 'easy-going extravagance, the fox hunting, the huge slaughter of pheasants, the 60-horsepower motors, the incessant golf of pre-war days'.[43]

This was a plausible motive, at least for the backwoodsmen who abandoned the social season's diversions for the Lords debates in August 1911. A glance through the *Tatler* for 1910 and 1911 suggests that a high proportion of diehards were manic sportsmen. The bushy-bearded Lord Harrington, who had feared that the new taxes would drive him to get rid of his dogs, was a keen polo player and Master of Foxhounds who 'after abusing the motor with some violence for many years' had recently recanted and taken to driving to meets. It was felt that the political crisis had cast a shadow over the season; 'Glorious' Goodwood became 'Gloomy' Goodwood because the King had been compelled to stay in London and not, as was customary, attend the races.[44]

Seeking to preserve their pleasures, the peers had forfeited power. The Parliament Act was not a revolution; it merely confirmed what had been constitutional custom since 1832. Nonetheless, it and the battle over the Peoples' Budget showed plainly that the political power of the aristocracy had been curtailed for ever and would never be revived. Yet, had the peers taken their stand on Home Rule, then the outcome may have been very different, for it was deeply unpopular in Britain and among the Liberals. As it was, they needed the Irish to beat the peers and, therefore, conceded Irish self-government. In retaliation, the Lords imposed their two-year delaying veto on the third Home Rule Bill of 1912. Tory bile, stirred up during the 1910–11 crises, was redirected towards Ireland. During the next two years the party dallied with treason by backing the Ulster Unionists, who raised and armed a private militia to defy Parliament and fight Home Rule.

After 1911, the politically active peers lost heart. Early in 1914, and after a career in the Commons, the twenty-sixth Earl of Crawford was dismayed by what he discovered when he took his seat in the Lords. 'The atmosphere . . . is so soporific, spreading to atrophy . . . that it is hopeless to arouse vital interests in its members.'[45] The peers may have been in a coma, but they were not quite dead.

25

Dangers and Honours: War, Empire and the Aristocracy

During the elections of 1910 Tory propaganda urged voters to remember the debt owed by the nation to generations of aristocrats who had won the battles which had enlarged the British Empire and who had governed it wisely. One postcard showed a South African hillside covered with the gravestones of peers who had died in the recent Boer War. In the foreground is Lloyd George, disguised as a policeman, slinking away from a meeting in Birmingham at which he had provoked a riot by speaking in favour of the Boer cause.

Heroic and honourable self-sacrifice for the greater Britain was starkly contrasted with the poltroonery of Lloyd George, (then) a notorious Little Englander. Victories in South Africa and on other imperial frontiers over the past ninety years had affirmed the validity of the aristocratic principle in the services at a time when it was being challenged in the civilian world. The culture of the army and navy was blatantly aristocratic in that it regarded gentle lineage as a prime qualification for leadership and exalted stringent codes of personal honour. Gentlemen cherished honour while the money-obsessed middle classes cherished profits and dividends, or so Lord Elcho claimed in 1855 when he told the Lords that no businessman would purchase a commission for his son since it was an investment unlikely to yield any return.[1] Frugal and financially astute peers made no comment.

Honour distinguished the officer in his own and his equals' eyes. A cavalry colonel accused of cowardliness by a mere trumpeter after the Battle of Chillianwala (now Pakistan) in 1849 shot himself rather than endure public disgrace. The redemption of an officer condemned as a coward formed the narrative of A. E. W. Mason's best-selling 1902 novel *The Four Feathers*, which sees the hero undergo self-imposed, gruelling tests of courage and stamina to regain his honour in the manner of a medieval knight.

As ever, honour defined the gentleman and the terms 'officer' and 'gentleman' remained synonymous. The proprieties of the mess or wardroom and their rules of conduct were those of gentlemen. Officers who flouted them were ostracised and humiliated, sometimes harshly. In 1854 Cornet Thomas Ames of the 4th Hussars was knocked about by his fellow officers, forced to eat pabulum and had his moustaches clipped. *The Times* was appalled and asked why 'wealthy and titled libertines' were allowed to drive 'a man of different disposition' out of his regiment? One of Ames's tormentors, Lord Ernest Vane Tempest, fourth son of the third Marquess of Londonderry, replied. His victim's 'peculiar English and pronunciation of the letter "h"' had been obnoxious to his brother officers. Poor Ames clearly had not mastered the languid, lisping drawl of the mid-Victorian upper class.[2]

The middle classes might wince at this snobbishness, but

they were prepared to tolerate the aristocratic values of the armed forces. Lord Palmerston explained why in 1855. He warned the Commons that if the aristocracy ever shrank 'from partaking in the dangers and honours of the battlefield and fatigues of the campaign' then the nation would fall.[3] Britain and its Empire remained secure because the ancient martial traditions of the aristocracy were enjoying a fresh and extremely vigorous lease of life. The proof was as clear as the print in newspapers which reported the advance of imperial frontiers. By 1849 the conquest of India had been completed, between 1840 and 1860 British fleets and armies had browbeaten China into accepting the doctrines of free trade, and, from 1879 onwards, large swathes of Africa were conquered and subjugated. All these operations had been undertaken by soldiers and sailors invariably led by the younger sons of peers and squires and Anglican clergymen. Each campaign produced a crop of stirring exploits which were detailed in the newspapers and the illustrated weeklies.

In every imperial garrison and on every quarterdeck there were young men of birth with absolute self-assurance, a sincere faith in their country's imperial mission and a willingness to risk their lives to fulfil it. For all it meant the routine acceptance of sickness, discomfort and peril, and for some it was a glorious adventure. After 1842, all survivors of imperial campaigns were awarded handsome silver medals attached to coloured ribbons with the names of the recipients' engagements engraved on small clasps. These decorations were worn publicly and were tokens of honour and bravery like the regalia of the old chivalric orders. A new one was created in 1855, the Order of the Victoria Cross, which was awarded for outstanding courage and open to all ranks.

Ancestral pride animated many aristocrats as they went to war. In his autobiography, Admiral Lord Charles Beresford, a younger son of the fourth Marquess of Waterford, was immensely proud of a pedigree that stretched back to the medieval counts of Brittany and the legendary King of Ireland, Brian Boru. Lord Charles believed that the courage of these warriors ran in their descendants' blood so that 'every scion of the house is judged by the stern company of his ancestors'.

Their warlike spirits must have cheered Lord Charles and his brothers. He commanded HMS *Condor* in a plucky inshore attack on the Egyptian batteries during the bombardment of Alexandria in 1882 and stood, firm-jawed, in the squares which repelled Dervish charges in the Sudan two years later. Lord William Beresford of the 9th Lancers was 'renowned for reckless hardihood', won a Victoria Cross fighting with sabre against assegai during the Zulu War of 1879, and was military secretary to five successive Viceroys of India. Another brother managed the royal stud and a fourth was a rancher in America. According to Lord Charles, all were 'keen sportsmen, hard riders, men of their hands, high couraged, adventurous, talented in affairs, winning friendship and affection wherever they went'.[4]

As in the Middle Ages, the aristocracy and gentry elevated that honour and courage of the kind which Beresford sincerely believed he possessed. During the Crimean War, there were allegations that this genetic élan encouraged rashness on the battlefield.[5] This was civilian bleating, for officers knew that by setting examples of audacity they inspired their men. Moreover, the rank and file were mentally conditioned to follow their betters into danger. 'I always found the private soldier anxious to save my life because he looked up to me as the officer as being the person to lead him to victory,' recalled the fifth Duke of Richmond, a veteran of the Peninsular War and Waterloo. He added that the 'labouring classes' possessed an instinctive trust in the intelligence, as well as the bravery of a gentleman and were, therefore, happy to place their fate in his hands.[6]

This formula worked and became embedded in the consciousness of officers at all levels. In March 1914, when some officers resigned their commissions rather than suppress the Ulster Unionists who were arming to resist Irish Home Rule, one officer told his sister: 'As regards the men, the type of man we get has no feeling beyond his pocket and his stomach, the reasons being that he is uneducated and unintelligent.'[7]

Trust had to be won and repaid. The ordinary soldier or sailor expected his officers to show a paternal concern for his physical welfare and morale. Both, together with discipline, were at a low ebb in the 63rd Regiment during the Crimean War, which found itself encamped before Sebastopol in 1855. The state of the sick, hungry and ragged soldiers was blamed on the negligence of their Colonel, Robert Dalzell, the fourteenth son of the ninth Earl of Carnwath. He blamed his men ('the very scum of Dublin'), an excuse which failed to impress his superiors, who insisted on Dalzell's resignation.[8] He had doubly failed as officer and gentleman through his indifference to the principle of the moral reciprocity between those in command and those below them. Translated into a civilian context, Dalzell was the equivalent of an idle landlord who cared nothing for his tenants and labourers.

The armed services remained a stronghold of the old moral economy. A regiment or a man-o'-war was like a landed estate and a colonel or a captain was the equivalent of a squire. Ideally, they exercised a firm, fatherly authority over their men, who, in return, gave them obedience and devotion. There were misfits. Captain George Cadogan, later the fifth Earl of Cadogan, was a martinet who commanded through fear and flogged the crew of HMS *Ferret* mercilessly to the point where some mutinied in 1806. A brave man, Cadogan faced the rebels stark naked and brandishing a pistol and a cutlass, telling them he had one life to live. They flinched and then submitted; afterwards he told one that he would not have him shot 'for I am more of a gentleman'. The spared man turned evidence against the other mutineers. Cadogan rose to the rank of admiral.

Cadogan died in 1864 when flogging had become rare in both services. A more humane spirit prevailed with the public, and many officers now preferred a style of leadership which relied upon kindness and moral persuasion. Captain Lord Gillford, later Admiral the Earl of Clanwilliam, led by example and encouraged professional pride among the sailors and officers of HMS *Tribune* in the 1860s. Lord Charles Beresford, then a midshipman, recalled his pride at earning Gillford's approval for some minor task correctly undertaken and was impressed by his insistence that every officer mastered all the skills of seamanship. 'If a man is a lubber over a job, you ought to be able to *show* him how to do it, not *tell* him how to do it.' Technical and mathematical expertise were vital in sailing and navigating a ship and so naval officers needed both practical and book learning and, as readers of the Hornblower novels will know, promotion required the passing of exams. Likewise, artillery and engineer officers in the army needed professional instruction.

None was required by infantry and cavalry officers. The army adhered to the cult of the gentleman amateur who led through force of character. Until 1870 commissions and promotion up to the rank of lieutenant-colonel were purchased from the Treasury, irrespective of merit or experience. The scale of charges was fixed, but there were variations according to a regiment's social status. Fashionable units such as the Guards and all cavalry regiments were the most expensive and the laws of supply and demand often drove up prices far beyond the official limits. The third Lord Lucan was alleged to have paid £25,000 for the lieutenant-colonelcy of the 17th Lancers, nearly four times the regulation price. At the bottom of the scale, a cornet in a light dragoon regiment paid £632 for his commission and a further £134 for his uniform. His pay was eight shillings a day, out of which he paid two shillings and sixpence for his evening dinner in the mess and a further two shillings and sixpence a week to his batman.

There were additional expenses for his charger and horses for hunting and steeplechasing. All officers needed private incomes; the minimum in an infantry regiment was a hundred pounds a year and in the Guards and the cavalry three to five times that amount. William MakepeaceThackeray's fictional young cavalry officer declares: 'Must hunt you know. A man couldn't live in the wedgment if he didn't. Mess expenses enawmuth. Must dine at mess. Must drink champagne and claret. Ours ain't a port and sherry light-infantry mess'.[9] The drawl is authentic and so are the obligatory expenses in a mess where the tone is aristocratic, and where officers spent their plentiful spare time following the pursuits of landed gentlemen. If Thackeray's plunger had been attached to the 13th Light Dragoons in the 1850s he would have needed as much as £500 a year to cover all his expenses, including three horses and contributions to the upkeep of the regimental pack of harriers.[10]

Sport was sacred to the Victorian officer. It was central to his daily existence, filled his off-duty hours and was of immeasurable value in the cultivation of the qualities needed to lead others. In 1916 Major-General Sir Harry Knox, a veteran of North-West Frontier and Ugandan punitive campaigns, declared that no man had 'done as much as the fox and the fox-hound to foster the cult of character, quick decision, and nerve so necessary for leadership in war'.[11] He was then a senior staff officer in France and must have been delighted to know that old sporting traditions were flourishing behind the lines, where the officers of many regiments had established packs of hounds and hunted whenever they could, much to the annoyance of French farmers.[12]

Regretting the absence of many familiar faces from race courses during the 1855 season, a sporting journal drew great satisfaction from the fact that the 'gallant race brigade' was now attending 'meetings before Sebastopol'.[13] There were indeed impromptu races held in the Crimea where officer jockeys

showed their prowess, watched and cheered on by private soldiers. Some may have been followers of the Turf in peacetime
and would have awarded sporting officers the same adulation
they gave to sporting peers.

Sporting officers won the hearts of their men. 'The same
qualities which bring a man to the front at polo are required by
anyone who aspires to lead men,' claimed a Lancer colonel in a
1922 polo handbook.[14] For over sixty years, polo had mesmerised the British officer corps. It originated in India and soon
surpassed in popularity such imported sports as hunting, shooting, cricket, tennis and billiards. A young Hussar subaltern in
Bangalore in the 1890s, Winston Churchill, recalled that the
'hour of polo' was the high spot of his day. By this date, polo
mania had reached such an intensity that senior officers became
anxious about its harmful side effects: players were killed or
injured, and the costs of maintaining a string of ponies were
stretching the resources of officers to breaking point. In polo's
favour was the fact that it reduced drinking and gambling in
messes.

Next to polo, Churchill relished pig-sticking: hunting wild
boar on horseback with short lances. All officers indulged in
every form of hunting whenever they had the opportunity. Like
the medieval and renaissance knight, the Victorian officer treated
sport as a physical and mental preparation for war. Sometimes,
the two were complementary. A former naval officer and obses-
sive sportsman, Sir Claude de Crespigny Bt. recalled that in
1905: 'I went out to East Africa for a little big-game shooting,
and had the luck to arrive just in time to join the Sotik punitive
expedition, so that I was able to combine a certain amount of
fighting with some excellent sport.'[15] Other officers' memoirs
are full of references to shooting game of all kinds during pauses
in campaigns. When their ships anchored, naval officers never
missed an opportunity to go ashore for some shooting.

The essentially aristocratic sporting ethos formed a bond

between officers and their men. Failure to conform estranged an officer from his brothers and led to unpleasantness in the mess. In 1894 a subaltern in the 4th Hussars who was the son of a retired naval officer and had an allowance of £300 a year admitted to his colleagues that he lacked the wherewithal to keep hunters and racehorses. He was threatened, assaulted and told: 'It is not what you do, Hodge, but what you don't do.' He resigned and his replacement was told that his private income of £500 a year was insufficient 'for the pace of this regiment'.[16] One of his fellow subalterns, Winston Churchill, underwrote his own mess and stable bills by being a war correspondent.

A similar case surfaced in 1903 and involved the Grenadier Guards. It was exposed by Rear Admiral Sir Arthur Cochrane, the son of the Napoleonic naval hero, the tenth Earl of Dundonald. He complained to *The Times* that his nephew, an Oxford graduate who was studying Russian and strategy as a Sub-Lieutenant in the Guards, was threatened with a beating by the senior subaltern unless he rode with the Guards' draghounds at a meeting at Windsor. It seemed that conformity in the mess was enforced by a subalterns' court martial, which frequently ordered miscreants to be caned on their bare buttocks. Leaving aside the homoerotic undertones of this ritual, it suggests the lengths to which officers would go to uphold the aristocratic ethos of their regiment.[17] Interestingly, prefects were allowed to administer such punishments in public schools where sports mania was also rampant.

The aristocratic tone of the army had survived the abolition of purchase. The late-Victorian officer still needed a private income to keep up appearances in the mess, at the racecourse and on the polo pitch. The fifty pounds a year allowed George Younghusband as subaltern in the 17th Regiment in the late 1870s proved inadequate even in a comparatively modest mess, and so he secured a transfer to an Indian regiment, the Guides Cavalry. Indian pay and allowances were far higher than in the British army, and so a deliriously happy Younghusband could now 'play polo, hunt, shoot, and be merry' without any fear of being out of pocket. And there was always the prospect of action against some 'pretty tough customer' on the North-West Frontier.[18]

Younghusband was proud to be commanding what he called 'the fighting classes' of India. They were 'splendid men, brave and fearless in action', but 'to be at their best, they require to be led by British officers'. Their age was irrelevant, what mattered was that they were British and, it went without saying, were gentlemen; the Indian belonged to a layered, hierarchical society and was historically conditioned to obey his superiors. He knew a sahib when he saw one and responded accordingly, and so too did the hereditary princes of India, whose collaboration was vital to the British government.

Since the turn of the eighteenth century, when the East India Company underwent a change from a commercial enterprise to a politico-military power with administrative responsibilities, it had preferred gentlemen as its servants. The aristocratic principle was implanted in the government of the Company's territories by Richard Wellesley, Earl of Mornington and later Marquess Wellesley, who served as Governor-General between 1797 and 1805. Typically, he recommended his brother Arthur, the future Duke of Wellington, as an ambassador to the ruler of Poona on the grounds that his 'firmness, integrity [and] temper' would overawe the prince.[19]

Imperial government, like domestic, was an aristocratic duty. Offered the governor-generalship of Bengal in 1784, Lord Cornwallis asked himself, 'Why should you volunteer plague and misery?' 'Duty' dictated the answer. 'You are not here to please yourself . . . try to be of some use; serve your country and your friends.'[20] Cornwallis imposed high standards of humanity, probity and decorum on the Company's staff. 'Exemplary punishment' was inflicted on an officer who struck an Indian, and another who refused to pay his debts to an Indian moneylender was judged 'unworthy' of being an officer and a gentleman and sacked. Another aristocratic proconsul, Montstuart Elphinstone, fourth son of Lord Elphinstone and Governor of Bombay between 1819 and 1827, was admired for his gracious bearing and courtesy towards Indians of all ranks.[21]

As Talleyrand once remarked, 'Empire is the art of putting men in their places.' This was something which aristocrats understood and so they were indispensable to governing the Empire. Since its infancy, the British had been acutely aware that they were acquiring power over races which adhered to and practised the principles of hierarchy.[22] In 1710 four Iroquois chiefs visiting London were held to be 'kings' and one an 'emperor' and people were struck by their 'awful and majestic' presence. One High Church Tory hailed them as:

Four kings – each God's viceregent
With Right divine inherent.[23]

Such men of rank were naturally susceptible to the aristocratic principle and, it therefore followed, would gladly accept imported aristocrats as their rulers. Mornington was right to believe that Indian princes had sensitive social antennae which made them infallible judges of who was, or was not, a gentleman. This was important when it came to observing the nuances of Indian court protocol and following the proper linguistic forms in political and social intercourse with princes. One raja contrasted the finesse and bearing of Lord Hastings, Governor-General of Bengal between 1813 and 1822, with his predecessor, whose manners revealed that he was from the 'weaver caste'.[24] The man concerned, Sir George Barlow, had been a middle-class civil servant.

The romantic medievalism of the early nineteenth century made it easy for proconsuls to identify Indian landowners of all ranks with barons and knights. The comparison was made by Colonel James Tod during his survey in Rajasthan, where he was enthralled to find a ruling elite devoted to war, horsemanship and hunting. 'The Rajput', he wrote, 'slays buffaloes, hunts and eats the boar and the deer . . . he worships his horse, his sword . . . and attends more to the martial song of the bard than to the litany of the Brahmin.'[25] He might easily have stepped from the pages of Scott's *Ivanhoe*.

Addicted to chivalric literature, T. E. Lawrence was spellbound when he first encountered the Sharif Husain of Mecca and his sons Faisal and Abdullah in 1917. They and their armies of spear- and sword-armed camelry and horsemen brought to life Lawrence's romantic vision of the Middle Ages. Faisal and his brothers were aristocrats whose bloodlines and character gave them the right to rule others in a stratified society that had been unchanged for centuries. Lawrence, the illegitimate son of an Anglo-Irish baronet, was determined to preserve this old order and played kingmaker, setting Faisal on the throne of Iraq and Abdullah on that of Jordan. The objective was British paramountcy in the Middle East and regional stability through the preservation of what seemed an immutable order. Lawrence's accomplices in this exercise in freezing societies were Winston Churchill, Sir Mark Sykes Bt., a Yorkshire landowner, and Aubrey Herbert, half-brother of the fifth Earl of Carnarvon.[26] British patronage of local aristocracies extended to the Persian Gulf, where old Arab dynasties were placed in mothballs and protected.

Here, as elsewhere in the Middle East, India and Nigeria, Burkean ideology was adapted. Native societies had developed organically, fulfilling peculiar needs and, in most instances, aristocracies had emerged. They were invaluable allies and, like British aristocrats in the past, could be made into servants of the

Crown. Many needed close supervision and lessons in the arts of benevolent paternalism from British residents, and their sons and grandsons were packed off to British public schools, Oxford and Cambridge and Sandhurst to acquire the accomplishments of gentlemen.

Every effort was made to assimilate the Indian princes (nominal rulers of three-fifths of the subcontinent) into the British aristocracy. Shared passions for bloodstock and hunting helped, and Indian princes were invited to London for royal celebrations such as jubilees and coronations. Many gravitated towards Britain's racecourses.

When maharajas were presented to Queen Victoria, they appeared before their Queen Empress wearing the regalia of pseudo-chivalric orders of knighthood. These had been invented during the second half of the nineteenth century as a device which would bind together Indian rulers and British administrators in a layered brotherhood of honour. As in the Middle Ages, membership of one of these orders was a mark of special royal favour and a reward for loyalty. Most prestigious and, therefore, most desirable was the Most Exalted Order of the Star of India, which was open to all Indian princes, Malayan sultans and high-ranking British proconsuls. Awards reflected the recipient's place in the imperial pecking order. Viceroys, governors and the richest maharajas were Knights Grand Commander of the Order and wore a splendid regalia with fur-lined robes, sashes and collars reminiscent of the British orders of chivalry. Lesser creatures, mostly middle-ranking civil servants, were awarded the Most Eminent Order of the Star of India. Wives of proconsuls, princes and British princesses were awarded the Imperial Order of the Crown of India. Like other British orders, it was also scattered among foreign princes. In 1910 the sisterhood of the Order included the Grand Duchess Cyril of Russia.

A Maltese order, the Most Distinguished Order of St Michael and St George, was annexed in 1868 and sub-divided into ranks and distributed amongst imperial administrators and dominion politicians. The rank and file were Commanders (CMG), governors of lesser colonies were Knight Commanders (KCMG) and governors of larger colonies Grand Commanders (GCMG). Some wit rendered the initials as 'Call Me God', 'Kindly Call Me God' and 'God Calls Me God'. These titles were no laughing matter for those who craved them; the ninth Earl of Elgin, Viceroy of India between 1894 and 1897, wrote that 'in the colonies, premiers and chief justices fight for stars and ribbons like little boys for toys, and scream at us if we stop them'.[27]

The creation of chivalric orders for the Empire was a psychological masterstroke; the imperial honours system 'tied together' the white dominions, India and the colonies 'in one integrated, ordered, titular transracial hierarchy'.[28] Its members, whether the Maharaja of Gwalior, the Governor of St Kitts or the Prime Minister of Canada, were an aristocracy distinguished by dedicated service to the Crown rather than land or ancestry.

Paradoxically, since the 1870s the great majority of the Indian and colonial administrators who received these decorations had acquired their posts through competitive examinations. Most came from upper-middle-class backgrounds and were attracted by what Ralph Furse, who interviewed all candidates for the colonial service, called the 'prestige and renown' of the imperial bureaucracy. For most of the first half of the twentieth century, he examined young men who wished to join it, and looked for signs of 'initiative, hardihood, self-sacrifice, and a spirit of adventure'. A shifting eye or 'languid handshake' were disqualifications for entry into the imperial elite.[29]

The aristocratic principle made no headway in the white dominions. The constitutions of Canada, Newfoundland, Cape Colony, Natal, New Zealand and the Australian states included no provision for upper chambers filled by hereditary peers. The idea had been mooted for Canada in 1789, when George III suggested baronetcies for the most distinguished members of the legislative council. This plan was briefly revived in 1819, but the Governor-General, the fifth Duke of Richmond, told the Colonial Office that titles were utterly inappropriate for 'the low description of merchant' and 'shopkeepers' who sat in Canada's upper house.[30] There was another, insurmountable stumbling block: local opinion. Canadians never wanted an aristocracy and said so, vehemently. In 1919 the Canadian government asked George V to suspend peerages to native Canadians, and in 1951 the former Canadian Prime Minister Vincent Massey was banned from accepting an offer of the Garter. Fifty years later the entrepreneur Conrad Black had to forfeit his Canadian citizenship when he accepted a life peerage.

There was the same antipathy to the notion of an aristocracy in Australia. In the 1820s John Macarthur, the Governor of New South Wales, hoped that the colony's major landowners might act as a kind of aristocracy, but feared that the idea would outrage the colonists, whose temper was egalitarian and democratic. A third of them were convicts or the descendants of convicts with no affection for British institutions and the premises on which they rested. They and the immigrants who came of their own free will believed that they were settling in a country in which all men and women enjoyed an equality of opportunity, and in which talent counted more than birth. Moreover, in all the dominions the abundance of cheap land meant that its possession was open to all, and so it did not have the same social prestige as it did in Britain. It was the American colonial experience all over again, but this time proconsuls and successive colonial secretaries in London were sensitive to the mood of the settlers. They were fiercely loyal to the mother country and the Crown, but wished to create their own form of society in which there was no place for hereditary privilege or deference to lineage.

Hierarchies did emerge in all the colonies and were based on achievement and wealth rather than birth. There was a flow of younger sons of peers to Australia, New Zealand and Canada, where they farmed large estates, built fine mansions and spent their spare time hunting, shooting and fishing. In 1871 Trollope remarked that Australian landowners enjoyed lives similar to that of an eighteenth-century squire, although many were self-made men. Had he visited the country, he would have found familiar lines of social demarcation. Until the late 1880s, farmers were segregated from the 'gentry' at the annual ball in York, Western Australia.[31]

By the close of the century, there were public schools in Australia and New Zealand which, like their British counterparts, upheld the cult of the gentleman and the publishers of *Burke's Peerage* were producing a regularly updated *Colonial Gentry*. Those listed would have been on the invitation lists of the aristocratic governors and governor-generals appointed by the Crown, but they and their wives would have rubbed shoulders with elected politicians who, alone, made the laws in the dominions.

Customary respect for rank of any kind was not part of the colonial psyche. Its absence was frequently and sometimes dramatically revealed during the First World War, when Australian and, to a lesser extent, New Zealand troops were disrespectful to British officers and showed amazement at the apathetic submissiveness of their British comrades. Antipodean recalcitrance tried the admittedly limited patience of Field Marshal Lord Haig in France. In Egypt, a large body of Aussies and Kiwis faced down and barracked the fiery-tempered Field Marshal Lord Allenby when he castigated them for gross indiscipline.

Haig and Allenby had made their reputations fighting the wars of Empire and, like many other successful generals, the latter ended his career as a proconsul. Both men were products of the late Victorian army, an institution which, like the navy, was aristocratic in spirit. It was expressed with characteristic brio a few moments before the Dervish attack during the Battle of

Abu Klea in 1885, when officers regretted that it would be a pity
to die before knowing the result of the Derby. A *Punch* cartoon
of 1909 showed a quartet of elegant cavalry officers (one mono-
cled) enjoying cigarettes and whisky and sodas in their mess
nonchalantly discussing a war with Germany. A major observes:
'It's pretty certain we shall have to fight 'em in the course of next
few years.' 'Well, let's hope it'll come between the polo and the
huntin', remarks a subaltern. All may have had aristocratic connections, but it is highly likely that one or more was the son of,
say, a judge or a senior civil servant. About a quarter of army
officers at the time were, but visitors to messes would not have
noticed. Whatever his background, an officer could survive only
if he assimilated to the aristocratic ethos of his service.

If one accepts the principle that all modern armed services are
a reflection of the nation which employs them, then Britain's
army and navy in 1914 were an anomaly. For the past century,
the aristocratic principle had been in retreat in political life, yet
it remained entrenched in the mindset of British officers. They
were gentlemen, an elevated species, isolated from the civilian
world and proud to be so. In 1914 the Labour MP James
Ramsay Macdonald reviled those army officers who had made
plain their unwillingness to enforce Home Rule in Ireland.
Major Alexander Baird, a baronet's son and veteran of campaigns in Burma and South Africa, rebuked him in an angry
letter. Macdonald and his kind served themselves and their parties to the exclusion of all else. By contrast, Baird insisted, 'The
King, Empire and the Flag' were the lodestars of men like himself who prized honour above expediency.

For the past hundred years the Empire had become an outlet
for aristocratic energies and ambitions. Peers had a monopoly of
the viceroyalty of India and dominion governorships, often, like
Lord Curzon, alternating imperial offices with cabinet ministries.
Beneath them was an imperial civil service whose members were
expected to show the frank manliness of gentlemen and who, if

their careers flourished, might find themselves bound together in a stratified chivalric order. Many would have dedicated themselves to the perpetuation of the aristocratic principle as mentors to hereditary native rulers who had thrown in their lot with the British.

The public did not mind. It was broadly in favour of an Empire which gave Britain prestige and power in the world and was periodically excited by wars in distant places. People were largely content that these and the everyday governance of the Empire were delegated to aristocrats and gentlemen. On the whole this arrangement worked very well, although the dismal performances of Lord Raglan in the Crimea and Lord Chelmsford in Zululand provoked sharp criticism. Victorious commanders were lionised by the press, had statues erected to them and were given titles and the wherewithal to support them by Parliament. Lords Roberts of Kandahar and Kitchener of Khartoum were national heroes who could do no wrong, which was why the latter was made Minister of War in 1914.

Peers in khaki added lustre to the Lords. For the rest of the nobility, imperial and military service were compensation for the slow loss of political power at home and an opportunity for displaying their continued usefulness to the nation. Moreover, in those parts of the Empire which were governed directly, aristocrats could still exercise considerable personal power, giving orders and dispensing patronage. In India, they could even initiate wars, as Lords Auckland and Lytton did against Afghanistan in 1838 and 1878 and Lord Curzon did against Tibet in 1903.

In fact, the British Raj in India became the last stronghold of the aristocratic principle. It was governed by imported lords, home-grown princes and commoners for whom the absorption of aristocratic conventions and tastes was vital for social acceptance, both by Europeans and natives. Lording it over the natives was perhaps some compensation for the loss of influence at home.

26

Always Keep Hold of
Nurse: Aristocratic
Twilight

The twentieth century was an unkind age for the traditional aristocracies of Europe. Historical forces in the form of total war, the expansion of democracy, the replacement of monarchies by republics and the spread of socialist ideologies left them politically and economically vulnerable. There were many casualties. The Russian aristocracy was extinguished by the 1917 revolutions and subsequent civil war, and the nobility of the Baltic states, Poland, East Germany, Czechoslovakia, Hungary, Rumania, Bulgaria and Yugoslavia lost titles and lands under the Communist regimes established between 1944 and 1948. German, Austrian, Spanish and Italian noblemen kept their titles and estates, and some embraced Nazism or Fascism, creeds which, although egalitarian on one level, were reassuringly anti-communist. In inter-war Britain, a small but not insignificant coterie of peers lost faith in conventional politics and attached themselves to Sir Oswald Mosley's Fascist movement and pro-Nazi lobby groups dedicated to Anglo-German cooperation.

Yet on the whole, the British aristocracy kept its head and its nerve in a country which, by 1928, had become a full democracy and whose political temper became increasingly equalitarian, especially during and immediately after the Second World War. The aristocracy survived, sometimes in reduced circumstances and, by and large, was tolerated even during periods of acute economic distress when class tensions intensified. How did it accomplish what appears to be a remarkable act of survival?

There are no simple answers to a complex and often emotive question. This chapter analyses some of the reasons why the aristocracy has endured, as well as tracing the further paring down of its constitutional power. In the most general terms, one explanation of the survival of the aristocracy lies in its history. It has always been integral to national life, it has shown versatility and inventiveness in handling its financial affairs, and a capacity for political compromise. It is always worth remembering that the diehards lost in 1832, 1846 and 1911 because there were enough peers who recognised the supremacy of the public will and were willing to come to terms with it. As one peer remarked during the 1911 debate on the Lords veto, his fellows had no wish to lose the goodwill of their countrymen.

It is also important to remember that the British aristocracy had always been an open and fluid elite. Its 'aristos' [i.e. the best] element was never a matter of birth alone, although some peers and their admirers continued to make much of genetic virtue. 'The Scots have a wonderful pride of race that positively makes itself felt', wrote a guest at the 1922 London Caledonian Ball, 'especially . . . where all the most ancient and noble, and the youngest and most beautful of them are collected.'[1] Ancestry mattered less in many quarters as the century progressed. In the 1960s one peer remarked with insouciant candour: 'We got the barony in the eighteenth century . . . one of those political manouevres to pack the House of Lords and get a bill through . . . I forget what on earth the bill was about.'[2]

Self-confidence did not wilt in a demotic age, particularly among the older generation. In 1977 the noted diarist James Lees-Milne was struck by the 'Edwardian patrician accent' of the Countess of Westmorland. Its timbre seemed to him to epitomise the ancient spirit of the aristocracy. It was 'a proud voice' which resonated 'assurance without swank' and that 'devil-may-care, dismissive manner of the well-bred' which took nothing too seriously.[3]

Like the Scottish ballgoers and the diffident peer, the Countess was a member of a clan with its own language, shared pastimes and often common blood. The largely nineteenth-century social and sporting rituals of the London season with its balls, Cowes week, the August exodus to Scotland and autumnal and winter house parties continued. In 1958 Elizabeth II (1952–) ended the custom of presenting eighteen-year-old debutantes to the reigning monarch, but girls still 'come out', many the daughters of new money.

The aristocracy suffered losses through natural causes and world wars; it was calculated that two hundred direct heirs to titles or major landed estates were killed between 1914 and 1918.[4] Numbers were quickly replenished. Following eighteenth-century precedent, senior generals and admirals were ennobled at the end of the war, irrespective of their performance, which in some instances had been dire.

Mediocre commanders were joined in the post-war Lords by financiers and businessmen who had made fortunes by supplying and arming Britain's mass armies. Some paid Lloyd George for their titles and he placed their cheques in the coffers of his faction of a now divided Liberal Party, which was in the first stages of terminal decline. These shenanigans provoked an outcry, and blatant trafficking in honours was made illegal. At the turn of the century, there were rumours of an identical scandal which prompted a police investigation into the sale of life peerages by Tony Blair and some of his entourage. No conclusive evidence was found.

These recent allegations have an extraordinary social significance. Titles have retained their old magic in a country which, since the 1960s, had flattered itself on the steady advance of egalitarianism. This was suddenly exposed as skin-deep when it became clear that the super rich and successful still craved for peerages and were happy to pay for them, even though they could no longer pass them on to their children. The rigid social hierarchy of Lloyd George's time may have been eroded, but there were plenty of individuals who believed that their accomplishments and wealth deserved the public prestige and respect which a title still represented. The drive for social equality had not eliminated old-fashioned snobbery. Or, as one peer observed during the 1999 debate on the future of the Lords, 'Lords would like to be millionaires, but all millionaires want to be Lords.'

This ambition of millionaires has been legitimised and satisfied by Conservative and, to a much lesser extent, Labour governments. The number of peerage creations spiralled and outpaced natural wastage; there were 596 members of the Lords in 1911 and 851 in 1960. With the introduction of life peers and peeresses in 1957 and 1963 the flow of hereditary creations all but ceased. There was no political mileage in swelling the ranks of the hereditary peers and anyone who wanted the cachet of a title had to be content to accept a life peerage.

Life peerages were a Conservative measure contrived to assuage critics, mostly on the left, who wished to abolish the Lords as an anachronism rooted in ancient inequality. Life peerages reduced but did not eliminate the inbuilt Tory majority in the Lords and accorded with the old aristocratic principle, insofar as they were distributed among men and women of distinction with a broad range of experience and expertise, often gained beyond the narrow world of politics.

It was hoped that their proven wisdom, experience and talents would reinvigorate the Lords and give weight and dynamism to its debates and committees. One life peer, Robert Boothby, a talented Tory maverick, thought that his kind were 'gingering the whole thing up, and keeping it up to date, and making it better'. A broad base was a stronger one, he added. 'I mean, you have all sorts of people, Sainsbury, Crowther, God knows who, who are the rulers of industry . . . you have all the retired Chiefs of Staff who know a hell of a lot about it all [who] can speak with much more authority than any member of the House of Commons could hope to.'[5] Such luminaries also existed among the hereditary titles, who at the time –1970 – included a retired bus driver, Lord Teviot. Between 1958 and 1978 nearly five hundred life peerages were granted, and recipients included academics, scientists, entertainers, former trade unionists, worthies from local government and charitable organisations and the inevitable contingent of superannuated politicians and party hacks.

Hereditary peers remained in what had become a hybrid assembly. Their value and virtues were remembered by one life peer, William Rees-Mogg, a former editor of *The Times*. The old aristocracy were 'reserve troops of common sense', many had had military careers and roots in the countryside, and all were conscious of their families' historic traditions, which qualified them to serve as a 'sort of grand jury of the nation'.[6] This was exactly how the fourth Marquess of Salisbury had justified the existence of the Lords in 1933, when he proposed a relaxation of the restrictions on the chamber's veto. 'The hereditary principle is woven into the public life of the nation,' he declared, and, one day, it might fall to the independent-minded peers to protect the liberties of the nation from a House of Commons in which the majority party ruled by diktat. Or, more pertinently, from a coup of the sort which Hitler had recently accomplished in Germany.[7] This was a well-worn argument that would be resuscitated whenever the existence of the Lords was called into question.

Yet, when Salisbury was defending the Lords, at least fifteen peers, including a quartet of dukes, openly discarded conventional politics and the historic principles which underpinned them by embarking on a brief but intense flirtation with the radical right. Many had fallen under the spell of a dashing but essentially meretricious political adventurer, Sir Oswald Mosley. He was a baronet and a rich landowner whose British Union of Fascists, founded in 1932, was an ostentatiously classless party (the blackshirt uniform obliterated social distinctions) dedicated to national rebirth. Its organisation and objectives were modelled first on Mussolini's Fascism and, later on, Hitler's Nazism. British Fascists hated Jews and Communists and proposed submission to a monolithic state as the prime duty of all citizens.

The history of the aristocratic engagement with British Fascism and its Italian and German prototypes has been thoroughly uncovered and dissected by Richard Griffith and Stephen Dorril. What emerges is a picture of a knot of peers adrift in an uncongenial world, united by paranoia, pessimism and panic. All blamed the misfortunes of their times and class on an immensely powerful but clandestine Judaeo-Bolshevik global conspiracy which could be thwarted only by Fascism and Nazism. Mosley exploited this nightmare version of modern history; he had charisma, intimate connections with aristocratic circles and, for all his populism, was an aristocrat at heart. He had been 'reared in upper-class society and had become accustomed to giving orders because of [his] personal wealth and social position', thought Herbert Morrison, who had worked alongside Mosley when he had been a prominent figure in the Labour Party.[8]

Mosley, Mussolini and Hitler offered bewildered and frightened aristocrats the prospect of a world in which their status and property would be secure from Red revolution and gave a validity to private prejudices, chiefly anti-Semitic. When they met, the second Lord Redesdale was captivated by Hitler's dynamism and will, and Lady Redesdale told her daughter Jessica that the 'Socialists want everyone to be poor.'[9] Another admirer of Hitler, the second Duke of Westminster ('Bend Or') was a host to fantasies about the subversion of Britain by Jewish 'gold' and spent the first nine months of the war demanding an immediate peace with Nazi Germany. That Casanova of Kenya's 'Happy Valley', the twenty-second Earl of Erroll, was mesmerised by Mosley, and, when he returned to the colony, he promised his fellow settlers that he would introduce Fascism to East Africa. Amazingly, he listed its ingredients as 'complete religious social freedom', 'no dictatorship' and a self-supporting Empire which would not 'trade with the dirty foreigner'.[10]

The third Lord Brocket fawned over Nazi bigwigs, whom he invited to his houses in Hertfordshire and Hampshire, attended Hitler's fiftieth birthday celebrations in 1939 and deluded himself that he was an invaluable link between the leaders of Britain and the Third Reich. During the Blitz it was rumoured that he lit fires on his Hertfordshire estates to guide German bombers.[11] James Lees-Milne summed up this buffoon as 'a fundamentally nice man' but 'stupid'.[12]

From the standpoint of this book, the importance of Brocket and his kind lies not so much in their political opinions, but in the fact that they ingenuously imagined that their status gave them public credibility, particularly between September 1939 and May 1940, when they joined Mosley in calls for an accommodation with Hitler. The government kept these peers under intelligence surveillance, but they were not treated as a serious threat and none was interned, unlike Mosley and his wife Diana, a daughter of Lord Curzon and lifelong devotee of Hitler. Nevertheless, when he flew to England in May 1941, Rudolf Hess, Hitler's deputy in the Nazi Party, imagined that he would find peers sympathetic to a peace with Germany, but then he was probably three-parts mad.

If this episode revealed anything, it was the sheer lack of influence of men like Westminster, Redesdale, Brocket and Erroll, and, indeed, it may have been an awareness of their impotence which had propelled them into the un-English politics of Fascism, with its intolerance, bombast and violence. Although the Fascist peers stressed their patriotism, none had ever expressed it through a conventional political career in an established party or as a crossbencher in the Lords. Their attachment to Germany during a national emergency was a rejection of their duty to the state and its political ideals and institutions. In this respect, they were taking their cue from a kindred spirit Edward VIII (1936), who had abandoned his birthright when he abdicated. As Duke of Windsor, he revealingly wrote in the spring of 1940 that Britain urgently needed a purge of the 'old lot of politicians and much of our out-of-date system of government'.[13] These were treasonous sentiments, which Mosley would have applauded, but they were enticing for those aristocrats who found themselves stranded on the periphery of politics and out of step with their times.

To these disappointments were added a visceral anti-Semitism which permeated the upper classes between the wars. Jews were vilified as flashy and pushy arrivistes with a knack of enriching themselves at a time when the aristocracy was grumbling about an often exaggerated downturn in their fortunes. As ever, old money resented new, but what made the anti-Semitic ramblings of figures like Westminster so odious was that they continued long after Hitler's persecution of Germany's Jews had become public knowledge.

In terms of the political history of the peerage, the behaviour of a handful of right-wing extremists was a reminder that aristocratic power, as it had been understood in the past, was now moribund. After 1918, peers who chose a political career could no longer expect to attain the highest offices of state; since 1902 no peer has served as Prime Minister, Chancellor of the Exchequer, or Minister of Health, though there have been four titled Foreign Secretaries and one Minister of Defence. Six of the ministers in Churchill's wartime coalition were peers, which was about average for the past forty years. All held junior and unglamorous offices, with the exception of the Canadian newspaper proprietor Lord Beaverbrook, who oversaw aircraft production during 1940.

An unwritten constitution had now acquired an unwritten protocol which demanded that the prime minister was always a Member of the Commons. It was invoked in May 1940 by Lord Halifax when he stood down in favour of Churchill, although the truth was that the peer regarded the prime ministership with apprehension and considered himself temperamentally unfitted to provide the leadership needed in wartime.

Churchill, grandson of the Duke of Marlborough, was supremely confident that he had all the necessary qualities. He was forthright, cocksure, pugnacious and possessed a patrician sense of public duty, a faith in his own talents and judgement, and an emotional attachment to his country. Churchill was deeply conscious of his illustrious ancestry (he wrote a life of the first Duke of Marlborough) and, born in 1874, he had the mindset of a Victorian aristocrat with a birthright to rule. This made him the last representative of a tradition of leadership which stretched back through Palmerston to Wellington and beyond to the Whig and Tory grandees of the eighteenth century. Yet Churchill was distrusted and disliked by the Conservative aristocracy, because of his apostasy in 1904 and subsequent, often savage assaults on the Lords during the 1910 and 1911 crises. In May 1940 many peers would have preferred one of their own kind, Halifax, who, although a dull dog, was solid and reliable.[14]

Churchill's finest hour was also that of the old aristocratic ideal, although, paradoxically, he later refused a dukedom and remained fiercely proud of being a commoner and a Member of the Commons.

Churchill was right: twentieth-century political life revolved around the Commons. This was why in 1960 the ambitious Anthony Wedgwood Benn disclaimed the peerage he had inherited on the death of his father, Lord Stansgate. After three years of legal quibbling the hitherto cast iron laws of inheritance were relaxed and Wedgwood Benn remained a 'Mr' and an MP. A trickle of similar renunciations followed, most notably that of Alec Douglas-Home, fourteenth Earl of Home, who abandoned his title before becoming Prime Minister in 1964. A hereditary title was now a handicap for an ambitious young politician.

For all the occasional sparkle of its debates and its benches filled with talented and experienced men and women, the mid-century House of Lords was essentially a passive institution. It could suggest, amend and plead for the reconsideration of bills, but, in the event of an impasse, it could merely delay their implementation for a year. It grew and grew, so that by 1979 there were 1,150 peers of whom 408 were nominally Conservatives, 151 Labour and 42 Liberal and the rest cross-benchers.[15] The old Tory predominance remained, and the Lords was still what it had been a hundred years before: the Tory party's poodle. It was, therefore, a potential embarrassment to a Party which went to great lengths to project itself as modern, democratic and representative of the interests of every section of society. For this reason, the Conservative leadership endeavoured to keep its dog on a tight leash to forestall a clash with a Labour Party which could easily provoke a 'peers versus people' contest.

Sometimes the dog growled. In 1949 the Lords dragged their heels over the nationalisation of steel, and in June 1968 it gave a defiant bark. The peers rejected Labour Prime Minister Harold Wilson's implementation of United Nations sanctions against the technically rebellious former colony of Rhodesia (Zimbabwe). There was widespread sympathy with the white settlers ('in Rhodesia you are dealing with men, not with the helots of a discredited dictatorship') and anger that the United Nations was meddling in Britain's affairs. The Conservative leader in the Lords, Lord Carrington, urged the peers to accept a measure which fulfilled Britain's international obligations as a member of the United Nations.[16] His party was bounding ahead in the opinion polls, and was disinclined to become embroiled in a contest over the future of the Lords.

This episode gave the Labour government the opportunity to introduce the first ever bill to abolish the Lords. There were two debates, the first in June, when the quirky Willie Hamilton (notorious for his sniping at the royal family) introduced a private member's bill for the immediate abolition of the chamber and titles. In November, and on the government's initiative, the Commons discussed how the Lords might be replaced. These debates were not welcomed by Wilson, who, while presenting himself and his party to the voters as catalysts for the long-overdue modernisation of Britain, would have preferred to leave the Lords alone.[17] After his resignation in 1976 he became Lord Wilson of Rievaulx.

Wilson's caution displeased the left of his party. Hitherto, Labour had been in a vague way committed to the dissolution of the Lords, but pragmatism had always intervened: what, if anything, would replace the chamber? As one MP observed, quoting Hilaire Belloc:

> *Always keep a hold of nurse,*
> *For fear of finding something worse.*[18]

Nurse's qualifications were ridiculed by Hamilton. His rant included sneers at peers' deafness, senility – which infuriated older Labour MPs – and eccentricity. Over the past thirteen years, the tenth Duke of Atholl had spoken on the Game Laws, birds' eggs and grey squirrels (which, as a countryman, he presumbly knew something about) and then Rhodesia![19] Such men were invaluable; the late Lord Borthwick felt that his veterinary training enabled him to speak with authority in debates concerning animals. At the time there were no former vets in the Commons.

Replacing the Lords presented many hurdles. The Liberal MP and future party leader Jeremy Thorpe warned that if the new chamber was elected, it could challenge the Commons. A nominated chamber would be a dangerous extension of government patronage and the party in power could easily secure a permanent majority by packing it with placemen and toadies. Most prescient were the comments of Sir Dingle Foot, a Labour jurist. The new Lords would strengthen 'a class of professional politicians who have no other occupation but politics' while the present system filled the Lords with 'men from all walks of life who can speak from first-hand experience, men from the services, the law, banking, industry, agriculture, the shop floor and the mine'.[20] The Conservative MP Enoch Powell saw the Lords as 'an intrinsic part of the national tradition of the government of the country'. Taking a purely pragmatic view, the Tory Lord Lambton, the eldest son of the Earl of Durham, argued that there was nothing to be gained from arguing over the future of the Lords since the peers had effectively lost their political power in 1832. He later renounced his father's title to stay in the Commons.

This debate turned out be academic, for the government dropped the bill in April 1969. Labour was in no position to embark on what might be a prolonged constitutional wrangle over an issue which excited little public interest. The party was trailing miserably in the opinion polls (only 24 per cent favoured it) and was distracted by economic problems. Its supporters may have been disappointed; in the 1977 Labour conference 6.2 million voted for abolition of the Lords, but, given the dominance of the trade union block vote, this was no reflection of opinion within the country. The House of Lords would survive for a further twenty years.

In terms of economic survival, the aristocracy was doing rather well in the 1960s. Land values had risen since the war and stood at an average of £240 an acre in 1967. A 54,000 acre estate in Gloucestershire produced a rent roll of £15,000 for Lord Bathurst.[21] By 1984 English prices were £2,000 an acre, Scottish between £300 and £1,700 and in Wales roughly £1,000.[22] Agriculture was now flourishing, although its recuperation and present health had been achieved only through injections of state and then European Union subsidies.

The late twentieth-century prospects for agriculture would have amazed landowners of sixty years before. Between 1918 and 1924 between 6 and 8 million acres had been sold, prompting predictions that the old landed aristocracy would soon become extinct.[23] Sales of paintings and town and country residences confirmed this bleak picture. Between 1920 and 1938 over one hundred country houses were demolished by owners who could no longer afford to maintain them, and then and later there were protests against the destruction not of the properties of the individuals, but the 'national heritage'. There were similar outcries when peers sold outstanding works of art, the assumption being that they were integral to the country's culture and therefore never to be sold abroad. The sums raised were invariably used to pay death duties, or for investment.

Between the wars, a handful of peers, including the eleventh Duke of Manchester and the seventh Duke of Montrose, purchased estates in Kenya's Happy Valley and Rhodesia. There, they and other aristocratic exiles could make money, live in a truly patrician manner with legions of cheap servants and enjoy all the sybaritic indulgences of their recent forebears. Those provided by Happy Valley were listed by Evelyn Waugh as fights, adultery, arson, bankruptcies, card-sharping, insanity, suicides, even duels'.[24] The flavour of life in Happy Valley is vividly described in James Fox's *White Mischief*, published in 1980, who reminds us that the proprieties were never entirely abandoned. When the Prince of Wales was dining at the Muthaiga Club, one rake offered him cocaine and was bundled out of the room. The man who had done the evicting remarked afterwards: 'Well, there is a limit even in Kenya, and when someone offers cocaine to the heir to the Throne, something has to be done about it, particularly when it is between courses at the dinner table.' Murder was added to the vices of Happy Valley in 1941 when the twenty-second Earl of Erroll was shot. Sir Jock Delves Broughton Bt., one of the many husbands Erroll had cuckolded, was tried for the murder and acquitted. He returned to England and shot himself, bringing the episode to an appropriately melodramatic conclusion.

Regency England under the sun was also an agreeable alternative to post-1945 austerity Britain under Labour. 'Seldom have I witnessed gentry living in such squalor even in post-war days,' Lees-Milne wrote after visiting one country house in Wiltshire in 1948. Elsewhere, he encountered a field marshal's wife polishing the silver and stairs, abandoned gardens and rooms covered with dustsheets.[25]

Paid employment offered relief to many peers. The number of aristocratic directors rose from 167 in 1896 to 232 in 1920 and has increased steadily since.[26] During the 1950s a knot of peers with financial and social foresight were actively engaged in the funding and creation of local commercial television stations.[27] Another form of showmanship was now attracting more and more peers: the imaginative exploitation of their country houses and parks. Since the eighteenth century, many houses and parks had been open to the public when their owners were away and interiors could be inspected on payment of a small charge to the housekeeper. In the 1730s up to five hundred local people a day visited the second Duke of Richmond's menagerie at Goodwood in Sussex. They were amazed by, among other beasts, an armadillo, a lion, wolves, bears, vultures, a 'woman tiger', a 'Greenland dog' and cassowaries.[28]

Menageries, renamed 'safari parks', proved equally popular in the second part of the twentieth century. Lions and later other creatures drew visitors to the Marquess of Bath's house at Longleat and the Duke of Bedford established a zoo at Woburn in Bedfordshire. As leisure and tourist industries expanded, the aristocracy responded to the tastes and interests of their predominantly middle- and working-class customers. There were funfairs, specialist museums, newly designed and spectacular gardens, occasional pop concerts (such as at Knebworth House in Hertfordshire) and spectacles such as tournaments. Country houses became the backdrop for corporate conferences, weddings, concerts and advertising promotions. At Kelburn in Ayrshire the Earl of Glasgow and his son Viscount Kelburn achieved a delightful coup de théatre by inviting Brazilian graffiti artists to paint the walls of the castle, to quite stunning effect.

Modern visitors to houses and parks had been preconditioned as to what to expect by television. Popular series such as *Upstairs Downstairs,* which traced the parallel lives of the families of the master and his servants during the early part of the century, perennial adaptations of Jane Austen's novels and P. G. Wodehouse's Jeeves and Wooster stories, as well as Evelyn Waugh's *Brideshead Revisited* have reconstructed the world of the aristocracy. Many were filmed in aristocratic houses. The latter was shot at Castle Howard and in 1984 visitors were invited to 'see the real thing' in an advertisement headed 'Revisit Brideshead'.[29]

Fiction replaced reality: a mansion built by a historic family was now the seat of a fictional one, Waugh's Flytes.

There was also a new tendency to emphasise the duality of the country house with visitors being conducted through the servants' quarters, kitchens and laundries as well as the state rooms. Every house had its shop, often marketing products which suggested its past ambience, particularly brands of preserves and chutneys whose labels indicated that their recipes had once been concocted for exclusive use of the aristocracy and gentry. Garden centres also proliferated to satisfy the demands of what had become one of the most popular pastimes in the country.

Sporting estates secured a fresh and valuable lease of life. They were now status symbols purchased by the super-rich who had made fortunes in the City. Those who could not afford to buy shoots could rent them and fishing rights. In the boom time of 1990, it was estimated that bagging a deer would cost a corporate shooter £30,000 and landing a salmon, £13,000, figures that fell by over a half when the City went through a sticky patch.[30] Providing game for fund managers led to tensions in some areas, particularly Scotland. Here, gamekeepers were regularly charged with killing rare protected predators, including eagles and kites. Making shooting profitable was apparently an imperative which overrode even the law; on one estate owned by a City figure locals blamed 'imported' English gamekeepers ordered to rear large numbers of grouse.[31] Defenders of grouse shooting claimed it annually provided £10 million for the Scottish economy. On occasions, aristocratic landowners themselves played host to paying shooting parties. (An anecdote from the 1980s claimed that one noble host joined a party of paying guns and, irritated by the enthusiasm of his dogs, shouted, 'Get down! Get down!' Several of the waiting businessmen went down on their knees.)

What is significant about corporate lawyers paying large amounts to pot grouse and the rest of the public paying to visit country houses is that both are seeking to share the aristocratic experience. In the broadest sense, the aristocratic sector of the leisure industry was driven by a nostalgia for a past which has been sanitised to make it attractive and marketable. The paying gun bringing down a pheasant was part of an aristocratic sporting tradition which was reproduced in the paintings and prints which hung on the walls of country houses. The visitors who wandered through them caught a glimpse of a distant and glamorous world. Yet, my experience of walking through these places is that many tourists are excited by evidence such as toys and a television set which suggest that the house is still inhabited by a family. Continuity is often emphasised by guides who talk familiarly and affectionately about present owners.

Tourism has guaranteed that the aristocracy remains part of the fabric of national life. Popular curiosity about the actual lives of aristocrats, past and present, has also been satisifed by individual and family biographies with a distinct preference for eccentric subjects. The six Mitford girls, daughters of the second Lord Redesdale, have generated a thriving literary industry, not surprisingly since their lives have embraced, among other things, an elopement, conversion to Communism, and high melodrama in the form of Unity's manic passion for Hitler and attempted suicide.

Roughly until 1980, the misdeeds, misadventures and trivial activities of real aristocrats remained the stock-in-trade of newspaper gossip columns, but their perceived interest to readers has diminished rapidly. Of course the drug-taking and bad driving of peers still make headlines, but now they compete for attention with a new class: celebrities. They are actors, actresses, pop musicians, television personalities, models, self-promoters and sportsmen and -women, particularly footballers, and nearly all have lower-middle- or working-class backgrounds. Like some aristocrats in the past, many modern celebrities have convinced themselves that they are beyond the law and the older moral conventions, including good manners. To use a not altogether defunct expression, celebrities are mostly 'vulgar', yet some spend their fortunes on acquiring rural properties and the trappings of squiredom.

Reacting to this social phenomenon, Tom Blofeld, a Norfolk squire and proprietor of a tourist attraction in Norfolk, feels obliged to shed ancestral instincts. 'It's a meritocratic, democratic world now. Being an ordinary geezer gets you a lot of opportunities, whereas being a toff doesn't corner you in some way,' he observed in May 2008.[32] Yet, at the same time, a journalist contemplating the recent success of two Old Etonians, Boris Johnson and David Cameron, regarded disparingly by the Left as 'toffs', wondered whether the time had come for such creatures to regain their 'birthright' of leadership.[33]

Noblesse oblige has not completely faded away. Blofeld's life is dedicated to maintaining his estate to pass on to his heirs, and other peers strive towards the same end. Others have had to make their own living, like Lord Lichfield, the photographer. Some fell by the wayside; in 1984 there were eleven peers who earning their livings in humble but useful occupations, including a policeman, a bus conductor and a municipal gardener.[34] Given that there were nearly eight hundred hereditary peers, this number was remarkably small.

In purely Darwinian terms, the twentieth-century aristocracy had shown extraordinary flexibility and a capacity to adapt to circumstances. Lord Montagu of Beaulieu, who attached a popular motor museum to his Hampshire house, attributed this general success to breeding. 'It is fashionable to dismiss, as irrelevant, breeding and background in human beings,' he wrote in 1970. 'But when you compare the difference in price of a pedigree bull or stallion, and that of an equally fine but non-pedigree animal . . . it can run into thousands of pounds.'[35] This was perhaps a riposte to the gibe made two years before in the Commons by William Hamilton, who observed: 'As a method of ensuring quality, the hereditary principle is rather less selective than the methods adopted on a stud farm.'[36] Lord Lichfield concurred: an ancestor who had gained a title for his exploits at sea gave him no automatic right to 'speak in public on important issues'.[37]

Hereditary and life peers continued to do so until 1997. In that year New Labour secured power with a large majority and the promise to regenerate and modernise the nation and its system of government. One of its targets was the Aunt Sally of the old Labour party, the House of Lords. The first offensive was undertaken in 1998 with a bill to expel four hundred hereditary peers, leaving a token ninety-five who had to be elected by their fellows. It was probably more than coincidence that the trimming of the hereditary peers was accompanied by a successful campaign to outlaw fox-hunting, which was widely supported by rank-and-file Labour supporters, for whom men and women on horseback were symbolic of a feudal past. Aristocrats hunted, but their preferred sport was shooting. One outcome of this skirmish in the class war was the Countryside Alliance, which defended fox-hunting and complained of the government's indifference to rural issues.

The debate on remaking the Lords followed predictable lines. Defenders of the Lords repeated the argument that it acted as a brake on the Commons and could, in some circumstances, reflect public opinion more accurately than a chamber in which MPs were constrained and hustled by party whips. The peers stood between the country and an elected dictatorship. Many peers were fulfilling what they sincerely believed to be a public duty incumbent on them because of their family traditions. According to Lord Arran, these men and women 'asked for nothing . . . other than their offspring should be allowed to serve in the same selfless way' as their ancestors had.[38]

In the Commons, the former Prime Minister Sir John Major

stressed the independence of the peers and wondered whether this could be reproduced in a yet-to-be devised replacement chamber. New Labour ministers reiterated Tom Paine's taunt about hereditary judges and poet laureates, and the Lord Chancellor, Lord Irvine, expressed amazement that the country had for so long tolerated a chamber which gave hereditary peers the right to 'sit and vote' on the making of laws.[39]

By a bizarre paradox, the period in which the future of the Lords was in jeopardy witnessed a massive inflation of peerages. Tony Blair created 376 life peers between 1997 and 2007, just under the total made by Mrs Thatcher and John Major during their eighteen years in office. Nearly all New Labour's peers were from those sections of society already over-represented in the Commons: the law, the media, corporate bigwigs and professional politicians. Some were 'people's peers' (a Blairite invention) who had been nominated by the public and finally chosen by one of the Prime Minister's friends. The result was more of the same thing: Lord Brown, the Chief Executive of British Petroleum, Lady Howe, the wife of a Tory Foreign Secretary, and Sir Claus Moser, a merchant banker. No wonder Robin Cook, the Foreign Secretary who broke ranks with Blair over the invasion of Iraq, drolly observed in 2004 that the House of Lords had shifted 'from the fifteenth-century principle of hereditary to the eighteenth-century principle of patronage'.[40] George III would have envied Blair's powers of patronage. Many of these men and women, hungry for power, often interconnected by marriage, friendship and blood and based in London, were intrinsically hostile to the Lords and the hereditary peers in particular, more than half of whom had rural backgrounds and many of whom had had a greater experience of the world than any professional politician. The nineth Duke of Buccleuch who died in 2007 was an expert on forestry and had served throughout the war as an ordinary seaman.

The everyday work of the Lords continues, now largely

undertaken by life peers and peeresses. A handful have their own blogs, which, in the spring of 2008, revealed that during the past year over eight hundred thousand people had corresponded with members of the Lords. Individual peers were performing their public duties in the manner of their predecessors: one had helped expose government subterfuge over British Aerospace's arms sales to Saudi Arabia and between seventy and eighty had listened to the debate over the Treaty of Lisbon, during which a former European Union mandarin, Lord Williamson, explained some of the more arcane legal matters. Other busied themselves with humdrum committee work.[41]

Who or what will replace these men and women? In his *In Defence of Aristocracy* of 2004, Sir Peregrine Worsthorne played a modern Burke, emphasising the enlightened disinterest of the hereditary peers and contrasting the spirit of *noblesse oblige* with the modern plutocrat's selfishness and philistinism. The extinction of the Lords would create a vacuum in public life and a dangerous one, for proposals were in hand to supersede it with a chamber in which the nominees of the party in power would dominate. The old Tory poodle would be New Labour's lapdog.

This has not yet happened. There is no consensus, even within New Labour, as to the form and powers of a new second chamber. In March 2008 an elected chamber was proposed whose members would serve for fifteen years with a third being replaced every five years. This is still a matter of great contention, not least because it would create two potentially rival chambers each with a popular mandate. An American journalist asked whether 'by moving from an upper chamber of ornery old buffers to one of political grandees, would the Brits be doing themselves a favour?'[42] The resolution of the impasse over the Lords may be postponed for some years, not least because politicians are now preoccupied with the chronic recession created by the sudden disintegration of the banking system during the summer and autumn of 2008.

In the meantime, life peers predominate in the Lords and have become imbued by the audacious and independent spirit of their hereditary predecessors. The Lords has again become a bulwark against arbitrary government and the protectors of ancient popular liberties. Over the past four years, peers have treated the government as they once treated overbearing monarchs. Successive cabinets have uncritically succumbed to the alarms sounded by police chiefs, assorted 'security' gurus and secret service supremos running scared from real and illusory terrorist threats and whittled away established liberties and legal processes. The Lords have blocked these measures: they have resisted the erosion of the right to trial by jury, the suspension of the Habeas Corpus Act, and a bill contrived to suppress freedom of expression in religious matters and the peacetime introduction of identity cards. For good measure, the peers have also swept aside the exemption of MP's expenses from the Freedom of Information Act, which has led to some disconcerting revelations.

The last ten years has witnessed the strange rebirth of the House of Lords. Its members, overwhelmingly life peers, have somehow unconsciously absorbed the historic independence and vigilance of the old hereditary nobility. Of course, these qualities were often more apparent than real, but there were crucial moments when they were not, and the early twenty-first century is one. Today, the Lords are applying their traditional dispassion and watchfulness to restrain an executive whose inclinations are authoritarian and which tends to dismiss the ancient legal rights and liberties of the individual as hindrances to administrative efficiency. There is nothing new in this: King John and Charles I would have approved of on-the-spot fines and the 2006 Terrorism Act. Nor is there anything new in the House of Lords' position as the guardian of ancestral freedoms and a defence against tyranny. The power of the hereditary aristocracy may have disappeared, but its sense of public duty remains strong among its modern successor.

Notes

The works referred to here are cited in full in the Bibliography.

Abbreviations
BL = British Library
BodL = Bodleian Library
BP = Blenheim Palace
CP = *The Complete Peerage*
CPR = *Calendar of Patent Rolls*
CSP = *Calendar of State Papers*
DNB = *Dictionary of National Biography*
HMC = Historic Manuscripts Commission
HP = History of Parliament
ILN = *Illustrated London News*
LP = *Letters and Papers Foreign and Domestic of the Reign of Henry VIII*
MCO = Magdalen College, Oxford
NA = National Archives
NAS = National Archives of Scotland
NLS = National Library of Scotland
PL = *Paston Letters*
SR = *Statutes of the Realm*

Part One: Ascendancy

Chapter 1. A Game of Dice: The Growth of Aristocratic Power

1. Tristram, *passim*.
2. *Calendar of Inquisitions Post Mortem*, VIII, 1968, p. 46, p. 51, p. 55, p. 70.
3. Maddicott, pp. 43–5.
4. Sayles (ed.), p. 227.
5. *Stonor Letters*, I, pp. 116–17.
6. *The Lisle Letters*, I, p. 585.

Chapter 2. Manners and Virtue: The Cult of Chivalry and the Culture of the Aristocracy

1. Rawcliffe, pp. 29–30, pp. 93–4; *Lisle Letters*, I, p. 13.
2. Dyboski, R., and Arend, M. (eds.), p. 11.
3. Keen, p. 119, p. 122.
4. St John Hope, *passim*.
5. Sinclair, pp. 87–9.
6. ed. Miller, p. 559.
7. Anglo, I, p. 20.
8. Turville-Petre, pp. 336–7.
9. Westfall, pp. 175–8.
10. Hanna III, p. 897, p. 910.
11. Smyth, *Lives of the Berkeleys*, II, p. 34.
12. Both are large and were made in 1401; one is at Dyrham and the other at Chipping Campden.
13. Aldwell, p. 56.
14. MCO, Miscellaneous Manuscripts, 270.
15. HMC, *De Lisle and Dudley*, I, p. 199.
16. Saul, *passim*.
17. Virgoe, 'Some Ancient Indictments', pp. 254–5.
18. Offord (ed.), pp. 2-4.
19. Smyth, *Lives*, II, pp. 5–6.

Chapter 3. Their Plenty was Our Scarcity: Resistance.

1. By far the best account is Professor Barry Dobson's collection of documents; I have relied upon it and his comments.
2. Dobson, p. 258.
3. Owst, p. 301.
4. Fryde, p. 78.
5. Fryde, p. 76, p. 119.
6. Smyth, *Lives*, II, p. 6.

Chapter 4. Weeds Which Must Be Mown Down: The Wars of the Roses 1450–87

1. Hamner, p. 285.
2. Hicks, pp. 310–12.
3. *Henry VI, Part Two*, IV, i.
4. Virgoe, 'The Death of William de la Pole', p. 499.
5. Pugh, p. 55.
6. Hughes, *Arthurian Myths and Alchemy*, pp. 47–8.
7. Hughes, *Arthurian Myths*, p. 71.
8. Scattergood, p. 205.
9. Hicks, p. 293.

Chapter 5. As a True Knight: Honour and Violence in the Wars of the Roses

1. Lander, Attainder, p. 106n.
2. Griffiths, p. 35.
3. *PL*, III, p. 4.
4. Hughes, *Arthurian Myths*, p. 196, p. 197, p. 241.
5. *CPR, 1452–1461*, pp. 93–102.
6. *PL*, I, pp. 96–7.
7. Virgoe, 'William Tailboys and Lord Cromwell', p. 469, p. 472.
8. Payling, p. 893.
9. NA, C 1/26/76.
10. NA, KB 9/118/22.
11. Hicks, pp. 48–9.
12. Smyth, *Lives*, II, pp. 65–8, pp. 110–14.
13. *PL*, II, 230.
14. NA, C 1/31; KB 9/296, 297; C 1/29, 193; C 1/40, 60–63.
15. NA, E 404/ 74, 31, 79.
16. Dunham, p. 16.
17. Macfarlane, P. 250.
18. *CPR, 1452–1461*, pp. 552–3.
19. HMC, 3rd *Report*, Appendix 4, pp. 2–4.
20. Chrimes, p. 308.

Chapter 6. In Foolish Submission: Irish and Scottish Aristocracies

1. Miller (ed.), p. 565.
2. HMC, 12th *Report*, Appendix 4, p. 35.
3. Gwynfor Jones, pp. 104–16.
4. Ellis, p. 67.
5. *Clan Campbell Letters*, p. 153.

6. Dawson, p. 8.
7. Muldoon, p. 90.
8. Fradenburg, p. 154, p. 239.
9. Brown, "'Rejoice to hear of Douglas'", pp. 168–70.
10. Stringer, pp. 217–18.
11. Connolly, pp. 52–3.
12. *CSP, Scotland*, V, pp. 253–63, and *CSP, Scotland*, VII, p. 558, p. 577.
13. Brown, *Bloodfeud in Scotland 1573–1625*, p. 5.
14. Burnet, p. 11.

Chapter 7. Obeyed and Looked Up To: The Tudors and Their Lords

1. Henderson, p. 11, p. 31.
2. Archer, *Religion, Politics and Society*, p. 130.
3. Bernard, 'The Downfall of Thomas Seymour', pp. 221–2.
4. Nicholls, (ed.), p. 9.
5. *CSP, Domestic, Mary I*, I, 44.
6. *CSP, Domestic, Mary I*, I, 30.
7. HMC, *Salisbury*, I, pp. 443–7.
8. *Letters of the Clifford Lords and Earls of Cumberland, c.1500–c.1565*, p. 34.
9. *Lisle Letters*, II, pp. 468–9.
10. *LP, Henry VIII*, XI, p. 371.
11. Stone, p. 747.
12. Woodward, pp. 15–17.
13. Wall, p. 37.

Chapter 8. Stir Up Your Fame: A New Breed of Noblemen

1. *LP, Henry VIII*, XXI, i, p. 284.
2. Stone, p. 791.
3. Stone, p. 677.
4. Markham (ed.), pp. 42–3.
5. Scott (ed.), p. 497.
6. Low, p. 18.
7. Stone, p. 236.
8. Stone, pp. 274–5.
9. *The Wentworth Papers 1597–1628*, p. 16.
10. Hamner, p. 57.
11. Spiers (ed.), pp. 62–3.
12. HMC, *Rutland*, I, pp. 397–9.
13. HMC, *Hastings*, III, p. 309.
14. Lightbrown, p. 158.

15. Elyot, p. 103.
16. Weber, p. 121.
17. Rosenberg, p. 128.
18. Lamb, p. 164.
19. Lamb, p. 165.
20. Woodfill, pp. 59–60.
21. Woodfill, pp. 66–7.
22. Rothenberg, pp. 350–1.

Part Two: Equilibrium: 1603–1815

Chapter 9. I Honour the King as Much as I Love Parliament: The Road to Civil War

1. James, *English Politics and the Concept of Honour*, p. 85.
2. Malcolm, p. 136.
3. Trevor Roper, p. 354.
4. Ibid., p. 348.
5. *Register of the Privy Seal of Scotland*, VII, pp. 185–6.
6. HMC, *13th Report*, II, p. 133.
7. Zagorin, p. 53.
8. Gardiner (ed.), p. 217.
9. Trevor Roper, p. 297.
10. Malcolm, p. 158.
11. Zagorin, p. 332.
12. Fletcher, p. 285, p. 289.
13. HMC, *13th Report*, I, p. 87.
14. Hughes, *Politics, Society and Civil War in Warwickshire, 1620–1660*, p. 155; *The Diary of Bulstrode Whitelock, 1605–1675*, pp. 138–9.

Chapter 10. A Circular Motion: Revolution and Restoration 1642–60

1. Carlton, pp. 211–14.
2. *CSP, America and the West Indies, 1574-1660*, p. 380, p. 387.
3. *CP*, XII, ii, pp. 706–8.
4. Kelsey, pp. 55–6, p. 116, pp. 120–1.
5. Bush, p. 134.
6. Malcolm, p. 147.
7. Ibid., p. 157.
8. Warmington, p. 103; Underdown, p. 133.
9. Hughes, *Politics, Society*, p. 202, p. 251.
10. *DNB*, 49, pp. 124–7.

11. *Calendar of the Proceedings of the Committee for Compounding, 1643–1660*, I, pp. 839–40; *CP*, XII, i, pp. 691–2.
12. *Calendar of the Proceedings*, I, pp. 914–15; *CP*, XI, pp. 26–7.
13. Ward, pp. 23–4.
14. Ibid., p. 31.
15. Thirsk, p. 188.
16. Durston, pp. 47–8.
17. Gentles, 'The Sales of Crown Lands during the English Revolution', *passim*; Gentles, 'The Purchasers of Northamptonshire Lands', p. 217.
18. Thirsk, p. 188.
19. O'Hart, pp. 248–304.
20. Ohlmeyer, p. 284.
21. *CSP, Ireland, 1647–1660*, pp. 624–5; *CSP, Ireland, 1660–1662*, p. 318.
22. Ohlmeyer, p. 242.
23. Ibid., pp. 263–4.
24. Hughes, *Politics, Society*, pp. 293–4.
25. Bush, p. 135.
26. Zagorin, p. 14.

Chapter 11. Signal Deliverances: Restoration 1660–85

1. *SR*, V, 12 Charles II c. xxiv.
2. *SR*, V, 12 Charles II c xiv.
3. Slater, p. 133.
4. Harris, p. 22.
5. *Register of the Privy Council of Scotland, 1681*, pp. 69–70; *Register of the Privy Council of Scotland, 1683–1684*, p. 30.
6. A. N., p. 2.
7. Stillingfleet, pp. 27–8.
8. L'Estrange, p. 24.
9. Clark, *English Society 1688–1832*, pp. 16–17.
10. Bush, p. 29.
11. *The Late Apology in Behalf of the Papists Re-Printed and Answered in Behalf of the Royalists*, p. 46.
12. *Depositions from the Castle of York Relating to Offences Committed in the Northern Counties in the Seventeenth Century*, p. 230.
13. Clark, *English Society*, pp. 16–17.
14. Slater, pp. 129–30.
15. HP, *House of Commons, 1660–1690*, I, p. 2, p. 16.
16. Ibid., II, pp. 419–20.
17. *SR*, V, 16 Charles II, c.iv.
18. *SR*, V, 30 Charles II, c. 1.
19. Slater, pp. 141–2.

20. Evelyn, IV, pp. 225–34.
21. Halifax, p. 255, p. 234.
22. *The Diary of Samuel Pepys*, III, pp. 209–10; *Pepys*, IX, 335–6.
23. Kenyon, p. 330.
24. Keeton, pp. 266–7.
25. Halifax, p. 49, p. 101, p. 195, p. 216.

Chapter 12. The People Assembled and Freely Chose Them: The Glorious Revolution and After

1. Harris, p. 285.
2. Lindsay, pp. 39–41.
3. Slater, p. 167.
4. HMC, *Buccleuch and Queensbury*, II, p. 31.
5. Harris, p. 265.
6. Slater, p. 181.
7. Lindsay, p. 18, p. 20.
8. *Register of the Privy Seal of Scotland*, XIII, p. 352, p. 355.
9. HMC, *Le Fleming*, p. 214, p. 220, p. 223, p. 226.
10. *Letters and Papers chiefly addressed to George Earl of Melville, Secretary of State for Scotland 1689–1691*, p. 12.
11. Clark, *English Society*, p. 120.
12. *Charges to the Grand Jury, 1689–1803*, p. 37.
13. Ibid., p. 67–8, p. 73.
14. *The Letterbooks of John Hervey First Earl of Bristol*, I, pp. 74–5, p. 139.

Chapter 13. I'll Share the Fate of My Prince: Jacobites

1. NLS, MS 7104, pp. 3-4.
2. James, *Warrior Race*, pp. 109–12.
3. Lindsay, iv.
4. NLS, MS 7044, p. 50.
5. NLS, MS 7104, pp. 128–9, p. 143.

Chapter 14. Magnificence: Grand Houses and Grand Tours

1. Henderson, p. 11.
2. Tinniswood, p. 81.
3. Ibid., pp. 21–2; Peck, pp. 197–200.
4. HMC, *Mar and Kellie*, II, pp. 77–9.
5. Nashe, pp. 300-1.
6. HMC, *Mar and Kellie*, II, p. 98.
7. Stoye, p. 134.
8. Bacon's *The Advancement of Learning* quoted in Strong, p. 50.

9. HMC, *Twelfth Earl of Lindsey*, p. 279.
10. Stoye, p. 146.
11. Strong, p. 29.
12. Tinniswood, pp. 42–3.
13. Ibid., p. 42; HMC, *De Lisle and Dudley*, I, pp. 290–1.
14. Strong, p. 50.
15. Hesemer (ed.), I, pp. 87–8.
16. Shakeshaft, p. 123.
17. Ibid., pp. 123–4.
18. Whalley, *passim*.
19. Wootton, pp. 18–19, pp. 20–1.
20. Stone, pp. 719–20.
21. Smuts, *passim*.
22. Cohen, pp. 55–6.
23. Uglow, pp. 322–3.
24. *Lady's Magazine*, IV (1773), p. 8.
25. Burke, *A Philosophical Enquiry into the Origin of Our Ideas on the Sublime and Beautiful*, p. 136, p. 140.

Chapter 15. Public Character: The Aristocratic Century 1714–1815

1. Cannon, *Aristocratic Century*, and Clark, *English Society, 1688–1832*.
2. *The Creevey Papers*, I, p. 275; Burke, *A General and Heraldic Dictionary of the Peerage and Baronetage of the British Empire*, p. vii.
3. *SR, George III*, XXXI, c. xxxi.
4. *The Speeches of the Duke of Wellington in Parliament*, I, p. 406.
5. Colley, pp. 177–93.
6. Cannon, p. 40, p. 42, p. 44.
7. Maxwell Lyte, p. 431; *CP*, VI, p. 326n.
8. Bourne, p. 9.
9. Yonge, I, pp. 7–8.
10. *Creevey Papers*, I, p. 4, pp. 50–1, 260; *Creevey Papers*, II, p. 117.
11. HMC, *Egmont*, I, p. 34.
12. *The Correspondence of the Dukes of Richmond and Newcastle 1724–1750*, p. xxvi, p. 4, p. 7, p. 8, p. 40, p. 63, p. 46.
13. Ibid., p. 6, p. 13.
14. BL, Add. MSS 32,995, p. 162, p. 252.
15. BL, Add. MSS 32,998, p. 407, p. 409.
16. BL, Add. MSS 32,995, p. 262d.
17. Wraxall,
18. Beckett, *The Aristocracy of England 1660–1914*, pp. 428–9.
19. BL, Add. MSS 32,995, pp. 175–9.
20. Clay, p. 19.

21. MacCahill, p. 273.
22. HMC, *10th Report*, pp. 6–7.
23. Wraxall, 413–14.
24. Clark, *English Society*, pp. 212–13.
25. *Gentleman's Magazine*, August 1784, p. 577.
26. NAS, GD 51/1/36.
27. NAS, GD 51/1/120, p. 2.
28. NAS, GD 51/26/31; *CP*, V, p. 607.
29. HMC, *Bathurst*, p. 278.
30. *Speeches of the Duke of Wellington*, I, p. 80, p. 81, p. 91.
31. HMC, *Egmont*, p. 420–6.
32. HMC, *10th Report*, p. 15.
33. McCahill, p. 273.
34. NAS, GD 22/1/318, p. 1, p. 4, p. 5.
35. *The Later Correspondence of George III*, I, 183n.
36. *Gentleman's Magazine*, LX, ii (1785), p. 619.

Chapter 16. A Fair Kingdom: Fame, Taste and Fashion

1. *Public Advertiser*, 18 and 20 January 1758.
2. Saville, *Secret Comment*, pp. 92–3.
3. *Bell's London Life and Sporting Chronicle*, 1 August 1824.
4. *The Oracle and Daily Advertiser*, 16 June 1800.
5. *The Universal Register*, 14 April 1785.
6. Lady Caroline Lamb, I, p. 184, p. 186.
7. *Lady's Magazine*, IV (1773), p. 4 (the novel was serialised in this publication).
8. Tillyard, pp. 65–6.
9. *The Connoisseur*, 16 January 1754.
10. *The Connoisseur*, 27 June 1754.
11. Postle (ed.), p. 29.
12. Brewer, pp. 256–9.
13. *The Universal Register,* 14 June 1785.
14. Brewer, pp. 256–9.
15. Ibid., p. 285.
16. *The Art Journal* (1849), p. 165.
17. *John Constable's Correspondence*, pp. 180–1; Haydon, III, p. 386.
18. See Brewer and Porter.
19. Schultz, pp. 1–2; Gay, p. 80.
20. Deutsch, p. 746.
21. Ibid., p. 426.
22. *The Connoisseur*, 6 June 1754.
23. *Gentleman's Magazine*, August 1784.
24. Tait, 439–441.

25. NAS, GD 248/589/1, p. 11, p. 32, p. 34, p. 37, p. 44.
26. NAS, GD 248/589/1, p. 18, p. 47.
27. NAS, GD 248/589/1, p. 19.
28. HMC, *10th Report*, p. 6.
29. Clark, *English Society*, p. 112 n. ·
30. *The Oracle: Bell's New World*, 3 June 1789.
31. Lord John Hervey, pp. xxviii–xix; NA, WO 71/85, p. 176.
32. *Bell's London Life and Sporting Chronicle*, 8 February 1824 and 11 April 1824.
33. *The Connoisseur*, 28 November 1754.
34. *The Oracle: Bell's New World*, 11 June 1789.
35. Lady Caroline Lamb, I, pp. 199–200, p. 206.
36. *Anti-Jacobin*, VII (October 1800), p. 144.
37. Clark, *English Society*, p. 110.
38. Andrew, p. 429, p. 433.
39. Ibid., p. 423.
40. Hall-Witt, p. 224.
41. *The General Advertiser*, 1 March 1780.
42. Brewer, p. 457, p. 461.
43. Robbins Landon, p. 165.
44. Weber, Did People Listen?, pp. 688–90.
45. Weber, Did People Listen?, p. 690.
46. *Art Journal* (1849), 3-5.
47. Haydon, V, p. 471.
48. *The Greville Diary*, II, p. 26.
49. Hansard, 3rd Series, 146, 333–4, 1152.
50. Rhodes James, p. 107.

Chapter 17. We Come for Pheasants: Peers and Poachers

1. Munsche, p. 222.
2. HMC, *Stopford-Sackville*, II, p. 17.
3. Munsche, p. 63.
4. Archer, 'Poachers Abroad', p. 63.
5. Thompson, *Whigs and Hunters*, pp. 101–2, 110–12.
6. Hay, p. 190.
7. Archer, 'Poachers', p. 54; Hansard, 1st Series, 38, 542; Hansard 3rd Series, 47, 939, 956.
8. *The Times*, 11 March 1844.
9. Hay, p. 239 (e.g. *Public Advertiser*, 10 June 1758).
10. Munsche, p. 222.
11. King, p. 104–5.
12. Cirket, p. 83.
13. Hansard, 3rd Series, 47, 940.

14. *The Times*, 4 April 1859.
15. *Spectator*, I, 413.
16. *Correspondence of the Dukes of Richmond and Newcastle*, p. 25, p. 241.
17. Hansard, 1st Series, 39, 1086–7.
18. Hansard, 3rd Series, 47, 925.
19. Oerlemans, pp. 71–4.
20. Hansard, 1st Series, 39, 937, 1082–7; *The Times*, 23 March 1819.
21. *The Economist*, 11 January 1845.

Chapter 18: A Gang of Ruffians: Americans and Aristocracy

1. *Pennsylvania Evening Post*, 23 and 28 November 1776.
2. Paine, *Common Sense*, p. 8, pp. 17–19.
3. Foner, p. 208.
4. *Journals of the Continental Congress 1774–1789*, V, p. 804.
5. *Pennsylvania Evening Post*, 11 January 1777.
6. Kramer. p. 230.
7. *Maryland Gazette*, 29 December 1780.
8. Roeber, p. 29, p. 44.
9. Kay, p. 74, p. 75, p. 104.
10. Foner, p. 195.
11. Marshall, p. 112.
12. Devine, p. 218.
13. Yarborough, pp. 89–95.
14. Calhoun, pp. 140–1, p. 209.
15. HMC, *Hastings*, I, p. 157, p. 170, p. 179.
16. *Documents of the American Revolution 1770–1783*, VI, pp. 72–3.
17. *Correspondence of Charles First Marquis Cornwallis*, I, p. 67, p. 75, p. 78.
18. Conway, pp. 393–4.
19. Wyatt Brown, p. 146.
20. *Maryland Gazette*, 18 September and 27 November 1780.
21. Evan Davies, pp. 5–13.
22. De Tocqueville, pp. 24, 53.
23. Goodrich, pp. 93–4.
24. *Gorgon*, 24 April 1819.
25. Shelley, IV, pp. 11–12.

Chapter 19: The Aristocrat to Quell: Peers, Paineites and Patriots 1789–1815

1. Burke, *The Works of the Right Honourable Edmund Burke*, IV, p. 150–1.
2. Goodrich, pp. 46–9.
3. Paine, *The Rights of Man*, 62.

4. Hansard, 6th Series, 319, 959–60 and 324, 741; 6th Series (Lords), 559, 26.
5. *The Letter Journal of George Canning 1793–1795*, p. 59.
6. James, *Mutiny,* pp. 39–40.
7. Elmsley, p. 96.
8. Royle, pp. 40–1.
9. Goodrich, p. 117.
10. Macleod, *A War of Ideas*, pp. 84–5.
11. Goodrich, p. 95.
12. Ibid., p. 117.
13. *Anti-Jacobin*, January 1799, p. 104.
14. Macleod, *War of Ideas*, 84-85.
15. Davies (ed.), VI, p. 275, p. 282.
16. Royle, p. 33.
17. *Aberdeen Chronicle*, 30 June and 9 September 1794.
18. *True Briton*, 16 July 1800.
19. *Naval Chronicle*, IX (1804), pp. 317–25.
20. *The Times*, 4 March 1814.
21. NAS, GD 22/1/318, p. 2.
22. For the history of the militia see Cookson, *passim*.
23. NAS, GD 46/6/43, p. 1.
24. NLS, Sep 313/3270, p. 3171.
25. These incidents are described in J. Prebble, *Mutiny* (1975).
26. *Edinburgh Review*, V (October 1804), pp. 5-6, p. 11.
27. Hudson, 'Volunteer Soldiers in Sussex during the Revolutionary and Napoleonic Wars', p. 172, p. 173, p. 179.
28. *The Times*, 25 March 1814.
29. *The Times* 14 April 1814.
30. James, *The Iron Duke*, p. 10.
31. Ibid., p. 172, quoting W. P. Woodberry, 'The Idle Companion of a Young Hussar in the Year 1813' (National Army Museum).
32. *CP*, X, p. 580.
33. *Edinburgh Review*, XXIII (April 1814), pp. 35–7.

Part Three: Decline: 1815–

Chapter 20. Rats: Crisis and Compromise

1. NLS, MS 11,865, p. 58d.
2. NLS, MS 11,981, p. 2d–3.
3. Haydon, IV, p. 15.
4. Shelley, IV, p. 7.
5. NLS, MS 11,980, pp. 2–8.

6. NLS, MS 11,982, pp. 7-8, p. 11.
7. *The Economist*, 11 January 1845.
8. Hansard, 3rd Series, 11, 110–11; *CP*, XII, ii, 421.
9. Harling, pp. 100–1.
10. Clark, *English Society*, p. 399.
11. Jaggard, p. 85, p. 92.
12. Eastwood, *passim*.
13. Beckett, *Aristocracy of England*, *passim*.
14. NLS, MS 11,865, p. 58.
15. Haydon, IV, p. 561, p. 573; *Greville Diary*, I, p. 348.
16. NLS, MS 11,865, p. 15.
17. Hansard, 3rd Series, 12, 7.
18. Hansard, 3rd Series, 12, 49–50.
19. Hansard, 3rd Series, 13, 25.
20. Haydon, IV, p. 83.
21. Hansard, 3rd Series, 13, 292–3.
22. Clark, *English Society*, p. 93.
23. NAS, GD 46/6/43, p. 7.
24. NLS, MS 12,338, pp. 117–18; Ms 12,339, p. 44. These files contain many entertaining appeals for patronage and some sad ones.
25. Rowe, p. 88, pp. 91–8.
26. Bromond, *passim*.
27. *The Times*, 1, 3 and 6 September 1866.
28. *Dod's Parliamentary Companion for 1859*.
29. Thompson, *English Landed Society in the Nineteenth Century*, p. 48.

Chapter 21. Thoroughbred: Sport and Manliness

1. *King's Counsellor: Abdication and War: The Diaries of Sir Alan Lascelles*, pp. 150–1.
2. Apperley, *The Chace, The Turf, and the Road*, p. 83.
3. Seth-Smith, pp. 147–8.
4. *Bell's London Life and Sporting Chronicle*, 18 July 1842.
5. *The Diary: or Woodfall's Register*, 18 January 1791.
6. *Bell's London Life and Sporting Chronicle*, 2 and 25 November 1855.
7. Egan, I, pp. 3–4, 12-13.
8. Cassidy, p. 3.
9. Ibid., p. 43, p. 116.
10. E.g. HMC, *Hastings*, I, pp. 366–7.
11. Ashton, pp. 84–5.
12. Ibid., pp. 105–6.
13. Ibid., pp. 139–40; *CP*, III, p. 415.
14. Connor and Lambourne, p. 54.

15. Apperley, *The Chace*, p. 71.
16. Ashton, p. 197.
17. Gash, p. 254–5.
18. *Bell's London Life and Sporting Chronicle*, 1 July 1855.
19. Ashton, p. 221.
20. *The Tatler*, 5 July 1911.
21. Gash, p. 257.
22. Apperley, *Nimrod's Hunting Tours*, p. 229.
23. Corballis, p. 44, p. 47.
24. Apperley, *Nimrod's Hunting Tours*, p. 10.
25. Ibid., pp. 238–9, pp. 323–4.
26. MacKenzie, p. 46.
27. Girouard, *The Return to Camelot*, Chapter 16.
28. Ibid., pp. 6–7.
29. Ibid., pp. 276–8.
30. Wagg, pp. 33–4.
31. Jarvie and Jackson, p. 29.

Chapter 22. The Surrender of Feudalism to Industry: The Mid-Victorian Peerage 1846–87

1. NLS, Dep 313/769, p. 588.
2. *Greville Diary*, I, p. 29.
3. Hansard, 3rd Series, 251, 193.
4. *Greville Diary*, I, p. 39.
5. *Gentleman's Magazine*, 3rd Series, XIV, p. 657.
6. *Gentleman's Magazine*, 2nd Series, XX, p. 532.
7. *Gentleman's Magazine*, 3rd Series, XV, p. 288.
8. *Gentleman's Magazine*, 4th Series, II, p. 625–7.
9. *Saturday Review*, 11 April 1868.
10. Details of Cardigan's multiple indiscretions can be found in Saul David's excellent *The Homicidal Earl: The Life of Lord Cardigan* (1997).
11. Hansard, 3rd Series, 130, 1535.
12. Roberts, *Salisbury*, p. 834.
13. Ibid., p. 127.
14. *Blackwood's Magazine*, 1880, pp. 240–3.
15. *The Economist*, 25 January 1846.
16. Hansard, 3rd Series, 87, 953–4, 963.
17. Fisher, p. 97.
18. Thompson, *English Landed Society*, 242-243.
19. *Edinburgh Review*, CXXIII (1866), p. 186.
20. Cragoe, pp. 37–8.
21. Cannadine, *The Decline and Fall of the British Aristocracy*, p. 93.

22. Thompson, *English Landed Society*, p. 257, p. 259, p. 262.
23. Rubenstein, pp. 206–8; Cannadine, *Decline and Fall*, 91.
24. Roberts, *Salisbury*, pp. 101–3.
25. Pumphrey, p. 5; *The Times*, 26 August 1856.
26. BP, Marlborough Letters, IV, pp. 455–6.
27. Roberts, *Salisbury*, p. 74.
28. Adonis, p. 225.
29. Hansard, 3rd Series, 251, 163, 165 and 255, 1743.
30. Hansard, 3rd Series, 256, 782.
31. Adonis, p. 283.
32. Roberts, *Salisbury*, p. 259.
33. Rhodes James, p. 117.
34. Ibid., p. 113.
35. Lord Rosebery, pp. 131–2, p. 165.

Chapter 23. Revolvers Prominently Displayed: The Downfall of the Irish Aristocracy

1. *Edinburgh Review*, CXXIII (1864), p. 197.
2. Curtis Jr., p. 332, p. 359; Vaughan, p. 119.
3. Hamilton, p. 46.
4. Hoppen, p. 115; Curtis Jr., p. 320n.
5. Trench, pp. 53–6, pp. 70–1.
6. *Thom's Official Directory of the United Kingdom of Great Britain and Ireland for the year 1883*, p. 751; Hoppen, p. 109; Vaughan, pp. 3–4, p. 11.
7. *ILN*, 5 February 1881.
8. Hansard, 4th Series, 16, 1652.
9. BP, Marlborough Letters, IV, 406.
10. *Spectator*, 15 January 1881.
11. Fleming, p. 11.
12. *Spectator*, 10 June 1893.
13. Hoppen, p. 414
14. Ibid., pp. 419–20.
15. *ILN*, 8 January 1881. There is a dramatic engraving of this scene which took place during a rainstorm.
16. Gladstone, p. 542.
17. Ibid., p. 538; Hoppen, 143.
18. *The Times*, 3, 4, 5 and 11 April 1878; *CP*, VII, p. 582; Vaughan, pp. 119–20.
19. Pole, p. 395.
20. Clark, 'Social Composition of the Land League', p. 457.
21. Vaughan, p. 143.
22. Pole, p. 395.

23. BP, Marlborough Letters, III, p. 405.
24. Curtis Jr., p. 348.
25. Gladstone, p. 541.
26. *Spectator*, 16 September 1893.
27. Adonis, 131.
28. Hansard, 4th Series, 16, 1621–2.
29. *The Times*, 1 September 1893.
30. Hansard, 4th Series, 17, 54, 63, 70, 248, 257–8, 434.
31. Hansard, 4th Series, 17, 30, 277–8.

Chapter 24. Like Chaff Before Us: Hanging On 1887–1914

1. Lord Chandos, p. 26.
2. Macleod, *The Last Summer*, pp. 12–13.
3. *The Sphere*, 16 August 1919.
4. *The Times*, 1 September 1893.
5. Blewett, p. 230.
6. Wasson, p. 205.
7. *Spectator*, 16 September 1893.
8. Adonis, p. 145.
9. Burke, *A Genealogical and Heraldic History of the Landed Gentry . . . 1913*, Introduction, np.
10. *The Times*, 14 May 1919.
11. Cannadine, *Decline and Fall*, p. 98.
12. Thompson, English Aristocracy in the Twentieth Century, i, 19.
13. Rhodes James, p. 45.
14. Adonis, p. 245.
15. *Country Life*, 3 August 1901.
16. BodL, Carrington Diaries, 29 March 1909.
17. Wilson Fox, pp. 81–2; *The Times*, 14 June 1928.
18. Lord Rosebery, p. 34.
19. ed. Boyce, vii.
20. Roberts, 'The Holy Fox', pp. 6–9.
21. Fleming, p. 16.
22. Ibid., p. 19; Hansard, 4th Series, 187, 529.
23. Grigg, p. 174; Masterman, p. 150, p. 211.
24. Quoted in *Spectator*, 23 September 1893.
25. Adonis, p. 183.
26. Ibid., pp. 189–90, p. 284.
27. Ibid., p. 264.
28. Ibid., pp. 155–6.
29. BodL, Carrington Diaries, 3 August and 29 December 1909.
30. Grigg, p. 174.

31. Ibid., pp. 203–8.
32. Gilmour, pp. 384–5.
33. Thompson, 'English Landed Society in the Twentieth Century, I (Poverty and Survival)', p. 7.
34. BodL, Carrington Diaries, 31 January and 3 March 1910.
35. Ibid., 2 March 1910.
36. Masterman, 143.
37. Adonis, p. 267.
38. Grigg, p. 305; BodL, Carrington Diaries, 24 July 1911.
39. *The Letters of Arthur Balfour and Lady Elcho 1885–1917*, p. 267.
40. BodL, Carrington Diaries, 16 March 1911.
42. *National Review,* LVII (September 1911–February 1912), p. 25, p. 40.
43. Adonis, p. 272.
44. *The Tatler,* 5 October 1910, and 2 and 9 August 1911.
45. Thompson, 'English Landed Society in the Twentieth Century, II (New Poor and New Rich)', p. 8.

Chapter 25. Dangers and Honours: War, Empire and the Aristocracy

1. Hansard, 3rd Series, 136, 2136.
2. The Marquess of Anglesey, I, p. 172.
3. Hansard, 3rd Series, 137, 1895–6.
4. Lord Charles Beresford, p. xiii.
5. Hansard, 3rd Series, 137, 1206–7.
6. *The Economist,* 25 January 1845.
7. Beckett, *The Army and the Curragh Incident,* p. 124.
8. Mawson, *passim.*
9. Thackeray, p. 421.
10. The Marquess of Anglesey, II, p. 359.
11. Riedi, pp. 246–7.
12. Gibson, p. 190.
13. *Bell's Life in London and Sporting Chronicle,* 1 July 1855.
14. Riedi, p. 247.
15. de Crespigny, p. 248.
16. *The Times,* 20 June 1896.
17. *The Times,* 10 February 1903.
18. Younghusband, 31.
19. *The Despatches, Minutes and Correspondence of the Marquess of Wellesley,* V, p. 19.
20. *Correspondence of Charles First Marquis Cornwallis,* I, pp. 168–9.
21. Kaye, I, p. 288.
22. Cannadine, *Ornamentalism,* p. 5.
23. Hinderaker, p. 501.

24. James, *Raj*, p. 164.
25. Tod, I, p. 82.
26. Cannadine, *Ornamentalism*, p. 73.
27. Ibid., p. 88.
28. Ibid., p. 90.
29. HMC, *Bathurst*, 460–1, pp. 471–2.
30. Bolton, pp. 320–1.
31. Becket, *Curragh Incident*, pp. 369–70.

Chapter 26. *Always Keep Hold of Nurse: Aristocratic Twilight*

1. *The Tatler*, 7 June 1922.
2. Perrott, p. 260.
3. Lees-Milne, *Diaries 1975–1978*, p. 175.
4. *Burke's Peerage* (1920), Introduction.
5. Lord Montagu of Beaulieu, p. 186.
6. *The Times*, 24 March 2004.
7. Hansard, 6th Series (Lords), p. 90, p. 613.
8. Dorril, p. 157.
9. Ibid., pp. 439–40; *Decca: The Letters of Jessica Mitford*, p. 3.
10. Dorril, p. 327.
11. Private information.
12. Griffiths, *Patriotism Perverted*, p. 206.
13. Dorril, p. 494.
14. Roberts, *Eminent Churchillians*, p. 137, pp. 140–1.
15. Butler and Sloman, p. 198.
16. Hansard, 5th Series, 295, 367, 403, 423, 531.
17. Hansard, 5th Series, 760, 1611.
18. Hansard, 5th Series, 773, 1326.
19. Hansard, 5th Series, 767, 469.
20. Hansard, 5th Series, 773, 1162.
21. Perrott, p. 150.
22. *Country Life*, 19 April 1984.
23. Cannadine, *Decline and Fall*, pp. 106–11.
24. Ibid., p. 624.
25. Lees-Milne, *Caves of Ice, passim; Midway on the Waves: Diaries 1948–1949*, p. 114.
26. *CP*, V, pp. 780–3.
27. Cannadine, *Decline and Fall*, pp. 648–9.
28. Richmond, p. xxvi.
29. *Country Life*, 17 May 1984.
30. Jarvie and Jackson, p. 47.
31. Private information.

32. *Financial Times*, 4 May 2008.
33. *The Times,* 3 May 2008.
34. Thompson, 'English Landed Society in the Twentieth Century, I (Poverty and Survival)', p. 14.
35. Lord Montagu of Beaulieu, p. 182.
36. Hansard, 5th Series, 466, 760.
37. *Montague*, 183.
38. Hansard, 6th Series (Lords), 599, 175.
39. Hansard, 6th Series, 760, 337, 741, 768–9, 959–60; Lords, 599, 204.
40. Oborne, p. 207.
41. Lord of the Blog net.
42. www.economist/democracy/2007/British aristocracy overthrown.cfm.

Bibliography

Unpublished Sources

Blenheim Palace, Woodstock, John Winston Spencer Churchill, Duke of
    Marlborough, Papers.
Bodleian Library, Oxford: Carrington Diaries (B.P.D. 1649 microfilm)
Magdalen College, Oxford: Miscellaneous Manuscripts
National Archives, Kew: Adm 1; C.1; E.404; K.B.9; WO 71
National Archives of Scotland, Edinburgh: Melville Papers (GD 51);
    Findlater Papers (GD 248)
National Library of Scotland, Edinburgh: Tweeddale Papers (MSS 7045;
    7046: 7104); Sutherland Papers (Dep 313); Minto Papers (MSS
    11,865, 11,889, 11,980, 11,981, 11,982, 12,338, 12,339)

Published Sources

All books published in London unless otherwise stated. The dates given are
    those of the editions consulted by the author.

Adams, S., '"Because I am of that Country and Mynde to Plant myself
    there"': Robert Dudley Earl of Leicester in the West Midlands',
    Midlands History 20 (1995)
Adonis, A., *Making Aristocracy Work: The Peerage and the Political System
    1880–1914* (Oxford, 1993)
Aldwell, S. H., *Wingfield, its Church, Castle and College* (Ipswich, n.d.)

A. N., *The Royal Favourite Cleared with an Admonition to the Roman Catholics and an Address to his Royal Highness the Duke of York* (1662)

Andrew, D. T., 'The Code of Honour and its Critics: The Opposition to Duelling in England', *Social History* 5 (1980)

The Marquess of Anglesey, *A History of the British Cavalry*, I, 1815–1851 (1988), and II, 1851–1871 (1975)

Anglo, S., *The Great Tournament Rolls of Westminster* (2 volumes, Oxford, 1968)

Apperley, C. J. ('Nimrod'), *Nimrod's Hunting Tours interspersed with characteristic anecdotes, sayings and doings of Sporting Men including notices of the principal Crack riders of England* (1835)

— *The Chace, The Turf, and the Road* (1870)

Archer, I. W. (ed.), *Religion, Politics and Society in Sixteenth-Century England* (Camden Society, 2005)

Archer, J. E., 'Poachers Abroad', in G. E. Mingay (ed.), *The Unquiet Countryside* (1989)

Ashton, J., *A History of Gambling in England* (1898)

Aston, M., 'Lollardry and Sedition', in R. H. Hilton (ed.), *Peasants, Knights and Heretics: Studies in Medieval English Society* (Cambridge, 1976)

The Letters of Arthur Balfour and Lady Elcho 1885–1917, eds. J. Ridley and C. Percy (1992)

Barclay, A., *The Life of St George*, ed. W. Nelson (Early English Text Society, 1955)

Beales, D., 'The Electorate Before and After 1832: The Right to Vote and the Opportunity', *Parliamentary History* 11 (1993)

Beckett, I. F. W., *The Army and the Curragh Incident* (Army Records Society, 1986)

Beckett, J. V., 'English Landowning in the Later Seventeenth and Eighteenth Centuries', *Economic History Review* 30 (1977)

— *The Aristocracy of England 1660–1914* (Oxford, 1986)

Beeman, R. R., 'Deference, Republicanism and the Emergence of Popular Politics in Eighteenth-Century America', *William and Mary Quarterly* 49 (1992)

Beer, B. L., *Rebellion and Revolt: Popular Disorder in England during the reign of Edward VI* (Kent State University Press, 1982)

Lord Charles Beresford, *The Memoirs of Admiral Lord Charles Beresford written by himself* (1916)

Bernard, G. W., 'The Downfall of Thomas Seymour', in. G. W. Bernard (ed.), *The Tudor Aristocracy* (Manchester, 1992)

Bernard, S., and Burke, A. P., *A Genealogical and Heraldic History of the Landed Gentry of Great Britain*, ed. A. Winton Hope (1921)

de Berners, J., *The Book Containing the Treatise of Hawking; Coat Armour; Fishing; and the Blasing of Armes As Printed at Westminster by Wynkyn de Worde* (1496, facsimile edition 1810)

Black, J., *George III: America's Last King* (2006)

Blamires, A. 'The Twin Demons of Aristocratic Society', in N. MacDonald (ed.), *Pulp Fictions of Medieval England: Essays on Popular Romance* (Manchester, 2004)

Blewett, N., *The Peers, the Parties and the People: The General Elections of 1910* (1972)

Bolton, G. C., 'The Idea of a Colonial Gentry', *Historical Studies* 13 (1967–69)

Bower, W., *Scotichronicon*, vol. 7, eds. A.B. Scott and R. Webb (1986), and vol. 8, ed. D. E. R. Watt (1987)

Boyce, G. (ed.), *The Crisis of Unionism: Lord Selborne's Domestic and Political Papers, 1885–1922* (1987)

Boyd, M., *Reminiscences of Fifty Years* (1870)

Brewer, J., *Party Ideology and Popular Politics at the Accession of George III* (Cambridge, 1976)

— *Pleasures of the Imagination: English Culture in the Eighteenth Century* (1997)

Bromond, T., '"A Complete Fool's Paradise": The Attack on the Fitzwilliam Interest in Peterborough in 1852', *Parliamentary History* 12 (1992)

Brown, K. M., *Bloodfeud in Scotland 1573–1625: Violence, Justice and Politics in Early Modern Scotland* (Edinburgh, 1986)

— '"Rejoice to hear of Douglas": The Presentation of Magnate Powers in Late-Medieval Scotland', *Scottish Historical Review* 78 (1987)

— 'Aristocratic Finances and the Origins of the Scottish Revolution', *English Historical Review* CIV (1989)

— 'Scotland Tamed? Kings and Magnates in Late-Medieval Scotland: A Review of Recent Work', *Innes Review* 45 (1994)

Brown, R. E., *Virginia 1705–1786: Democracy or Aristocracy* (Lansing, Michigan, 1964)

Burke B., *A Genealogical and Heraldic History of the Landed Gentry of Great Britain* (1914)

Burke, E., *A Philosophical Enquiry into the Origin of our Ideas on the Sublime and Beautiful* (1770)

— *The Works of the Right Honourable Edmund Burke* (5 volumes, Oxford, 1907)

Burke, J., *A General and Heraldic Dictionary of the Peerage and Baronetage of the British Empire* (1829)

Burke's Peerage (1920)

Burnet's History of His Own Times (1883)

Burnley, D., *Courtliness in Medieval England* (1998)

Burns, A., and Innes, J., *Rethinking the Age of Reform, Britain 1780–1850* (2003)

Bush, M. L., *The English Aristocracy: A Comparative Study* (Manchester, 1984)

Butler, D., and Sloman, A., *British Political Facts 1900–1979* (1908)

Buxton, A., 'There Is No "Right" to Roam', *Contemporary Review* 274 (1999)

Calendar of Inquisitions Miscellaneous, VIII (1399–1422) (1968)

Calendar of Patent Rolls, 1452–1461 (1910)

Calendar of the Proceedings of the Committee for Compounding, 1643–1660 (2 volumes, 1889–90)

CSP, America and the West Indies, 1574–1660 (1860)

CSP, America and the West Indies, 1661–1668 (1880)

CSP, America and the West Indies, 1689–1692 (1902)

CSP, Domestic, 1595–1597 (1869)

CSP, Edward VI, III 1549–1551 (1925)

CSP, Ireland: Adventurers for Land, 1643–1649 (1903)

CSP, Ireland, 1647–1660 (1903)

CSP, Ireland, 1660–1662 (1908)

CSP, Mary I, 1553–1558 (1998)

CSP, Philip and Mary, 1553–1554 (1937)

CSP, Scotland, V 1574–1581 (Edinburgh, 1907)

CSP, Scotland, VII 1584–1589 (Edinburgh, 1913)

Calhoun, R. H., *The Loyalists in Revolutionary America 1700–1781* (New York, 1973)

Clan Campbell Letters, 1559–1583, ed. J. E. A. Dawson (Scottish History Society, 1997)

Cannadine, D., *The Decline and Fall of the British Aristocracy* (1990)

— *Ornamentalism: How the British Saw Their Empire* (2001)

The Letter Journal of George Canning 1793–1795, ed. P. Jupp (Camden Society, 1991)

Cannon, J., *Aristocratic Century: The Peerage of Eighteenth-Century England* (Cambridge, 1984)

Carlton, C., *Going to the Wars: The Experience of the British Civil Wars, 1638–1651* (1995)

Cassidy, R., *The Sport of Kings: Kinship, Class and Thoroughbred Breeding at Newmarket* (Cambridge, 2002)

Lord Chandos, *The Memoirs of Lord Chandos* (1962)

Chibnale, M. (ed.), *The Ecclesiastical History of Ordericus Vitalis*, V (Oxford, 1975)

Chrimes, S. B., *Henry VII* (1972)

Cirket, A. F., 'The 1830 Riots in Bedfordshire: Background and Events', *Bedfordshire Historical Society* 37 (1978)

Chaucer, G., *The Canterbury Tales*, trans. N. Coghill (1954)

Clark, J. C. D., *English Society 1688–1832* (Cambridge, 1985)

Clark, S., 'Social Composition of the Land League', *Irish Historical Studies* XVII (1971)

The Clarke Papers, II, ed. C. H. Firth (Camden Society, 1894)

Clay, C., 'Property Settlement, Financial Provision for Family and the Sale of Land by the Greater Landowners 1660–1790', *Journal of British Studies* 21 (1981)

Letters of the Clifford Lords and Earls of Cumberland, c.1500–c.1565, ed. R. W. Hoyle, *Camden Miscellany*, 31 Camden Society 4th Series, 43 (1992)

Cockburn, J. S. (ed.), *Crime in England 1550–1800* (1977)

— *Calendar of Assize Records: Kent Indictments Elizabeth I* (1979)

Cohen, M., *Fashioning Masculinity: National Identity and Language in the Eighteenth Century* (1997)

Colley, L., *Britons: Forging the Nation 1707–1837* (1994)

Collins, H. E. L., *The Order of the Garter 1348–1461: Chivalry and Politics in Late-Medieval England* (Oxford, 2000)

The Complete Peerage, ed. G. E. Cockayne and revised by V. Gibbs, H. A. Doubleday and Lord Howard de Walden (13 volumes, 1910–57)

Connolly, M., 'The Dethe of the Kynge of Scotis: A New Edition', *Scottish Historical Review* 71 (1992)

Connor, P., and Lambourne, L., *Derby Day 200* (1979)

John Constable's Correspondence, ed. R. B. Beckett, IV (Suffolk Records Society, 1966)

Conway, J., 'To Subdue America: British Army Officers and the Conduct of the Revolutionary War', *William and Mary Quarterly* XLIII (1986)

Cookson, J. E., *The British Nation Armed* (Oxford, 1997)

Correspondence of Charles First Marquis Cornwallis, ed. C. Ross (3 volumes, 1859)

Coss, P., and Keen, M., *Heraldry, Pageantry and Social Display in Medieval England* (Weybridge, 2002)

Cragoe, M., *An Anglican Aristocracy: The Moral Economy of the Landed Estates in Carmarthenshire, 1832–1895* (Oxford, 1996)

Crawford, A. (ed.), *The Household Books of John Howard 1462–1471, 1481–1483* (Stroud, 1992)

The Creevey Papers, ed. H. Maxwell (2 volumes, 1903)

de Crespigny, C. C., *Forty Years of a Sportsman Life* (1925)

Crouch, D., *The Image of the Aristocracy in Britain, 1000–1300* (1992)

Curtis Jr., L. P., 'Encumbered Land Indebtedness in Post-Famine Ireland', *American Historical Review* 85 (1980)

Dalton, M., *The Country Justice* (1630)

Darrell, W., *A Gentleman Instructed in the Conduct of a Virtuous and Happy Life* (1704)

Dawson, J., 'The Fifth Earl of Argyle: Gaelic Lordship and Political Power in Sixteenth-Century Scotland', *Scottish History Review* 67 (1988)

David, S., *The Homicidal Earl: The Life of Lord Cadogan* (1997)

Davies, M. T. (ed.), *London Corresponding Society* (7 volumes, 2002)

Depositions from the Castle of York Relating to Offences Committed in the Northern Counties in the Seventeenth Century (Surtees Society, 1861)

Deutsch, G. E., *Handel: A Biography* (1955)

Devine, T. M., *Scotland's Empire, 1600–1815* (2003)

The Journals of Sir Simonds D'Ewes, ed. W. Notestein (New Haven, 1923)

Diamond, A., 'Sir Degrevant', in N. McDonald (ed.), *Pulp Fictions of Medieval England: Essays on Popular Romance* (Manchester, 2004)

Dickinson, H. T., 'Popular Conservatism and Militant Loyalism', in H. T. Dickinson (ed.), *Britain and the French Revolution* (1989)

Dictionary of National Biography, 64 vols (Oxford, 2004)

Disraeli, B., *Coningsby* (1907)

Documents of the American Revolution, 1770–1783, VI

Dobson, B., *The Peasants' Revolt* (1993)

Dod's Parliamentary Companion for 1855 (1855)

Dod's Parliamentary Companion for 1859 (1859)

Dunham, W. J., *Lord Hastings' Indentured Retainers, 1461–1483* (New Haven, 1955)

Durston, C., *The Family in the English Revolution* (Oxford, 1989)

Dorril, S., *Blackshirt: Sir Oswald Mosley and British Fascism* (2006)

Dyboski, R., and Arend, M. (eds.), *Knyghthood and Bataile* (Early English Text Society, 1935)

Eastwood, D., 'Toryism, Reform and Political Culture in Oxfordshire, 1826–1837', *Parliamentary History* VII (1988)

Egan, P., *Boxiana: Sketches of Ancient and Modern Pugilism* (2 volumes, 1818)

Ellis, S. G., *Tudor Frontiers and Noble Power: The Making of the British State* (Oxford, 1995)

Elmsley, C. E., 'The Military and Public Disorder in England, 1790–1801', *Journal of the Society for Historical Research* 61 (1983–4)

Elyot, T., *The Book Named the Governor* (1975)

Emmison, F. G., *Elizabethan Life: Disorder* (Chelmsford, 1970)

Evan Davies, W., 'The Society of Cincinnati in New England 1783–1800', *William and Mary Quarterly* V (1948)

Evelyn, J., *The Diary of John Evelyn*, 6 vols (1955)

Lady Fanshawe, *Memoirs of Lady Fanshawe wife of the Right Honourable Sir Richard Fanshawe, Bart* (1829)

Fisher, J. R., 'The Limits of Deference: Agricultural Communities and a Mid-Nineteenth Century Election Campaign', *Journal of British Studies* 31 (1981)

Fleming, N. C., *The Marquess of Londonderry: Aristocracy, Power and Politics in Britain and Ireland* (2005)

Fletcher, A., *A County Community in Peace and War: Sussex 1600–1660* (1975)

Foner, E., 'Tom Paine's Republic: Radical Ideology and Social Change', in
    A. F. Young (ed.) *The American Revolution in the History of American
    Radicalism* (De Kalb, Illinois, 1976)

Formier, E., 'Tom Paine's Republic: Radical Ideology and Social Change',
    in A. F. Young (ed.), *The American Revolution: Explorations in the
    History of American Radicalism* (De Kalb, Illinois, 1976)

Fosbroke, T. D., *Abstracts and Records and Manuscripts Respecting the County of
    Gloucestershire Formed into a History* (2 volumes, 1807)

Lord Fountainhall, *Chronological Notes on Scottish Affairs from 1660 to 1701*
    (Edinburgh, 1822)

Fradenburg, L. O., *City, Marriage, Tournament: Arts of Rule in Late Medieval
    Scotland* (Madison, Wisconsin, 1991)

Furse, R., *Acuparius: Recollections of a Recruiting Officer* (1962)

Fryde, E. B., *Peasants and Landlords in Later Medieval England c.1380–c.1525*
    (Stroud, 1996)

Gardiner, S. R. (ed.), *Notes on the Debates in the House of Lords, 1624 and
    1626*, (Camden Society, 1879)

Gash, N., *Robert Surtees and Early Victorian Society* (Oxford, 1993)

The Letters of John Gay, C. F. Burgess (ed.) (Oxford, 1966)

Gentles, I., 'The Sales of Crown Lands during the English Revolution',
    Economic History Review 26 (1973)

— 'The Purchasers of Northamptonshire Lands', *Midland History* 3 (1979)

The Later Correspondence of George III, ed. A. Aspinall (5 volumes,
    Cambridge, 1962)

Gibson, C., 'The British Army, French Farmers and the War on the
    Western Front, 1914–1918', *Past and Present* 180 (2003)

Gilmour, D., *Curzon* (1995)

Girouard, M., *Life in an English Country House* (1978)

— *The Return to Camelot* (1981)

Given Wilson, G. (ed.), *Chronicles of the Revolution 1397–1400* (Manchester,
    1993)

Gladstone, H., 'Forster and Ireland 1881–2, Select Documents, I', *Journal of
    Irish History* 17 (1970–1)

Goodrich, A., *Debating England's Aristocracy in the 1790s: Pamphlets, Polemics
    and Political Ideas* (Woodbridge, 2005)

Gray, T. (ed.), *Devon Household Accounts*, II, *Henry Bourchier Fifth Earl of
    Bath and Rachel Countess of Bath, 1637–1655* (Devon and Cornwall
    Record Society, 1996)

Green, J. A., *The Aristocracy of Norman England* (Cambridge, 1997)

The Greville Diary, ed. P. Wilson (2 volumes, 1927)

Griffiths, R., *Patriotism Perverted: Captain Ramsay, the Right Club and British
    Anti-Semitism 1939–40* (1998)

Griffiths, R. A., 'The Crown and the Royal Family in Late Medieval

England', in R. A. Griffiths and J. Sherborne (eds.), *Kings and Nobles in the Later Middle Ages: A Tribute to Charles Ross* (Gloucester, 1986)

— *King and Country: England and Wales in the Fifteenth Century* (1991)

— (ed.), *The Household Books (1510–1551) of Sir Edward Don: An Anglo-Welsh Knight and His Circle* (Buckinghamshire Records Society, 2004)

Grigg, J., *Lloyd George: The People's Champion* (1978)

Gunn, S. J., 'Henry Bourchier, Earl of Essex (1472–1540)', in G. W. Bernard (ed.), *The Tudor Aristocracy* (Manchester, 1992)

Gwynfor Jones, J., *Concepts of Order and Gentility in Wales, 1540–1640* (Llandysul, Dyfed, 1992)

Lord Halifax, *Complete Works*, ed. J. P. Kenyon (1969)

Hall-Witt, J. L., 'Reforming the Aristocracy: Opera and Elite Cultures in Britain', in A. Burns and J. Innes (eds.), *Rethinking the Age of Reform in Britain 1780–1850* (2003)

Hamilton, J., *Sixty Years Experience as an Irish Landlord* (1894)

Hamner, P. E. J., *The Polarisation of Elizabethan Politics: The Political Career of Robert Devereux, 2nd Earl of Essex, 1585–1597* (Cambridge, 1999)

Hanna III, R., 'Sir Thomas Berkeley and His Patronage', *Speculum* 64 (1989)

Hardacre, P. H., *The Royalists during the Puritan Revolution* (The Hague, 1956)

Hare, A. J. C., *Biographical Sketches* (1895)

Harling, P., 'Parliament and the State and the Old Corruption', in A. Burns and J. Innes (eds.), *Rethinking the Age of Reform in Britain 1780–1850* (2003)

Harris, T., *Revolution: The Great Crises of the British Monarchy, 1685–1720* (2006)

The Letters of Francis Hastings, 1574–1609, ed. C. Cross (Somerset Record Society, 1969)

Hay, D., 'Poaching and the Game Laws on Cannock Chase', in *Albion's Fatal Tree: Crime and Society in Eighteenth Century England*, (1975)

The Diary of Benjamin Haydon, W. B. Pope (ed.), 5 vols (Cambridge, Massachusetts, 1960–3)

Henderson, P., *The Tudor House and Garden* (Yale, 2005)

The Letterbooks of John Hervey First Earl of Bristol (3 volumes, Wells, 1894)

Lord John Hervey, *Some Materials Towards Memoirs on the Reign of George III*, ed. R. Sedgwick (3 volumes, 1931)

Hesemer, F. (ed.), *Corpus Rubenianum Ludwig Burchard, Portraits*, I (1977)

Hicks, M., *Richard III and His Rivals: Magnates and their Motives in the Wars of the Roses* (Stroud, 2003)

E. Hinderaker, 'The "Four Indian Kings" and the Imaginative Construction of the British Empire', *William and Mary Quarterly* LII

HMC, *Bathurst* (1923)

HMC, *Buccleuch and Queensbury*, II, i (1903)

HMC, *De Lisle and Dudley*, I (1925)

HMC, *Egmont* (3 volumes, 1920–1923)

HMC, *Hastings*, III (1934)

HMC, *Hastings*, I (1928)

HMC, *House of Lords, 1689–1690* (1889)

HMC, *Le Fleming* (1890)

HMC, *Lindsey, 1660–1702* (1942)

HMC, *Mar and Kellie*, II (1930)

HMC, *Rutland*, I (1911)

HMC, *Rutland*, IV (1905)

HMC, *Salisbury*, I (1883), and XXI (1970)

HMC, *Stopford-Sackville*, II (1916)

HMC, *Twelfth Earl of Lindsey* (1942)

HMC, *3rd Report* (1872)

HMC, *10th Report*, part 6 (1887)

HMC, *12th Report* (1891)

HMC, *13th Report*, I, Portland Manuscripts (1891), and II, Portland Manuscripts (1893)

HP, *The House of Commons, 1386–1421*, ed. J. S. Roskell (4 volumes, 1992)

HP, *The House of Commons, 1660–1690*, ed. B. D. Hemming (3 volumes, 1983)

HP, *The House of Commons, 1690–1715*, ed. D. W. Heyton (5 volumes, 2002)

Hoccleve's Works, II, *The Regiment of Princes*, ed. F. J. Furnivall (Early English Text Society, 1897)

The Letters of John Holles 1587–1637, ed. P. R. Seddon, I (1975, Thoroton Society of Nottinghamshire), and II (1983, Thoroton Society of Nottinghamshire)

Holmes, G., and Szechi, D., *The Age of Oligarchy 1722–1783* (1993)

Hoock, H., 'Reforming Culture: National Art Institutions in the Age of Reform', in A. Burns and J. Innes (eds.), *Rethinking the Age of Reform in Britain, 1780–1850* (2003)

Hopkins, E., 'The Re-leasing of the Ellesmere Estates, 1637–1642', *Agricultural History Review* 10 (1982)

Hoppen, K., *Elections, Politics and Society in Ireland 1832–1885* (Oxford, 1984)

Howard, D. (ed.), *Art and Patronage in the Caroline Court: Essays in Honour of Sir Oliver Miller* (Cambridge, 1993)

Howard, M., and Wilson, E., *The Vyne: A Tudor House Revealed* (2003)

Hudson, A., 'Volunteer Soldiers in Sussex during the Revolutionary and Napoleonic Wars', *Sussex Archaeological Collections* 122 (1984)

Hudson, H., 'Construction of Class, Family and Gender in Some Middle English Romances', in B. J. Harwood and G. R. Overing (eds.),

Class and Gender in Early English Literature (Bloomington, Indiana, 1994)

Hughes, A., *Politics, Society and Civil War in Warwickshire, 1620–1660* (Cambridge, 1987)

Hughes, J., *Arthurian Myths and Alchemy: The Kingship of Edward IV* (Stroud, 2002)

Hutton, R., *The Royalist War Effort, 1642–1646* (1982)

I. M., *A Health to the Gentlemanly Profession of Serving Men; or, The Servingman's Comfort* (1598)

Innes, J., '"Reform" in English Public Life: The Fortunes of a Word', in A. Burns and J. Innes (eds.), *Rethinking the Age of Reform, Britain 1780–1850* (2003)

Jaggard, E., 'Cornwall Politics, 1826–1832: Another Face of Reform?', *Journal of British Studies* 22 (1983)

James, L., *Mutiny: In the British and Commonwealth Forces, 1797–1956* (1987)
— *The Iron Duke: A Military Biography of Wellington* (1992)
— *Raj: the Making and Unmaking of British India* (1997)
— *Warrior Race: A History of the British at War* (2001)
— *The Middle Class: A History* (2006)

James, M., *English Politics and the Concept of Honour* (1978)

Jarvie, G., and Jackson, L., 'Deer Forests, Sporting Estates and the Aristocracy', *The Sports Historian* 18 (1998)

Journals of the Continental Congress 1774–1789, V (1776) (Washington, 1906)

Journals of the House of Commons 40 (1803)

Kaenper, W. *Chivalry and Violence in Medieval Europe* (Oxford, 1999)

Kaminsky, H., 'Estate, Nobility, and the Exhibition of Estate in the Late Middle Ages', *Speculum* 68 (1993)

Karsten, P., *Patriot Heroes in England and America: Political Symbolism and Changing Values in Three Centuries* (Madison, 1978)

Kay, M. L. M., 'The North Carolina Regulators 1760–1766: A Class Conflict', in A. F. Young (ed.) *The American Revolution: Explorations in the History of American Radicalism* (De Kalb, Illinois, 1976)

Kaye, J. W., *Lives of the Indian Officers* (2 volumes, 1867)

Keeble, K. H., *Restoration: England in the 1660s* (2002)

Keen, M., *Chivalry* (1984)

Keeton, G. W., *Lord Chancellor Jeffreys and the Stuart Cause* (1965)

Kelsey, S., *Inventing a Republic: The Political Culture of the English Commonwealth 1649–1653* (Manchester, 1997)

Kent, J., *Records and Reminiscences of Goodwood and the Duke of Richmond* (1896)

Kenyon, J. P., *Robert Spencer Earl of Sunderland 1641–1702* (Westport, Connecticut, 1976)

King, P., *Crime, Justice and Dissension in England 1746–1820* (Oxford, 2000)

King's Counsellor: Abdication and War: The Diaries of Sir Alan Lascelles, ed. D. Hart-Davies (2006)

Kramer, L. S., 'America's Lafayette and Lafayette's America: A European in the American Revolution', *William and Mary Quarterly* XXXVIII (1981)

Kurtz, S. G., and Hutton, J. H., *Essays in the American Revolution* (Chapel Hill, N.Y., 1974)

Lady Caroline Lamb, *Glenarvon* (2 volumes, 1816)

Lamb, M. E., 'The Countess of Pembroke's Patronage', *English Literary Renaissance* 12 (1982)

Lamoine, G., *Charges to the Grand Jury, 1689–1803* (Camden Society, 1992)

Lander, J. R., *Conflict and Stability in Fifteenth-Century England* (1969)

Lander, J. R., 'Attainder and Forfeiture, 1453–1509', in E. B. Fryde and E. Miller (eds) *Historical Studies of the English Parliament 2 (1399 to 1603)*, (Cambridge 1970)

The Late Apology in Behalf of the Papists Re-Printed and Answered in Behalf of the Royalists (1667)

Leahy, W., *Elizabethan Triumphal Processions* (2005)

Lees-Milne, J., *Another Self* (1970)

— *Caves of Ice* (1983)

— *Midway on the Waves: Diaries 1948–1949* (1985)

— *Ancient as the Hills: Diaries 1973–1974* (1997)

— *Diaries 1975–1978* (1998)

— *Deep Romantic Chasm: Diaries 1979–1981* (2000)

L'Estrange, R., *Citt and Bumpkin in a Dialogue and a Pot of Ale Concerning Matters of Religion* (1680)

Letters and Papers Foreign and Domestic of the Reign of Henry VIII, VII, ii (1888); XI, ii (1889); XXI, i (1910)

Lewis, J., *Cyril Connolly: A Life* (1997)

Lightbrown, R., 'The Sculpture of Isaac Besnier', in D. Howard (ed.), *Art and Patronage in the Caroline Court: Essays in Honour of Sir Oliver Miller* (Cambridge, 1993)

Lindsay, C., 3rd Earl of Balcarres, *An Account of the Affairs of Scotland Relating to the Revolution in 1688* (1714)

The Lisle Letters, ed. M. St C. Byrnes (5 volumes, Chicago, 1981)

Loades, D., *John Dudley, Duke of Northumberland, 1504–1553* (Oxford, 1996)

Low, J., *Manhood and Honour* (2003)

McCahill, M. W., 'Peerage Creations and the Changing Character of the British Nobility 1750–1850', *English Historical Review* 96 (1981)

Macfarlane, K. B., *The Nobility of Later Medieval England* (Oxford, 1973)

MacKenzie, J. M., *The Empire of Nature: Hunting, Conservation and British Imperialism* (Manchester, 1988)

MacLeod, E. V., *A War of Ideas: British Attitudes to the Wars against Revolutionary France* (Aldershot, 1998)

McLeod, K., *The Last Summer: May to September 1914* (1983)

Maddicott, J. R., *Thomas of Lancaster, 1307–1322* (Oxford, 1970)

Malcolm, J. L., *Caesar's Due: Loyalty and King Charles, 1642–1646* (1983)

Sir Thomas Malory, *Le Mort Darthur*, ed. S. H. A. Shepherd (2000)

Manning, R. B., *Village Revolts: Social Protest and Popular Disturbance in England, 1509–1640* (Oxford, 1988)

Markham, J. H. (ed.), *Instructions by Henry Ninth Earl of Northumberland to his Son Algernon Percy* (1838)

Marshall, P. J., 'Empire and Authority in the Later Eighteenth Century', *Journal of Imperial and Commonwealth History* 15 (1987)

Masterman, L., *C.F.G. Masterman: A Biography* (1968)

Mawson, H. H., 'Not a Very Nice Regiment: Her Majesty's 63rd (The West Suffolk Regiment of Foot)', *Journal of the Society for Army Historical Research*, 76 (1998)

Meikle, M. M., 'The Invisible Divide: The Greater Lords and the Nobility of Jacobean Scotland', *Scottish Historical Review* 71 (1992)

George, Earl of Melville, *Letters and Papers chiefly addressed to George Earl of Melville, Secretary of State for Scotland 1689–1691* (Edinburgh, 1843)

The Memoirs of Sir James Melville of Halhill, ed. G. Scott (Edinburgh, 1735)

Mendyk, S. A. E., *'Speculum Britanniae': Regional Study, Antiquarianism and Science in Britain to 1700* (Toronto, 1989)

Mertes, K., *The English Noble Household 1250–1600* (Oxford, 1988)

Miller, K. (ed.), *The Agrarian History of England and Wales*, III, 1348–1500, (Cambridge, 1991)

Decca: The Letters of Jessica Mitford, ed. P. Y. Sussman (2007)

Lord Montagu of Beaulieu, *More Equal than Others* (1970)

Mowl, T., *Elizabethan and Jacobean Style* (1993)

Muldoon, J., *Identity and the Medieval Irish Frontier* (Gainesville, Florida 2003)

Munby, L. M. (ed.), *Early Stuart Household Accounts* (Hertfordshire Record Society, 1986)

Munsche, R. M., 'The Game Laws in Wiltshire 1750–1800', in J. S. Cockburn (ed.), *Crime in England 1550–1800* (1977)

Nashe, T., *The Unfortunate Traveller*, in R. B. Kerrow (ed.), *The Works of Thomas Nashe*, II (1910)

Nicholls, J. G. (ed.), *Chronicles of Queen Jane* (Camden Society, 1850)

Oborne, P., *The Triumph of the Political Class* (2007)

Oerlemans, O., *Romanticism and the Materiality of Nature* (Toronto, 2000)

Offord, M. (ed.), *The Parlement of Three Ages* (Early English Text Society, 1959)

O'Gorman, F., 'Pitt and the Tory Reaction to the French Revolution

1789–1815', in H. T. Dickinson (ed.), *Britain and the French Revolution* (1989)

O'Hart, J., *The Irish and Anglo-Irish Gentry* (Dublin, 1969)

Ohlmeyer, J. H., *Civil War and Restoration in the Three Stuart Kingdoms: The Career of Randal MacDonald, Marquis of Antrim* (Cambridge, 1993)

Owst, G. R., *Literature and the Pulpit in Medieval England* (1933)

Paine, T., *Common Sense* (1791)

— *The Rights of Man*, ed. A. Seldon (1963)

The Paston Letters, ed. J. Gairdner (4 volumes, 1900)

Payling, S. J., 'The Ampthill Dispute: A Study in Aristocratic Lawlessness and the Breakdown of Lancastrian Government', *English Historical Review* 104 (1989)

Peck, L. L., *Consuming Splendour: Society and Culture in Seventeenth-Century England* (Cambridge, 2005)

The Diary of Samuel Pepys, eds. R. C. Letham and W. K. Matthews (11 volumes, 1974–94)

Perkin, H., 'Recruitment of Elites in British Society since 1800', *Journal of Social History* 12 (1978–9)

Perrott, R., *The Aristocrats* (1968)

Physick, J., *Five Monuments from Eastwell* (1973)

Pilbrow, F., 'The Knights of the Bath: Dubbing to Knighthood in Lancastrian England', in P. Coss and M. Keen (eds.), *Heraldry, Pageantry and Display in Medieval England* (Weybridge, 2002)

Pole, A., 'Sheriffs' Sales during the Land War 1879–82', *Irish Historical Studies* XXXIV (2005)

Porter, R., *English Society in the Eighteenth Century* (1991)

Postle, M. (ed.), *Joshua Reynolds: The Creation of Celebrity* (2005)

Prebble, J., *Mutiny: Highland Regiments in Revolt, 1743–1804* (1975)

Prinsep, H. T., *A Narrative of the Political and Military Transactions of British India under the Administration of the Marquess of Hastings, 1813 to 1818* (1820)

Pugh, T. B., *Henry V and the Southampton Plot of 1415* (Southampton Record Series, 1986)

Pumphrey, R. E., 'The Introduction of Industrialists into the British Peerage: A Study in Adaptation and a Social Institution', *American Historical Review* 65 (1959)

Rawcliffe, C., *The Staffords, Earls of Stafford and Dukes of Buckingham* (Cambridge, 1978)

Register of the Privy Council of Scotland, VII (Edinburgh, 1897)

Register of the Privy Council of Scotland, 1681 (Edinburgh, 1922)

Register of the Privy Council of Scotland, XI, 1686–1689 (Edinburgh, 1932)

Register of the Privy Seal of Scotland, 1604–1607 (Edinburgh, 1885)

Register of the Privy Seal of Scotland, 1683–1684 (Edinburgh, 1915)

Register of the Privy Seal of Scotland, 1689 (Edinburgh, 1933)
Register of the Privy Seal of Scotland, 1690 (Edinburgh, 1967)
Rhodes James, R., Lord Randolph Churchill (1959)
Richmond, C., 'Patronage and Polemic', in J. L. Watts (ed.), The End of the
    Middle Ages? England in the Sixteenth and Seventeenth Centuries (Stroud,
    1998)
The Correspondence of the Dukes of Richmond and Newcastle 1724–1750, ed.
    T. S. McCann (Sussex Record Society, 1984)
Riedi, E., 'Brains or Polo? Equestrian Sport, Army Reform and the
    Gentlemanly Officer Tradition', Journal of the Society for Army
    Historical Research LXXXIV (2006)
Robbins Landon, H. C., Haydn in England 1791–1795 (1976)
Roberts, A., 'The Holy Fox': A Biography of Lord Halifax (1991)
— Eminent Churchillians (1994)
— Salisbury: Victorian Titan (1999)
Roeber, A. G., 'Authority, Law and Custom: The Rituals of Court Day in
    Tidewater Virginia 1720 to 1750', William and Mary Quarterly
    XXXVII (1980)
Rosenberg, E., Leicester: Patron of Letters (New York, 1955)
Lord Rosebery, Lord Randolph Churchill (1906)
Rowe, V., 'The Hertford Borough Bill of 1834', Parliamentary History 11
    (1992)
Royle, E., Revolutionary Britannia? (Manchester, 2000)
Rubenstein, W. B., 'Wealth, Elites and the Class Structure of Modern
    Britain', in Past and Present, 74 (1977)
Sanderson, M. H. B., Scottish Rural Society in the Sixteenth Century (1982)
Saul, N., 'The Contract for the Brass of Richard Willoughby (d. 1471) at
    Wollaton (Notts)', Nottingham Medieval Studies L (2006)
Saville, A. (ed.), Secret Comment: The Diaries of Gertrude Saville 1721–1757
    (Thoroton Society of Nottinghamshire, 1997)
Sayles, G. O. (ed.), Select Cases in the Court of King's Bench under Richard II,
    Henry IV and Henry V (Seldon Society, 1971)
Scattergood, V. J., Politics and Poetry in Fifteenth-Century England (1969)
Seth-Smith, M., Lord Paramount of the Turf (1971)
Schultz, W. E., Gay's Beggar's Opera: Its Content and Influence (New Haven,
    1924)
Scott, W. (ed.), A Collection of Scarce and Valuable Tracts, I (1809)
Shakeshaft, P., 'Documents for the History of Collecting, I', The Burlington
    Magazine CXXVIII (1986)
Sharp, B., In Contempt of All Authority: Rural Artisans and Riot in the West of
    England, 1586–1660 (Berkeley, California, 1982)
The Complete Works of Shelley, T. Hutchinson (ed.) 10 vols (1965)
Sinclair

Sinclair, A., *The Last of the Best: The Aristocracy of Europe in the Twentieth Century* (1969)

Slater, V. L., *Noble Government: The Stuart Lord Lieutenantcy and the Transformation of English Politics* (Allen, Georgia, 1994)

Smith, D. L., *The Stuart Parliaments 1603–1689* (1999)

Smuts, R. M., *Court Culture and the Origins of the Royalist Tradition in Early Stuart England* (Philadelphia, 1987)

Smyth, J., *Lives of the Berkeleys* (4 volumes, 1883–5)

Spiers, W. I., *The Notebook and Account Book of Nicholas Stone*, 7 (Walpole Society, 1918–19)

Squier, C. L., *Sir John Suckling* (Boston, Massachusetts 1978)

Statutes of the Realm, 9 vols (1810–22)

Steer, F. W. (ed.), *A Catalogue of the Earl Marshal's Papers at Arundel Castle* (Harleian Society, 1964)

Stillingfleet, E., *Separation Convicted . . . being further Evidence of the Mischief of Separation* (1681)

Stinger, K. J., *Essays on the Nobility of Scotland* (1985)

Stone, L., *The Crisis of the Aristocracy, 1558–1641* (Oxford, 1965)

The Stonor Letters and Papers, ed., C. L. Kingsford, 2 vols, Camden Society, third series, 29–30 (1919)

Stoye, J., *English Travellers Abroad 1604–1667* (1989)

Stringer, K. J., ed., *Essays on the Nobility of Scotland* (Edinburgh, 1985)

Strong, R., *The English Icon: Elizabethan and Jacobean Portraiture* (1969)

Tait, A. A., 'Lord Findlater, Architect', *The Burlington Magazine* CXXVIII (1986)

Thackeray, W. M., *Book of Snobs* (1869)

Thirsk, J., 'The Sale of Royalist Land during the Interregnum', *Economic History Review* 5, ii, (1952)

Thomas, D., 'The Social Origins of Marriage Partners of the British Peerage in the Eighteenth and Nineteenth Centuries', *Population Studies* 26, i (1972)

Thomas, P. W., 'Two Cultures? Court and Country under Charles I', in C. Russell (ed.), *The Origins of the English Civil War* (1973)

Thompson, E. P., *Whigs and Hunters: The Origin of the Black Act* (1975)

Thompson, F. M. L., *English Landed Society in the Nineteenth Century* (1963)

— 'English Landed Society in the Twentieth Century, I (Prosperity and Survival)', *Transactions of the Royal Historical Society*, 6th Series, L (1990)

— 'English Landed Society in the Twentieth Century, II (New Poor and New Rich)', *Transactions of the Royal Historical Society*, 6th series, I (1991)

— 'English Landed Society in the Twentieth Century, III (Self Help and Children)', *Transactions of the Royal Historical Society*, 6th Series, II (1992)

Thom's Official Directory of the United Kingdom of Great Britain and Ireland for the year 1883 (1883)

Tinniswood, A., *The Polite Tourist* (1998)

Tillyard, S., '"Paths of Glory": Fame and Fortune and the Public in Eighteenth Century London' in M. Postle (ed.) *Joshua Reynolds: The Creation of Celebrity* (2005)

Tocqueville, A. de, *Democracy in America*, D. Mayer and M. Lerner (eds) (1968)

Tod, J., *Annals and Antiquities of Rajasthan* (3 volumes, New Delhi, 1993)

Trench, W. S., *Realities of Irish Life* (1869)

Trevor-Roper, H. R., *Religion, the Reformation and Social Change* (1967)

Tristram, E. W., 'The Wall Paintings at South Newington', *The Burlington Magazine*, March 1933

Turberville, A. S., *The House of Lords in the XVIIth Century* (Westport, Connecticut, 1970)

Turville-Petre, T., 'The Lament for Sir John Berkeley', *Speculum* 57 (1982)

Uglow, J., *Hogarth: A Life and a World* (1997)

Underdown, D., *Somerset in the Civil War and Interregnum* (Newton Abbot, 1973)

Vaughan, W. E., *Landlords and Tenants in Mid-Victorian Ireland* (Oxford, 1994)

Virgoe, R., 'The Death of William de la Pole, Duke of Suffolk', *Bulletin of the John Rylands Library* XLVII (1965)

— 'William Tailboys and Lord Cromwell: Politics in Lancastrian England', *Bulletin of the John Rylands Library* LV (1973)

— 'Some Ancient Indictments in the King's Bench Referring to Kent, 1450–1452', in *Documents Illustrative of Medieval Kentish Society* (Kent Archaeological Society, Kent Records, 18, (1964)

Wagg, S. A., '"Time Gentleman Please": The Decline of Amateur Captaincy in English County Cricket', *Contemporary British History* 14 (2000)

Wall, A., *Power and Protest in England, 1525–1640* (2000)

Ward, I., 'Rental Policy on the Estates of the English Peerage, 1649–60', *Agricultural History Review* 40 (1992)

Warmington, A. R., *Civil War, Interregnum and Restoration in Gloucestershire 1640–1672* (1997)

Wasson, E. A., 'The Crisis of the Aristocracy: Parliamentary Reform, the Peerage and the House of Commons, 1750–1914', *Parliamentary History* 13 (1994)

Weber, K., *Lucius Second Viscount Falkland* (New York, 1940)

Weber, W., 'Did People Listen?' *Early Music*, 25 (1997)

The Despatches, Minutes and Correspondence of the Marquess of Wellesley KG during his Administration in India, ed. M. Martin (5 volumes, 1837)

The Speeches of the Duke of Wellington in Parliament, ed. Colonel Gurwood (2 volumes, 1874)

The Wentworth Papers 1597–1628, ed. J. P. Cooper (Camden Society, 1974)

Westfall, S. R., 'The Chapel: The Theatrical Performance in Early Tudor Households', *English Literary Renaissance* 18 (1988)

Whalley, J. I., 'Italian Art and English Taste: An Early Seventeenth Century Letter', *Apollo* 94 (1971)

The Diary of Bulstrode Whitelock, 1605–1675, ed. R. Spalding (1996)

Williamson, A. H., 'A Patriot Nobility? Calvinism, Kin Ties and Civic Humanism', *Scottish Historical Review* 73 (1993)

Wilson Fox, A., *The Earl of Halsbury Lord High Chancellor (1823–1921)* (1929)

Wingfield Digby, G., and Hefford, W., *The Devonshire Hunting Tapestries* (1971)

Woolley, L., *Medieval Life and Leisure in the Devonshire Hunting Tapestries* (2002)

Woodfill, W. L., *Musicians in English Society from Elizabeth I to Charles I* (Princeton, 1958)

Woodward, J., *The Theatre of Death: The Ritual Management of Royal Funerals in Renaissance England, 1570–1625* (Woodbridge, 1997)

Wootton, H., *The Characters of Robert Devereux Earl of Essex; and George Villiers Duke of Buckingham: Compared and Contrasted* (1814)

L. Worsley, 'Building and Family: William Cavendish First Duke of Newcastle and the Construction of Bolsover and Nottingham Castles', *The Seventeenth Century* 19 (2004)

Worsthorne, P., *In Defence of Aristocracy* (2004)

Wraxall, F. N., Historical Memoirs of My Own Times (1904)

Wyatt Brown, B., *Honour and Violence in the Old South* (Oxford, 1986)

Yarborough, J. M., *American Virtues: Thomas Jefferson on the Character of a Free People* (Lawrence, Kansas, 1998)

Yonge, C., *The Life and Administration of Robert Banks, Second Earl of Liverpool* (3 volumes, 1868)

Young, A. F., *The American Revolution: Explorations in the History of American Radicalism* (De Kalb, Illinois, 1976)

Young, K., *Harry, Lord Rosebery* (1974)

Younghusband, G., *Forty Years a Soldier* (1923)

Zagorin, P., *The Court and the Country: The Beginning of the English Revolution* (1969)

Index

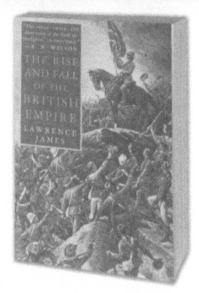